In the first six decades of the 19th century, Delhi was at the cusp of two regimes—on the one hand, the East India Company, which was a growing political power and the de facto ruler, and on the other, the Mughal dynasty, which was increasingly irrelevant politically but had great cultural, symbolic and emotional influence.

Swapna Liddle describes in rich detail the reigns of the last two Mughal Emperors—Akbar II and Bahadur Shah Zafar, going beyond the usual cliches and incorporating a significant amount of material not published so far. Her study of the key figures of the East India Company—Sir David Ochterlony, Lord Metcalfe, William Fraser and others—their relationship with the Mughal royal family and their administration in Delhi, provides a ground level look at the workings of early British rule in India.

In discussing the Revolt of 1857, the book challenges some commonly held assumptions—e.g., that it was a sectarian divide that weakened the revolt. The inclusion of the Urdu poetry written in the immediate aftermath of 1857, is a new contribution to the study of the Revolt. Bahadur Shah Zafar's tragic death in exile in Rangoon and the events that led to it, make this an invaluable work on the end of one of the greatest dynasties in the world.

Swapna Liddle's abiding love for the history of Delhi has translated into a PhD as well as several books and articles. She also seeks to raise awareness about the city's historic precincts through her work for the Indian National Trust for Art and Cultural Heritage (INTACH). She has written *Delhi: 14 Historic Walks*, *Chandni Chowk: The Mughal City of Old Delhi*, *Connaught Place and the Making of New Delhi*, and has edited and annotated a translation of *Sair-ul-Manazil*.

PRAISE FOR *THE BROKEN SCRIPT*

'Liddle's study is illuminating, and reflective of how complex even a relatively narrow historical canvas and geographical space can prove. It is a gratifying read, about a dynasty and a city navigating the end of an old world, and the creeping advent of a new, unfriendly one.'

—Manu Pillai, *Frontline Magazine*

'With an eclectic scholarship and impressive storytelling, the author tells the story of a great city in perpetual transition.'

—Saleem Rashid Shah, *Deccan Herald*

'Written in a story-telling style, the book is rich in details based on a variety of sources. It is a grasping, fascinating account of the travails, trials and tribulations of the national capital in the period under scrutiny.'

—Meena Bhargava, *The Book Review*

'Drawing upon various sources, Swapna Liddle writes a luminous account of the history of Delhi from 1803 to 1857 relevant to contemporary times.'

—Rakhshanda Jalil, *The Hindu*

'Liddle's vivid account of the people and events bring a long-lost Delhi to life, and reminds readers of a great city in transition.'

—Antara Raghavan, *Open India*

'Strikingly well-researched and with terrific prose, the book knits together a rich narrative history of the time. Perhaps there are lessons we can draw from it for our contemporary times.'

—Naorem Anuja, *India Today*

'A very good book studded with unknown gems of information.'

—Rudrangshu Mukherjee, *Business Standard*

The Broken Script

Delhi Under the East India Company and the Fall of the Mughal Dynasty
{ 1803-1857 }

SWAPNA LIDDLE

SPEAKING TIGER

SPEAKING TIGER BOOKS LLP
125A, Ground Floor, Shahpur Jat, near Asiad Village,
New Delhi 110049

First published by Speaking Tiger Books 2022
This edition published by Speaking Tiger Books 2025

All images courtesy Swapna Liddle, except where mentioned otherwise.

ISBN: 978-93-6336-184-3
eISBN: 978-93-5447-387-6

10 9 8 7 6 5 4 3 2 1

Typeset in Sabon Roman by SÜRYA, New Delhi
Printed at Chaman Enterprises, New Delhi

bas ke bedad se tute hain makan e dehli
ho raqam khat e shikastah se bayan e dehli

So unjustly have the buildings been razed in Delhi,
It is fitting to inscribe in the broken script, the account of Delhi

—Qadir Baksh 'Sabir'

CONTENTS

PART FIVE: 1857 and Its Aftermath

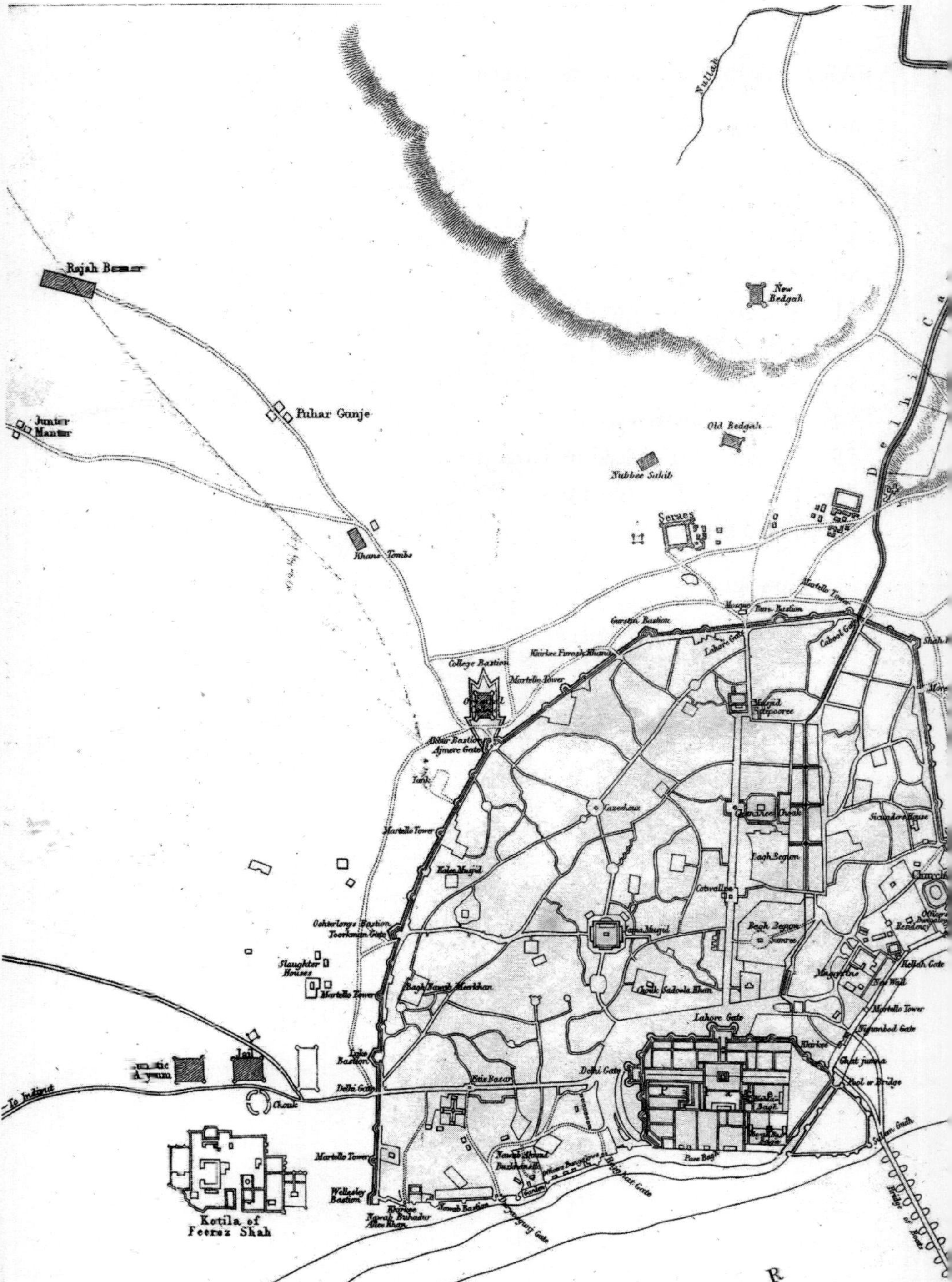
New Bedgah
Nullah
Puhar Gunje
Old Bedgah
Nubbee Sahib
Seraes
Khans Tombs
Gurstin Bastion
Martello Tower
Lahore Gate
Cabool Gate
Kairkee Furash Khana
College Bastion
Martello Tower
Ajmere Gate
Tank
Gazeehous
Masjid Futtepooree
Martello Tower
Sicunders House
Bagh Begum
Cotwallee
Kalee Musjid
Jama Musjid
Bagh Begum
Sumroo
Ochterlonys Bastion
Toorkman Gate
Slaughter Houses
Martello Tower
Bagh Nawab Meerkhan
Chouk Sadoola Khan
Magazine
New Wall
Kellah Gate
Residency
Martello Tower
Lahore Gate
Delhi Gate
Ghat jumna
Pool or Bridge
Jail
Chouk
Delhi Gate
Martello Tower
Wellesley Bastion
Nawab Bastion
Nawab Ahmad Buxkhan
Garden
Officers Bungalows
Raj Ghat Gate
Pure Bagh
Salem Gudh
Bridge of Boats
Kotila of Feeroz Shah
R
E
V
I

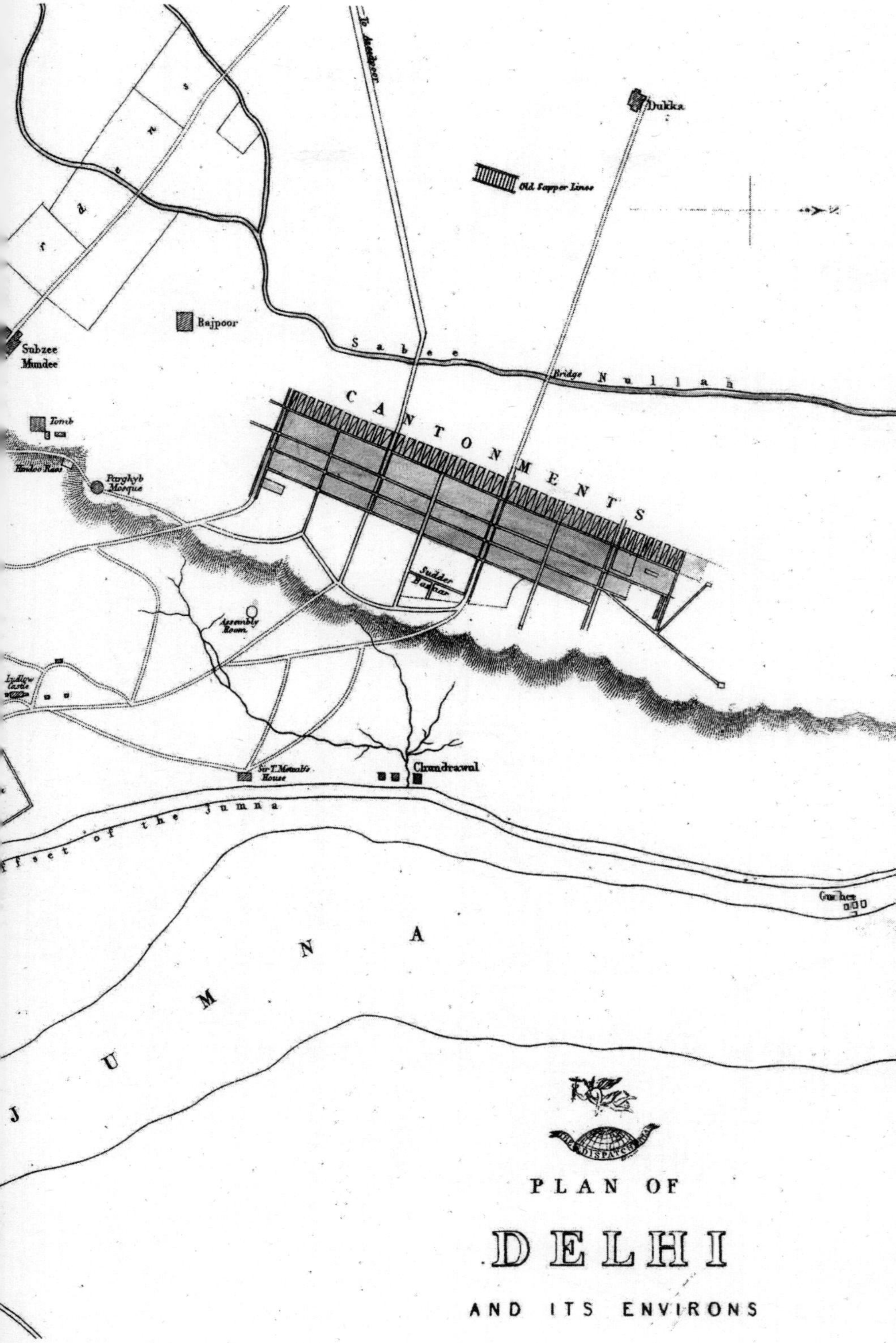

PLAN OF

DELHI

AND ITS ENVIRONS

Mughal Emperors and Contenders to the Mughal Throne in the Nineteenth Century

Shah Alam II (r. 1760-1806)
- Akbar II (son of Qudsia Begum)
- Sulaiman Shukoh (son of Qudsia Begum)

Akbar II (r. 1806-1837)
- Bahadur Shah II (son of Lal Bai)
- Mirza Jahangir (son of Mumtaz Mahal)
- Mirza Babur (son of Mumtaz Mahal)
- Mirza Salim (son of Mumtaz Mahal)

Bahadur Shah II (r. 1837-1857)
- Dara Bakht (son of ?)
- Mirza Shah Rukh (son of ?)
- Mirza Fakhru (son of Rahim Baksh Bai)
- Mirza Koeash (son of Moti Bai)
- Mirza Mughal (son of Sharafat Mahal Begum)
- Mirza Jawan Bakht (son of Zeenat Mahal)

Mirza Fakhru
- Mirza Abu Bakr (son of Asa Rafat Sultan Begum)

British Officials in Charge of the Administration of Delhi

The primary official appointed to manage the English East India Company's affairs in Delhi was to begin with called the 'Resident', though the name of office was changed from time to time—Agent to the Governor General, Agent to the Lt Governor of the North-Western Provinces, and Commissioner. The names given below (along with their periods of tenure) feature prominently in the pages that follow.

David Ochterlony (1803-06 and 1819-20)
Archibald Seton (1806-11)
Charles Metcalfe (1811-18 and 1825-27)
H. Middleton (1821-22)
Alexander Ross (1822-23)
Charles Elliot (1823-25)
Edward Colebrooke (1827-29)
Francis Hawkins (1829-30)
W.B. Martin (1830-32)
William Fraser (1832-35)
Thomas Metcalfe (1835-53)
Simon Fraser (1835-57)

Introduction

This is the account of an important era in the history of Delhi, when it was ruled by the East India Company, from 1803 to just after the revolt of 1857. This was the period not only of the East India Company's administration in Delhi, but also a time when the last vestiges of the Mughal empire were still in evidence, in the person of three emperors in succession, the last of them being Bahadur Shah 'Zafar'. This point of overlap provides an insight into the often divergent premises on which the two different regimes worked.

This is also the story of the people of Delhi in this period, some already well known, such as the poet Ghalib, others who are largely forgotten. They include the cultural and intellectual elite, business magnates, the landed nobility—both old and new, and the new ruling class—the British, who were relative newcomers. It tells of the ways in which a new political regime affected the everyday lives of citizens of Delhi, as well as the ways in which they were still grounded in inherited traditions and the continuing influence of the old regime. It looks at the economic and social climate, literature, education, beliefs, ways of thinking and belonging, and how all of these evolved in this period.

I have attempted this complex task with some trepidation, because some of these aspects have already been made the subject of detailed study. In fact many may feel that, for instance, the poetry of this period deserves a separate book. I have nevertheless knit these into a single narrative, telling the story of administrative change alongside an account of cultural developments, such as the proliferation of print technology.

The story I tell has many strands, which intertwine, for lives are not lived in compartments. Social status is tied up with economic and political power, and sovereignty is as much about emotive symbols as it is about legal statutes. Intellectual endeavours can be directed towards the production of sublime poetry, as much as towards an education promising a secure job. Language itself can be highly political, separating those of high and low status, the ruler and the ruled. The larger picture is indeed more than the sum of its parts, and it is in studying them side by side that their connections can be perceived. Also, it is only by studying these over a relatively long span of time that the process of change can be fully appreciated. That is why I have taken a period of about half a century as my subject of study.

This investigation into the many different aspects of the lives of the many different kinds of people who populated Delhi in that time reveals a city that was in the midst of profound changes. Some of these were gradual, such as the slow erosion of the status of the Mughal Emperor, the growth of Western education, and changes in the world of Urdu literature. Others were sudden, and of these none more so, or more devastating, than the revolt of 1857. This cataclysmic event, which affected the city profoundly, forms a large part of the book. Here too, placing the revolt in the context of what had gone before helps us to see aspects that might not otherwise be apparent.

This story of Delhi under the rule of the East India Company is relevant for understanding processes at work in the wider world. It answers many questions about the course of India's transformation under colonial rule, and in particular, changes in culture and intellectual life. These were developments that had a greater impact on the development of modern India and its institutions than is generally understood. I hope this book will be a contribution to that understanding as well.

PART ONE

Akbar II: The Beleaguered Emperor

Akbar II

1

A New Power

At the opening of the nineteenth century, there was a Mughal Emperor on the throne of Hind, but the Mughal empire was practically gone, having been in decline for almost a century. From the mid-eighteenth century onwards it had slowly lost its territories to newly expanding regional powers—the Marathas, Jats, and Sikhs, among others. Its own regional governors had worked themselves free of imperial control, founding independent states. Awadh, Bengal, and Hyderabad, were the most important of these. Simultaneously, control over what remained of the empire increasingly slipped from the hands of the Emperor, who became the puppet of powerful courtiers and regional potentates who fought for power with each other. The Emperor Shah Alam II had come to the throne in 1758, but in exile in Bihar, away from the capital Dehli, or Shahjahanabad, as it was then called, after its founder Shahjahan, and which was now torn apart by civil strife. When he came to Delhi in 1771 to occupy his capital, it was under the protection and control of the Marathas. The Marathas were a power that had arisen from local revolt against Mughal rule in western India, but had come to dominate large parts of central and North India as well. One particular Maratha chieftain, Mahadji Sindhia (and later his successor Daulat Rao), controlled Delhi. By the beginning of the nineteenth century the old and blind Emperor lived in the Red Fort, the palace complex within the city, as a mere puppet and pensioner, though one with considerable symbolic authority over the vast territories that were still legally considered a part of the Mughal empire.

At the same time as the Mughal empire had slowly declined, a new power had gradually emerged—the British East India Company. The Company had begun its journey in India as one of the several European trading companies—the Portuguese, Dutch, Danish, French and British—seeking to secure supplies in India. In time it had established strongholds in the form of forts along the coast—the ones at Calcutta, Madras and Bombay being the most prominent of these. The Company's efforts to secure its trading interests led to increasing interference in the affairs of Indian states, and to armed conflict with not only its competitors, most notably the French East India Company, but also local rulers. It emerged victorious in these conflicts, and succeeded not only in protecting its trading interests but in acquiring territorial possessions as a state in its own right. Victory in the Battle of Plassey in 1757 had made the Company the ruler of Bengal, Bihar and Orissa, and in the Carnatic and Mysore wars had given it control over extensive territories in South India.

Finally, the Company also went to war with the Marathas, who controlled territories in western, central and north India. The second Anglo-Maratha war in 1803 brought the action into the upper Doab region, where Delhi was situated. Here the prize worth fighting for was not only control over rich territory, but over the city of Delhi and the person of the Emperor. The Mughals had ruled a vast empire for centuries. More than that, they had established a hold on the popular imagination as the rightful sovereigns of the realm, and this charisma persisted even in decline. Any power that sought to rule over what had once been part of the Mughal empire, wanted legitimacy to be granted as a mandate from the Emperor. To any power seeking all-India domination, control over Delhi and the Emperor was, therefore, of great advantage.

In September 1803 the British captured Delhi and the surrounding territory after defeating the Maratha forces (which were commanded by the French mercenary, General Perron) at the battle of Patparganj, across the river Yamuna from Shahjahanabad. Shah Alam welcomed the commander of the victorious British forces, Lord Lake, and gave over to the East India Company the role of the protector of the Emperor, and at least in form, the principal functionary of the empire on his behalf. This was not out of a partiality for the East India Company. Shah Alam, blind and helpless, was long habituated to giving in to the strongest power of the day. He would have done the same for the Maratha commander, had the latter been victorious.[1]

From now on the British were the de facto rulers in the city. A thin veil of nomenclature and ceremony continued for a while, not so much to obscure reality, as to dress it up. Thus, the principal British functionary was known as the 'Resident', as if to suggest that he was merely a representative of his government at the Court of the Emperor. In fact, he was the head of the administration of the city and its surrounding territory, as well as the channel for diplomatic dealings with independent states on the northern frontier of the Company's territories. Vis-a-vis the Emperor, he was a representative at his court, but he represented the power that had considerable control over the Emperor. He was ultimately answerable only to the Company's government, with its capital in Calcutta. The government in Calcutta was in turn responsible to the executive body of the Company—the 'Court of Directors', located in London, and in turn under a loose overall supervision of the British Government through a 'Board of Commissioners for the affairs of India'.

The first Resident at Delhi after the takeover was General David Ochterlony. Born in America, he had spent most of his adult life in India. He was a colourful character, the quintessential so-called 'White Mughal'. In Delhi he went by the title bestowed on him by the Mughal Emperor—Nasir ud daulah ('defender of the state'). Contemporary descriptions and paintings depict him wearing Indian clothes, smoking a hookah, and being entertained by Indian dancing. Add to this a (rumoured) veritable harem of women, and a procession of camels, elephants and palanquins, and you have all the superficial trappings of a stereotypical Indian nobleman.[2]

Ochterlony was also a rich man, having accumulated considerable wealth during his career in India. Out of his private funds he bought one of the grandest mansions of Delhi, located just within the Kashmiri Gate. This had once belonged to Dara Shukoh, the son of Shahjahan, and had changed hands many times since the death of that prince.[3] Ochterlony also bought a piece of ground from the consort of Shah Alam within the city wall, close to Kashmiri Gate. In association with a wealthy Delhi merchant, Harsukh Rai, he had constructed in it a walled enclosure containing several shops, and the space was named Nasir Ganj, after Nasir ud daulah—his title.[4]

An important role of the Resident at Delhi, in those early years after the conquest, was a military one. The second Anglo-Maratha war had brought the British into conflict with many of the independent Maratha chiefs. Though the war with Daulat Rao Sindhia had ended with the treaty of Surji-Anjangaon in December 1803, that against Jaswant Rao Holkar, another Maratha chieftain, continued till 1805. Thus, much of North India remained a theatre of war. Holkar's forces besieged Delhi itself in October 1804, but were repulsed. While his energies were concentrated on dealing with military threats, Ochterlony, who was also responsible for organizing the administration of the city and the territories around, did not make many changes. In the first years therefore, the systems already in place during Maratha administration were largely carried on.

According to the terms of the agreement entered into between the British Government and Shah Alam, a swathe of territory on the right bank of the Yamuna was set aside as Crown lands for the Emperor, formally referred to as 'Assigned Territory', i.e. assigned for the support of the Mughal Emperor. These were to be administered by the officers of the Company, but in the name of the Emperor, and the accounts of the revenue office were to be scrutinized by officers of the Emperor's royal treasury. It was further specified that certain fixed amounts were to be paid every month by the government for the maintenance of the royal family—Rs 60,000 for the Emperor, Rs 10,000 to the heir apparent, and so forth, coming to a total of Rs 90,000 per month. This was considered necessary because the revenue collections were uncertain at the time, and one couldn't be sure if the income of the assigned territory would be adequate for the support of the royal family. It was, however, envisaged that increases in revenue from the assigned territory would soon enable an increase in the allowances. In a letter to Ochterlony, the Governor General, Lord Wellesley (Richard Wellesley, Governor General between 1798 and 1805), wrote: 'If the produce of the revenue of the assigned territory should hereafter admit of it, the monthly sum to be advanced to His Majesty, for his private expenses may be increased to the extent of one lac of rupees'. An *ikrarnama*, or agreement, which had been handed over by Ochterlony to the Emperor, further stated, 'that in case the revenue arising from the Crown lands should increase, in consequence of improved cultivation and better conditions of the *ryots* or peasantry, a proportionate augmentation shall take place in the Royal Stipends.'[5]

It was further stipulated that two *qazis* and a *mufti* (judges and magistrate respectively) were to be 'appointed from among the most learned of the inhabitants of Delhi for the administration of justice'. By the same agreement, every death sentence had to be confirmed by the Emperor. Coins struck in the name of the Emperor were to be current in the city and in the crown lands. *Nazars*—ceremonial offerings—of ten thousand rupees would be presented by the Resident to the Emperor at each of the seven important festivals celebrated at the Mughal court. These festivals were the two Eids, Nauroz (the Persian New Year), Basant (Basant Panchmi), Holi, Ramzan, and the anniversary of the Emperor's accession.

The agreement gave considerable importance to existing structures and the position of the Emperor. It was based on an offer that had been made by the British to Shah Alam before the conquest of the city. It was generous, with a view to making the bargain an attractive one for Shah Alam. Apart from the written agreements, it was also taken for granted that British officials would participate in the elaborate court ceremonial, which often put them in a position of submission. This included the practice of bowing down low while greeting the Emperor with a *salaam*, and remaining standing in his presence.

In the Emperor's court, British officials also had to participate in the ceremony of *khilat*, an old practice at the Mughal court which had a deep symbolic value attached to it. The Emperor would present rich garments, and other articles of personal use, such as a cloak, a headdress, a turban ornament, to specially honoured subjects. It was a ceremony that underlined a relationship of fealty between the giver and the receiver.[6] The Governor General himself, seated at the British Indian capital in Calcutta, was expected to display servility during correspondence with the Emperor. This correspondence, incidentally, was carried out in the Persian language, the official language of the Mughal court. It was drafted by the Persian Secretary to the Governor General. The seal the Governor General used in such correspondence was engraved with the words '*fidwi* e Shah Alam Padshah', fidwi being literally, 'devoted servant'.

Those, like Ochterlony, who had been part of the politics of North India for several decades, took these ceremonials for granted. From 1803 they softened the reality that it was the British who controlled important portions of the erstwhile empire, and the capital itself. Though they were often spoken of within British official circles as simply humouring the old Emperor, their significance was greater. The Mughals still enjoyed considerable symbolic importance within India, and it was important for the Company's officials to be seen to be treating the Emperor with respect. Archibald Seton, who succeeded Ochterlony as Resident, therefore continued these practices scrupulously.

2

A New Emperor

Shah Alam died in November 1806, at the age of seventy-eight. He was buried at Mehrauli, a suburb of Delhi, in the same marble enclosure that held the grave of his great-grandfather, Bahadur Shah I, the son and successor of Aurangzeb. Shah Alam was succeeded by his oldest surviving son Akbar, who ascended the throne as Akbar II.

The accession of a new Mughal Emperor was an occasion that had great significance for the ruling houses all over India. Though the Emperor had long had little real power, he still continued to be seen as a symbolic fount of authority. As news of the new Emperor having ascended the throne spread, letters with nazars of gold *mohurs* began to arrive spontaneously from many different rulers around India. If they were ever in doubt, the British now certainly realized the extent to which the sovereign status of the Mughals was acknowledged by the ruling powers of India. They also understood that if they wanted to eventually supplant the Mughals as the sovereign of India in the minds of the people, they would have to deal with some tricky issues of the symbolic delegation of authority from the Mughal throne.

Khilat was one very powerful vehicle of this delegation, and it was customary for the new Emperor to send these articles of clothing to his vassals to underline ties of loyalty to the new occupant of the throne. The British decided that it was time to set down new precedents, and Akbar was at once dissuaded from sending ceremonial robes that would signify his sovereign position vis-a-vis the rulers of independent states.[7]

Another way in which the Mughal Emperors symbolically delegated authority, was by giving titles. Many of the rulers of principalities all across India, big and small, had received such titles. With the accession of a new Emperor, various rulers sent applications expecting and sometimes explicitly requesting that their titles, given by the previous Emperor, be confirmed, or even enhanced.[8] The British Government had to decide how it was to deal with this situation. The only titles enjoyed by several important rulers such as the Nizam of the Deccan, the Nawabs of Awadh, Carnatic, and Bengal, were those given by the Mughal rulers. These states had been founded by those who had at one time been part of the Mughal bureaucracy. Though their rulers were now completely independent of Mughal control, they continued to use their hereditary titles. They could not reasonably be stopped from sending formal applications to the new incumbent on the throne to confirm them. The British also realized that helping to secure these titles from the throne was a useful way of obliging friends and allies.

The Company's government did, however, make it clear that any titles given were at the instance of the British Government, and it was a message that was quickly understood. The titular Nawab of Bengal, Zain ud din Ali Khan wrote to the Governor General expressing his gratitude for the address from the throne 'at your Excellency's kind instance'.[9] The British Government also thought it prudent to discourage the impression that the Emperor had any right to even nominally confirm any ruler's right to rule. So, when Zain ud din Ali Khan's predecessor, Baber Ali Khan had applied to the Emperor for 'a renewal of the Sunnud conferring on His Highness the office of the Soubahdar of the provinces of Bengal, Behar and Orissa', the British authorities had decided not to forward the application to Delhi.[10] Similarly, when the newly ascended rulers of Jodhpur and Jaipur desired to be honoured with a *tika* of investiture from the Emperor, the British Government turned down the request.[11] On the succession of Malhar Rao Holkar, the authorities at Calcutta again had to say unequivocally that a khilat or any other sign of investiture from the Mughal Emperor was neither required nor permissible.[12]

The importance that the ties to the Mughal Emperor carried in the minds of the princely rulers becomes evident in the case of the Nizam of Hyderabad. The arrival of the Emperor's *shuqqa* (literally, 'royal order') bestowing imperial titles on the ruler at Hyderabad was treated by the Nizam with a display of great reverence. The occasion was given additional significance by the presence of all the local British civil and military officers who turned up in the *durbar* for the ceremony. When the report of this event reached the British Government at Calcutta, it expressed its discomfort with this overt display of subordination by the ruler of Hyderabad to the Mughal Emperor. The local British authorities at Hyderabad were instructed that in future it would be better to stay away from such ceremonies.[13]

By asking for titles and accepting them, the Nizam of Hyderabad was of course not really suggesting that he was a vassal of the Mughal Emperor. The nature of the allegiance was a complex one, involving a far greater reciprocity than the simple 'giving' and 'accepting' of khilats or titles. The Nizam, for instance, did not attempt to hide his 'chagrin' and 'disappointment' when his titles did not match his expectations. The British on their part supported his demands for enhanced titles, and the Resident at Delhi was told to make it clear to Akbar that he must give the desired titles. Thus, while the form was one of an overlord conferring a favour and being given a nazar in gratitude, in actual fact the Emperor did not have any real discretion in the matter. This was an expectation that existed on the part of the Nizam quite independently of the views of the British Government.[14] Though the Nizam, and for that matter, many other rulers, had long ceased to recognize the overlordship of the Mughal Emperor, the name of the Emperor held great currency throughout the land, in the minds of high and low. Recognition from the source, however symbolic, helped to establish the ruler's own status.

Apart from rulers of independent principalities, other people, who happened to be residents of British territory, also sought titles and khilats, for similar reasons. On the succession of Akbar II, the commercial magnate Jagat Seth wrote to the British Government, saying that it had been the tradition of his business house to present nazars to a newly ascended Emperor. Following from that, he added, 'Although I now hold no intercourse with, nor desire the favour of any government but that of the Hon'ble Company...yet some of the principal inhabitants of this place, who are my old and intimate acquaintance [*sic*], have suggested to me the propriety of my continuing the observance of this established custom'. Public opinion may indeed have prompted this move, but the desire of Jagat Seth to re-open a branch of his business in Delhi may also have been a factor.[15]

What the British Government was really interested in, at least in the long term, was a complete indifference on the part of the princes and people of India towards the Mughal throne. But there were no signs of this happening in a hurry. Several of the rulers posted *vakils* or agents in Delhi to keep them in constant communication with the throne. Matters such as who had been declared the heir apparent were eagerly enquired into. Samples of the new coins struck at Delhi in the name of the new Emperor were eagerly asked for.[16] The coinage of the states themselves reflected the traditional ties with the Mughal throne. Coins almost all through India, including in the East India Company's territories, were struck in the name of the Emperor. So much so, that an unfamiliar Sanskrit inscription on a new coin issued by Jaswant Rao Holkar in 1808 caused a sensation, because it was misunderstood as not including the name of the Emperor. To avoid controversy, Holkar decided to withdraw the coin and replace it with a coin bearing the familiar and unambiguous inscription.[17]

3

The 'House of Timur'

The death of his father had put Akbar at the head of his large extended family, which also lived in the fort. The members of the royal family did not use for themselves the word 'Mughal'—the appellation commonly used by the Western world. They instead identified themselves as the descendants of Timur, the fourteenth century Turko-Mongol conqueror known in the West as Tamerlane. Those members of the family closely related to the reigning Emperor were known as *shahzadas*, the more distantly related, as *salateen*. The exact numbers were not always easy to determine, as information from the palace was not readily made public, but in 1810 there were said to be about 5,000 persons in the fort.[18] They included men and women related in various degrees to the Emperor (and his dependents—wives, concubines, etc.) who were subject to his authority and received an allowance from him. According to a report in 1814, these included the king's twenty-three brothers, twenty sisters, six aunts, four uncles, and six cousins.[19]

Though some of them had alternate means of their own, many were entirely dependent on the allowance they received from the head of the family. The size of a person's allowance was usually proportionate to the closeness of his or her relationship with the Emperor. The allowances were small, because they had to be paid out of the relatively modest allowance the Emperor received from the British, and some of his own private resources. The latter included rents from personal lands in the vicinity of Delhi, which amounted to about 1,50,000 rupees, and rents from houses, shops, etc., which were royal property within the city.[20] Though the allowances given out were small, the Emperor was expected to play the role of the generous head of the family, and so he helped out with wedding and funeral expenses and generally in times of need, such as illness and house building. Several of the poor received small salaries/allowances from various royal *karkhanas*, or workshops, on a purely charitable basis. The poor were also objects of charity through the periodic distribution of alms, as when the Emperor or a close relative of his were ill.[21]

Unlike the population in the city outside, the inhabitants of the fort were not subject to the jurisdiction of the British Government, but of the Emperor, who in theory exercised considerable power over them. Not only were they in many cases utterly dependent on him for their financial needs, they were subject to his authority in a variety of other ways too. He would decide their internal disputes. He would give orders regarding their financial affairs; for instance, mediating between a man and his creditors, ordering that part of his allowance would be deducted to pay the creditors. Even their marriages were approved by the Emperor, held in his presence and on his summoning the qazi, who was specially appointed by him to conduct the family's weddings.[22] Their important correspondence was brought to the notice of the Emperor too.[23]

There were on the other hand certain members of the family who wielded great influence over the Emperor. Most important among these were three ladies close to him—his favourite wife Mumtaz Mahal, his mother Qudsia Begum and his aunt Daulat un Nissa Begum. They frequently attended court, seated behind a screen, and interjected in his interactions with the Resident and others. Mumtaz Mahal also had great control over the financial affairs of the palace.

The Emperor's authority over members of the royal family within the fort, fairly comprehensive in theory, was not unquestioned.

Moreover, those who had a grievance against the Emperor realized that they could now appeal to the British authorities, exploiting to their own advantage the power the British Government undoubtedly had over him. Akbar II's succession itself was occasion for dissention. The widow of Shah Alam's eldest son (who had predeceased him) put forward a claim to the throne on behalf of her son Mirza Khurram Bakht. The British Government turned down her application, pointing out that Islamic law did not provide for a grandson inheriting directly from the grandfather, and Shah Alam had selected Akbar II, his eldest surviving son, as his heir.[24]

This was just the beginning of a prolonged tussle, often on minor points, between the Emperor and members of his family. Not long after the succession, the Emperor's brother Ezad Baksh sent a letter to the government, complaining against his treatment at the hands of his brother. He said he was not allowed to attend the *namaz* at the Jama Masjid on the two Eids, and he could not enter into conversation with any of the royal attendants.[25] Akbar's brothers also complained that their offspring were excluded from the lessons that were given to the more privileged children of the royal family.[26]

The tension between a newly crowned Emperor and his brothers was traditionally the result of tussles for the crown. The Mughals had not followed the custom of primogeniture, where the oldest male offspring would automatically be the heir. Instead, all male offspring grew up in hope and expectation that they had a very real chance of being the next ruler. That was why successions to the throne were often bitterly contested, even though a reigning Emperor often made his own preference known, by way of declaring one of his sons the heir apparent. As a result, with the accession of every new Emperor, all brothers and cousins who were potential candidates to the throne were automatically treated with suspicion, deprived of resources and made to live in a state of semi-confinement to prevent them from becoming rival centres of power. By the time of Akbar II, the stakes were not high, since the Company had turned the Emperor into a mere figurehead. The practice nevertheless continued, fuelled by personal rivalries. The prime mover behind Akbar's less than generous treatment of his brothers was his mother, Qudsia Begum. She was the one who, soon after her son's accession, demanded that the arms and horses of her late husband's other sons (by other wives) be confiscated.[27]

Archibald Seton, the Resident, intervened, and persuaded Akbar II to allow his brothers the right to enter the hall of audience. He also attempted to persuade Qudsia Begum to include Akbar's brothers in family gatherings and other occasions, though not always with success. At any rate, Seton was happy to report a 'reconciliation', when His Majesty's brothers were included in the royal *sawari* (procession) and allowed to go to their father's tomb. The Governor General, Lord Minto, fixed a seal of approval by writing to Akbar that the event had 'filled your devoted servant with the most lively joy and satisfaction'.[28]

4

Revisiting a Relationship

The accession of Akbar II set the stage for a re-opening of important questions about the relationship between the Emperor and the British. One of the new Emperor's first acts was to write to the Governor General regarding an increase in the stipend payable to him by the Company, according to the agreement it had entered into with his father. He pointed out that, as the expenses of the royal household had increased with his accession, it was time for the government to fulfil the promises given to Shah Alam.[29] As a second point, he asserted his right to appoint his own successor, the young prince Jahangir, the son of Mumtaz Mahal, instead of his first born, Abu Zafar, who had the approval of the British.

On neither of these did he receive a positive response. The stipend was in fact reduced, from a total of Rs 90,000 to Rs 80,500, on the grounds that certain allowances that had been made during Shah Alam's time, i.e. a separate allowance of Rs 7,000 to Akbar as the heir apparent, and Rs 2,500 to a *mukhtar* (chief functionary or minister) who had recently died, were now not warranted. The sum was further reduced to Rs 79,800 rupees sometime soon after.[30] The government was equally unreasonable on the question of the right to appoint an heir apparent. They continued to hold that by right it was the firstborn who must succeed as the heir, completely ignoring the fact that as per Mughal tradition, the Emperor had always been free to choose from among his sons. These two issues, of the augmentation of the stipend and the right of the Emperor to appoint his successor, were to be a constant feature of Mughal-British relations till 1857.

What Seton tried instead was a policy of trying to console and conciliate the Emperor through gestures. He frequently visited the palace, sent small gifts to the Emperor and other members of the royal family, and on days he did not visit himself, sent messengers to enquire politely about the Emperor's well-being.[31] He also participated in various religious ceremonies important to the royal family. He accompanied the princes who went to the tomb of Shah Alam, near the Qutub Minar, to perform certain religious ceremonies six months after the burial. He also went to the palace every evening during the first twelve days of Rabi ul awwal (the period when the birth and death anniversaries of the Prophet Mohammad were commemorated). On this occasion, noted *maulvis* and *pirzadas* of Delhi joined with the Emperor and the princes in recitations from the scriptures. The Emperor apparently was pleased with this and introduced him to the various religious divines. According to the Persian newsletters, Seton also went to pay his respects at the holy relic of the footprint of the Prophet, which was kept in a shrine in the garden known as Mahtab Bagh, located within the fort.[32]

These were diplomatic gestures, and Seton confessed to his superiors in Calcutta that the ceremony and gestures of submission involved in an audience with the Emperor were tiresome for him, which he was willing to put up with only because he thought it was necessary for him to discuss important issues with the Emperor personally.[33] All the same, Seton was not immune to the charisma of the royal family. He felt honoured when one of the young royal princesses was presented before him.[34] Moreover, the courtesies extended by the Resident to the royal family were never one-sided, but graciously reciprocated. The Emperor frequently sent small presents to the Resident, such as a basket containing a flower garland and a *paandan* or betel leaf case full of prepared *paans*. On one occasion Abu Zafar wrote and presented a few verses in praise of Seton.[35]

The relationship overall was not without tensions. Both sides were well aware of the actual balance of power, and the fact that the British only needed the Emperor as a prop to legitimize their position in India. At the same time, both sides wanted to manipulate the situation in their own favour. The British were eager to treat the Mughals with courtesy, but equally keen to make it clear that they were not really subordinate to or dependent on the Emperor. The Emperor, on the other hand, wanted to exploit the British need to keep up the fiction, in order to extract some real benefits.

One important tool that the royal family could employ in their favour was that of symbols and ceremonials. The political culture of the Mughals in India had developed a complex of symbolic objects and ceremonies that were expressive of power and incorporation. As the British felt constrained by expediency to pay at least nominal homage to the Mughal heritage, this involved them in frequent contestations around these symbols. Even though these interactions took place within the limited space of the Mughal court, their impact was felt over a much larger area. These events were widely reported by the news writers who were maintained at Delhi by the British Government, as well as the independent chiefs, to report occurrences at the court on a daily basis. This gave the royal family a peculiar power to deploy court ceremonies to convey powerful messages to the independent chiefs of India and the general population.

Most important among these symbols were those that emphasized the Emperor's suzerainty. The Emperor was understandably interested in the retention of these symbols. The British response was to try and prevent the Emperor from deploying these tools, and instead appropriating them to increase their own power.

Coinage was one such symbol. At the beginning of the nineteenth century, the coins of the East India Company were struck in the name of the Mughal Emperor, as were those of practically every independent ruling chief over much of India. With the accession of Akbar II, new coins bearing his name were struck at Delhi. It was, however, decided that the old dies, bearing the name of

Shah Alam, would be retained in the Company's territories. The measure was supposed to be one dictated by 'convenience'.[36] In effect however, a powerful symbol of the claim to sovereignty of the reigning Mughal Emperor was thus being devalued. The message being sent to the minds of the people through the length and breadth of the Company's territories was a subtle one. The Company was demonstrating a relationship to a late Emperor and thus the legitimacy of its own claim to rule, without explicitly declaring itself a vassal of the present Emperor.

A similar question arose about the seal used by the Governor General in official correspondence with the Emperor. The Governor General's first letter to the newly ascended Akbar bore the seal used during the previous Emperor's time, and was engraved with the words 'fidwi e Shah Alam Padshah'. The Emperor received the letter with a thoughtful silence and Seton, eager to placate, volunteered an explanation before it had been asked for. He explained that no slight had been intended. It was not the intention of the Governor General to deny the present Emperor the status accorded to the last. Rather, the use of the old seal was due to a delay in producing a new one, because the 'engravers of the Persian character at Calcutta worked slowly and unskillfully'! The matter, however, did not end there, as Seton's quick thinking put him in some further difficulty. The Emperor proceeded to order a new appropriate seal to be engraved at Delhi and had it sent to Calcutta. Seton took pains to explain to the government at Calcutta the circumstances out of which the action had occurred, and that it should not be interpreted as demonstrating the right of the Emperor to confirm the titles of the Governor General.[37]

The problem was that, conventionally, the sending of a seal denoted a delegation of authority, and thus the sending of the seal by the Emperor to the Governor General was likely to be interpreted as such. The government did not have any objection to the use of a seal bearing the new Emperor's name; in fact, in the meanwhile one had already been cut in Calcutta. It inadvertently differed in certain aspects from the one sent by Akbar—the former was inscribed with 'Akbar Sanee' (Akbar II), whereas the Emperor wanted just 'Akbar'. The Governor General politely but firmly insisted on using a seal that would be cut anew at his orders in Calcutta, 'precisely according to the inscription in that sent by His Majesty'.[38] The important point was that the seal the Governor General used would not be the one sent by the Emperor.

The ceremony of khilat too became a matter of controversy. If the Company was in theory merely governing on behalf of the Mughal Emperor, its highest officials should receive these robes as symbols of royal favour and delegation. Akbar, therefore, soon after his accession, expressed his determination to send khilats to the Governor General and the other members of his council. The government was, however, adamant that he should desist, advising Seton that if it came to it, he should tell the Emperor that the khilats would be returned. The objection was that the presentation of the khilats would involve the recipients in the exhibition of 'a degree of exterior ceremony and submission inconsistent with the real rank and ascendancy which the British Government holds among the states of India' and would be a 'public acknowledgement of vassalage'.[39]

The Emperor did not give in easily. He wrote a shuqqa to Seton pointing out that as this intention to send the khilats had become common knowledge and had gained publicity in the newspapers, it could not now be gone back upon. In any case, he did not see the reason behind the reluctance. 'If anyone should have a thought of not carrying into execution this necessary plan let him dismiss such a thought', he added with a definite tone of command, as 'our satisfaction depends upon its fulfilment'.[40] Seton tried hard to persuade Akbar to give up the plan. Finally, the latter agreed that a mission under a certain Shah Haji Abdul Majeed and a Raja Sedh Mal would be sent to Calcutta, without the khilat, but with the intention of having a personal audience with the Governor General. Evidently the audience was desired because the Emperor felt that direct communication through persons in his confidence would be more efficacious in putting forward his case with regard to the questions of succession and the increase in stipend. Seton requested the government that this be agreed to, if only in order to prove to the Emperor that the opinion of the government was no different from what was conveyed through the Resident. The government would rather have seen the plan abandoned altogether, but agreed to Seton's proposal.[41]

This, however, was not the end of the story. When Shah Haji and Sedh Mal arrived in Calcutta it was discovered that they had brought the khilats after all. They also carried a letter from Qudsia Begum, as well as shawls, in effect a khilat, from herself and Mumtaz Mahal.[42] After much discussion it was decided that they would be given a private audience with the Governor General. They would, however, not formally hand over the letter and cloak sent by the Emperor. Those would be sent through the Persian Secretary to the Government (in charge of all Persian correspondence, hence, in effect, responsible for all communications with Indians of influence). This was intended to obviate the Governor General from the necessity of observing any ceremony during its presentation.[43] One can, however, speculate that as far as Akbar II was concerned, the purpose had been served. This was because the news was broadcast through the newspapers that the khilats had been sent and accepted at Calcutta.

While the operation of these symbols of authority was contested at the highest levels, the Company's government did not mind the Emperor giving khilats to British officials of a lower rank, or granting titles to them, or if these officials presented nazars to the royal family. Those who interacted with the Emperor in an official capacity, such as the Resident, the commander of the palace guards (a post created somewhat later, which will be discussed below), or the British doctor who provided his services to the royal family, were invariably given royal titles.[44] There were also those British officials and non-officials who were not related in any official capacity to the Emperor but also wished for and received titles. One of these was Lady Hood, Mary Elizabeth Frederica Mackenzie. Mary was a Scotswoman of a noble family, who had impressed Sir Walter Scott enough for him to model his character of Ellen in the *Lady of the Lake* after her. When she visited Delhi in 1814 she was thirty years old, and the wife of the Naval Commander of the East Indies, though she travelled to Delhi without her husband. Lady Hood was a spirited woman, reputed to smoke hookahs and famous for having shot a tiger. In Delhi, she visited the palace and was introduced to the Emperor and the begums, and was given a title.[45] Even senior army officers actually applied for and were permitted to receive titles, such as Brigadier General John Arnold in 1818.[46]

Nazars or presents, usually of money, were made to the Emperor and important members of the royal family such as the chief consort and the heir apparent. Though a gesture of submission, it was free of connotations of delegation of authority, such as the khilat carried. Apart from the nazars presented by the Resident to the Emperor on state occasions as per the formal agreement with Shah Alam, nazars were frequently presented by a variety of individuals. They were offered by the Resident and other officials, either resident in Delhi or visiting, on their own behalf on a variety of other occasions, such as when an officer was first introduced to the Emperor, on the Emperor's birthday, on family celebrations like the wedding of a prince, when the princes visited the Residency for some celebration, such as the birthday of the British monarch, or when the Emperor made a present (often it was a present of his own poetry). The presentation of nazars by British officials also took place in contexts that were peculiarly personal, such as when the Emperor was bled during an illness, or 'on the commencement of the rains in consequence of His Majesty's prayers'! Customary presents, called *inam* instead of nazar, were also made to a number of royal attendants on the occasion of the anniversary of the Emperor's succession to the throne.[47]

5

'The Abode of War'?

While Akbar II negotiated with the British over the limits of his power, the citizens of Delhi were working out their own position vis-a-vis the new regime. The renowned Islamic scholar Shah Abdul Aziz, assessed the advent of British rule in 1803 in the following words:

> 'In this city [of Delhi] the *Imam al-Muslimin* wields no authority, while the decrees of the Christian leaders are obeyed without fear [of the consequence]. Promulgation of the command of *kufr* means that in the matter of administration and the control of the people, in the levy of land-tax, tribute, tolls and customs, in the punishment of thieves and robbers, in the settlement of disputes, in the punishment of offences, the *kafirs* act according to their discretion. There are indeed, certain Islamic rituals...with which they do not interfere. But that is of no account. The basic principle of these rituals are of no value to them, for they demolish mosques without the least hesitation and no Muslim or *dhimmi* can enter the city or its suburbs except with their permission....From here to Calcutta the Christians are in complete control.'[48]

In the eyes of one of the most devout and learned Muslims of Delhi, therefore, Delhi was now *dar ul harb*, 'the abode of war'; as opposed to *dar ul Islam*, 'the abode of peace'. The kafirs (unbelievers) were in control and kufr (unbelief) was the basis of their rule. Incidentally, the *fatwa* made a clear distinction between kafirs and dhimmis—those non-Muslims accorded protection and freedom to practice their own religion in an Islamic state (in this case, mostly Hindus and Jains).

The question of loss of political power was one with which the *ulema*, Islamic scholars, had been grappling for much of the eighteenth century too, as the Mughal empire continued headlong into decline, and eventually Delhi itself came to be controlled by the Marathas. In the eighteenth century, Shah Abdul Aziz's father Shah Waliullah, also a noted Islamic scholar, had turned instead to the role he felt the ulema could play in guiding Muslims to regulate their lives in accordance with the law. An important aspect of this was proper education in the original sources of Islamic law—the Quran, and the *hadis*, the traditions and sayings of the Prophet. For Shah Waliullah, one important means of achieving this was through teaching in the Madrasa e Rahimiya. This theological college had been set up by his father, and students flocked to it from all over North India. Another important aspect of his work was the attempt to make the tenets of Islam known more widely to the faithful, without the intermediacy of commentaries and interpreters. To this end he translated the Quran from Arabic into Persian, which was at the time the lingua franca for much of India.

Shah Waliullah also combined his learning in Islamic law with participation in the Sufi tradition, which sought to establish a close personal relationship between God and creation. This made him one of the most influential Islamic scholars and spiritual leaders of his time. After his death in 1763, his legacy was continued by his sons, of whom the eldest, Shah Abdul Aziz, was the most respected. He and his brothers carried on this tradition of reform of the customs and practices of Muslims into the nineteenth century. In addition to formally teaching their students, who came from far and wide, and giving spiritual guidance to initiated disciples in the Sufi tradition, they attempted to reach out to a broader public, for instance through the sermons they preached in the mosques of Delhi. An even more important instrument to this end was the fatwa. The fatwa was an opinion given by a scholar on a specific point of Islamic law. A significantly greater number of these were given during the lifetimes of the sons of Waliullah than before. They became the source of fairly detailed guidance for individual Muslims seeking to lead a life in accordance with the *shari'at*, particularly in the context of alien rule.[49]

Abdul Aziz's position on British rule was more equivocal than the fatwa quoted at the beginning of this section seems to suggest. His characterization of Delhi as a dar ul harb has to be examined carefully, and in the context of pronouncements on other, related, subjects. He did not advocate the taking up of arms or immigrating—the options open to Muslims living in a hostile state. In fact, he was not against Muslims taking up employment in the Company's government, as long as their duties did not go against their faith or harm their fellow Muslims in any way.[50]

Shah Abdul Aziz of course represented only one of several points of view, though an influential one. There was the occasional religious divine who called for a complete avoidance of service with the government. This was particularly true of the Sufis of the *khanqah*, or convent, of Mirza Jan e Janan.[51] But even in this case, it may be argued that it was an extension of their general policy to distance themselves from the polluting effects of political power, rather than a specific opposition to British rule.

In any event, many men of influential families in fact did take up employment in the middle rungs of the colonial administration. One of these was Khwaja Farid ud din, the maternal grandfather of the later reformer and educationist Sir Syed Ahmad Khan. He belonged to a Delhi family, and had joined the Company's service in middle age, in 1797. He served in various capacities—educational, administrative and diplomatic; in Calcutta, Iran, Ava (Upper Burma), and Bundelkhand. He returned to Delhi in 1810 and was to play an important role in the city.

Another was Fazl e Imam, originally from Khairabad (in modern-day Uttar Pradesh), and a noted scholar in the *ma'qulat* tradition. The latter emphasized the study of the rational sciences—Arabic grammar and rhetoric, logic, mathematics, philosophy, theology, Islamic law and jurisprudence. This was a position distinct from the *manqulat* tradition of the Waliullahi family, which emphasized the Quran and hadis above all else. Fazl e Imam migrated to Delhi at the beginning of the nineteenth century, and worked in the judicial service. He soon reached the position of *sadr us sudur*, the chief Indian judge in Delhi.

Government service at this level provided a good livelihood. Moreover, there was an apparent persistence of pre-colonial forms in administration. Persian was used as the official language in courts of law and in official correspondence. Islamic law was applied, and Muslim law officers were appointed in the courts to interpret that law. It was not difficult for the Muslim service elite to fit into this ethos, and it was not difficult for a Muslim to reconcile service in the British administration with his religious conscience.[52]

6

The British Power and the New Elite

The service elite was only one of the several categories of people who had to adjust to life under a new dispensation. A number of military chiefs, big bankers and merchants found it quite easy to make the transition from Maratha to Company rule in the early nineteenth century. In its war with the Marathas, the Company had sought military support from local chieftains and financial resources from the big bankers and merchants. To secure this support it had made promises of generous grants of revenue free lands, or *jagirs*, and recognized the claims of several small independent rulers.

Several *jagirdaris*, or minor princely states in the Delhi region, owed their origin to the British. They had all provided arms to the British cause at a crucial time, and were rewarded with territory. Ahmad Baksh Khan received the lands of Ferozepur Jhirka and Loharu; Abdus Samad Khan, Dujana; and Faiz Talab Khan, Pataudi. Nijabat Ali Khan became the ruler of Jhajjar, and his brother Ismail Khan that of Bahadurgarh. Others, like Bahadur Singh of Ballabgarh, and Begum Samru of Sardhana, had the possession of their estates confirmed.

Begum Samru was the widow of an unscrupulous and bold military adventurer, Walter Reinhardt, who was a native of Trier, in Germany. Arriving in India around 1750, he had successively served the British East India Company, the French at Chandernagore,

Safdarjang, the Nawab of Awadh, and a host of smaller powers. He eventually wound up in Delhi, serving Najaf Khan, the most able of the late Mughal chief ministers. Najaf Khan gave him the jagir or principality of Sardhana, which continued in his possession till his death in 1778. Reinhardt had acquired the sobriquet 'Sombre' or 'dark', which was corrupted to Samru, the nickname by which many Indians knew him. He had at some point in his sojourn in North India married Farzana, a Kashmiri girl, popularly known as Begum Samru. After his death, his widow not only took control of the jagir, but of her husband's troops, with the blessings of the Mughal Emperor, and acquiescence of Mahadji Sindhia, to both of whom she proved loyal as well as militarily useful. Reinhardt had a son from an earlier wife, called Louis Balthazar Sombre, alias Zafaryab Khan, who lived quietly at Delhi, though some opponents of the Begum did briefly try to put him up as a rival in Sardhana. After the British conquest of Delhi in 1803, Begum Samru shrewdly threw in her lot with them, and therefore had her jagir confirmed, though only for her own lifetime.[53]

A number of military men who had been employed by the Marathas but had come over to the British side were rewarded either with pensions or employment. Prominent among these was the D'Eremao family, consisting of Manuel, his son Domingo, and his nephew Anthony. This family had been resident in Delhi for generations. One of their illustrious ancestors was Juliana Diaz da Costa, a Portuguese lady who had been an influential figure at the Mughal court in the first half of the eighteenth century. Manuel D'Eremao was given an allowance of Rs 400 per month, and his son and nephew, Rs 40 and Rs 60 respectively.[54] Mirza Ashraf Beg had also served under the Marathas, and he was re-employed, and put in command of *najeeb* battalions—consisting of 'irregular' (as in, not in the main army) infantrymen, to guard the city gates and other locations around the city and outside its walls as well.[55]

A pension was also granted to Madame le Marchand, the widow of Captain le Marchand, a French officer who had been the *kotwal*, or chief of police, of Delhi during the Maratha administration, and had died before the takeover of the city by the British. Her case had been approved on the recommendation of a Catholic priest, Padre Gregorio, resident at Delhi, who reported that the lady was 'in the greatest distress'. It was decided that the pension of Rs 30 per month, which she had been getting from the Marathas, be continued to her.[56]

There was one military leader of outstanding merit who was treated less generously—James Skinner. His father was a British soldier in the army of the East India Company, and his mother an Indian. When their sons James and Robert wanted to become officers in the Company's army, they found that this was an avenue that was closed to men of a mixed parentage. James therefore used his father's military connections to obtain employment in 1796 in the armed forces under General Benoit de Boigne, a French mercenary, who commanded troops in the service of the Maratha chieftain Daulat Rao Sindhia. Over the next several years he distinguished himself in Sindhia's army, which, under the command of Perron (who had succeeded de Boigne), by 1801 became the most powerful force in North India. James' brother Robert had by then also joined him in service.[57]

Towards the end of August 1803, when the Anglo-Maratha war had commenced, two soldiers of British ancestry resigned from Perron's service, saying they would not fight against the East India Company's army. In consequence, all the other soldiers of a similar background, including the Skinners, were dismissed. At the same time, on 29 August, a proclamation by the British Governor General offered good terms to all soldiers and commanders, whether British, other European, or from other parts of British India and Awadh, who were serving in the Maratha armies, if they came over to the British side. Robert had already joined the service of Begum Samru, and James, after some misgivings, presented himself to Lord Lake. Shortly afterwards, with the defeat of the Maratha forces at Delhi, some of Perron's cavalry troops came over to the British side, and were placed under the command of Skinner, who agreed to command them, with the stipulation that he would never be asked to take up arms against Sindhia.[58]

This troop formed the nucleus of Skinner's famous body of

soldiers, called Skinner's Horse, or informally, 'Yellow Boys', after the colour of their uniforms. Because of his mixed parentage, Skinner was for many years not given a regular commission in the East India Company's army, and his troop remained an 'irregular' part of the army. In 1804, Robert joined his brother's troop.[59] Though their brave service in the cause of the Company was officially recognized, the Skinners were treated rather shabbily. In 1806 Lord Lake promised them a jagir worth Rs 20,000 a year, but when this proposal was put before the government at Calcutta, the Governor General, George Barlow, turned it down on the grounds that being British subjects, they could not be permitted to hold land in India. Instead James was offered a relatively paltry pension of Rs 300 per month, and his brother Robert, Rs 120.[60] They found, therefore, that their mixed parentage was a double disadvantage.

This, however, was not the end of the Skinners' story. In 1808, Robert Skinner was involved in a legal dispute, and the judicial decision arising from that also settled the question that they should be considered 'native subjects'. As a consequence their pensions were commuted to jagirs of equal worth, i.e. yielding Rs 3,600 and Rs 1,440 per year, respectively.[61]

In the meanwhile, Skinner's Horse was needed for active military service again. At first this involved bringing to order rebellious landowners in the territory around Delhi; but soon became more intense as the Company engaged in war with Nepal (the so-called Gorkha War, 1814-16), and once again, the Marathas (the third Anglo-Maratha war, 1817-18). With the end of these campaigns, Skinner and his body of horsemen more or less retired, except for brief stints in action against Bharatpur (in 1825-26). Around 1,000 of them, a third of the total, were put under James and located at Hansi, in present-day Haryana. As a reward for their further military services, the brothers' jagirs were made hereditary. Finally, in 1826, as a special case, the title of 'Commander of the Bath' and the rank of Lt Colonel was bestowed by the order of the British monarch on James Skinner. Unfortunately, this measure was not implemented till 1830, due to resistance in army quarters in India itself.[62]

The British also rewarded those who had given non-military support during the war with the Marathas. Bhawani Shankar had been the *bakshi* or paymaster of the troops of the Marathas, and had switched sides. He was granted the jagir of Najafgarh, and his son an additional four villages, as a reward for having extended financial support in provisioning the Company's troops. His grand mansion in Delhi, close to the Fatehpuri mosque, came to be known popularly as the '*namak haram ki haveli*'—'the house of he who had not been true to his salt'—evidently a reference to his betrayal of his masters, the Marathas.

The banker Harsukh Rai also received a jagir. His family had lived in Delhi ever since his ancestor Dip Chand Sah had been invited by Shahjahan to establish his banking business in the new city of Shahjahanabad in the mid-seventeenth century.[63] Harsukh Rai's business and political importance had stemmed from his position as hereditary treasurer to Emperor Shah Alam, and to the Marathas, and the loans he had given to several other states, particularly in Rajputana. His social status was underlined by the title of 'Raja', given by the Emperor. Under the new dispensation he became the treasurer for the Company's government in Delhi.[64] The British also recognized a range of hereditary revenue-free holdings and stipends that were a legacy of the earlier regime.

7

Peace...and Strife

The end of the second Anglo-Maratha war (1803-05) brought about peace in North India, such as it had not seen for several decades. Once armies ceased to march up and down the countryside, and the political situation stabilized, the impact was felt in both town and country. Cultivation improved, and with it, rural prosperity. Trade received a boost, both from higher rural outputs and from the improved security of the highways. In Delhi, the value of property—both land and houses—was said in 1806 to have increased nearly a hundred per cent compared to the period before the takeover by the British.

Seton, in a letter to the government at the end of 1806, was effusive in his positive assessment of the tranquillity of the city and the contentment of the people. He was convinced that 'the community at large seems to perceive the great and new advantages of security of person and property and of impartial justice which it enjoys through the mild, equitable and moderate system of the British Government.' He was happy to report, 'At Delhi and in its vicinity the most perfect tranquillity continues to prevail' and that 'breaches of the peace seldom occur and murder is hardly ever committed.'[65]

Soon, however, the peace was to be shattered, and the reason was sectarian strife. The city had a diverse population, in numerical terms fairly equally divided between Muslims on the one hand, and Jains and Hindus on the other. It was Muslims who mostly made up the military and service elite, and the Islamic scholars, all of whom were an influential section of the population. Their fortunes, however, had declined with the decline in fortunes of the Mughal empire. The mercantile class, mostly composed of Hindus and Jains, fared better. Their growing economic status found an outlet in construction activity. This included houses, but more significantly, temples, of which several were built in the eighteenth century.

Public assertion of the religious identity of the Hindus and Jains received a boost under the Marathas, when cow slaughter in the city was banned. Though this order was revoked under the British administration,[66] apparently without protest, there was soon a flexing of muscles by opposing groups. The broad issue was, what was to be the balance of power in Delhi? Traditionally, it was a city which was not only the seat of the Mughal Emperor, who was himself a Muslim, but one which was an important centre of Islamic learning, and where the powerful citizens—the landed aristocracy and bureaucracy of the empire—had been largely Muslim. Against this, the Hindus and Jains had prospered economically. They had also become politically more influential, through their financial dealings as bankers to various ruling powers including the Emperor, the Marathas and the British. They were now ready to assert their position.

The lead was taken by Harsukh Rai, the banker, a pious Jain known for his charitable works and the building of several temples. In 1807 he had a new temple constructed outside the city, in the nearby suburb of Jaisinghpura.[67] It also became known that the idol to be installed there would be taken in an ostentatious procession through the city before it reached its final destination. Seton decided to dissuade him, deeming that such an act, 'from its being unusual, would have been offensive to the feelings of the Mussulmans'.[68] Traditionally, Seton felt, big non-Muslim religious processions had not taken place in Delhi, and therefore the status quo should be maintained. The rumours, however, persisted, and some troublemakers started to attack the house of Harsukh Rai.

The incident grew into a riot, and in suppressing it, the government forces killed a few people. Soon a crowd of Muslims collected at the Jama Masjid in protest.

Maulana Rafi ud din, brother of Shah Abdul Aziz, and a highly influential scholar in his own right, appealed to the Emperor to exert his influence on behalf of the Muslims who had been arrested. He also demanded an apology from Harsukh Rai, to be made to the Emperor, presumably as representing the Muslims of the city. In the meanwhile, the British local authorities also appealed to the Emperor to issue a proclamation that would induce the protestors to go home. Akbar vacillated, particularly in view of the arguments of some of his own relations that he was bound by faith to support the Muslims. Ultimately, Seton worked on him in his usual subtle way, reminding him that he was the king of the Hindus (in this category, Seton, like most British officials, included the Jains) as much as of the Muslims, and that violence and looting were not to be tolerated.

This was an argument that Akbar was more than willing to listen to, but Seton went to the extreme of asking that an order banishing Rafi ud din to a distance of 100 miles from Delhi be given under the seal of the Emperor himself.[69] With some reluctance Akbar conceded. The Emperor's only alternative probably would have been to refuse to lend his name to such an order. But for Akbar, who was seeking to extract a raise in his stipend and an acknowledgement of Jahangir as his heir, resistance was unwise, particularly as the Resident could actually take such action without reference to the Emperor at all. The Mughal Emperors had traditionally played the role of mediators and been quite even-handed on sectarian questions. Left to himself, Akbar would probably have found a gentler solution, particularly as Rafi ud din had clearly condemned the violence and looting that had accompanied the affair. In a letter to Seton he had remarked that 'the ignorant and common people were the cause of this improper riot, which, both according to the law of our religion and the maxims of the world, is bad.'[70]

Though Rafi ud din's departure was uneventful, certain murmurs of discontent came to Seton's ears. He learnt through the various newsletters of the city that somebody had made a representation to the Emperor, saying that the British intended to exile all the Muslim religious scholars and holy men from the city. Seton, who was probably coming to a realization of the esteem in which Shah Abdul Aziz and his brothers were held, immediately set out to do some damage control. He paid a visit to Shah Abdul Aziz in his home, and was cordially received. Seton was impressed with the venerable teacher as well as his disciples, who were according to him, 'very numerous and uncommonly respectable in appearance'.

On being asked by Seton if there was anything that he wished done, one of the disciples of Abdul Aziz pointed out two things. One was the case of fifty-one *bighas* of land in Jor Bagh, at some distance to the south of Shahjahanabad. This had been granted to Shah Waliullah during the reign of the Emperor Alamgir II (1754-59), but the grant had at a later date been withdrawn, due to some internal politics at the Mughal court. Seton agreed to the restoration of the grant of this land, which now yielded a revenue of twenty-seven rupees a year. The other point was the repair of the garden of Mehndian, just outside the city wall, which was the burial place of Abdul Aziz's parents. Gujars had destroyed this, and Seton immediately ordered its repair.[71]

Evidently, the question of the banishment of Rafi ud din did not cause rancour during the visit, and was not even mentioned. Nevertheless, Seton wrote to the government asking that the banishment of Rafi ud din may now be cancelled, as his brother probably pined for him. The Emperor too had informally asked Seton that Rafi ud din be allowed to return. And so, the latter was back after the absence of a few months.[72]

At the same time as he visited Abdul Aziz, Seton also visited Shah Sabir Baksh, a respected Sufi teacher of the Chishti *silsila*. He apparently chose Sabir Baksh and Abdul Aziz because among the holy men of Delhi, they were the best known 'for learning, sanctity and general respectability of character and conduct.' According to Seton, Sabir Baksh compared the British administration favourably to that of the Marathas.[73]

Seton also made other attempts to project the British administration as being sensitive to the feelings of the people of Delhi. He ordered repairs to be carried out in the Jama Masjid and the Zeenat ul Masajid—the two major mosques of the city.[74] He was clearly anxious that the British be well thought of in Delhi, and in his letters to the government at Calcutta, was optimistic that his efforts were bearing fruit. On the occasion of Eid ul Fitr in November 1809, he accompanied the Emperor, as the latter went in procession through the streets of the city to the Eidgah. He wrote in his letter to Calcutta the next day that he 'distinctly heard the praises of the British Government blended with the shouts of blessings' and praises of the Emperor shouted out by the onlookers.[75]

8

The Question of Succession

Seton also had to push the limits of his tact and diplomacy in the palace, where the nomination of the heir apparent had arisen as a contentious issue. Akbar's oldest son was Abu Zafar, scholarly, courteous, and a favourite with the people of Delhi. The British had decided that he was the fit heir to Akbar, but there were other powers at work within the palace. Mumtaz Mahal had succeeded in pushing the cause of her son Jahangir, a rather spoilt youth. Though the response from the government at Calcutta was a negative one, the pressure was kept up, mainly on two fronts. One being repeated correspondence and missions, and the other, the creative use of symbolic gestures and ceremonies.

One occasion where the latter tactic was deployed was the so-called 'adoption' of Seton by Mumtaz Mahal. Seton had been informed that the Begum had decided to adopt him (a favour that Seton could not possibly refuse) and would like to invest him with a '*khilat e farzandi*', i.e. khilat of adoption, at a suitable date. Seton dutifully wrote to the government at Fort William for instructions.[76]

While such instructions were awaited, one day at the durbar Seton was informed that that very day had been picked by the Begum as an auspicious one on which to perform the ceremony, it being the birthday of the British king. Seton was, not to put too fine a point on it, trapped. As he explained later, 'The complimentary manner in which this unexpected proposal took place, and the circumstance of its being made at the King's Durbar, and of the Begum expecting me, as it were, immediately, rendered it somewhat difficult for me to persist in my declining to accept.' The ceremony took place, with Mirza Jahangir placing the '*dastar e farzandi*', i.e. turban of adoption, on his head. Rather lamely Seton added that he had 'made it clear' that this was totally unconnected to the efforts that were being made to ensure Jahangir's succession.[77]

As the government saw it, however, the damage had been done. Seton had assured the government that the ceremony would not involve anything that gave the impression that Jahangir had been accepted as heir apparent. Yet the newspapers of Delhi and Lucknow had reported that Seton had been 'invested with a khelaut on the occasion of his...being appointed on the part of the Prince Jehangeer, to the office of Naib Wullee Ahud, or Deputy Heir Apparent'—thus suggesting that the ceremony had also involved accepting Jahangir as the heir apparent. There was nothing left for the British to do but try to counter the reports through the news writers and British Residents at the various courts.[78]

Events surrounding Jahangir were soon to reach an even higher pitch. In the several accounts that have been written about the incidents, the prince has often been described as a wayward, wilful child who invited punishment through his reckless behaviour.[79] It is recounted that he would frequently make insulting remarks about the Resident behind his back, and one day out of the blue he got it into his head to barricade the fort and fire on Seton, who was entering with a small entourage of guards. It makes for a colourful story, and one historian has dismissed it as one of the 'breaches of etiquette' on the part of the Mughals, in the face of consistently correct behaviour from the British, represented by the 'hyper-polite Seton'.[80]

The contemporary official correspondence, however, reveals a darker side to the episode. This was a period when Britain was particularly concerned about defending its interests in India against European rivals. In mid-1807 Britain's nemesis, Napoleon, had cemented an alliance with Tsar Alexander I of Russia through the treaty of Tilsit, which committed Russia to supporting France in its war against Britain. The direct result of this was the declaration of war by Russia against Britain in late 1807. Though this war was never aggressively pursued by Russia, it made a move by Russia on British possessions in North India a very real possibility. In May 1809, therefore, the government at Calcutta wrote a secret letter asking Seton to explore the possibility of removing the Emperor and the royal family from the fort in case of the approach of a 'European enemy'. Seton responded by saying, that though they would never leave willingly, it would be possible to evict them with minimal bloodshed if British troops were already in strategic possession of the two main gates of the fort. Seton hoped that 'circumstances might arise' which would persuade the Emperor that the stationing of British troops in the palace was necessary.[81]

The 'circumstances' in fact arose just a month after Seton's letter was dispatched. The Emperor was persuaded to give an order to the *qiladar*, the commander of the Emperor's troops in the fort, to prevent any wine entering the fort. That same night the commander caught someone trying to smuggle wine in, and that person was sent back. Soon after, however, a man with a sword entered the house of the commander, allegedly to kill him, failing in the intention because the latter was out. It is not unlikely that this sequence of events was clandestinely engineered by Seton. If not, they were certainly used by him to serve the ends of the government. In a petition to the Emperor, Seton regretted this flouting of the Emperor's orders and expressed concern over the possible threat to the Emperor's person. Pleading that if anything untoward were to happen to His Majesty, the Resident would be blamed, he begged the Emperor to temporarily allow British troops to be stationed at the palace gates.[82]

Akbar II consented reluctantly to the measure, and two companies of soldiers were posted at each of the palace gates. It was after this that Jahangir with his armed followers took up positions in the windows and galleries of buildings commanding a view of the British post. Seton arrived on the scene, and as he was advancing, with the intention, as he later described, of reasoning with the prince, he was fired upon. The bullet went harmlessly through the cap of a soldier next to him. Seton retreated, and after some attempt at negotiation, British guns were turned on the gates of the fort, which were blown open. After a brief skirmish in which some lives were lost, Jahangir was taken into custody and the Company's troops occupied the fort.[83]

Seton was convinced that the Emperor had at no time supported the prince's action; he had simply not been able to prevent it, though he pleaded. The Emperor's troops, the najeebs, were, however, a cause for worry. During the incident, they had either sided with Jahangir, or at least, had done nothing to oppose him. To neutralize this threat, Seton then proceeded to put into position a system that would give the Resident effective control within the fort. The Emperor objected to the presence of the Company's soldiers within the fort, and also rejected the plan of instead using najeebs under the command of James Skinner. He finally agreed, albeit reluctantly, to the proposal that the Company's troops would retain control of the two gates but vacate the interior. The latter would be guarded by the Emperor's najeebs under the command of Mirza Ashraf Beg, who enjoyed Seton's confidence. Seton explained to the authorities in Calcutta that the reason Ashraf Beg was a good choice was that, apart from his general efficiency, he would be the means of supplying 'authentic information of everything of importance that occurred in the palace'. In effect, Seton hoped he would be a British spy in the palace.

Within a few days the plan had been implemented. The perimeter of the fort now came to be guarded by troops in the pay of the Company—the armed *barqandazes* or guards, stationed along the river side of the wall, and regular soldiers on the main gates.[84] A British officer was stationed in command of the Company's troops guarding the gates, and this officer soon became 'the means of procuring interesting information...beneficial to the public service.'[85] The incident had been used successfully by the British to gain important strategic control of the palace.

With the royal family on the defensive, Seton sought to

further consolidate British control over the affairs of the palace. The immediate pretext for greater interference was the supposed misappropriation of the royal allowance. The financial affairs of the Emperor, which crucially included the distribution of the allowance, were managed by Raja Jai Sukh Rai, a merchant who was a favourite of Mumtaz Mahal. Seton felt that 'the lowness of the origin of this person', and his general unfitness for the job, which was 'the public talk of Delhi', made his removal desirable. This was in fact not true, since Jai Sukh Rai was from one of the old banking families of North India. His forbear, Sah Ranbir, had founded the town of Saharanpur during the reign of the Emperor Akbar. Nevertheless, Seton felt it was 'highly expedient to introduce into the palace and to place about the king one or two persons whose integrity, ability and attachment to the British Government might be relied upon'.[86] Accordingly, the Emperor appointed people expressly approved of by Seton. Raja Jai Sukh Rai was not only dismissed but also banished 'to the other side of the river'. He later returned at the request of the Emperor, but was given a relatively inferior position.[87]

9

Exile

Akbar agreed to all these measures because Seton had a bargaining point that he could not possibly counter—the custody of Jahangir. What was to be done with the young man was still uncertain. Seton himself had suggested sending him to Agra, but he then vacillated. He evidently had a conversation with the prince where he took the moral high ground. Rather hypocritically, he reminded the prince:

> 'that what had been done had solely proceeded from the absolute necessity of supporting the royal authority which had been usurped and abused... that what had taken place had been a source of deep and painful regret to me; and concluded with an assurance that I should be most happy in promoting any of his wishes which might not be contrary to the commands of the king.'[88]

Jahangir, according to Seton's letter to the authorities in Calcutta, then expressed great repentance, saying that his eyes had been opened. He also expressed the view that the fault lay with his evil ex-associates, the troopers. Seton in fact got sufficiently carried away with his own fiction to write to the government that it was his aim to reform the prince, hoping that 'ere long the pleasing office may be mine, of restoring the prince, in a state of progressive reform, to his royal parents'. The reform would be implemented in a way that gave the impression that it was the Emperor's 'fatherly correction' that was being applied. Since this impression would be difficult to maintain at a distance, it might be best not to send Jahangir away to another city. Soon, however, Seton went back to the view that exile was the best solution.[89]

Through all these subtle manoeuvrings, Seton kept up a facade of polite courtesy in the palace. He made it a rule, he said, 'to go to the durbar twice every day, as I know the attention to be peculiarly gratifying during the agitation which his [the Emperor's] separation from his son may be supposed to cause'.[90] He also visited the prince frequently, presenting him a musical box, a backgammon board, a table, two glasses and saucers, with a view to providing him the means of 'innocent amusement'. It was decided finally that Jahangir would be exiled to Allahabad. Seton saw him off at Patparganj, presenting him with some pieces of muslin and a copy of the Gulistan of Sadi.[91] The latter was one of the standard texts of the basic Persian curriculum, and so, quite in keeping with Seton's determination to reform the young man!

In Allahabad, away from parental controls, Jahangir took to an extravagant lifestyle, funded out of a generous allowance from his parents. He had a natural charm, which made him popular with the various British officials and other local residents who came to visit him, presumably out of curiosity, since he was after all a royal prince. He took to drink, which had always been a weakness with him, indulging in gin, brandy and port wine. He associated with 'loose women', causing his wife to complain to her relations in the palace in Delhi. He was also reported to have adopted 'the dress and manner of Europeans'. This was the influence of his local British minders, who often breakfasted with him, and now and then took him out in a carriage to see a play.[92]

In Delhi, the Emperor and those close to him resorted to desperate measures following the frustration of their plans. A certain Babu Pran Kishan was secretly dispatched to Calcutta, with a letter in Akbar II's own hand appointing him ambassador to 'our son the Governor General, to the Members of Council, and to the Supreme Court...[and if necessary, i.e. if the application in Calcutta should fail]...to the King of England'.[93] He carried letters with him addressed to various of these personages, which were chiefly complaints against Seton, and also mentioned the questions of the allowance and the appointment of Jahangir as heir apparent. These letters had not been prepared, like all official correspondence, in the royal office, the *munshi khana*. They had been clandestinely written in the palace interior, by the female *munshis* or *chitthee navees* employed there. In Calcutta Pran Kishan tried to approach a senior official with a bribe of a lakh of rupees, said to have been given by Mumtaz Mahal. This, however, yielded no result.

Pran Kishan kept his lack of success a secret from the royal family. He wrote letters back to Delhi claiming that he had met the Chief Justice and the members of the Council, and that a solution to His Majesty's problems was at hand. Letters, patent forgeries, purporting to be from Lord Russell (the Chief Justice of the Supreme Court) had been forwarded to the Emperor to keep his hopes up. Interestingly, Pran Kishan had been introduced to the Mughal court by the son of Maulana Rafi ud din, Maulvi Ghulam Mustafa, who was said to be the prime mover behind the plan.[94]

The facts of this secret mission to Calcutta did not come to light until much later. In the meanwhile, the British authorities had discovered some interesting correspondence with the state of Awadh. One was a shuqqa sent by Qudsia Begum to Bahu Begum (mother of Nawab Asaf ud daulah) at Awadh. It cautioned against the 'machinations of the English' and complained of the 'acts of violence and degradation' committed against the royal family at Delhi. Yet the only remedy suggested was that a letter be written to the Presidency so that the harm may be redressed and 'the good name of the Company may be restored'.[95] A letter from one of the royal princes to Bahu Begum similarly asked her to consult the Governor General and his council at Calcutta to appoint 'agents of good character, wisdom and discrimination to conduct the affairs of the state'. In the meanwhile the Nawab of Awadh was to resume his 'own hereditary office of Vizier'.[96] Safdarjang, the second nawab of the independent principality of Awadh, and his successor Shuja ud daulah, had been the prime ministers of the

Mughal empire. Ever since then the nawabs of Awadh had enjoyed the title of 'nawab wazir'.

Clearly the attack was against Seton and not the British Government as such. When later confronted with this correspondence, Akbar and his family could only protest that they had been misguided and misled by people into writing these letters in a 'moment of doubt and distress'.[97] Qudsia Begum was induced to send a shuqqa to Bahu Begum at Lucknow disavowing the mission of Mohammad Beg Khan (who had taken the letters), and the matter was allowed to rest without an official representation from Calcutta to the Emperor on the subject.[98]

In the meanwhile, however, the government had decided to allow Jahangir to return to Delhi. It was presumed that he had learnt his lesson, but as a special precaution, he was made to sign a written code of conduct. Seton believed that this liberality towards Jahangir would disarm the Emperor and expose the malicious lies of those who encouraged him to distrust the British. Moreover, Jahangir's exile had served one important purpose, as it had been used effectively as a bargaining point with the Emperor. The latter went out of his way to conciliate Seton in the hope that his son would be allowed to return. To this end, he gave up one of his dearest wishes, and invested Abu Zafar as the heir apparent. The reward was the return of Jahangir, and the prince arrived back in Delhi in November 1810, after an absence of a little over a year.[99]

During his absence, his distraught mother had vowed that she would offer a canopy and coverlet of flowers at the shrine of Qutb ud din Bakhtiyar Kaki, if her son returned. Qutub Sahab, as he was popularly called, was the much-revered Sufi whose shrine in Mehrauli had been the focus of pilgrimage since his death in 1235. With Jahangir back in Delhi, the vow was fulfilled with great pomp. It immediately became an annual event sponsored by the palace, and continues to this day. The flower sellers of the city, who were commissioned to prepare the floral offerings, added *pankhas* or fans to the procession of their own accord, and in time these became the main feature of the fair. The fair was celebrated each year sometime in the monsoon, the date being fixed by the Emperor at the request of the flower sellers. The Emperor would also donate a large sum of money for the purpose. The *mela* became a huge affair and a social occasion, referred to as 'Phoolwalon ki Sair'. It also became an occasion for religious harmony, as pankhas were also offered at the Hindu temple of Jogmaya.[100]

10

Charles Metcalfe as Resident

In 1811 Seton was succeeded as Resident by Charles Metcalfe, just twenty-six years old, and ambitious. He had been Seton's 'First Assistant', or deputy, from October 1806 to August 1808, and believed that his new post was 'without exception in every respect the highest in the country beneath the members of government.'[101] A subtle change in attitude, a greater impatience with the trappings of the Mughal court, distinguished him from Seton. As Seton's deputy he had been privately critical of what he felt was the former's 'submission of manner and conduct' towards the Emperor, which, he believed, 'destroys entirely the dignity which ought to be attached to him who represents the British Government, and who, in reality, is to govern at Dihlee; and it raises...ideas of imperial power and sway, which ought to be put to sleep for ever'.[102] On his first being presented to Akbar as the new Resident, he was given the customary titles. In a letter to the government he made it clear that he had accepted them, against his own natural inclination, in order to indulge the Emperor's wishes and because it was a matter of 'little importance'.[103]

On the part of Akbar there was an understandable caution. Whereas Shah Alam had acknowledged the appointment of Seton simply with the confidence that the latter 'will render the most essential services to our Royal Person',[104] his son could take nothing for granted. Akbar wrote to the Governor General to give instructions to the new functionary, 'enjoining him in the strongest terms, that he should do nothing without our consent, that he should not neglect to execute whatever orders may be issued by us, that he should not attend to the representations of anyone, either verbal or in writing, to the prejudice of our Royal Person...'.[105] Though couched in the usual imperious style, in substance this was an anxious application of an insecure man.

Soon after Charles Metcalfe took over charge, the news broke of Pran Kishan's secret mission to Calcutta, to push the Emperor's case directly with members of the government. The government's displeasure was conveyed to the Emperor. Much was made of the clandestine nature of the mission, and the ingratitude towards the good and kind Seton.[106] The fact remained, however, that to the royal family there had seemed no other way out. The alarming erosion of the Emperor's privileges and powers was immediately attributable to Seton's actions, and the only appeal lay with the latter's superiors in Calcutta. Letters addressed by the Emperor to them 'officially' needed to be conveyed through Seton himself. The only alternative was to go behind Seton's back. The letters had to be written secretly because there were people even within the palace who could not be trusted. Akbar had nothing left to say in the end except that he had been misled by his advisors. He put forward his demands and grievances before Metcalfe and they were, as expected, rejected. Three individuals at Delhi who were alleged to have been involved in the 'plot' were dismissed from his service, and Metcalfe intended to make sure that they never entered the palace again.[107]

A few months later, rather unexpectedly, Metcalfe was informed that Jahangir wished to leave Delhi and live elsewhere. Akbar put his son's hand into that of Metcalfe and 'committed him to the special protection of the British Government.' Metcalfe concluded that one of the reasons for this was that they were both convinced now that he could never aspire to the throne. Further, if his father died while Jahangir was at Delhi, he would be under the authority of Zafar, who would be Emperor. In addition, felt Metcalfe,

Jahangir had become accustomed to the liberty he had enjoyed in Allahabad and was restive in Delhi. The prince had acquired English tastes during his stay in Allahabad, and he enjoyed wearing English clothes, driving English carriages, and building apartments in an English style within the Red Fort. Metcalfe recommended the application on the ground that the prince was a disruptive influence within the palace.[108]

The government was willing to accommodate the desire, with a few conditions. Jahangir was not to be allowed to visit Delhi except with prior permission of the government. Neither was he to have a separate allowance. His expenses were to be paid out of the royal stipend. He was to be under the control of the designated authority of his place of residence and governed by the rules and ordinances of the country. The government would determine the number of attendants he would be permitted to have.[109]

Jahangir left for Allahabad and was never to return to Delhi again. His stay in Allahabad was a source of friction on a number of points over the years. The point of etiquette was one that arose immediately. The prince expected the magistrate and commanding officers of the troops at Allahabad to pay an official visit, present nazars, receive khilats and remain standing in his presence. The magistrate applied to the government for instructions and was told that they of course could not be expected to remain standing in Jahangir's presence. For the rest, they should refer to the Resident at Banaras for the forms in practice with respect to members of the Mughal royal family who were resident there.[110]

Within a year another controversy had arisen. In early 1813 Jahangir set off for Lucknow via Kanpur on a visit not sanctioned by the government. The ostensible reason for the visit was to attend the wedding of a relative and to meet his uncles, the brothers of Akbar II, who lived there. While this escapade caused frantic correspondence between the various British authorities at Allahabad, Lucknow, Calcutta and Delhi, the climax of the episode was the discovery that this was yet another 'plot'. It was found that the hidden motive behind the visit was to make overtures to the Nawab of Awadh on behalf of the Emperor. The Nawab, Saadat

Ali Khan, was to be told that it was his duty as a functionary of the Mughal state to pursue the interests of the Emperor at Calcutta and London.[111]

The Nawab initially received Mirza Jahangir with all the required ceremony—going nine miles out of the city with all his courtiers to welcome him. However, when he learnt that the British Government positively disapproved of Jahangir's visit, he declined to visit the prince even when the latter expressly sent word that he expected a personal send-off. In addition, he handed over various documents to the British Resident at his court, which led to the unveiling of the 'plot'.[112]

The revelation of these details by the Nawab invited significant recriminations. The prince was ordered back to Allahabad, with orders that force may be employed to ensure his return. More seriously, it was decided 'that after what has passed he can on no account be permitted to return to Dilhi or to retain in any situation that degree of freedom...he has lately been allowed to enjoy'.[113] The allowance he got from his father and the household establishment he kept up was drastically reduced under direct British supervision. His movements were also more closely restricted. For a while he was entirely confined to the compound of the garden known as Khusro Bagh where he lived either in tents or a one-room bungalow. Later, he was permitted to go out for 'air and exercise'.[114]

The Emperor was made to feel the consequences of his behaviour too. An addition to the royal stipend had been sanctioned in 1809, which brought the total stipend to one lakh rupees. Of this, that portion which was intended for the Emperor's personal use (the Emperor's stipend had been increased from 60,000 to 73,000 rupees), was to be withheld. That part of it which was for the benefit of the heir apparent and others, was to be paid directly by the Resident.[115] The Emperor was also informed, that 'the deceit which Your Majesty has condescended to practice in these instances has excited the utmost astonishment and displeasure in the mind of the Right Hon'ble the Governor General.' Regret was expressed over his dissatisfaction with the Company's government, to which he was 'indebted for great advantages'. Finally, 'the Governor General cannot any longer repose confidence in Your Majesty's word...[and] has therefore judged it necessary to show Your Majesty that such proceedings cannot be entered into without danger'.[116]

Akbar's reaction was pitiful. In a conference with Metcalfe 'he called himself a fool, he called himself a wretch, he pulled his own ears, in token of deserving punishment, and humiliated himself...'; he offered to ask pardon of Metcalfe 'in public, with his hands together in a posture of supplication'.[117] Akbar's humiliation was complete. There was no pretence left as to his real position vis-a-vis the Company and its officials. Metcalfe felt that as the lesson had been learnt, the increase in stipend might be restored, but it was unwise to allow Jahangir to return. The government agreed but decided that a slight delay in the restoration of the allowance was required to make the desired impression.[118]

Jahangir's repeated requests to be allowed to go to Delhi were turned down. Among other reasons, it was felt that his presence might cause a disturbance during a future succession. He continued to live in Allahabad in cramped dwellings, in financial straits, and in ill health. His expenses were looked into by the local authorities, and revealed that the prince had been living on an extravagant scale. He employed 1,564 people at salaries totalling Rs 14,315 per month. Among this large retinue were 465 employed in the stables, fifteen pigeon-keepers, four sets of dancing girls, in addition to a large number of flag bearers and ceremonial musicians, singers, etc. Expenses of the birds and beasts alone came to Rs 2,012. These expenses were sharply pruned, to a maximum of Rs 1,500 per month.[119]

The magistrate of Allahabad was soon given full control over him—to appoint and dismiss his servants, to regulate his expenditure. His father was not to be consulted in these matters at all.[120] Most of his employees were dismissed, leaving a 'mere' 120 who received a total salary of Rs 425 per month.[121] In 1821 he again applied for permission to go to Delhi, saying that he was ill and hoped that a 'change of air' would do him good.

The magistrate informed the government that the prince looked perfectly well to him and that the government doctor had said that a change of air was unnecessary. The government sent back a message to the prince hoping that he was better, as a trip to Delhi was not 'expedient'. Within a few weeks Jahangir was dead, at the age of thirty.[122] His body was brought back to Delhi and buried at the shrine of Nizam ud din, in an enclosure of beautifully carved marble screens.

11

Keeping Up Appearances

While the royal family, particularly the Emperor, tried to work out important issues of legal and symbolic status with the British, both parties were also very aware that a public image had to be maintained, in the country at large, but also in the city. The Emperor already had the benefit of a relationship with the people of Delhi that went back several generations, and involved rituals and traditions that had been evolved at least as far back as the reign of Shahjahan in the seventeenth century. One such tradition was the ceremonial procession. Every time the Emperor moved out of the palace, whether to the Jama Masjid or the Eidgah on important festivals, or as he went to suburbs such as Mehrauli, he went in state. The procession included the Emperor and some close male family members on richly caparisoned elephants, the royal ladies in covered howdahs on elephants or in carriages. They were accompanied by armed guards, banners and insignia of royalty, and musicians. A crowd gathered to see the Emperor as he passed, and his officers stood outside their respective houses and tendered nazars as he went by.[123]

These were also occasions for charity, as the poor looked forward to coins that were scattered by the royal officials. The recipients also seem to have treated this as a matter of their right. Charles Metcalfe related the incident of accompanying Akbar II on one such outing, when the retinue was followed as usual 'by a party of the sturdy beggars...demanding rather than begging money' and he 'heard one of them roar out to the king "we got money when prince Jehangeer was here"'.[124] Jahangir, before his exile, had been liberally supplied with money by his parents, which he lavishly distributed on such occasions.

For the Emperor and other members of the royal family, this display was an important way to establish their status. Soon after he ascended the throne, the new Emperor spent money on the production of some rich howdahs and chairs of state to be used on such occasions of public display.[125] The new 'protectors' of the Emperor were also keen to be a part of this ritual of ceremonial processions. This was essentially to let the public at large know that they were treating the Emperor with respect. If the Mughal Emperor was the fount of sovereignty, an overt alliance with that sovereignty was crucial for the maintenance of the legitimacy of the de facto rulers. The practice of accompanying the Emperor on important ceremonial processions was therefore continued by successive Residents. When Sir George Nugent, the Commander in Chief of the British Army in India, was on a visit to Delhi in December 1812, he too accompanied the Emperor to the Eidgah on the occasion of Eid.[126]

Apart from the state procession, it was also felt that if the palace presented a respectable appearance, it would reflect well on the British Government. It would demonstrate that the government was treating the royal family with generosity. So, in 1808, in keeping with a demand the Emperor had himself made during the mission of Shah Haji and Sedh Mal to Calcutta, the government decided to gift the Emperor with new curtains for the Diwan e Khas. This was the famous Lal Purdah that all visitors to the court had to pass before entering the presence of the Emperor, and had over the years become rather tattered. The project became a fairly comprehensive one, as carpets, awnings, mirrors, window panes and crystal chandeliers were added to the gift. The carpets were ordered from Mirzapur, with samples of patterns being sent beforehand for approval. Broadcloth was sent from Calcutta as it was cheaper there, arriving only towards the end of 1812. The work finally was completed only by 1815.[127]

Repairs and renovations in the fort were motivated by a mix of practical necessity and diplomacy. In the British attack on the fort during the fracas involving Jahangir, the timber leaves of both the main gates had been destroyed. It was felt that these needed to be repaired with careful attention to the original pattern, and they were restored at a cost of little over four and a half thousand rupees. Further, once a British guard was moved into the fort, the bastions of the Delhi and Lahori Gates, which housed the officers, had to be repaired. Simultaneously, the decayed bridges at these two locations were replaced with masonry structures.[128] The inscription installed to commemorate this development noted that the construction had taken place in the fifth year of the reign of Akbar II, and was undertaken by Robert McPherson (the commandant of the palace guard).[129]

In his list of demands presented to the government in 1809, Akbar had included the repair of the parapet wall of the fort and of the Asad Burj, a bastion in the south-eastern corner. This was eventually done several years later, as a part of a project for strengthening the defences of the city, whence the repair of the outer perimeter of the fort was considered necessary. But in the repair of the Asad bastion, no attempt was made to match it to the other bastions of the fort, and all ornamentation was dispensed with in the interests of economy, though the magnitude of the project still involved the expense of almost fifteen thousand rupees.[130]

Political considerations were also behind the administration's decision to carry out repairs to the Jama Masjid in 1808-09, at a cost of Rs 3,430. The project was justified as being 'worthy of a great and powerful government and...a measure most gratifying to the Mahomedan Inhabitants of Delhi of every Rank and description'.[131] Moreover, the move could also serve an added purpose of conciliating the Emperor, because the Jama Masjid was a royal mosque. From the time of its foundation during the reign of Shahjahan, no *waqf* properties had been set aside for its upkeep, which was considered a prerogative of the Emperor himself. Apart from upkeep, the Emperor also played an important role in the organization of this religious institution, for he appointed the functionaries of the mosque and his soldiers guarded it. He went to the mosque in state on important occasions, and conferred khilats on functionaries such as the imam, and *darogha* (superintendent), and his name was included in the *khutba* or sermon on Friday. On his accession, he had been ceremonially presented with a sabre and shield by the functionaries of the mosque. Periodically, he would send for the relics enshrined in the mosque to be brought to the fort so that he and others could pay their respects.[132] By carrying out repairs to the mosque the British could reassure the people that the Emperor was being supported in his hereditary duties. Over the next several decades, periodic repairs continued to be carried out at government expense, including the repair of the machinery that raised the well water to the tank in the courtyard of the mosque, and repair of a tower that was struck by lightning.[133]

There were other measures which could be adopted to demonstrate to the people of Delhi that cordial relations existed between the royal family and the British Government. One was the invitation that was extended every year to the important princes to visit the Residency to witness the celebrations of the British monarch's birthday. The princes were ceremonially welcomed with nazars, and the celebrations included fireworks, and began with a dance performance by tawaifs, or courtesans.[134]

In these early years, the British administration found it useful to use the regard with which the Emperor was held among the people, to further its own policies. Thus, it was considered a significant step forward when Dr John Reid, the Surgeon, explained the principles of smallpox vaccination to Akbar and convinced him of its benefits. He then presented a set of lancets to him, so that the Emperor could inoculate the royal grandchildren with his own hands. The news was reported in the Persian newspapers, and Seton believed that it would do more than anything else to popularize vaccination among the people. Reid had been regularly treating members of the royal family too.[135]

In the attempt to create and foster ties with the people of Delhi, particularly the elite, the British used a range of devices borrowed from the Mughal tradition, but deployed independently of the Emperor. One of these was the khilat. So, for instance, khilats of condolence were routinely bestowed by the Resident on various people on the occasion of deaths of their fathers—individuals such as Bhawani Shankar and Harsukh Rai who were particular supporters of the British, and on big landholders and independent rulers (in the latter case on their vakils or representatives at Delhi).[136] The British administration also found several ways of obliging important people in the city. The Resident was sanctioned an additional number of peons with government badges, for the purpose of stationing them at the houses of foreign vakils, chiefs and other important people of Delhi, when the latter wished for them.[137] Elephants maintained at the Residency, for the use of the Resident and others on public occasions, were also lent from time to time to members of the royal family and others.[138]

This wide range of attempts to conciliate and befriend stemmed in large part from a deliberate self-interested policy. In the first decades of rule in North India, the British East India Company felt a certain insecurity. The conflict with the Marathas was not yet over, and the Mughal Emperor was potentially an alternative centre of power. In 1809, Seton justified the measures taken by him to prevent famine in Delhi in view of the 'unsettled character and the irregular habits of the people of Dehli' who were 'apt to be tumultuous and disorderly, and in times of difficulty to be guilty of excesses...endangering the peace of the city'.[139] In 1813 Charles Metcalfe still felt that it was not safe to feel secure in the fidelity of the 'natives'.[140]

On their part, the people of Delhi, too, were adept at negotiating the changing situations within the triangle of which they formed one corner, with the administration and the Emperor forming the other two. The Emperor had a tradition of maintaining relationships with citizens through close interactions. One avenue for this was the durbar held every evening in the Diwan e Khas, the hall of special audience in the Red Fort. The *akhbars*, or newsletters, tell us about the various individuals who attended on various occasions. Bhawani Shankar was one of these, and we find him on one occasion bringing sweets on the occasion of the Urs of the saint Ghaus e Azam Abd ul Qadir Jilani. Another frequent visitor was Maulvi Ghulam Qutb ud din (also known as Kale Sahab), the spiritual guide of the Emperor. Begum Samru not only came to visit the Emperor when he was in his private palace with the women of his family, she also corresponded with the ladies on an almost daily basis.

Many of these individuals had relationships with the British as well. In the case of Bhawani Shankar and Begum Samru who had jagirs awarded by the British, this was not surprising, but other connections were being made too. So we find Ghulam Qutb ud din being invited to the Residency to attend the celebrations of the British monarch's birthday. Among the others invited for the birthday celebrations was Shah Sabir Baksh—a Sufi—and other learned and spiritual figures.[141] There was clearly an attempt, by both parties, to forge relationships that would be independent of the Emperor. The court astrologer of Akbar II also made an overture to the British authorities by forwarding an almanac, or *panchang*, for the New Year to the Governor General.[142]

12

The British Enclave

In the early years following the Company's conquest of Delhi, its presence in the city was largely confined to a particular enclave, which was identified closely with the new rulers, their residences and institutions. This area lay between the Red Fort and the northern, or Kashmiri Gate of the city. This was relatively open land, overlooking the river, and therefore prime real estate. A start had been made when a mansion dating to the time of Shahjahan had been acquired by the Resident, General Ochterlony, out of his private funds for a residence. The government decided to purchase this from him when he left Delhi in mid-1806, to turn it into a permanent 'Residency'. This cost just under sixty thousand rupees, which included the price paid to Ochterlony, as well as the cost of some modifications and repairs that were underway.[143] Great pains and expense were expended to transform the building into a European-style one. Thus the fluted pillars and arches of the Mughal original were covered over to produce a facade of pillars in the neoclassical style. Seton's successor, Charles Metcalfe, spent another large sum, nearly sixty-eight thousand rupees, on repairing, refurbishing and furnishing the house. Another old building in the same complex, that might have served as a house for the Resident, received similar treatment.[144]

The British military establishment was also concentrated at

Kashmiri Gate. Nasir Ganj, which had been set up as a commercial enterprise by Ochterlony, was purchased by the government for eighteen thousand rupees in 1807. The ganj, or wholesale mart, was removed, and a military cantonment was set up there.[145] The old mansion of Safdarjang, who had been the prime minister of the Mughal empire in the mid-eighteenth century, was located close to the Residency. This was occupied by the officers of the garrison.[146]

So strong was the identification of Kashmiri Gate with British society, that it occurred to at least some who were aspiring to be part of that class, that this was the place to live. James Skinner, who had built a house just south of Chandni Chowk, had by the early 1820s sold it to Nawab Ahmad Baksh Khan, and shifted to another house near Kashmiri Gate.[147] His great social and architectural coup came soon after, as he began work in the mid-1820s on St James' Church. The church was located on what had earlier been Nasir Ganj and then a cantonment, until the troops were moved to Dariyaganj.[148] Consecrated in 1836, St James' became the place where all of British officialdom worshipped.[149]

There was a concentration of the British official class within the Kashmiri Gate area, and to some extent its social life revolved around the Residency. In the early years, the number of officials was small. As a result, the Resident in a sense acted as the head of a fairly close-knit family of officials. For instance, he frequently dined and breakfasted with the other officers in a communal arrangement.[150] The Residency was also where prayer services were held, before the construction of St James' Church.[151] A marked feature was the relative scarcity of British women. As Charles Metcalfe wrote to his sister, who was hinting that she might enjoy a trip to India, at Delhi 'there would be a total want of female society such as you would like—such, I mean, as in education, manners &c., would be suited to your tastes and habits. We are not without our share of good amiable and respectable Women of all Colours, but out of Calcutta a *Lady* is a rarity.'[152] What Charles was referring to was the invariable tendency of British men to make up for the lack of their countrywomen by keeping Indian mistresses.

Though British society at Delhi was small, its social life was considerably enhanced by the many important visitors from the Bengal Presidency that the city frequently received. Delhi was the last important outpost of the British territories at the time, and the gateway to territories further north. Many of these important official British visitors to the city stayed at the Residency, and their visits were inevitably the occasion for parties, and sightseeing trips among the rich, monumental treasures of Delhi and its environs.

The accounts and travelogues left behind by some of these visitors also throws interesting light on life at the Residency. For instance, an important ritual of the breakfast table was the reading of the newspaper. A lady who visited the city in 1808 remarked on what to her was the singular experience of 'a man, with a long white beard marching into the room...and, beginning to read as fast and loud as he was able, all the news of the day, from a paper in manuscript called the *Ackbar*; in which he related every, the most minute circumstances respecting the Royal Family, somewhat resembling a bulletin, which I understood was the practice at this hour in the house of every great personage. The Emperor is, in like manner, entertained with anecdotes of the Resident's family, the city news, etc.'[153] The news was indeed of the most detailed and intimate nature; an akhbar of 13 June 1810 reported that Seton had not eaten his breakfast as he had a hangover![154]

There was a small number of people who did not strictly belong to the British official class but to an extent were participants in the social life of the British enclave. One of these was of course James Skinner; another was Begum Samru. This remarkable lady was a typical example of an individual who successfully straddled the Indian and European social spheres, and modified her behaviour to suit the circumstances. She did not appear in public or in her own durbar unveiled, and even when interacting with her own officers, she usually sat behind a screen. On the other hand, she appeared unveiled on the frequent occasions when she hosted banquets in a European style where only Europeans, men as well as women, were invited. No Indian men were present on these occasions, and the food was served by the women in her household.[155] She was a frequent guest at the Residency, where too, observers often remarked on her comfort with male company. After dinner, as the European ladies retired, she continued to sit with the gentlemen and smoke her hookah.[156]

Though the main British enclave was just within the city walls near Kashmiri Gate, British officials also undertook several construction projects, often in a quasi-official capacity, outside the walls of the city. Charles Metcalfe established a mart outside the Lahori Gate at the site of the old Eidgah, which became known as Shah Ganj. Also, during his first term as Resident, he renovated the royal garden called Shalimar Bagh, established when the city was founded in the mid-seventeenth century. He had some buildings constructed in it for the use of his Indian mistress and family. Ochterlony, who later came back for a second term in Delhi, also added a few houses to this garden, and laid out another one called Mubarak Bagh, named after his wife, Mubarak un Nissa. In the latter was a building in which he is said to have wished to be buried. Ochterlony died in 1825 and was buried in Meerut, and Mubarak Bagh became a picnic area for British officers.[157]

Another prominent structure outside the walls was the house of Doctor Ludlow, who occupied the post of Civil Surgeon in Delhi for many years. Doctor Ludlow used to attend to the medical needs of the royal family as well, for which he was paid an allowance of Rs 300 per month by Akbar II from 1813 onwards.[158] This generous addition to his salary enabled him to acquire a large estate spread over forty-three bighas of land, situated right outside the Kashmiri Gate. On this he built a grand house, adorned with crenellations. Its rather pretentious architecture led to it being facetiously referred to as 'Ludlow Castle', in reference to an actual castle of that name in England.[159] Abu Zafar seems to have visited the house, and was impressed that it was excellently furnished and had '5,000 volumes of books and many pictures'.[160]

In 1828, Dr Ludlow was keen to sell the house and the Emperor wanted to buy it, with its furniture and attached land, for his son Babur. The house was valued at around fifty thousand rupees, and Akbar proposed that the mode of payment would be a monthly payment of three hundred rupees to Dr Ludlow, and after him to his son, till the end of their lives. Since this commitment involved a decision to alienate a portion of the Emperor's stipend beyond his own lifetime, the government prohibited the transaction.[161]

Another house constructed outside the city walls was that of William Fraser, the First Assistant to Charles Metcalfe. He built his residence on the Ridge, a part of the ancient Aravalli range, around 1819-20, and in contrast to Dr Ludlow's house, which was of an entirely British architectural style, it was more Anglo-Indian, incorporating features from both traditions.[162] Thomas Metcalfe, the younger brother of Charles Metcalfe and also serving in Delhi, later built a palatial home north of the city, beside the river.

13

Cultural Crossover

The building of St James' Church by James Skinner gave the Skinners social acceptance of sorts, with the visiting Bishop staying at his house, and conducting service in the church.[163] Nevertheless, where exactly families like the Skinners fitted into British Indian society, was a problematic question. Unions between European men and Indian women have often been romanticized, as the product of an age of greater racial intermingling and understanding, the era of the 'White Mughal'. It must be remembered, however, that there were complex questions of power, class and gender, as well as race, that were involved in these alliances. James Skinner's mother was a young girl of fourteen when she was taken prisoner during a war that the East India Company was fighting to extend its control over the region of Banaras in the 1770s. James' father was the soldier 'into whose hands she fell', and to whom she bore six children. Though a friend and biographer of James Skinner claimed that he 'treated her with great kindness' this seems doubtful, since she killed herself when James was twelve years old, heartbroken that her daughters had been forcibly taken from her and sent to boarding school.[164]

A happier story was that of William Linnaeus Gardner, who had served for a while in the British Army, and then some years under the Maratha chief, Jaswant Rao Holkar, before raising an 'irregular horse' troop, much as Skinner had, for the Company. In 1798 he had married a princess of the state of Cambay or Khambat, whom he had been assigned to protect, as she and her mother had fled to Surat after political intrigues in Cambay. In this case it was the young woman's elite status which probably smoothed the path, as Akbar II recognized the marriage, and granted the lady a high title as well as a jagir. Gardner and his young family settled in Delhi in 1809, dividing their time between the city and the jagir in Kasganj, in present-day Uttar Pradesh.[165]

Gardner moved easily within British society, independently of his wife, who observed purdah, and had her own, mostly Indian, social circle. The Skinner ladies (James had married an Indian, and had several sons and daughters by her) did not observe purdah, and were, therefore, free to mix with the British social circle. This, however, brought its own problems, because, though James Skinner was personally well respected because of his military service, his family were often the butt of jokes for they 'were all, of course very dark in complexion, and spoke English with an extraordinary accent...although they looked upon themselves as English people.'[166] David Ochterlony, who served two terms as Resident of Delhi, also had an Indian wife, though unkind rumours hinted at a greater number. Lady Ochterlony, otherwise known as Generalee Begum, does not seem to have had a role to play in the small society at Kashmiri Gate, though she had no trouble interacting with the Mughal royal family and the jagirdars and rulers of the independent principalities who reported to Ochterlony in his official capacity. In fact a certain amount of notoriety surrounded her activities, for it was averred that she was taking bribes in return for favours secured from her powerful husband.[167]

Simply put, James Skinner's father, William Gardner and David Ochterlony seemed the products of a different world, an era now past, where racial or religious differences did not matter as much. Younger men in the Company's Civil or Military service, were far more discreet about their liaisons with Indian women. Charles Metcalfe, during his tenure as Resident in Delhi, was raising a young family, though little information is forthcoming about the nature of this relationship, and certainly no public mention of the woman in question. Similarly, in the case of Fraser, he appears to have had at least one Indian wife/mistress, but there is no indication of her having mixed with even the female component of British society, as Gardner's wife did.

What had changed? At one level, not that much. Even in the eighteenth century, while numerous British officers took Indian concubines, and some even legitimate wives, never had such wives and their children ever been actually accepted as equals by the British colonial state and society in India. Begum Samru was socially important to British officialdom in Delhi because of her political significance as a loyal and powerful jagirdar. None of the children of these mixed marriages—the Skinners, or Gardners, actually rose in the mainstream of the colonial civil or military service. James Skinner faced discrimination despite long years of loyal and valuable service to the Company's government. Only in 1829, barely a decade before his death, did he get a formal army rank.[168]

This insuperable racial barrier was recognized by Ochterlony, who wrote to a friend: 'My children are uncommonly fair, but if educated [in India] in the European manner they will in spite of complexion labour under all the disadvantages of being known as the NATURAL DAUGHTERS OF OCHTERLONY BY A NATIVE WOMAN—In that one sentence is compressed all that ill nature and illiberality can convey, of which you must have seen numerous instances during your Residence in this country.'[169] Their future in England was not bright either. When Ochterlony died in 1825, obituaries printed in Britain simply said, 'Sir David was never married'.[170]

It was no surprise that Indian wives and children were far more common among those officers of the Company who had spent most of their careers posted in the Indian states. People like Skinner had in fact come into being largely in the context of 'native' society presided over by the independent Indian states. These had accorded a space in their service and society to Europeans, and had probably even encouraged marriages that would promote political ties.

A case in point is that of the Indian captain of cavalry who astutely tried to cover all bases in the 1770-80s by giving one daughter in marriage to William Palmer, the British Resident at the Sindhia court, and another to Benoit de Boigne, the French commander of Sindhia's forces. The blessing given to such marriages through titles, jagirs, etc., bestowed by the Mughal Emperor on the ladies—for example the wives of William Gardner and William Palmer—endorses the view that at least the Indians looked on them as political alliances.[171] The children from such mixed marriages were given similar opportunities for advancement as their fathers. James Skinner owed his rise in the first instance to opportunities provided by the Maratha army and later had to settle for an 'irregular' troop within the Company's army, despite his skill as a soldier and the men and resources he brought over with him.

What was new about the nineteenth century was that the native powers had been effectively subordinated to the East India Company's military and political might. For a British or mixed race man of a certain class, the latter soon afforded the most desirable avenue for employment. But, unlike the Indian states, the British colonial state was run on racial premises—admitting no one of Indian blood into the upper ranks of its service. To be able to establish one's membership of the ruling race was now of great importance. Hence the efforts of the Skinners and several other similar families in Delhi, all trying hard to fit into British society, and only succeeding in being objects of ridicule, or at best, pity.[172] It was soon obvious that these attempts could not in fact erase one's racial past. This realization must have in great part been the factor discouraging further mixed marriages, thus eliminating an important meeting point between individual representatives of the colonial state and Indian society.

At best, what lasted for a while was informal liaisons, such as that of Charles Metcalfe. He never married his mistress, though he had three sons by her, who were then separated from her and sent to England to be educated. In this case too, he worried for their future. He said of his oldest son's possible future avocation, 'I do not recommend his coming to this Country, out of Company's

Service, and there is no chance of an appointment in it'.[173] The son of David Ochterlony too decided to resign from his relatively minor job in the customs department in Delhi, and move to Europe, saying that it was for the sake of his children's education.[174]

Under the circumstances, it was not surprising that marriages with Indians became less common not only among Europeans, but also but also among those of mixed blood. There was a desire to restrict marriages either to Europeans or within similarly mixed families. One of Ochterlony's daughters was married to Henry Middleton, a civil servant who was for a while Deputy Superintendent at Delhi. Another daughter appears to have been married to a Skinner.[175]

Here the Gardners remained different. Mrs Gardner's social standing probably gave her a degree of power within the relationship that was very different from the position of, say, James Skinner's mother. The Gardners mutually came to an agreement that their sons would be brought up Christian, and their daughters Muslim. The daughters would also be brought up according to the norms of Indian society, secluded from the company and gaze of unrelated males. As it happened, their only daughter died young, but the same rules then applied to their granddaughters, from two surviving sons. Many years later, in 1835, though William was in favour of his granddaughters marrying Europeans, he gave in to his wife's desire to have a match made with one of the princes of the royal family at Delhi—a nephew of Akbar II. Another granddaughter was engaged to the Mughal emperor Bahadur Shah Zafar's son some years later.[176]

PART TWO

Winds of Change

Charles Metcalfe

14

Increasing Economic Control

The era of Charles Metcalfe as Resident marked a distinctly new phase in the evolution of the East India Company's role in Delhi and the surrounding territory. The early years, under Ochterlony, and even Seton, had seen the Company taking over the administration, but continuing with many older systems and institutions. It was on the whole slow to introduce innovations, partly because it was reluctant to interfere with what were considered established 'prejudices', but often this was the inadvertent result of a gradual, staggered replacement of the existing administrative apparatus. The process gathered momentum with the arrival of Charles Metcalfe.

The Residency of Charles Metcalfe inaugurated an era of some far-reaching changes in the land revenue administration in the territory of Delhi, and it was Metcalfe's First Assistant, William Fraser, who was directly connected with some of these measures. Two features of this assessment regime stood out. One was a high, some even said harsh, rate of assessment, and a strict enforcement of recovery of revenues in the district. High and rising revenue assessments were a feature that continued well into the 1820s.[177] A few simple figures clearly demonstrate the rate at which the total revenue demand increased:[178]

Year	*Demand in Rs*	*Collection in Rs*
1810-11	8,91,187	8,77,259
1815-16	14,14,943	12,14,195
1820-21	27,80,942	25,73,458
1825-26	30,40,878	28,63,710

The other prominent feature of Charles Metcalfe's period of administration was a new policy towards jagirs. These were revenue-free assignments of land, some of which dated from the heyday of the Mughal Empire, and many others were of a later date, that is, the eighteenth century, when the practice of giving jagirs became more common. This process in fact accelerated with the advent of the Company in the early nineteenth century. Jagirs had been given out with a fair amount of generosity at the time when Lord Lake was in charge of the campaign against the Marathas and needed the support of bankers and military chiefs. Older land grants had been continued from similar motives. As the situation stood in 1805, whereas 328 villages yielding a revenue of Rs 4,52,681 were held as jagirs awarded during the previous regime, 568 villages yielding Rs 7,41,284, had been given by the British.[179] The practice of giving out jagirs was more or less discontinued soon after the Company established itself in Delhi, as the need to win friends and influence people was thought to be less imperative.[180]

In fact, with the end of the Anglo-Maratha war and the resultant peace, agriculture and agricultural revenues had been growing, and now the government regretted the earlier alienation of lands as grants. So, a more determined reversal of the process began, which was, the resumption of jagirs—the cancellation of the grants by the government. There were two mechanisms through which this took place. One, as the original grantees died in the following years, existing grants were resumed and the jagirs reclaimed, and applications from the heirs praying for a continuation were rejected.[181] For instance, Bhawani Shankar was murdered in 1816, and his jagir reverted to the government.[182] Manuel D'Eremao's request to have his own jagir turned into a hereditary tenure in favour of his son was, however, accepted in 1821.[183]

Whereas these were cases mostly of jagirs granted by the Company itself, more controversial was another move of the administration—that of questioning the validity of all grants that had been given by the earlier regime. Many of these were grants made to individuals, such as the villages of Jaitpur and Ghosipur, that had been granted by Shah Alam to a very prominent practitioner of Yunani medicine, *Hakim* Sharif Khan. These were resumed, as his heirs later complained, 'without any ground whatsoever or any fault' on their part. The government's contention was that these had been granted at a time when grants from Shah Alam's court were easily available. This was in fact a rather flimsy ground, since Hakim Sharif Khan was highly respected by the Emperor as well as the general population, and therefore the grant had no doubt been given with great deliberation. A rather inadequate pension of one rupee per month was later granted to the sons of the hakim.[184]

The category of older grants also covered many villages that had been granted for the upkeep of shrines and tombs and other religious purposes. One of the earliest resumptions of such grants was of the one that had been made to Padre Gregorio, of the Catholic mission of Tibet and Hindustan, by Shah Nizam ud din, the Governor of Delhi in the late eighteenth century. This was resumed on the priest's death in 1812, though Father Angelo, the Prefect of the mission, challenged the resumption on the ground that it was a grant to the mission and not to Padre Gregorio personally.[185] Other cases of grants that were now being investigated included the village of Mehrauli, that had been granted for the upkeep of the *dargah* of Qutb ud din Bakhtiyar Kaki; the village of Bahapur that had been granted for the upkeep of the temple of Kalkaji; and the villages of Wazeerpur and Khanpur, that were granted for the expense of 'repairs and illumination' of the tomb of Safdarjang. The government at Calcutta, while against a general resumption, was willing to allow it in cases where the grant was 'legally resumable', tempered with political expediency, leniency, and recompense through monetary pensions wherever justified. In effect, the ultimate decision was in large part left to local discretion.[186]

Between 1813 and 1819, of the 328 villages granted by the previous regime, 188 valued at Rs 2,51,671 had been resumed. Of the 568 granted by the Company itself, 158, valued at Rs 2,85,292, were resumed.[187] The justification given for resumption was usually that title to the grant was unclear, based on forged documents, or on grants made by an authority that was at that time not authorized to make such grants. Frequent changes of administration had taken place during the second half of the eighteenth century, with multiple authorities at various times being authorized to make grants, therefore it was in fact very difficult to get to the root of the matter. Yet, when it came to the question of why now, several years later, the government had awoken to the need to set its house in order, the reason was very clear—the value of the jagirs had risen significantly in the last few years. For this reason, the government wanted to resume jagirs even if it had to give cash compensations.[188]

These policies of the Company's government were not popular in Delhi. The high revenue assessments in the Delhi territory led to increasing distress and eventually famine in 1824. The resumption of jagirs caused distress among the class of the barely or even reasonably well-to-do in Delhi, who were dependent partly or wholly on income from these land rights. In these measures, though Charles Metcalfe was a driving force, William Fraser played the role of the man on the ground, on whose reports the ultimate decisions were taken. Not surprisingly, this did not make him popular among the people of Delhi. The extent of his unpopularity was proved by an assassination attempt on him in 1819, in which he was wounded but recovered.[189]

Within the city itself, the government was moving to gain greater control of property, under the assumption that it now had a right over all manner of public property in the city. To take control of public property, the first step was to ascertain the details of what existed. Even during the time of Seton, the government had begun to make serious investigations into public property in the city, and a survey of such property in both the city and the surrounding countryside had been ordered in 1808.[190] Under Charles Metcalfe this was taken up in a more systematic manner, and one of the first steps was a comprehensive documentation. The aim of this was to identify certain categories of property—waqf (endowments e.g. for mosques), *taiul* (royal estates), *zabt* (confiscated) and *lawaris* (unclaimed)—in regard to which the government could lay claim to the right either of disposal or of management. The results of the investigation were laid before the government in the form of a report.[191]

By trying to take charge of these public properties, the Company was directly challenging the prerogative of the Emperor, who considered himself entitled to manage not only the royal estates, but also, by tradition, some other categories of public properties. The government alleged that these properties, particularly those that were part of the endowment of mosques, were being misappropriated and mismanaged, often with the connivance of members of the royal family. It asserted a right to appoint an official to identify such properties and 'to have the entire management of all the funds, as well in paying the establishments as in allotting money for necessary repairs'.[192]

It was, however, clear that the government's intentions were not altogether altruistic. The purpose of the enquiry into the precise number and extent of grants was also to identify those that might be resumed. As a result, there was a listing in minute detail of every tenant and owner of every house, shop and stall that was considered part of public property. These included buildings like the Dar ul shifa, which was an old hospital ancillary to the Jama Masjid and with regard to which the Emperor considered himself to have a special right—to grant tenancy to whom he wished. The government on the other hand wanted to overturn these claims entirely.[193]

The government's pecuniary motives became increasingly clear, since the disposal of various resumed or unclaimed properties began soon after. For instance, in 1822 several gardens were sold, to Nawab Ahmad Baksh Khan, Nawab Mubarak un Nissa Begum (the wife of David Ochterlony) and Dr Ludlow, the British

Surgeon, among others.[194] Sometime later, it was also laid down as a general principle that all land and houses that were escheated, or unclaimed property, would be sold for a fair price, augmenting the government's coffers.[195]

In other areas too there was a shift in policy in Delhi from the more generous attitude of an earlier period; which strongly suggested that the earlier generosity was dictated by political motives. In the early years the local government had disbursed sums regularly by way of 'inam and charity'—to the servants of the king and royal family and also to various other individuals such as *faqirs* (religious mendicants) and to shrines (such as the *khadims* of the dargah of Hasan Rasulnuma, and the dargah of Qutb ud din Bakhtiyar Kaki, and the Imam of the Jama Masjid). In 1822 the government had written from Calcutta that these payments, excepting those made to the servants of the palace, should be cut down. This was accordingly done, and notably the payment made to the khadims was missing from later accounts.[196]

To a culture which was attuned to rulers being generous with largesse, all these measures, aimed at increasing the government revenue at the expense of the people, stamped the new rulers as mean. The harshness of British exactions was the subject of popular lore. Just after the British victory at Bharatpur in 1826, Begum Samru hosted an entertainment at which the British officers were also invited. On this occasion, mimics enacted a short scene in which the dramatis personae 'were an English prize-agent, and a poor peasant of Bhurtpore. The former wore an immense cocked hat and sword, the latter was stark naked, with the exception of a most scanty dootee, or waistcloth. The prize-agent stops him, and demands his jewels and money. The half-starved wretch protests his poverty, and appeals to his own miserable appearance as the proof. The Englishman, upon this, makes him a furious speech, well garnished with G_d and d_ns, seizes on the trembling Bhurtporean, and, determined not to leave him without having extracted something from him, takes out a pair of scissors, cuts off his long shaggy hair close to his skull, crams it into his pocket, and exits, swearing.'[197]

15

Removing the Mask

The far-reaching changes taking place during the tenure of Metcalfe were related to a growing confidence on the part of the East India Company. By early 1819, it had subjugated its most formidable enemy, the Marathas, and it was ready to emerge from the shadow of the Mughal Emperor, as a power in its own right, and to formally announce itself as the real ruler of Delhi itself. So, by a resolution of early 1819, it was decided that the term 'Assigned Territory' that had been used so far, suggesting that it was territory assigned for the support of the royal family, be abolished. Instead, it would now be known simply as the Delhi Territory; so that 'the territory of Dihlee be in name, as it has long been in fact, a part of the British Dominions'.[198]

Some organizational changes were brought about in the Delhi administration itself, and these coincided with the departure of Charles Metcalfe, who left Delhi in December 1818. Up to this point, the administrative powers were concentrated in the hands of the deceptively named 'Resident', who was in fact much more than a representative of the East India Company at the court of the Mughal Emperor, as his name seemed to suggest. Now, the judicial and revenue duties were placed in the hands of a Civil Commissioner, T. Fortescue. The political functions, which mainly included relations with the royal family and relations with the independent and semi-independent rulers of the surrounding territories, were left in the care of the Resident, to which post General Ochterlony was now recalled.

With the division between the office of the Commissioner and the Resident, the revenue and judicial system was brought closer into line with the Regulation Provinces, i.e. the territories that had long been under British administration. Indian *sadr amins* (judicial officers) were appointed to try civil suits up to an amount of a thousand rupees, and criminal offences not exceeding a fine of fifty rupees or imprisonment without fetters for thirty days.[199] Prominent among the incumbents, appointed on a monthly salary of Rs 250, was Maulvi Mohammad Sadr ud din Khan, also known by his pen name, Azurda. He was a learned man, who immediately established a reputation for fairness and integrity.[200]

The return of Ochterlony as Resident did not signal a return to the old days of his previous residency, even with respect to his limited role as a mediator of the government's relations with the Emperor and the royal family. Many of Ochterlony's own inclinations, which were towards a greater consideration for 'fallen majesty' and the Emperor's feelings, were overruled by the government. As far as relations with the palace were concerned, there was a continuing shifting of the balance of power in favour of the Company, and an erosion of the Emperor's dignity as well as independence. As mentioned before, the process had begun early in the tenure of Metcalfe, with the removal of Jahangir, the establishment of Abu Zafar as the heir apparent, and positioning within the palace of functionaries that reported back to the Resident. These were the first steps in the Resident's growing control over the affairs of the royal family. Metcalfe was committed to wiping out what he thought was a hollow pretence of sovereignty which the deluded Mughals stubbornly clung to and the British Government had unnecessarily encouraged.

As the Company projected itself as the real ruler of Delhi, the Emperor's revised position within this scheme soon became very clear. In 1820, Akbar II wrote a letter to the newly ascended King of Britain, George IV, addressing the British monarch as 'brother' and speaking of the harmony and friendship between the two. The government at Calcutta chose not to forward this communication, deeming it 'inconsistent' with both the constitutional nature of the British Government and the relationship of Akbar II to it.[201]

Another important symbol of sovereignty, which the Company was eager to get rid of, was the coinage of rupees in the Delhi mint. The coins in the Delhi mint bore the name of Akbar II, whereas those of the Company, coined in the Farrukhabad mint, bore that of Shah Alam. In the second decade of the nineteenth century there had been a depreciation in the Delhi rupee that made it a significant 2.25 per cent less than the Company's Farrukhabad rupee. An important reason behind this was that it was not accepted in any of the government treasuries in other districts of the Company's territory. This government policy in effect had made sure that it would become devalued. At any rate, this was seen as a favourable opportunity to put a stop to the coinage of Delhi rupees and gradually supplant it entirely with the Farrukhabad coin. As the existence of a mint at Delhi was one of the symbols of royalty, it was expected that the Emperor might wish for its continuance. The solution, that had been suggested by the Financial Department of the government at Calcutta in 1812, was that the mint at Delhi would begin to coin the Farrukhabad rupee, with the exception of one or two hundred coins that 'might be struck as usual and presented to the king on the new year of the reign according to custom. By which means the name and appearance of the thing would be preserved for the gratification of His Majesty's feelings'. Metcalfe also felt that the Emperor would wish for his own allowance to be paid in the Farrukhabad rupee rather than the devalued Delhi coin.[202]

As expected, Akbar was not happy about the Delhi mint coining only Farrukhabad rupees, with the exception of a few commemorative coins in his name.[203] He was even more disappointed when it was decided some years later that the Delhi mint would be closed altogether. Support for Akbar's point of view within official circles came from David Ochterlony. He based his arguments on the supposed lack of favour for the move in the eyes of the people of the country, and the loss of employment of those working in the Delhi mint. Yet his primary motivation while pressing the case was the Emperor's 'earnest command to me to plead with his Lordship for the restoration of the only thing that remained to him of former dignity' and 'the fear that stood in his eye as he expressed his wishes'. Both Ochterlony and Akbar knew that the closure of the Delhi mint would remove the last symbol of the sovereignty of the Mughal emperor.[204] The government, however, was far less susceptible to these emotional considerations, and conceded only to the extent of allowing pensions to the old and infirm employees of the mint who could not otherwise have supported themselves.[205] The mint was closed and the limited coinage for the occasion of the anniversary of the Emperor's accession was shifted to the Farrukhabad mint. In 1824 the total coinage amounted to just nineteen gold mohurs and 400 rupees.[206] Within two years of this, the issue of the removal of Shah Alam's name from the Company's coinage was also being raised.[207]

Rules regarding the presentation of nazars to the Emperor were being revised too. In 1822 the government directed that in cases where British gentlemen visited the palace not on duty but out of 'curiosity', they would pay the nazars out of their own pockets.[208] A nazar of fifty-one gold mohurs used to be presented on behalf of the commander-in-chief on the two Eids and the anniversary of the Emperor's accession to the throne. Sometime after 1813 this practice was discontinued, perhaps inadvertently. When Akbar heard in 1823 of the arrival of a new commander-in-chief and asked why the nazar from him had not been given, Charles Elliott, who had recently taken over as Resident, asked for instructions. He was advised that the nazar, since it seemed to have been discontinued, was not to be revived.[209]

In 1828, the government also decided to discontinue the nazars from the Governor General on the ceremonial occasions agreed on with Shah Alam. There would be no monetary loss to the Emperor, as the government had decided that the sum would be added to the stipend instead. Akbar of course was not happy with this, as the point of the nazar was not monetary. He suggested that the money be paid as a consolidated nazar on a single occasion by the Resident.[210] The government, however, was adamant on the point. It was more difficult to do away with the nazars that were presented by individual officials and dignitaries during actual audiences with the Emperor. On the visit of the Lord Bishop of Calcutta in 1836, it was assumed that he would present a nazar, which would be paid for by the government. It was, however, decided that the sum of seventy gold mohurs and 150 rupees, given at the visit of Bishop Reginald Heber a number of years previously, had been excessive. This would have to be reduced to the extent possible without giving offence.[211]

Official communications from the Governor General to the Emperor had by tradition been in the form of an *arzdasht*, or petition, with the official seal of the Governor General, which styled him as the 'fidwi' or servant of the Emperor. By 1822 this had been dropped from the Governor General's official Persian seal, which was used in correspondence with the princely states. If, however, he were to write to Akbar II and not use the term, it was thought that the move might be 'misconstrued'![212] Though the Governor General would not assume a posture of subservience vis-a-vis the Emperor, this could not be put in so many words. Instead, a way out of the dilemma was found in an uneasy silence, and all direct correspondence was suspended. The attempt by the government in 1834 to resume addresses from the Governor General to the Emperor, after a gap of ten years, but without the subservient tone, gave offence to Akbar, and therefore direct correspondence once again ceased.[213]

Personal audiences with the Governor General, on the latter's very occasional visits to Delhi, were even more problematic. As early as 1815, the Marquess of Hastings had passed by Delhi, but declined coming into the city for an audience with the Emperor. The main objection was on the grounds of the protocol that might be required—he would have to remain standing in the Emperor's presence, and would have to offer a nazar in a gesture of submission.[214] During the visit of Governor General Lord Amherst in 1827, Akbar was so eager that the meeting actually take place, that he agreed to waive the protocols. The Emperor embraced the Governor General, and gave him a seat. No nazars were presented, and at the time of departure, the Emperor stood up and took the Governor General by the arm.[215]

During the visit, the Emperor presented a paper of requests to Lord Amherst, which listed, apart from the question of the stipend, some other privileges that the Emperor wanted restored. These included the right of the king to appoint his own functionaries, the right to appoint as many troops as he considered necessary, and the circulation in the Delhi territory of coins struck in his name.[216] Also included was the demand to 'let the English gentlemen generally and more especially the Resident receive titles from the Presence according to custom'.[217] The giving of titles by the Emperor, which had been a common practice, was now being opposed by the government, which had developed a policy to restrict titles to a very few British subjects, with its express approval. In response to the mention in the paper of requests, the government reiterated that the Emperor should restrict titles to his employees alone.[218] It is interesting to note, however, that the Company's government had systematically adopted the practice of conferring titles on its native subjects in its own right rather than through the medium of the Mughal court, and the principles governing such grants were formalized.[219]

The strengthening of the East India Company's position in North India was not the only reason behind its altered attitude towards the royal family at Delhi. With the defeat of Napoleon in 1815, Britain embarked on a long period of peace in Europe. Moreover, from the beginning of the century the country had also seen a remarkable acceleration of industrial growth. Politically it was on the path to long-term parliamentary reform, which itself was an outcome of complex social changes that were taking place. The self-confident representatives of a country that was simultaneously successful, prosperous and self-consciously modernizing, could not but be impatient of what they saw as the sad pretensions of an obsolete dynasty. For long they had not thought much of the Emperor, now they were also convinced that none of the chiefs or people of India could possibly do so. Or maybe, that even if they did, this did not pose any threat to the East India Company's government.

Whether or not the government cared about their opinion, the people of Delhi were unhappy with the nature of Lord Amherst's meeting with Akbar II. As William Gardner wrote, 'the not giving the nuzzur is what they complain of most...[and] they think it mean and pitiful that the Governor General should have left Delhi without an increased salary to the increased family. In short they think a great man should do things like a great man'.[220] This in fact sums up the reason why the British ultimately would find it impossible to supplant the Mughal rulers in the affections of the people. In this world view, generosity and a personal touch were an important part of the relationship between ruler and ruled, and the Mughals had set standards that the British on the whole failed to emulate.

16

Marginalized

Akbar soon came to the conclusion that in order to make headway with his claims against the Company, he had no option but to try and gain a better understanding of how the British Government in general worked, in the hope of being better able to negotiate that world. As an important step in achieving that, in 1814 he appointed a new chief functionary, or mukhtar, Khwaja Farid ud din Ahmad Khan. Khwaja Farid, in his sixties, was from an eminent Delhi family. He had just returned to Delhi after having been in the employment of the East India Company since 1797 in various locations. He had taught at the Calcutta Madrassa, the first higher educational institution founded by the East India Company, set up by the Governor General Warren Hastings in 1780. Khwaja Farid had then been part of diplomatic missions to Iran and Ava, and had worked in the revenue department in Bundelkhand. Not surprisingly, Akbar felt he would be a good mediator with the British.[221]

In fact, there was little Khwaja Farid could do with regard to the question of having the stipend raised, or getting the Emperor the power to appoint the heir apparent of his choice. These were matters of government policy at the highest levels, in which his mediation had no real role. Where he did play a role was in attempting to bring some order to the royal finances. Here too he made himself unpopular, as he tried to rationalize salaries and other expenditures within the fort, among the members of the royal family and household. He was therefore at the receiving end of many vested interests, and was victim to the personal politics and jockeying for position that continuously took place. As a result, he was dismissed after a year and a half, only to be reinstated later, for another term that lasted from early 1817 to mid-1819.[222]

In addition to his frustrating failure in negotiating a maintenance of his power and prestige vis-a-vis the government at Calcutta, during these years Akbar II found himself having to face resistance on the home front, Delhi, as well. He was subject to everyday challenges to his power from the city's administration and the Resident. An important cause for concern for the Emperor was the erosion of his position within the fort itself. The independent legal jurisdiction of the Emperor over the inhabitants of the fort, which had been guaranteed under the terms of the agreement with Shah Alam, was being continually eroded. In 1814 Charles Metcalfe summoned and examined the royal servants in order to investigate a charge that one of the Emperor's sons, Mirza Babur, had killed his own newborn daughter. This was humiliating, though Metcalfe concluded that the death was a natural one.[223] There was also, for the first time, an interest in the details of how the royal allowance was allocated within the palace. The Emperor was made to provide details of the sums he gave to all apart from his immediate family. Increments were suggested in some cases, though the discussions were kept secret as the government wanted the measure to appear to be an act of generosity from the king, independent of British pressure![224]

Increasingly, the civil administration of the city as well as the British commander of the palace guard were getting involved in the internal affairs of the palace. In 1822 the commander of the palace guard, Major McPherson, accused 'a person of rank' of distilling liquor in the palace. He also complained against Khwaja Farid, saying that the latter was deducting unnecessarily high amounts from the allowances of the princes in order to pay their debts. Both these matters were brought before Middleton, the acting Resident at the time. In the case of Khwaja Farid, he came to the conclusion that this gentleman, 'one of the most respectable and honest characters in Dehlee', 'particularly recommended to me by Sir David Ochterlony, whose friend he is' had acted completely within the bounds of his duty. Middleton also seems to have dismissed the other complaint. Mirza Ashraf Beg, who commanded the Emperor's troops, accused McPherson of trying to cause disturbances in the palace. In any event the fact that the complaints had been made, and investigated by Middleton, indicated a degree of interference in the affairs of the palace that was inconsistent with the theory of the Emperor's exclusive jurisdiction over the inhabitants of the fort.[225]

The issue of jurisdiction was also complicated because most of those employed in the fort, or those who had close dealings with the palace, were inhabitants of the city. They were thus in two jurisdictions simultaneously. These persons were sometimes subjected to punishment within the fort. On one occasion in 1828, one of them complained in the city court against Raja Sohan Lal, the mukhtar, or manager of the Emperor's finances, who had arrested him and exposed him to the heat of the sun for almost two hours. The judge and magistrate, Thomas Metcalfe, heard the case in his court and sent a letter to Sohan Lal in the palace, asking by what authority inhabitants of the city were confined in the fort. Sohan Lal answered equally forcefully that it was by 'the orders of His Majesty from long established usage at the palace'. He asserted that when he acted under the Emperor's orders he was not under the jurisdiction of the court, and moreover, the affairs of the palace were under the charge of the Resident. In fact, Edward Colebrooke, who was the Resident, had also taken up the matter with Thomas Metcalfe, objecting to the latter's direct communication with functionaries of the Emperor. The government expressed its disapproval of Metcalfe's action, saying that the palace was definitely outside the jurisdiction of the city courts and only the Resident was competent to take cognizance of acts within the palace.[226]

In effect what this incident highlighted was not the independence of jurisdiction within the palace as such, but its subordination to one wing of the British authority as distinct from another. In

1819 there had been a division of power between a Commissioner and a Resident. The former was in charge of civil and judicial administration, and the latter was responsible for the affairs of the palace and relations with the various princely states of the region.[227] There was no remedy in cases where the Resident himself did not object to interference in affairs that were thought to be completely internal to the palace.

One frequently raised issue revolved around escaped slaves. In 1812, the slave trade was prohibited by an order putting a 'stop to the sale of human beings in the town and country of Delhi.'[228] This new regulation gave the city's administration a handle to investigate the issue of the escape of women from the fort. From time to time women were caught just outside the palace walls, in the process of getting away. They were invariably released by the city authorities who found them. The royal family protested on the grounds that some of them were legally slaves, since they had been procured before the ban on slave trafficking, and that others were concubines. They also argued that they had made up stories of oppression in order to be set free. The British authorities were not inclined to believe this argument and usually came to the conclusion that they had in fact been kidnapped and illegally sold into bondage.[229]

The royal family had enjoyed a special legal status, even in matters outside the walls of the fort. By the late 1820s this was being questioned. In 1829, a relation of the Emperor, who lived in the city, was summoned to the court to give evidence. This was seen as a slight, and he did so under duress, and then immediately went and took refuge in the palace (which was considered a haven as in theory it was under the Emperor's jurisdiction alone).[230] By the time William Fraser became the Agent to the Governor General (a change in nomenclature for the Resident), in 1832, the question of civil jurisdiction was being seriously discussed. Fraser was of the view that the rent or revenue from crown property, directly under the control of the reigning Emperor, was also subject to the jurisdiction of the Company's courts, which could order that they be utilized for the settlement of the Emperor's debts.[231]

While the interference of British officials grew at one level, their everyday interactions with the Emperor were more impersonal. The immediate successors of Metcalfe in the early 1820s had short tenures, and except for Ochterlony, they lacked familiarity with what was going on in the palace. Residents such as Alexander Ross (who joined in 1822) and Charles Elliott (1823-25), relied heavily on a vakil or agent through whom all their correspondence with Akbar was carried out.[232] One important reason for this was an unwillingness to conform to the etiquette of the court, which required them to go through gestures of submission. Also, in the eyes of the British, the relative political significance of the Mughal royal family had declined over the years, and frequent attendance at the Emperor's court was not even considered necessary now.

There was also a perceptible decline in the courtesy extended to the Emperor and the palace at all levels in the British administration. Relations with the Resident reached a nadir in 1830 at the time of Francis Hawkins (1829-30), who peremptorily returned a letter from the Emperor intended to be forwarded to the Governor General, because it was not accompanied by a copy. All that the Emperor could do was write a letter complaining of the want of respect.[233] Then, in 1833, the government treasury decided that it would no longer issue the royal stipend on the first of the month if the day happened to be a holiday. R. Neave, the collector in charge of the treasury, flatly refused to go to office on Sunday, 'whatever may have been the practice of others'.[234]

Another mark of the casual treatment of the royal family was that the interior of the fort had become increasingly accessible to even casual British visitors and they often did not respect the dignity of their surroundings. In 1832 there was an incident where a party of two British officers and two ladies entered the Diwan e Khas, while the Emperor was not there. One of the officers sat down on the crystal throne which was reserved for the use of the Emperor, and struck the *chobdar* (mace bearer) who tried to stop him. Akbar had to be content with the explanation that the officer had committed the breach of etiquette 'unknowingly', and had merely pushed aside the chobdar, because the latter had been rude.[235]

The Emperor tried to keep up his dignity as best as he could. Elephants were ceremonially sent to the Residency on the first day of each month, to fetch the royal stipend, at least until this too was replaced by carts on the order of the authorities in 1830.[236] The Emperor made courteous enquiries after the health of the Resident, and periodically sent small presents—of fruit, paan, etc., to his home. When Bishop Reginald Heber visited Delhi in 1825 and stayed a few days, we find the Emperor ordering trays of food, and paan to be sent to the 'Lord Bishop Padri Sahab'.[237]

On the part of the British, though earlier there had been an anxiety and desire to know what was going on in the palace, as years went by, there was a growing indifference to the details of the intrigues and manoeuvring of the royal family. In 1831, Mirza Ashraf Beg, who had been placed in charge of the Royal najeeb*s* after the Jahangir incident, died. He had been loyal to the British and that had been the primary reason for his appointment under direct pressure from Seton. When the question of his likely successor was raised, the government decided that it was not an issue that warranted interference.[238] The perceived threat from what went on inside the palace was very different from what it had been twenty years before. It no longer mattered who was in control of such troops as the Emperor still had. In fact not long after, the number of the government's troops stationed at the palace gates was also reduced.[239]

Progressively less notice was being taken of the Emperor at all levels. Successive Governors General felt that a personal audience with Akbar, when passing through Delhi, was not worth the elaborate protocol that had to be gone through. Akbar on the other hand was eager for such meetings, willing to waive all formalities as in the case of Lord Amherst's visit in 1827. Apart from the satisfaction it gave that the sentiments of the Emperor on various issues had actually been directly communicated, the very fact of the audience could demonstrate that an amicable relationship existed. In 1831 therefore, strenuous but futile attempts were made by the royal family to arrange a meeting with Governor General William Bentinck, who was on a tour to North India. Akbar had private talks with Fraser, the Agent to the Governor General, on the subject and Mumtaz Mahal tried to enlist the help of Colonel Skinner, who pleaded his inability to help.[240] The meeting did not eventually take place.

17

Domestic Strife, and Rammohan Roy

Throughout his reign Akbar had faced challenges to his authority from within his own family. The perceived power of the government vis-a-vis the Emperor prompted many members of the royal family to seek the government's mediation in all sorts of personal conflicts with the Emperor. When Akbar had proposed that Mirza Jahangir be married to the daughter of Sulaiman Shukoh—his brother who was living in Lucknow—the latter promptly wrote to the Governor General. First of all, since the young prince had offended the government, he wanted permission in writing from the government that the match might be entered into. He also wished to have it made clear that, in case 'after the connection is made, through the Prince's unfortunate temper, of which your Lordship is aware, he should at any time misbehave towards my daughter, I shall have to represent it to your Lordship's notice.' The government informed him that he must do as he thought fit and not rely on the government's opinion or intervention.[241]

A major reason for domestic strife was also the Emperor's relationship with Abu Zafar, his firstborn. Zafar was acutely aware that his father wished to bypass him in the succession to the throne, first being in favour of Jahangir, and then, when that did not work out, pushing the case of another son, Salim. There were other ways in which the actions of his father threatened Zafar's future as

Emperor. In 1820, he complained to Ochterlony, that the Emperor had granted Begum Samru some fifty thousand yards of land in the city, near the garden known as Begum ka Bagh. This probably adjoined the plot of land the Begum had purchased in 1807, in the heart of the city, to build a grand house. Zafar complained that this grant was against the orders of Metcalfe, who had prohibited the alienation of crown property in this manner. Zafar also complained repeatedly against individuals around his father who he felt were conspiring against his interests. One such complaint in 1830 was directed against various people of 'vulgar origins' who had secured positions of importance under his father.[242]

A major threat, as far as Zafar was concerned, loomed in 1829, when his father engaged Rammohan Roy, the great Bengali reformer, with the task of proceeding as the Emperor's ambassador to the monarch of Britain. Since it was understood that the right of the Emperor to appoint his heir would be one of the points of the embassy, Zafar was understandably suspicious and resentful.[243]

Rammohan on his part did not want to be acting behind the back of the government at Calcutta, so he was careful to forward to Fort William a copy of Akbar's letter to George IV. The letter, which is likely to have been drafted by Rammohan Roy and approved by Akbar, provides an interesting insight into how the relationship between the new and the old powers in India was viewed. It said:

> Sire! My brother! It is with a mingled feeling of humility and pride that I approach your Majesty with the language of fraternal equality at the very time that the occasion of my addressing your Majesty compels me to consider myself rather as a supplicant at the footstool of your Majesty's throne than as a monarch entitled to assume the style and claim the privileges of royalty....I cannot forget that I am a king only in name...your Majesty is the rightful and acknowledged sovereign of a powerful, a wise and renowned people.'[244]

It was a letter that underlined the dignity of the house of Timur. Yet it acknowledged the realities of power and put forward the claims of the Emperor not as an entitlement due to regal status but based on the promises made by the British Government not so long ago. A major point the letter addressed was the issue of the stipend. The Emperor pointed to the meagre increases made in the allowance, in complete violation of the promises made to his father by the Company. With this letter, Rammohan proceeded to England, though the government refused to recognize his status as envoy of the Mughal Emperor, or indeed the title of 'Raja', which the Emperor had bestowed on his envoy. He circulated a document arguing the claims of the Emperor on the Company, but received no reply to either the letter or the document.[245]

Zafar complained to the British Government about the mission of Rammohan Roy to England. The Emperor had himself claimed that it was Khwaja Farid who had introduced Rammohan Roy to the court, because of an old Calcutta connection. Zafar refuted this claim, saying that the letter of introduction that purported to come from Khwaja Farid (who had died in 1828) was a forgery, perpetrated by some unscrupulous persons around the Emperor, including his mukhtar, Sohan Lal, another official named Afzal Beg, and Zafar's own brother, Mirza Salim. Zafar complained that an important aim of the conspiracy was to mislead the Emperor and to undermine Zafar's position as heir apparent. In his appeal to the government, Zafar projected his concern as not only for the safety of his own interests, but for the government's, saying, 'Since however the succession has been guaranteed to me by the Governor General and Council, who are the Naibs or Deputies of the Hon'ble Company, and as my enemies are the enemies of the British Government, so also whatever injures me, injures the latter.'[246] British interests were threatened, he wrote, because the conspirators had, 'in secret endeavoured to injure the government and by fraud and deceits laid the foundation of seditious proceedings'.[247]

This official complaint led to an open confrontation between Zafar and Rammohan, for when the latter heard of it, he wrote a strong letter to Zafar, which even the authorities at Calcutta agreed was of unsuitable 'style and tenor'. The government on its part sought to calm Zafar's fears with the assurance that, as the British Government always upheld the rights of all chiefs living under its protection, his interests were safe.[248]

Various other members of the royal family were also anxious to secure their interests, in the context of Rammohan Roy's mission. They wrote independently to the Governor General, and their complaint was against the Emperor's discretion in distributing the stipend within the palace. They claimed that the Emperor and those close to him, had been steadily reducing their share in the stipend. They requested that if an increase in the stipend were sanctioned, the government should make sure that it was more equitably distributed.[249]

The Court of Directors of the Company in England, which oversaw the functioning of the East India Company's government in India, agreed to sanction an increase in the royal stipend in 1833, raising it to fifteen lakhs of rupees per year. This increase was, however, on condition that the further claims being made in England be dropped, the increase be distributed within the royal family in proportions to be decided by the government, and a fixed portion be set aside for repairs of the palace. These were conditions that were unacceptable to Akbar, who, on the advice of Rammohan Roy, refused to accept the increase on these terms.[250]

An important reason for the refusal was the added instruction from Calcutta, directing the Agent to the Governor General at Delhi, 'to call upon the Palace authorities for the list of the members of the Royal Family who are now deriving subsistence from the stipend with a specification of the monthly allowance assigned to each and of the families which they respectively have to support.' Having gathered this information, the AGG had to report his 'sentiments as to the most equitable and expedient mode of distributing the increase among them.'[251] The government was proposing a degree of surveillance and control over the financial affairs of the palace which was considered highly objectionable by the Emperor.

Rammohan died in England in September 1833, and with his death, Akbar realized that no further mediation in England would be possible. Soon he was having second thoughts about his refusal to accept the increased allowance. He was dropping hints that he might be willing to accept the increase though he protested as to its inadequacy and the conditions attached to it. The main sticking point was the details of the distribution of this increase within the palace. The Company laid down the details of how it wished the money to be spent—allotting shares to Abu Zafar, the Emperor's other sons, grandsons, nephews, salateen, repairs of the palace, etc. It also suggested that around Rs 555 per month be set aside for the establishment of a college 'wherein the junior branches of the Royal Family might be instructed in such branches of liberal and useful knowledge as might...fit them for their duties in life and make them more valuable members of society.' Akbar objected strenuously to these conditions, not only because this was an unacceptable level of interference in his control over his family and household, but also because none of the increase was to go to him. In February 1837, he wrote a letter refusing to accept the increase on these terms.[252]

There was a further postscript to the Rammohan Roy mission. Later in 1837, a memorandum was sent to the government by Dwarkanath Tagore, a good friend of Rammohan. Dwarkanath drew attention to the fact that it had been the intention of the Emperor to set aside a considerable part of the increased stipend—Rs 1,875 out of the monthly increase of twenty-five thousand—as an allowance to Roy Radhaprasad and Roy Rumaprasad, the sons of Rammohan. The government's decision to dictate to the Emperor regarding how the stipend was to be spent, was hurting their interests as well.[253]

While these negotiations were on, Akbar, who was by now fairly advanced in years, suffered a bout of illness and suddenly the question of succession was revived. His son Salim was put forward as a candidate. Akbar forwarded to the AGG an application made to him by the prince, claiming that several specialists in Islamic law had given their legal opinion, or fatwa, in favour of the latter's claim as the rightful heir. Salim pointed out in the application that this was bound to find favour with the Company's government, because it believed in settling causes between Muslims according to Islamic law. Did it not after all spend thousands of rupees appointing sadr amins (judicial officers in the Company's courts) for this purpose? If this was an argument that was meant to put any sort of pressure on the government, it failed. The AGG was instructed to inform his majesty that none except Zafar could succeed to the throne.[254]

Zafar's insecurity regarding his own position caused him to continue to undermine the authority of Akbar vis-a-vis the British Government. He sent another letter alleging that Akbar was easily misled by bad advice from ill-motivated persons, as his mind was 'weak and imbecile from age'. Conspiracies were being hatched in the palace to install Mirza Salim as the heir apparent, though he, Zafar, had been proclaimed heir apparent 'by the acknowledged voice of the people and the government'. Among those who he felt were the chief instigators of the conspiracy against him was Radhaprasad, son of Rammohan Roy, who he said was preparing to be sent on another mission to England.[255]

18

Re-ordering Spaces

As Zafar struggled to safeguard his future within the fort, the city outside was seeing some significant changes. An important area of activity for any administration of the city was the taking up of projects of civic improvement. In the early years, British initiative in this area tended to be a direct response to public expectations and demands. One early measure the people of Delhi put pressure on the government to take up was the repair of the drains in Chandni Chowk and the replanting of trees that had once existed on that street. The trees were planted in 1809 with some difficulty, as it was found that the soil was very mixed with brick and lime, the result probably of construction that had encroached on the street and been recently removed. Fresh soil therefore had to be put into the pits dug for the purpose.[256] Clearing of encroachments on the streets seems to have been an ongoing process, since in 1830 the kotwal was again ordered to demolish unauthorized platforms that had been built in front of shops. Another responsibility of the kotwal, linked to civic control and order, was the killing of stray dogs.[257]

An important priority for the administration, however, was public works that could yield a direct economic benefit. One of these was the old canal of Ali Mardan Khan, which had been built in the seventeenth century to bring water from the Yamuna upstream, to Shahjahan's newly-founded capital. This had dried up through lack of maintenance in the decades immediately preceding the British conquest of Delhi. The government began considering plans to reopen this fairly soon after its capture of Delhi. There were proposals from entrepreneurs like Bhawani Shankar, who offered to do it on a commercial basis. These were turned down as the government decided to undertake this task itself. After army engineers prepared estimates which suggested that the costs would come to some three to four lakhs of rupees, sanction for the works to begin was finally given in 1817. The reasons that appear to have spurred the government were political as well economic. It was hoped that the extension of agriculture made possible by irrigation from the canal would keep the rural population away from marauding tendencies by 'providing them with peaceable occupation' and that 'the act of reviving so extraordinarily beneficial a work cannot fail to add both to the reputation and strength of the British Government.'[258]

Finally in 1820 the waters of the canal actually entered the city, 'amidst the acclamations and rejoicings of the inhabitants of Delhi, and a great concourse of people, hearing of their approach, went out some miles to meet them throwing flowers and sweetmeats into the stream in token of their gratitude.'[259] The stream entered the city at a western gate—Kabuli Darwaza, and one branch flowed down the Chandni Chowk street and another through the gardens to the north of that street. Both branches then reunited as they approached the fort, flowing out into the Yamuna at Nigambodh. As Akbar II had expressed a wish to have the waters flow through the fort, work was begun on that too. A few days later, on Eid, the waters entered the fort, and the begums washed their children in the stream.[260]

Not all interventions of the government were as popular. In the mid-1820s it was decided to buy land in Dariyaganj to accommodate the Delhi Provincial Battalion in addition to the infantry troops that were already stationed there. This battalion had thus far been located at Nasir Ganj lines, near Kashmiri Gate. The choice of Dariyaganj was an odd one because the area was fairly thickly inhabited and the land in question belonged to a large number of individual owners. In fact, the density of population in Dariyaganj had been vastly underestimated by the local administration. When the inhabitants of the area were asked to name their prices, a large number immediately presented a petition saying firmly that they were unable to accept the offer as they had nowhere else to live. The shopkeepers declared that only force could ensure their eviction. A visit to the area by the local official was marked by the gathering of a large and noisy crowd that included lamenting women. Under the circumstances, the government at Calcutta advised abandonment of this potentially expensive and unpopular measure.[261]

A certain amount of dissatisfaction was also occasioned by works on the fortifications of the city. The defence of Delhi was a matter of constant worry to the military, which had carried out a round of repairs shortly after the arrival of the British in Delhi. The context of this was that the Maratha chieftain Holkar had laid siege to the city briefly in 1804. This created an alarm among the authorities, who ordered a strengthening of the defences and clearing of the area immediately outside the city walls. Outside the Lahori Gate was a garden with several buildings in it, belonging to a Carmelite missionary, Padre Gregorio. This was cleared away, and he was compensated with a pension of Rs 100 per month for life. When Padre Gregorio died three years later, this lapsed. In addition, he had received the grant of a revenue free village when the territory was under Sindhia's administration. This was also resumed, leaving the mission in financial difficulties.[262] Others, such as Shah Nizam ud din, whose garden outside Ajmeri Gate was destroyed at the same time, were given no compensation at all.[263]

A more comprehensive project on the fortifications was taken up in the late 1810s, and continued well into the 1820s, under the superintendence of the Garrison Engineer, Robert W. Smith. This had been completed successfully, but a few areas of concern remained. One of these was the condition of the area just outside the city wall. It had been decided that to secure the safety of the wall, a strip of land to the distance of musket shot, three hundred yards, needed to be cleared of all buildings. Here the problem was a large number of labouring people, such as brick makers and lime burners who had occupied spaces close to the wall. These were people who had earlier been living in the ruins that surrounded the city, and now had come in closer to take advantage of the employment opportunities offered by the city. Apart from the security, Smith claimed that the fuel that was burnt, i.e. cowdung cakes, created 'a most offensive and insalubrious nuisance to the city.' It was decided that these should be removed.[264]

Though the homes of the poor could be removed without much thought, both the government at Calcutta and the civil administration were reluctant to be quite so severe in the removal of the dwellings of more 'important' people which compromised security. For instance, in the area overlooking the river in Dariyaganj, several bungalows had been built, even on the bastions. These bungalows belonged either to 'native gentlemen' or to civil and military officers of the British Government. The 'native gentlemen' in question were mostly the independent chiefs that were under the political control of the Resident at Delhi. They felt that it was useful to spend at least some of their time in Delhi so as to keep in touch with the authorities. They formed an important part of the elite of Delhi, and soon procured some of the best properties in Dariyaganj, which still had quite a bit of open space. Nawab Ahmad Baksh Khan already had ancestral property in Delhi but built a new estate in Dariyaganj, which overlooked the river and had an independent gate cut through the city wall to give access to the river. Later, the Nawab of Jhajjar bought an estate adjoining this one.[265] It was realized that considerable 'expense and inconvenience' would be involved in demolishing these accretions, and hence the matter was allowed to drop.[266]

The other category of structures that was spared was buildings of a religious nature. One of these was an old college, with an attached tomb and mosque. This was the Ghazi ud din *madrasa,* which was more than a hundred years old, and located just outside the Ajmeri Gate of the city. The college had suffered during the disorders of the late eighteenth century, and it was reported as being 'shut up, and without inhabitants' by a British visitor in 1793. In 1824, the situation was barely improved, and the institution had nine students.[267]

Eventually, it was decided that the madrasa should remain, though the huts surrounding it should be removed. The army reluctantly agreed to spare the madrasa, though which of its ancillary buildings would be destroyed became an issue for a minor confrontation between the local civil and military authorities. In the end, a compromise was reached with the decision to enclose the buildings within the city walls, by constructing a new bastion, which was named after the Emperor—Burj Akbar Shah.[268]

19

Religious Identities

It was not only the physical structures of the city that were changing in the early decades of Company rule. There were other developments in the lives of people that would have a long term impact. Among these was one that on the one hand succeeded in mobilizing a section of the Muslim population, but created sharp rifts within the community as well. This was the movement of Syed Ahmad Barelwi in the late 1810s and the 1820s. Having come to Delhi from Rae Bareily to get an education under Maulana Abdul Qadir (brother of Abdul Aziz), he soon became attracted to the Sufi path and received initiation from Shah Abdul Aziz. His spiritual stature quickly came to be widely acknowledged. After a short interlude in the service of Nawab Amir Khan of Tonk, he returned to Delhi and began gathering large numbers of followers. Among these were two close relatives of Abdul Aziz—his nephew Mohammad Ismail and his son-in-law Abdul Hayyi.[269]

The latter two actively took up the cause of Islamic reform and revival, and popularized it through their preaching and debates, for instance at the Jama Masjid.[270] No doubt the support of members of such a noted family was a factor in the popularity of Syed Ahmad's doctrines in Delhi. Another prominent citizen who became a follower of Syed Ahmad Barelwi was Momin Khan 'Momin', a noted poet. He wrote several Persian *qasidas* or panegyric odes, and an Urdu *masnavi* (narrative poem), in support of Syed Ahmad.[271]

Though Syed Ahmad's movement was critical of India's political subordination to the non-Islamic power of the East India Company, the latter was not his immediate target of attack.[272] The climax of his movement was his departure for the mountainous tribal areas of the North West Frontier, to wage *jehad* against the Sikh state of Ranjit Singh. With him were several thousand followers, gathered during his travels over large parts of the Gangetic plain. Among them were a number from Delhi, some of whom had resigned from government jobs to join the jehad. Defeat at Balakot in 1831, in which Syed Ahmad and hundreds of his followers, including Mohammad Ismail, were killed, all but finished the armed resistance.[273]

A more lasting legacy was the ideas of Syed Ahmad regarding the practice of Islam. The younger generation inspired by his writings and preaching followed a more radical line of reform, rejecting as anti-Islamic several popular practices that had not been given up by the older reformers (for instance Shah Abdul Aziz and his brothers).[274] These ideas furthermore reached a wide audience through active preaching by the reformers and the use of print media. Mohammad Ismail in particular was a charismatic speaker. People attributed an increase in attendance at the Jama Masjid to his preaching.[275]

Syed Ahmad's movement of course by no means united all or even most Muslims. In fact, his teachings by their very nature put the reformers on a course of conflict with important sections of their co-religionists. Sufism was sought to be cleansed of popular accretions such as meditation on the image of the saint, prostration at shrines, circumambulation and sanctifying water. This and other doctrinal stands generated considerable opposition, with eminent religious scholars such as Fazl e Haq Khairabadi ranged on the other side. The doctrinal strife was expressed through pamphleteering and public disputations.[276] The stage was in fact set for future occasions when potentially sensitive addresses at the Jama Masjid and other mosques would be attended by police presence.[277] Certain popular

Shia practices, such as the making of *taziyahs* during Moharram, were also denounced by the reformers with a vehemence that was uncharacteristic of the earlier generation—Abdul Aziz and his brothers.[278] This necessarily led to friction and sharp differences of opinion, and in 1830 the administration was making proclamations from the Kotwali Chabutra, the police station, urging Shias and Sunnis to observe Moharram together with amity. Through the 1840s and 50s, Moharram was an annual occasion for animosity between Shias and Sunnis, necessitating police arrangements and leading to occasional violent incidents.[279]

Interestingly, in contrast to developments later in the nineteenth century, the impetus for reform was less frequently expressed as a desire to do away with 'Hindu influence'.[280] In fact, popular religious practice and festivals often brought people of different faiths together. Delhi's leading Urdu newspaper, the *Dehli Urdu Akhbar* mentioned that Holi was celebrated by Muslims as well as Hindus.[281] The dargahs of Sufi saints were visited by Muslims and Hindus alike. Also, a number of holy men and women on the fringes of organized religion often attracted respect that worked across sectarian lines. Among these were the *majzub*, those ascetics who had given up many conventions of religion as well as society. They were often treated as oracles, and people visited them with their problems. One such, Shah Abdul Nabi, had among his devoted followers Bhawani Shankar, the prominent banker and landowner.[282] The cantonments of the soldiers of the British Indian army at Wazirabad and Rajpura were the venues for annual Ramlilas, organized by Hindu and Muslim soldiers together.[283]

, however, incidents related to religious practices did occasionally bring the Muslims into conflict with the Hindu and Jain population of the city. The colonial government in its early years in Delhi perceived its role essentially as a dual one—to ensure peace, and also to maintain the status quo ante. This it interpreted as a balance of power that slightly favoured the Muslims and their sensibilities. The Hindus would have to settle for a basic regard for their beliefs 'as in a Mahomedan city they could with reason expect'.[284] The British therefore took measures to undo some of the policies of the Marathas. For instance, the latter, when in control of the administration, had banned the killing of cattle in the city. This order was reversed by the British administration.[285]

In the early years of the nineteenth century the Hindus and Jains seem to have accepted this situation. The most prominent assertion of religious identity in this period was the construction of a number of temples, usually funded by the mercantile class, either as individuals or as a group. In the 1820s the rich Jain merchants of the city contributed several lakhs of rupees for a Jain temple, which for this reason came to be known also as the Panchayati Mandir—a reference to the communal effort. A new Jog Maya temple was built on the old site at Mehrauli by Raja Sedh Mal, the same employee of Akbar II who had been sent to Calcutta on a mission. The Kalkaji temple, another ancient shrine, was enlarged and embellished with funds donated by Raja Kedar Nath, a merchant who was also an employee of Akbar II. The number of temples built between 1803 and 1857 in fact significantly exceeded those built in any other period of Shahjahanabad's history.[286]

But there was a particular kind of tension that had been simmering under the surface. This was a difference of opinion between the Muslims on one hand and the Hindus and Jains on the other, regarding certain customary practices. The clash in 1807 that had arisen from Harsukh Rai's desire to take out an ostentatious religious procession in the city had been an early assertion of the growing relative strength of the Jains and Hindus, particularly the prosperous trading class, in relation to the Muslim landed and service elite, whose position under the Company's rule was declining—as jagirs were resumed, and higher posts in the administration were reserved for Europeans.

One of the first issues on which the Hindus began to assert themselves in opposition to Muslims as a group was that of cow sacrifice. It started with small groups of individuals petitioning the administration to define and restrict the scope of what was permitted. The government's response was to try and ascertain what the customary practice was, and to ensure that it was adhered to. There was generally a ban against butchers killing any animals within the city walls. The only exception was at Eid uz Zuha, when Muslims were allowed to sacrifice goats and cows within their own houses, away from the houses of Hindus. A violation of this rule around 1815 had invited a sentence of a fine of twenty rupees or imprisonment for six months.

In 1822 a petition from some Hindus induced the magistrate, an inexperienced Thomas Metcalfe, to actually issue a proclamation prohibiting outright any cow sacrifice during the approaching festival. A sensation was caused by this proclamation among the Muslims of the city, and since the Resident, Alexander Ross, felt that the order had not been justified, he ordered another proclamation, directing the kotwal that the customary practice from previous years should be followed. Though Ross reported that the 'Principal Hindoos' in the city were reconciled to this, a mob consisting of the 'lower and most numerous classes of the Hindoos' surrounded Akbar II on the day of the festival, as he was on his way to the Eidgah. They were eventually dispersed through force of arms, and the Emperor returned from the Eidgah under the escort of a company of soldiers.

Thomas Metcalfe was asked by his superiors to account for his decision to issue the proclamation. His response was that, though he was well aware of the rules in existence which allowed Muslims to sacrifice animals, including cows, on the occasion of Eid, as long as it was within their homes or away from the residences of Hindus, he feared that Muslims were not likely to comply with this. He 'conjectured...that the insolent overbearing character of the Mussulman would urge him to disobey this proviso, and induce him to seize the first opportunity of publicly insulting an "infidel" by the exposure of the slaughtered carcase.' His proclamation was in the nature of a preventive action, and had been taken on the basis of an assumption about a supposed essential Muslim character.[287]

The British saw themselves essentially as umpires in the contest between Hindus and Muslims. On the other hand, the Mughals over the centuries had evolved a courtly and family culture that sought to bridge the gaps between groups and their varied practices by setting a personal example. This had led to a great degree of heterogeneity in belief and practice within the palace, which they continued to uphold in the nineteenth century. The akhbars of 1830 give us an interesting insight into the daily life of the court and palace, including a wide variety of religious and social observances. The Emperor went to the Jama Masjid and the Eidgah on the occasion of the two Eids. Many ceremonies associated with important festivals in the Muslim calendar were observed, such as Shab e Barat. On a more everyday basis, the Emperor frequently attended devotional ceremonies at a shrine within the fort, which held relics of the Prophet. At the same time, we also see the Emperor practising mourning rituals during Moharram. We are told that he 'put on a green dress, chains on his hands and feet and a neck collar of silver and thus declared himself the faqir of Imam Husain.' Among the many dargahs visited by the Emperor, such as that of Nizam ud din and Qutb ud din Bakhtiyar Kaki, was also the dargah of Shah e Mardan, associated with the Shias. There were in fact members of the royal family, such as the Emperor's brother, Sulaiman Shukoh, who were Shia. Husaini Begum, the wife of Sulaiman Shukoh was buried at Shah e Mardan, as indeed was Qudsia Begum, the mother of Sulaiman and Akbar II.[288]

The same akhbars tell us how the Emperor celebrated Holi in the fort. He sat in the Musamman Burj, and enjoyed the spectacle of *swangs*—tableaux caricaturing respected institutions. Other customs on Holi included the Emperor being weighed against sweets, which were distributed. Playing with colour, an integral part of Holi, was not forgotten, and we are told that the Emperor 'applied the paste and ointment'.[289] The akhbars also mention the arrival of Raja Kedar Nath on the occasion of Rakshabandhan, to tie a rakhi on the wrist of the Emperor. This was a tradition that dated to the time of Shah Alam II; his 'sister' had been symbolically adopted as such in gratitude for her having stood watch over the body of his father, who had been treacherously murdered. Kedar Nath was the descendant of this woman and the tradition of members of his family tying a rakhi on the wrist of the Emperor had continued down the line.[290]

To a significant extent, patronage of a variety of religious ceremonies was part of the traditions the Mughals had evolved over centuries, to form ties of mutual understanding with their subjects. This feeling of noblesse oblige was still very much alive in the era of Akbar II. During the Phoolwalon ki Sair festival in 1830, the royal family was as usual in Mehrauli, when the heir apparent, Abu Zafar, sent word that as he was not well, he may not be able to join them. To this, Akbar replied, 'that he could do as he liked, but for the sake of the people, he should take part in the festival.'[291] On this occasion Zafar may have genuinely been indisposed, because in general, he enjoyed visits to Mehrauli, particularly in the monsoon. The prince was also a poet, and one of his best known poetic compositions was one set to *raga malhar*, written about the monsoon in Mehrauli:

jhoola kinne dalo ri amraiyan!
bagh andeheri taal kinare, mor jhangare, badar kare
barsan lageen boondein phuiyan phuiyan
jhoola kinne dalo ri amraiyan!
sab sakhi mil gayeen bhul bhulaiyan,
bhuli bhuli dolein shauq rang saiyyan
jhoola kinne dalo ri amraiyan![292]

Who has hung the swings in the mango groves!
The dark groves beside the tank,[293] the peacocks calling, the dark clouds
A light drizzle begins to fall
Who has hung the swings in the mango groves!
All the young women have gone to the Bhulbhulaiyan,[294]
they wander, lost, Shauq Rang,[295] the beloved
Who has hung the swings in the mango groves!

The people of the city must no doubt have seen this as a stark contrast to British officialdom, which tended to keep itself aloof on these occasions, apart from what were seen as official duties of accompanying the Emperor to the Eidgah. The akhbars relating to Charles Metcalfe's daily preoccupations note that he declined to share in the Holi revels as they are not 'our festival'.[296] An akhbar of 1825 tells us that 'the wakil of Ranjit Singh presented the nazr of the Holi festival, but was exempted (i.e. the nazr was not accepted). [The Resident] once again said that people coming with gifts should go back.'[297]

Interestingly, Charles' brother Thomas seems to have been somewhat more amicable. We see him granting leave to members of his staff for four days to visit the Phoolwalon ki Sair, and himself going to the Qutub during the festival, and enjoying musical performances there.[298] Thomas Metcalfe's engagement with Mehrauli was not without controversy. In 1844 he made himself a home here, called Dilkusha, or 'heart expanding'. Bizarrely, this building was a seventeenth century tomb. Rooms were added to this, around the central chamber, and other buildings around were modified to provide accommodation for staff and for other ancillary facilities. The visual landscape was changed by the construction of pavilions and follies in the surrounding open space.[299] Since Thomas at the time was the Commissioner of Delhi, no one probably dared to comment on what might have seemed a desecration to most.

Dilkusha was not the only controversial intervention in Mehrauli's landscape. In the late 1820s the Qutub Minar, which had been damaged in an earthquake in 1803, had been repaired by the army engineers, led by Robert Smith. The work, however, revealed a surprising degree of lack of understanding and sensitivity. The facing stones that had fallen down were put back, but randomly, so that the inscriptions were now jumbled and unreadable. Numerous additions were made that did not match the original structure in either style or spirit—balcony balustrades on four stories, an iron and brass balustrade for the fifth storey, a stone pavilion, and over it all an octagonal wooden cupola supporting a flagstaff.[300]

Neither was the work at the Qutub Minar only about repairs and additions to the structures. The area around the minar and mosque was at the time covered with mud huts and the remains of several other structures dating from various periods in the history of the complex. These were completely cleared away, the debris being piled up into 'ornamental mounds and seats of view'.

The buildings that had been cleared away from the area were not all old and abandoned structures. Some of them clearly were the houses of religious mendicants and khadims (keepers of a dargah) and steps were taken to ensure that they would be unable to return to the area. The area was to be guarded and maintained by a permanent staff and elaborate rules were promulgated regarding access to the buildings and the space around them. There were clear injunctions against defacing the buildings and plantations and against occupying any part of the grounds or buildings for any length of time. Camping was to be allowed only on areas specifically demarcated for the purpose. Finally, the notices in Persian and English laid down, 'Groups of natives of the lower classes are not to ascend the minar in a number exceeding ten at a time, and are not allowed to make any stay in the minar. No faqirs, beggars or vagrants are allowed to take up their post or demand money about the Kootub'.[301] As in the case of Dilkusha, no open public opposition was recorded, but criticism of a covert sort was expressed soon after the repairs were completed. The official record noted that the new balustrade was damaged by an anonymous vandal in 'mere wantonness'.[302]

20

Not Business as Usual

The advent of British rule in Delhi and North India in general, had brought an end to war, and promoted the interests of trade and commerce. Those who benefited most from the new regime were the big bankers who had supported the Company against the Marathas. Not only were they rewarded with jagirs, but some of them were entrusted with the handling of the financial business of the government. Over the years they were to discover that this connection could prove to be a double-edged sword. One banking house that epitomized this was that of Harsukh Rai.

Harsukh Rai had acted as a treasurer for the Marathas, had loaned money to the rulers of various states in the region, and even the tribute of several states of Rajputana had been paid to the Marathas through him. This necessarily gave him considerable political influence as well. When he had established himself as the treasurer of the Company's government in Delhi, he tried to act as a go-between in the diplomatic relations of these Rajputana states and the British. He approached the government at Calcutta directly with a proposal that the states in question—notably Jaipur, Udaipur and Kota, would like to be taken under British protection. The Company would consequently mediate with the Marathas on issues such as the payment of tribute and the depredations of the Marathas in the territories of these states. The government, however, looked unfavourably upon Harsukh Rai directly approaching the Calcutta government without going through the Resident, and the banker was snubbed.[303]

His position was otherwise unaffected, and after his death some months later, his son Shagun Chand and his partner Sant Lal were appointed to carry on as government treasurers; though they seem to have parted ways sometime in the early 1820s.[304] The two bankers' political and financial relations with the independent states continued, though separately. Harsukh Rai and Shagun Chand had lent large sums of money to the rulers of various states in Punjab and Rajputana, and these transactions were based to a great extent on an implicit support of the British Government to the bankers. The Company, however, brought about a major change in this arrangement, by an order of 1818, which made it clear that the government would not interfere in the recovery of debts of the independent chiefs to the bankers. Shagun Chand's firm suffered a loss of 15 lakhs in the following years as a direct consequence. For Shagun Chand, the political was inseparable from the financial. So when one of his clients, the Maha Rao of Kota, was threatened by rival factions in his state, Shagun Chand tried to put in a word for him with the British. This was viewed by the government as unacceptable political intrigue, though Shagun Chand was only motivated by the desire to see his creditor survive and be in a position to repay him at a later date.

This crisis in the recovery of loans had other consequences that further weakened Shagun Chand's financial position. His cousins, Ganga Das and Jamna Das, when they saw the firm in crisis, brought suits for their shares in the firm. In the litigation that ensued, they received an award to the tune of three and a half lakh rupees against Shagun Chand. In settlement of this award, many of his havelis were attached by a decree of the court, and many of his other clients lost faith in him and started demanding their deposits. Shagun Chand also complained that the court had not done him justice, and he had not been granted leave to appeal. He was heard to complain that 'he had lost all his reputation in this case, therefore he would also give his life'. William Fraser tried to mediate between the two parties and effect a compromise, by which Shagun Chand would give Ganga Das and his brothers a quarter of his property.

The dispute carried on for an inordinately long time without any definite settlement. The firm survived somehow, in part certainly due to informal help from individual officials of the Company it had connections with. So, for instance, Shagun Chand's son Girdhar Lal was made treasurer of the government Treasury in 1830, which must have done much to counter the crisis of confidence that the firm was facing. Finally, as the property of Shagun Chand was on the verge of being auctioned, his mother stepped in to mediate. She invited Ganga Das and Jamna Das to a meal, and persuaded them to accept a compromise, whereby they would accept what was due to them, in instalments, in the meanwhile receiving the mortgage on a garden, a ganj, and a haveli. The formal deed was written up in Hindi and Persian, and signed by both sides.[305]

This was, however, not the end of the matter. The promised money, property, and mortgage papers were handed over in 1830, but in 1834 the cousins won another claim against Shagun Chand, this time against income from a jagir (consisting of the villages of Alipur, Madipur and Salimpur) that had been granted to Shagun Chand for services rendered to the British Government by his father. The firm never recovered from its financial difficulties, and a business that had been established in Delhi by Harsukh Rai's ancestor, Dip Chand Sah, in the mid-seventeenth century, collapsed. Even the jagir was resumed on Shagun Chand's death in 1843.[306]

Another of those whose business interests suffered due to the changed British policy was Narain Das, whose father had been of help to British forces in the early nineteenth century. He continued to petition the government right up to 1857 (when he sent a petition to the Court of Directors), asking for help in the recovery of his loan to the Raja of Alwar. He was unconvinced by the British arguments in defence of their policy of non-interference. He pointed out that 'whenever any disturbance takes place among the native chiefs, the British authorities always interfere unreservedly in suppressing the same...but the poor bankers as suffering parties are told (although they are British subjects, and look to them for the necessary protection) that for want of jurisdiction and authority, they cannot interfere or see justice done. But that they should seek redress from the hands of their very aggressors.'[307]

Shagun Chand's erstwhile partner Sant Lal was also finding out, in a different way, that financial dealings arising from the Company's political arrangements could be an unviable business proposition. He had undertaken to be the medium for the payment of tribute by the Jaipur state to the Company's government. When, in 1830, the tribute was not forthcoming, he and his son Ajodhya Prasad were charged with embezzlement, and the government sought to attach portions of his immovable property in the city, though this was eventually prevented by orders from Calcutta.[308]

It was not only the complicated intertwined financial and political dealings of the business houses that were threatened by the new regime. The administration was also bringing about changes in relationships within organized commercial groups. A case in point was the institution of the *chaudhari* of *shroffs*. The shroffs or bankers, had a hereditary headman or chaudhari, who was supposed to generally represent their interests. This position had descended in the same family for generations, since the days of the initial foundation of Shahjahanabad. On the one hand the institution was dependent on recognition from members of the banking community, who paid the chaudhari a certain percentage on all *hundis*, or instruments of remittance. On the other hand, this position was dependent on acknowledgement from the state, with the chaudhari representing the shroffs at the Mughal court. The Marathas had continued to recognize the institution, and had sanctioned Rs 55 for a turban and shawl—in effect a khilat, to be given annually to the incumbent in recognition of his position. This was continued through the first three decades of British rule.[309]

In the late 1820s, however, the son of the then chaudhari became involved in an incident that completely eroded the family's position among the shroffs of the city. This was the famous Colebrooke case, which broke in 1829. Edward Colebrooke, the Resident of Delhi, was accused of corruption by his immediate junior, Charles Trevelyan. The Resident was accused of financial irregularities and the dispensing of favours in exchange for gifts. Lady Colebrooke was also accused as a medium through which this racket of bribery was carried out. Of the many bankers who were accused of having given bribes to the Colebrookes, was Shagun Chand and his son Girdhar Lal, who were said to have given trays of jewels to Lady Colebrooke, among other things, with a view to obtaining favourable orders in their disputes against Shagun Chand's creditors and cousins. The Colebrookes' son, also named Edward, was also involved in financial dealings which created a conflict of interest in view of his father's official position.[310]

In order to prove many of his charges, Trevelyan needed the account books of the bankers, who unanimously refused to hand them over. The chaudhari, Godha Mal, of course had the details of all the financial transactions (of which in fact he received a percentage). His son Bakhtawar Singh was induced by Trevelyan to reveal these and thus help prove the charges against Colebrooke. The immediate result of this was that the chaudhari lost the confidence of the shroffs, the majority of whom proceeded to withhold his customary share. Bakhtawar Singh in the process also had to suffer humiliation at the hands of Colebrooke, who had him imprisoned for a while.[311] The case created a crisis among the bankers in the city. Leading the protest against Trevelyan's proceedings were two prominent bankers—Shagun Chand and Saligram. The latter was the head of a very old banking family, and also enjoyed the post of a government treasurer.

If Bakhtawar Singh had been hoping for reward or compensation from the government, he was disappointed. The government refused to intervene in the decision of the shroffs to discontinue the payment of a percentage to the chaudhari. It was also decided that the khilat bestowed by the government on Godha Mal would not be continued in the case of Bakhtawar Singh. The rationale for this was that the khilat was recognition of a corporate regulation and control by an individual over the affairs of the group, which was incompatible with the liberal principles of British rule. Godha Mal had continued to enjoy the perquisite because the government had not wished to actually withdraw something he had received for a long time. But to extend the privilege to Bakhtawar Singh would 'be looked upon by everybody as a reward to this individual for the information and assistance he afforded in the prosecutions conducted by Mr Trevelyan'![312] Ironically, the justification for the withdrawal of the privilege was that Bakhtawar Singh should not be seen to be rewarded. It was decided instead that a life pension of Rs 100 per month would be adequate compensation for the loss and suffering he had incurred.[313]

The logic being applied by the government in this case was that the supposedly superior principles that were the foundation of British rule—financial honesty in public affairs, and free trade—justified their unfair treatment of an individual. That Bakhtawar Singh had jeopardized his interests and lost the trust of his fellow bankers in the help that he had rendered could not be weighed against the uprightness of British policy. Looked at from another point of view, the short message sent out to the Indians was that the rulers could use individuals for their own interest and then not reward their loyalty. On the other hand, ties with the now much less important Mughal court were much more lasting. Many years later, in 1851, the diary of palace events recorded that the son of chaudhari Bakhtawar Singh presented a nazar to the Emperor Bahadur Shah on the occasion of his marriage and was given the customary khilat.[314]

21

Uncertain Relationships

There were other ramifications of the Colebrooke episode too. It reflected a fundamental divergence in opinion among British officialdom. There were on the one hand those who were comfortable with carrying on business in the context of receiving nazars and gifts, and doing 'favours' on a very personal basis. This often went hand in hand with close personal ties between individual British officials and the Indian elite. In the early 1820s, the Indian wife of the Resident, David Ochterlony, personally received delegations from the independent rulers whose relations with the East India Company Ochterlony was in charge of. She was given gifts on the understanding that she would help to ensure the success of their applications to government.[315] Very similar conduct on the part of Lady Colebrooke was an important charge in the case brought against her husband.

Often such mediations were without pecuniary considerations; based simply on a network of acquaintance. Thus Khwaja Farid put in a word to his friend Ochterlony on behalf of the Maha Rao of Kota, and Fraser appealed to the government at a personal level in a case on behalf of the cousins of Ahmad Baksh Khan, Nawab of Ferozepur Jhirka, who was a close personal friend. Increasingly, as the affairs of Delhi were being brought under closer scrutiny by the government at Calcutta, these 'irregularities' were frowned upon. Thus Fraser was reprimanded for his application. Fraser also intervened on behalf of Shagun Chand with his cousins, who had secured a huge award against him in a litigation, trying to persuade them to come to some agreement, even though the litigation was over. Fraser's attempts to have the case reopened were snubbed by the Magistrate.[316]

During the whole episode between Colebrooke and Trevelyan, Fraser treated the former with great sympathy, and was reprimanded for it by the government. Colebrooke, in reply to the charges of corruption brought against him, projected the whole issue in terms of the relationship between the representatives of the British Government and Indians. He commented that exchanges of gifts—often simply baskets of fruit—were an important part of social relations with Indians. Too rigid a stand against these conventions was detrimental to such interactions. He lamented, 'I am a sacrifice to the resolution of putting an end to all interchange of courtesy between the British Functionaries and our native subjects and allies...of dinners, nautches and fireworks' for no Englishman would 'dare to accept of an entertainment from a native gentleman', resulting in 'total estrangement and alienation'.[317]

Colebrooke of course exaggerated. It was more than the gifts of mangoes and oranges that the government objected to. Neither was it simply a question of a straightforward difference between an old-style administrator sympathetic to the customs of the natives and the new cold and impersonal instrument of the rule of law. The situation was much more complex. Even relatively early on, there was a very basic arrogance that came across regularly in the behaviour of officials high and low, particularly in their interactions with Indians lower in the social scale. In the fairly small sample of letters written by William Gardner while at Delhi in 1820-21, more than one such instance is revealed. In mid-1820 he writes, 'People complain that the inhabitants have grown insolent but I cannot discover it—all the instances I have heard have been provoked by horsewhips—from tandem drivers'. In August 1821 he mentions the incident of an officer who in a drunken state attacked his tailor with a sword and killed him—leading to a strike by all the tailors of the city until a judicial enquiry was promised. Three months later he casually mentions other erring officers, including one, who 'used to amuse himself when on the Palace Guard in haranguing the sepoys and natives with the grossest abuse of the old Emperor—proper Galee.'[318]

It is also simplistic to assume that those officials who had 'gone native'—like Ochterlony and Fraser with their multiple Indian wives/concubines, their Indian clothes and lifestyle, and their Indian friends, were universally popular. Fraser made himself unpopular enough to have multiple assassination attempts against him. Gardner noted that the local Indian newspapers' reports of the venality surrounding the wife of Ochterlony would make his correspondent, an Englishman, 'blush for your country'.[319]

We do have evidence of frequent social interactions between the Indian elite and the British colonial officialdom, such as the friendship between Ochterlony and Khwaja Farid. Ochterlony was a frequent visitor to Farid's home, and was given a special velvet-covered chair next to Farid's *masnad*, or seat, every time he visited the house.[320] But there are also hints as to the fundamentally unequal nature of at least some of these relationships. For instance, Indians were inordinately eager to please their British 'friends'. Thus Nawab Ahmad Baksh Khan is reported to have complained that 'This many rupees were spent on a banquet for such-and-such an Englishman....That [English] gentleman came, I showed him around the stables. The pair of Kathiawar horses were standing there; he praised them. I had them harnessed to the buggy, and seated him in it, and sent him off home. And so on and so on'.[321]

It was often felt that entertaining British officials and generally 'keeping them happy' was a necessary part of getting your case heard, and your interests served. In one of the akhbars of 1830, we hear of Girdhar Lal, son of Shagun Chand, preparing a banquet for the 'great sahibs', for which he came to the Residency to borrow benches, chairs, etc. This was followed up by news of Francis Hawkins, who succeeded Colebrooke as Resident, visiting Shagun Chand's house and enjoying a banquet and an entertainment consisting of 'dancing, singing and the play of the actors.' This was while Shagun Chand's financial affairs were still under litigation. Soon after, we hear of Hawkins accepting the invitation of the ruler of Ferozepur Jhirka, Shams ud din Khan, to go and hunt on his estate.[322] Shams ud din Khan, who had succeeded his father Ahmad Baksh Khan, had an axe to grind, as he was fighting his half-brothers over a claim they had brought against him over shares in the inherited lands and property. A rather innovative means used by Shams ud din Khan to win over Colebrooke was the purchase by him of all the Residency furniture for the rather large sum of thirty thousand rupees. The 'purchase' in fact only involved the transfer of the money from the Nawab to Colebrooke, as the furniture remained in the Residency on 'loan'. This was just one of the many gifts made by Shams ud din Khan to the Colebrookes.[323]

Against this background, the Colebrooke case was a step in an increasing attempt by the government to address some of these issues. One was an attempt to reign in physical violence. An akhbar of early 1830 informs us that 'the chief of the court (Sahib e adalat) gave the order that if an Englishman beat a person for no fault of his, that person could lodge a complaint with the court and the case would be heard.'[324] The other aim was to place relations with Indians on a more impersonal footing, such that they would not be influenced by personal connections. The aim was a positive one, to make the system fair—not easily subverted by considerations of status and influence. But in its working, it came up against some well entrenched notions of status, and caused dissatisfaction. There were some who felt that British rules and regulations paid inadequate regard to status, respectability and lineage.

In 1832, members of the well-respected family of hakims, the sons of Hakim Sharif Khan, complained that their hereditary pension had not been paid to them by the Collector on the ground that they had not furnished descriptive rolls of themselves. They felt that this was demeaning. Besides, they said, there was no question of the pension of any one of them being drawn fraudulently by another. They were so well known, that their deaths would immediately become public knowledge. The government considered them not included within the category of political pensioners for whom the rules could be relaxed, and was unwilling to make exceptions in their case.[325]

There were also complaints that the British state, contrary to expectations, did not set any store by loyalty. These expectations were based on experience of the Mughal system, which was predicated on ties of fealty that lasted generations. Khwaja Zain ul abidin, the son of Khwaja Farid, served as head munshi in the office of the British Political Agent at Jaipur for five years. In 1832 he was replaced by the appointee of the new Agent. Zain ul abidin's petition to the government recalled the services of his father to it, and drew attention to his own unblemished record. The government's reply acknowledged that he had not been dismissed for any fault, but that the Agent had the authority to pick his candidate, and so no redressal was possible.[326]

Apart from specific complaints of unjust or insensitive treatment, there was the more elusive issue of friendliness and respect. In 1819, both Nawab Ahmad Baksh Khan and the Raja of Alwar complained of a lack of courtesy in the correspondence addressed to them by R. Cavendish, the Assistant Commissioner. In fact so insolent was Cavendish that he came to be known as 'ghamandi sahab'—'Mr Arrogant'.[327] The more astute and successful of the Residents had appreciated the importance of keeping lines of communication open. Charles Metcalfe, for instance, set aside one day every week to meet 'natives of all ranks (including the lowest)' who could talk to him in private if they wished.[328] As against this, a newspaper report of 1830 expressed sentiments against Hawkins, the then Resident, complaining of the lack of effort on his part to befriend the people of the city.[329]

One way in which colonial authorities could forge ties with the people of the city was by adopting long-held traditional practices that had been used by the Mughals, such as khilats. This was a language that Indians understood, and khilats and other similar signs of state patronage were much sought after. Badr ud din, acknowledged the best seal engraver in North India, used to engrave the seals of most of the rulers of the area, and was engaged to make the Persian seal of the Governor General as well. As remuneration, instead of a sum of money he requested a khilat. He also put forward a request that he be granted a monthly salary and 'thus have the honour of being a servant to the British Government'.[330] Similarly, durbars were further formal occasions for reinforcing the state's ties with individual elite. An invitation to attend a durbar held by the Resident, the Governor General or the Lieutenant Governor, the order accorded in the precedence there, and the khilats received, were crucial markers of status. When Bentinck visited Delhi, the poet Ghalib wrote to a friend giving a detailed account of exactly who was presented to the Governor General and what nazars they presented and what khilats they received.[331] The newspapers also regularly reported the durbars held by the Resident with lists of those attending.[332]

For the same reason, letters from those in authority were treasured. Ghalib stated with pride that the British Government had confirmed three privileges in his favour—the right to attend the durbar, to receive khilat, and to receive letters from officials. On another occasion he was extremely pleased when the Chief Secretary at Calcutta addressed him in a letter using epithets that were slightly more grand than those customarily used. The extent to which the mere arrival of a letter from a British official could boost an individual's standing is evident from an instance where Ghalib said of a certain nobleman that he was a very important man and 'received hundreds of English letters every day'![333]

The fact that the elite accepted and indeed actively sought to make connections with the colonial state should probably not be seen as an unequivocal endorsement of British rule. State recognition—expressed in the form of titles, khilats and pensions—was an important component of personal prestige. The fact that the state was now a colonial one did not change that fact much.

22

The Fraser Assassination Case

These tensions—caused by British regulations that seemed inherently unjust to Indians, or by complicated personal relationships—were thrown into sharp relief by the Fraser murder case in the mid-1830s. In 1832, William Fraser had risen to the post of Agent to the Governor General, the designation that had replaced the earlier one of 'Resident'. Fraser had survived an assassination attempt in 1819, and there were signs that he was not well liked. In mid-1834 a complaint was made against him by a head clerk. His allegations against Fraser ranged from misappropriation of government property, to having an authoritarian streak—evidently he had 'declared that he would wish always to be in the district having absolute power'. His subordinate officials were unhappy with his methods of working—which included making his circuits during the rainy and hot seasons, and having numerous drafts of letters made and torn up.[334] Some months later, on the night of 22 March 1835, Fraser was shot dead on his way home from a party.

The official investigation into the assassination was led by a newly arrived magistrate, Simon Fraser, who quickly arrived at a conclusion as to the guilty party. The investigation pointed the finger at Karim Khan, a man said to be acting under the orders of Shams ud din Khan, the ruler of Ferozepur Jhirka. Both were soon arrested and the process of assembling the proof and the trial began. Though the prosecutors had little doubt of Shams ud din and Karim Khan's guilt, they had great trouble in persuading people to give the evidence they wanted. Simon Fraser complained that he received from his own police 'not only no assistance but every concealed opposition.' Even the kotwal was believed to be conspiring with the agents of the Nawab. James Skinner, a friend of William, who was helping the investigation, was requested by Thomas Metcalfe to use his influence in the city (with the 'natives') with a view to obtaining information. He too remarked, 'I have never in my experience seen such an union amongst the natives of all ranks.'[335]

These developments in Delhi were overseen by the government of the North-Western Provinces, with its capital at Agra, that had come into existence as an independent entity in 1836, under a Lieutenant Governor, with a degree of independence from the Presidency of Bengal. The government of the North-Western Provinces was surprised at the opposition the local administration was facing in gathering evidence against the accused, and urged the latter to keep an open mind and consider other possibilities too. Maybe the police and people genuinely did not have much information to incriminate the two prisoners? The Agent to the Governor General, the newly appointed Thomas Metcalfe, was asked to be careful, that 'you may not be the instrument of inflicting unmerited punishment or injury on the innocent.'[336]

As a matter of fact, almost the only evidence against the accused that was forthcoming had been provided by people who were far from disinterested witnesses. The first one to denounce Shams ud din, and have Karim Khan arrested, was Fatehullah Beg Khan, a second cousin of Shams ud din, and by more than one account, his 'mortal enemy'. Fatehullah Beg Khan had a long-standing dispute over a share in a jagir that was paid to him through Shams ud din. Shams ud din Khan also had a dispute with his half-brothers Amin ud din Khan and Zia ud din Khan. This was a dispute that had arisen out of arrangements made by their father Ahmad Baksh Khan in his own lifetime. He had given over the jagir of Ferozepur to Shams ud din, and that of Loharu to his younger sons, while leaving the management of Loharu with Shams ud din. The dispute was a challenge from the younger sons about the proceeds from Loharu. At the same time, they claimed shares in the ancestral property in Delhi too.[337] In fact, it was with the aim of a favourable decision in this dispute that Shams ud din had bribed Colebrooke.

Evidence was also provided by Asadullah Khan, who we know better as the poet 'Ghalib'. Ghalib had a long-standing connection with the family of Shams ud din Khan. Ghalib was born in Agra in a family of noble birth, from a class of Central Asian military men who had immigrated to India in the eighteenth century. His father had died in 1802, when he was just five years old, and Ghalib was raised by his uncle. This uncle, Nasrullah Khan, had served the Marathas and then the Raja of Alwar. Like many other military commanders, he was also absorbed into the East India Company's establishment once the latter conquered the territory around Delhi in 1803, probably through the intervention of his wife's brother, Ahmad Baksh Khan. He was recruited as a leader of a troop of cavalry, and awarded a jagir for his support. Nasrullah Khan died soon after, when Ghalib was just eight years old, and his jagir was resumed. Ahmad Baksh Khan, however, entered into an agreement with the British in May 1806, whereby he would set aside ten thousand rupees a year from his own obligations to the latter, for the dependents of Nasrullah Khan. A month later, in June 1806, this agreement was reduced from ten thousand to five thousand. Among the dependents of Nasrullah Khan was Ghalib, whose share in the reduced allowance came to seven hundred and fifty rupees a year.[338]

Ghalib's connection to Ahmad Baksh Khan's family was strengthened when, at the age of thirteen, he was married to Umrao Begum, the daughter of Nawab Ilahi Baksh Khan, the brother of Ahmad Baksh Khan. Ilahi Baksh Khan was also a poet, who wrote poetry under the *takhallus,* or pen name, of 'Maruf' and lived in Delhi. This marriage brought Ghalib to Delhi, as he moved into his father-in-law's home. He made Delhi his home for the rest of his life, though he moved out of Ilahi Baksh's house after a while. This connection to the city by marriage, so to speak, bestowed on

Ghalib the nickname 'Nausha' (bridegroom), for the rest of his life, though he detested it.

Shortly after the death of Ahmad Baksh Khan, Ghalib entered into a long-drawn-out dispute with Shams ud din Khan, claiming that the agreement of June 1806 was a forgery, and he ought to have been getting double the allowance he was actually receiving. Ghalib pursued his application all the way to the government in Calcutta, making a trip there that lasted from 1827 to 1829. Even this did not get him anywhere and his case was dismissed, with bitter recriminations on both sides. Challenging the truth of some statements made by Ghalib, Shams ud din had sarcastically remarked that the former being a poet, had probably availed himself of the customary poetic latitude—in effect, told a lie.[339] On his part, Ghalib, in a petition to the government in Calcutta in 1830, complained that his dispute with Shams ud din Khan was going against him because 'all the persons attached to the Delhi Residency agree both in heart and speech, with the Ferozepur walla'.[340] It was true that the then Resident, Hawkins' report was in favour of Shams ud din Khan. Ghalib had sought to counter it with an appeal to the Governor General's Private Secretary, Andrew Stirling, whom he had met in Calcutta, and who he believed was more sympathetic to his cause. Unfortunately, Stirling's untimely death in early 1830 ended that hope.[341]

At the time of the Fraser murder, Ghalib had more serious worries than the perceived injustice done to him. He had been living beyond his means for quite a while, and finally two of his creditors had obtained a court decree against him. As a result, Ghalib had two options before him—to pay the money (which he did not have), or face arrest. The only latitude that was allowed to one of his respectable status was, that a constable could not enter his house and arrest him, but could only do so on the street. So, for many days, Ghalib had been lying low, virtually under house arrest, when the news of the murder broke. Ghalib informs us through one of his letters: 'The Magistrate of the City already knew me and felt the bond of mutual regard. In the seclusion I have spoken of, when like the owl I flew by night alone, from time to time I went to him at night to pass an hour or two in pleasant converse. When this event took place he made me his partner to pry into the mystery, until at last, the crime was brought home to the Lord of Firozpur.'[342]

To many people in the city, this seemed like collusion between an interested witness and the prosecution. Ghalib himself admitted that among the people of the city, who knew of the long-standing enmity between himself and Shams ud din, it was widely believed that Ghalib and Fatehullah Beg Khan had given evidence against the Nawab from personal enmity.[343]

The rather questionable methods adopted by the prosecution, and its very partisan approach, were repeatedly questioned by the family and other supporters of Shams ud din Khan. His mother, Bahu Khanam, wrote to the Governor General (this post at that time was occupied by Charles Metcalfe) and mentioned the vested interests of Fatehullah Beg Khan. She also complained that the representatives of the accused were not allowed to attend court to refute charges, and that rewards were offered to those who would come forward and give evidence against him.[344]

The vakil of the Nawab accused the magistrate of 'having quitted all rules and laws of equity.' He pointed out that all evidence that led in any other direction was wilfully disregarded. A *thanadar* who had put in a report saying that he had investigated the real murderer was dismissed from his situation, and his application destroyed. Simon Fraser in fact had dismissed the official, but according to him, it was for conniving with the supporters of the accused. The vakil also said that two other persons who had come to give statements regarding another suspect, were deliberately examined late, so that the person they incriminated could escape. He also claimed that the murder weapon, a carbine which was found in a well, had been planted, and in any case the shot did not fit it. He was also suspicious of the use of the English language in the recording of the evidence, accusing the magistrate of altering the statements when they were written in English. The vakil protested that the administration was taking the case to a personal level, having it proclaimed with the beat of the drum that 'anyone who should offer up prayers for him (Shumsoodeen Khan) or make any mention of him, should be punished'. In fact the vakil underlined his lack of confidence in the investigation by requesting that an Indian sadr amin (judicial officer) be appointed to investigate the case.[345]

Once the trial was over, Shams ud din sent a petition to the government protesting against the procedures adopted during it. He said that the procedure had been compromised because Simon Fraser was the committing magistrate, gaoler of the witnesses for the prosecution, and the public prosecutor, or vakil, all in one. He only allowed such witnesses to give evidence as would strengthen his case. Moreover, anyone changing his statement, saying that he had been coerced, was immediately sentenced for perjury. Shams ud din also complained that he himself had not been allowed to communicate with his vakil. The conduct of the judge, Russell Colvin, was also questioned. He had concurred with the magistrate's examination of the witnesses, without examining them himself, he had not heard any evidence for the defence, and had not allowed the representatives of the Nawab to say anything.[346]

The objections of the defence in the Shams ud din case were brushed aside. Russell Colvin replied to the accusation that he had not examined all witnesses himself with the argument that it was not his 'duty to carry out the preliminary enquiry again'. As for Shams ud din's accusation that only such witnesses as propped up the case against Karim Khan were produced, Colvin found it but natural that the 'magistrate as a matter of course adduced only such evidence as he considered would support the commitment, and rejected such as he deemed immaterial or suspicious'. The government of Agra expressed a mild curiosity that no investigation had been made as to the possible motive for the murder. To this, Colvin had no comment to make.[347]

The proceedings wrapped up quickly, with both Shams ud din and Karim Khan being sentenced to death. On 10 October 1835, the Nawab was hanged to death outside the Kashmiri Gate of the city. As a precaution, to prevent any rescue attempt, he had been brought from his jail in the cantonment to the Kashmiri Gate the previous night. He had seemed calm, and conversed as usual, but was unhappy that his request to be allowed to go to his death in clothes suitable to his station in life had been refused. He protested his innocence to the end. So nervous was the administration in the face of the massive public sympathy for the Nawab's cause, that a large body of troops—900 from Delhi plus two additional regiments from Meerut—were present at the execution.[348]

After hanging for an hour, the body was lowered and handed over to his father-in-law, Mughal Beg, for burial at Qadam Sharif, a fourteenth century shrine. Considering the extent of the support for the Nawab, there had not been too many people at the execution. Some said this was because the Kashmiri Gate had been shut by the orders of the government. There were, however, some important personages present—the rulers of Patiala, Nabha, Kaithal and Alwar, and Hindu Rao.[349] Hindu Rao, who was the uncle of the ruler of Gwalior, had been living in exile in Delhi since less than a year previously.[350] In fact, Hindu Rao had purchased Fraser's house on the Ridge, and lived there till his death in 1850. The house came to be known as Hindu Rao's house.

A few days after Shams ud din Khan was hanged, a curious petition was received in Calcutta to the address of the Governor General. It was from Ania Meo, the chief witness whose evidence had linked Shams ud din Khan with Karim Khan in the conspiracy to murder. He claimed that he had given his evidence as asked by James Skinner, Simon Fraser and others, 'to their entire satisfaction'. In return, he claimed, 'the above named gentlemen promised to bestow on me after the final settlement of the case, as a remuneration the sum of 35,000 rupees and to assign to me in perpetuity 3 villages and a monthly allowance of 100 rupees'. This promise had not been fulfilled. He complained that it was 'solely in consequence of my having given this evidence that territory and property to the amount of Lacks [*sic*] of Rupees have come into the possession of the Hon'ble Company...while I have, for my having done so, become separated from my country and cast out by my tribe, relations and family.' The government dismissed this embarrassing letter as being most probably a forgery, and nothing further was done.[351]

Doubts about whether the case had been tried fairly were again raised, in 1838, in a meeting of the shareholders of the East India Company, in London. The occasion was a vote to grant a sum of five thousand pounds to the estate of William Fraser (in effect his mother and surviving brother) as compensation, in addition to the two hundred pounds per year that had already been assigned to his mother for her lifetime. Though the vote was in the affirmative, one of the shareholders present persistently claimed that the grant could not be made without reopening the question of whether Shams ud din had received a fair trial. He himself was convinced, having seen some of the papers that had been made available to the shareholders, that there were serious doubts on the issue. In the absence of a fair trial, he added, it might even be said that Shams ud din had been murdered.[352]

Back in India, the impression that the government was using the case as a pretext for possessing itself of the jagir of Ferozepur Jhirka was reinforced in the public mind by the government's actions. Shortly after the arrest of Shams ud din, officials arrived in Ferozepur to take possession, ordering the Nawab's mother to leave for Delhi, leaving most of her valuable possessions behind.[353] After the execution of the Nawab and the resumption of the jagir, his family, including several dependants of his father, Ahmad Baksh Khan, were suddenly bereft of property and income. Their petitions for a restoration of the jagir, which they argued had been given to Ahmad Baksh Khan for personal services, were rejected. The property of the Nawab was auctioned and the proceeds went largely to settle various claims against the estate.[354]

Ghalib had in the meanwhile waited to see how the property would be disposed. Once Shams ud din had been hanged, he wrote to a friend, 'My eyes still wait to see the token of my triumph. To speak more plainly, what the Lord of Ferozpur used to pay me was less than was my due; and if the government pays no more than that sum, I shall not rest content.'[355] As it happened, Ghalib never did get the increment in pension he hoped for. His wife, Umrao Begum, who was a cousin of Shams ud din, also had a claim against the estate. She had been receiving an allowance of thirty rupees per month from her uncle, Ahmad Baksh Khan, which Shams ud din had discontinued. She fought for the restitution of this allowance till 1850, when her case was finally rejected. Ghalib does seem to have got some recompense. His immediate legal/financial problems seem to have been solved, as there is no further talk in his letters of being confined to the house for fear of arrest.

Fraser was as controversial in death as in life. His good friend James Skinner built a beautiful memorial to him in the ground of St James' Church, which was nearing completion. The poet Momin Khan 'Momin', in a letter to a friend, remembered bitterly the confiscation (in fact resumption), under orders of Fraser, of land he had inherited from his mother. He said, 'Before he (Fraser) was murdered...he raised the dust of torment and tyranny. No doubt in punishment of this oppression he perished and descended to the depths of hell.'[356]

PART THREE

Bahadur Shah Zafar: The People's Emperor

Bahadur Shah 'Zafar'

23

The New Emperor and His Court

Akbar II died on the 28 September 1837, at the age of eighty-two, some four months after the death of Mumtaz Mahal. Abu Zafar, the heir apparent, almost sixty-two years old, had waited impatiently and anxiously for many years. Now, when news of his father's passing, at six o'clock in the evening, was brought to him by the messengers in the palace, he could wait no more. He ordered that preparations be made immediately for the coronation. His astrologers advised against this unseemly haste, suggesting that daylight hours would be more auspicious. Zafar, however, probably insecure and expecting a last-minute coup by his brothers, insisted on ascending the throne in the middle of the night. He assumed the title of Bahadur Shah at a ceremonial durbar held at three a.m., while the body of the dead Emperor still lay unburied. Soon afterwards, there was a widespread famine in India, and the people of Delhi attributed the calamity to this inauspicious act of the new Emperor. Food riots took place when grain arrived from the east in boats at Delhi and this became a memorable landmark event in the lives of the people.[357]

On the whole, however, even as a prince, Zafar had been popular in Delhi. He was a polite, cultured man; a poet, who wrote Urdu and Persian poetry under the takhallus 'Zafar', and Braj and Punjabi poetry under the takhallus 'Shauq Rang'. He was accomplished in the scholarly skill of calligraphy, but also in the more military pursuit of archery.[358] As the heir apparent, acutely conscious of the fact that he was not his father's favourite, he had lived in insecurity and financial straits. Now, he could finally come into his own.

Though his writ ran only within the walls of the fort, and even that was increasingly circumscribed, Bahadur Shah presided over his tiny realm with all the dignity he could muster from his grand heritage. He held a daily durbar with his ministers in the Diwan e Khas. Here the business of state was transacted, which in effect amounted mainly to the affairs of the palace and its employees, disputes between individual members of the family, and relations with the British Government. Petitions were heard, orders were given, correspondence was dealt with. The diary of daily events at court, meticulously maintained, tells us of the fairly petty issues that the Emperor often personally dealt with—theft, cases of food poisoning, the complaint of the young wife of one of the Emperor's *chaprasis* (peons), who beat her.[359] On important occasions the durbar would include various important personages—British officials who were connected to palace affairs, various other holders of titles from the throne, bankers and merchants.

The most important offices in the fort were that of the mukhtar—the principal functionary of the Emperor, and the *nazir*—the superintendent of the household, a position invariably held by a eunuch. The mukhtar was in charge of the all-important finances. In fact, the office was frequently held by men of means who could make advances on their own account towards the royal finances. Several other royal employees were also creditors of the Emperor and farmers of royal revenues, and no doubt motives of speculation were a consideration when accepting royal office of importance. There were frequent allegations that money was made by individuals at the expense of the royal finances.[360]

In the early years of Bahadur Shah's reign, the post of mukhtar was held by Hamid Ali Khan, an important figure in Delhi society, the son-in-law and heir of Nawab Fazl Ali, the prime minister of the state of Awadh. He had a difficult time as mukhtar. He was in charge of distributing the monthly allowances that were given to a large number of people within the palace out of the Emperor's stipend. There were frequent complaints that these were not given out in time.[361] The picture was further muddied by the fact that he was also the revenue farmer of the *pargana* of Kot Qasim, which was a royal possession. Kot Qasim was a troublesome area, as the landowners often defaulted on their revenues and put up armed resistance against the revenue collectors. The problems with this revenue farm was probably the reason why Hamid Ali Khan was in financial difficulty and unable to run the palace finances efficiently. In any event, he made so many enemies that he was soon removed from his post.[362]

Another appointment was that of the captain of the royal troops, the najeebs. This post was occupied by Wilayat Ali, who was originally from Agra. Interestingly, he was married to the older, very wealthy widow of General Ochterlony, Mubarak un Nissa, the notorious 'Generalee Begum'. The marriage had its ups and downs, however,. Wilayat Ali got into trouble with the government for human trafficking, and his wife too complained to the Emperor against him, on the charge that he had defrauded her of large sums of money. The problem seems to have been that he had 'borrowed' her money in order to offer a *nazrana*, which would secure him the position of the captain of the najeebs.[363] The practice of candidates for royal office paying a nazrana—a sum in cash for the acceptance of their candidature, was a common one. To British observers, this payment, the amount of which was carefully negotiated, looked like a bribe. In fact, it is probably more accurate to view it as a sort of security deposit.

This impression is confirmed when we see the case of Wilayat Ali. He resigned in November 1840, and immediately demanded the money that was owed to him, i.e. the nazrana that he had presented on being appointed the captain. In response he was told to settle all accounts with the new appointee to the post. His wife also put in a word for the recovery of the dues, which were, she pointed out, actually her money. Clearly, the nazrana was refundable and adjustable against outstanding dues.[364]

It is possible that the appointment of Hamid Ali Khan and Wilayat Ali was an attempt by Bahadur Shah to bring fresh blood into the administration, and distance it from those who had dominated the palace during his father's time. This was probably due to a suspicion that the older regime had ties to those who had opposed Zafar in the old days, and were close to his rivals for the throne—his brothers. The dismissal of the new appointees after a relatively short time is probably indicative of how difficult it was to actually get away from established connections and practices. Hamid Ali Khan's position had been constantly undermined by Raja Sohan Lal, who went about claiming that he could eliminate mismanagement if he was appointed instead.

Hamid Ali Khan was replaced by one Zamir ud daulah Agha Hyder, and the deputy appointed with him was Debi Singh, the son of Raja Jai Sukh Rai, who had been the mukhtar during the early years of Akbar II. Hamid Ali made a last-ditch attempt to regain his position by proposing to forego all the money that was owed to him by the royal treasury, on condition that he was reinstated, to no avail. Finally, accounts were settled between Hamid Ali Khan and Debi Singh in June, with the latter paying the former fifteen thousand rupees. Interestingly, the person who replaced Wilayat Ali, being appointed to the *kul bakshigiri* (office of paymaster of the troops) and *kaptani*, was another son of Jai Sukh Rai, Saligram, who had the support of Bahadur Shah's son Mirza Shah Rukh, the prince who had considerable influence in the court at the time.[365]

There was one new entrant who had a long innings, and this was because he had an important supporter within the palace. Ahsanullah Khan, who had been a physician of the ruler of Jhajjar, was appointed physician to the Emperor in early 1840. Soon after, he became embroiled in the complex politics of the palace, and Mirza Shah Rukh recommended his dismissal. This was, however, turned down on the intervention of Zeenat Mahal, the Emperor's new wife. Bahadur Shah had married the daughter of Nawab Ahmad Quli Khan, a nobleman of his court, on 19 November 1840, and gave her the title Zeenat Mahal. The new queen soon established herself as an important and vocal influence at the court.

Less than a month after the wedding she reminded her husband that he had promised to give her father the revenues of Kot Qasim and Chandni Chowk, and extracted a promise that it would be seen to. Her special position was formally recognized by Bahadur Shah, who gave her the additional title of Mumtaz Mahal and instructed all the princes and employees of the state to honour her and pledge loyalty to her.[366]

Bahadur Shah's ancestors had been patrons of the arts, and Bahadur Shah aspired to be the same, despite his straitened circumstances. Delhi's strong musical tradition, in the form of the Dilli 'gharana', had its roots in the thirteenth century. It had developed along two strands, one associated with Sufi shrines, and the other with imperial courts. Bahadur Shah himself was not a mere patron but a serious practitioner, the *shagird*, or pupil, of the maestro Miyan Achpal. Another disciple of Miyan Achpal was Qutub Baksh, who eventually became the Emperor's chief court musician, and was honoured with the title 'Tanras Khan'.[367]

Another important figure in the royal entourage was the Emperor's *ustad*, or master in poetry. This position had been occupied, from the time Zafar was heir apparent, by Mohammad Ibrahim 'Zauq'. Zauq, the son of a humble soldier, was a prodigy. Born in 1789-90, he had become the ustad not only of Zafar, but of Ilahi Baksh 'Maruf', the brother of Ahmad Baksh Khan, when he was just nineteen. His reward for correcting the verses of Zafar was modest, in keeping with the impecunious heir apparent's means, but he gained prestige from the position. This was further enhanced when he impressed Akbar II so much that he was given the title of 'Khaqani e Hind' by him. This title, literally 'the Khaqani of India' was a reference to the famous twelfth-century Persian poet, Khaqani.[368]

24

Challenges from Company and Family

Much like his father, Bahadur Shah's days as Emperor were marked by complex negotiations with the East India Company's government, which were often complicated by a contentious relationship with members of his family. Nevertheless, he was determined to try and get off on the right foot, and one of his first acts as Emperor was to write to the Governor General condoling the death of William IV and expressing his good wishes for Queen Victoria, the new monarch.[369]

For the East India Company, the accession of a new Emperor was an occasion to re-examine the broader questions of the relationship between the Company and the Emperor, and an important aspect of this was centred on ceremonial practices. The Agent to the Governor General was authorized to give the usual nazars and receive khilats on the occasion of the succession to the throne.[370] With the death of Mumtaz Mahal just a few months before Akbar, however, it had been decided that queens would no longer be presented nazars.[371] Some confusion still remained regarding the official policy on titles, khilats and nazars. When the Commander-in-Chief, General Henry Fane, visited Bahadur Shah's court soon after the latter's accession, he was given titles. When news of this reached Calcutta, the government expressed its disapproval that these titles had been accepted by such a high functionary of the government.[372] Inconsistencies such as this are likely to have sprung from more than a mere ignorance or confusion about the official policy. It is likely that in the setting of the court, where the audience took place, it was difficult to control or resist specific parts of the ceremonial protocol. The atmosphere of the court, the dignity of the 'presence', were still powerful enough to draw the participant completely into the ritual.

There was nevertheless a steady erosion of these privileges of the Emperor. A few years after his accession Bahadur Shah tried to have a personal meeting arranged with the Governor General, Lord Ellenborough, who was on a visit to Delhi, primarily with the aim of putting certain of his wishes before the latter. The Emperor was informed that as to the meeting, 'it could only be conducted on terms of the most perfect equality'—i.e. dispensing with all of the customary protocol of an audience with the Emperor.[373]

Quite clearly the government was not in an accommodating mood, though to Bahadur Shah this protocol was very important, as it was the only way open to him of continuing to maintain his position in the eyes of his own family and court, as well as the outside world. The Governor General returned from his tour of Delhi without an audience with the Emperor. In addition, he expressed surprise that British officials were still in the habit of presenting nazars and receiving khilats from the Emperor. This practice was ordered to be immediately discontinued, to be replaced by 'presents indicative of friendship', and these too on the basis of strict reciprocity—'previous provision having been made that presents of equal value shall be returned'! As a consolation, the Agent was to behave towards the Emperor 'with the consideration and attention due to his misfortunes'. In fact it had for some years been acknowledged that the Agent attended the Emperor's durbar from time to time 'more from respect to the King than from any public utility'.[374] British magnanimity was to extend to a condescending acknowledgement of fallen majesty, but certainly not to a humouring of pretensions to sovereignty.

Many of Bahadur Shah's concerns and expectations vis-a-vis the British were strongly reminiscent of his father's. He wanted the government to recognize his second son, Mirza Shah Rukh, as heir apparent in place of Dara Bakht, the firstborn. He also wished to be allowed to bestow certain crown property in favour of his new bride, Zeenat Mahal, to continue in her possession after his lifetime. Ironically, these were the very points on which he had opposed his own father.[375] But his most urgent concern was the question of an increase in the stipend, a subject on which long-drawn-out negotiations between his father and the government, had failed. The Emperor's share of the stipend allotted to the royal family had remained stagnant at seventy-three thousand rupees since 1809. This despite the fact that a promise had been made in 1805, that this sum would be raised to a lakh of rupees as soon as revenues from the Assigned Territories increased.[376]

The Company, however, continued in its insistence on linking the question of the stipend to greater access to information about the numbers and condition of the inhabitants of the palace. Bahadur Shah obliged, to the extent that fairly detailed information about the number and identity of the members of the royal family who were paid allowances out of the stipend was supplied in 1838. The government, however, also asserted its right to determine the details of how the stipend was to be distributed among them, and the Emperor refused to accept the increase on these conditions.[377]

The reason Bahadur Shah insisted on this was that control over the distribution of allowances was practically the only tool he had in the exercise of authority over his family. His authority was, in fact, frequently challenged. Even before his succession, many of the salateen had, at the instigation of his brother Salim, and probably his father, signed a document against his succession, going as far as to produce a fatwa that declared that he was disqualified due to illegitimacy.[378] Though they did not succeed in this, they had other grievances, particularly over the allowance question. Unfortunately, the state of the finances had not improved with the change in functionaries, and there were considerable delays in paying allowances.[379]

With the passage of time their protest became more frequent and more insistent, in proportion with the worsening financial conditions within the palace. Matters sometimes reached a crisis, as in 1838, when the famine and high price of grain led to great distress. Bahadur Shah's recent refusal to accept an increase in the stipend further provoked the salateen. They gathered in a crowd on their rooftops night after night and shouted abuse against the mukhtar.[380] The voice of opposition in the palace also found an outlet in at least one newspaper, the *Dehli Urdu Akhbar*. Beginning in April 1841, there appeared a series of letters to the editor, criticizing the management of the finances, particularly the delay in payment of allowances. The author claimed that the actual mukhtar was a figurehead, and the blame for mismanagement lay squarely with the young and inexperienced sons of Jai Sukh Rai, and the young Hakim Ahsanullah Khan, who were said to dominate the palace. It was also claimed that the mukhtar in the time of Akbar II, Sohan Lal, had been more competent.[381]

The salateen were also aware of the British ability to exercise influence over the Emperor's actions, and frequently tried to use it to their own advantage. Over the years, in the time of Akbar II as well as Bahadur Shah, there were repeated letters addressed to the government, usually asking that the Emperor be made to give them enhanced shares in the royal stipend, or to safeguard property that they might have been deprived of. Bahadur Shah himself had often appealed to the British authorities against his father. The salateen now appealed to the government that they be allowed to draw their allowances directly from the government treasury instead of being paid by the Emperor.[382]

There was a price attached to an appeal to the British. For one, it gave the government a legitimate excuse to bring members of the family under its control in legal and administrative matters, and this in effect resulted in the erosion of the privileges they had enjoyed outside the walls of the fort. Many of the members of the royal family held crown lands rent free in areas that were now controlled by the Company. The government decided to examine more closely the title deeds to these, in the case of all except those most closely related to the Emperor. A list of all holders of such lands was demanded from the palace, and Thomas Metcalfe was in favour of a summary attachment of the doubtful estates until the claimants proved their cases satisfactorily.[383] New rules were proposed whereby tenants of crown estates were to be provided redress through the British courts. This posed a tricky problem for the Emperor. On the one hand he was given no assistance by the government in realizing rents, and on the other he had no power to punish defaulters himself. Zafar was, however, willing to let individual claims and disputes be examined and decided by the Agent to the Governor General, subject to his own confirmation.[384]

Another proposal involved bringing a larger number of the royal family within the jurisdiction of the British courts. It was made clear to the Emperor that while events occurring within the walls of the palace were outside the jurisdiction of the Company's courts, the Agent was to be consulted in important cases of administration of justice within the palace.[385] It was also proposed that the residents of the palace would be liable to British courts when outside the precincts of the palace, with certain exceptions. The exceptions were the Emperor and the heir apparent who would be exempt from both civil and criminal jurisdiction of such courts; and the sons and brothers of the present and former Emperors who were to be exempt from civil but not criminal jurisdiction. The rest would be indiscriminately liable. Bahadur Shah protested strongly against this proposal and wanted complete exemption not only for members of the royal family but for all royal servants when acting under his orders.[386]

The government was also now looking more closely at affairs inside the palace, and the outcome was not one that was of help to either the Emperor or other members of the family. While asking for details about the royal family immediately after the accession of Bahadur Shah, the government had curiously also called for a report on the 'conduct of this family', though it had already made up its mind about what the answer might be. The prevalent view in Calcutta, as reflected in a minute by the Governor General, was that the hundreds of inhabitants in the palace, among whom the women far outnumbered the men, were 'living in unrestrained profligacy, and many of them in a state bordering upon absolute penury, yet daily multiplying in number'.[387] In response to the query from the government at Calcutta, Thomas Metcalfe, making a report to Calcutta in 1838 regretted that the salateen were largely devoid of 'moral rectitude'; and that 'the rules of the purdah are but imperfectly attended to in any and totally disregarded in most instances. Incest and profligacy of all kinds is supposed to exist to a great extent, and His Majesty I regret to add does not seem disposed to adopt any salutary necessaries of reform.'[388] Metcalfe's comments reflected some common British ideas about Indian society, the place of women, and supposedly universal moral values. Judgement was being passed with a very imperfect understanding of the customs and practices followed within the palace.

In fact, seclusion of women within the royal family was not particularly strict and it seems that purdah, the veil, was not observed by the women in the presence of even fairly distant members of the family.[389] While polygamy and concubinage were almost universal among the princes, high-born women in particular were far from helpless victims. A case in point was that of Malka Zamani Begum the daughter of Sulaiman Shukoh (the brother of Akbar II). Malka Begum was married to her cousin Mirza Salim, the son of Akbar II, and her sister was married to the Nawab of Awadh, Nasir ud din Haider. When Salim's affections strayed, she promptly left for her parental home in Lucknow. While she was in Lucknow, a family crisis developed. Sulaiman Shukoh had married a third daughter of his to a man towards whose family Nawab Nasir ud din Haider was not favourably disposed. The retaliation of the Nawab against Sulaiman Shukoh included the abduction of Malka Begum. The young lady was eventually rescued, and the family, who had been evicted from Lucknow on the orders of the Nawab, were hospitably offered temporary shelter by William Gardner in his jagir at Kasganj. This led to further complications, as Malka Begum soon eloped with William Gardner's son James. Interestingly, these complicated relationships did not by any means lead to a rift between the two branches of the royal family. Malka Zamani Begum continued to visit Delhi and be received in the palace. Further matrimonial relationships were also initiated later. A niece of James—Susan Shabia, was married to Anjum Shukoh, a son of Sulaiman Shukoh; and James' daughter from an earlier marriage was married to Mirza Mughal, the son of Bahadur Shah.[390]

25

George Thompson: Advocate of the Mughal Cause

The interest in the details of the royal family, their condition and conduct, was in the context of certain long-term plans that were being contemplated by the higher echelons of the East India Company. By the early 1840s the Court of Directors was thinking along radical lines, proposing the ultimate exclusion 'of all illegitimate children and those beyond the third degree in descent from the throne both from the palace itself and the title of Salateen.'[391] Strong rumours were also abroad, and had in fact reached Bahadur Shah's ears, that major changes were contemplated after his death. The office of the Agent to the Governor General—who was an officer specifically designated to represent the British Government at the Emperor's court—would be abolished. It was also rumoured that no successor to the present Emperor would be appointed.[392]

Bahadur Shah responded to these drastic further inroads, actual or proposed, on his status in the only way he could—by sending a mission to England, much as his father had sent Rammohan Roy. Bahadur Shah's choice of emissary was a noted orator and activist in the cause of reform—George Thompson. Thompson, a British citizen, was well-known for his vocal support of the anti-slavery movement, both in Britain and the United States of

America. He was also at the forefront of the founding of the British India Society, set up in London in 1839, to draw attention to the 'oppressions and sufferings of the fellow-subjects...the Natives of British India'.[393]

Thompson's work for Indian reform brought him to Calcutta, on the invitation and sponsorship of Dwarkanath Tagore, commercial magnate, leading citizen of Calcutta, and founder of the Zamindari Association. In Calcutta, Thompson played a prominent role in the founding of the Bengal British India Society, closely along the same lines, but independent of the organization in Britain. Thompson's willingness to take up Indian causes, as well as his charismatic oratory, brought him to the attention of Bahadur Shah, who sent Ahsanullah Khan as an emissary to Calcutta, with the proposal that Thompson be appointed by Bahadur Shah to represent his case in England, with regard to his claims of an increase in stipend. Thompson agreed, and made a trip to Delhi to meet the Emperor in person. He arrived in Delhi on 9 July 1843 and was given a warm welcome. The Emperor's representatives, Debi Singh and Saligram, went as far as Shahadara to receive the visitor, who 'shook them both by the hand.' He then, together with Ahsanullah Khan, mounted an elephant that had been sent for him, and seated in a silver howdah, proceeded to Begum Samru's house, which had been prepared for his stay. On his audience with the Emperor, he was given suitable titles—'the Ambassador of the State', 'Counsellor' and 'Pacificator', and was also given a 'staff of office'. He spent the next several weeks preparing his case in Delhi. On his departure on 7 November, Bahadur Shah presented him with a shawl and traced on his forehead with his own finger a verse from the Quran—'victory rests with God and is at hand'.[394] The Emperor was also keen to send his son, Mirza Fakhr ud din, but the government forbade this. It also made it clear that Thompson's representation would not be sanctioned by it, but Thompson left despite the government's disapproval.[395]

Thompson was more successful in England than Rammohan Roy, perhaps because he was already a prominent figure there, due to his anti-slavery work. He was allowed to give an impassioned speech before the directors and shareholders of the East India Company on 18 December 1844; in which he castigated in strong terms what he considered a betrayal by the Company of the promises it had made to Shah Alam. He began with the battle of Buxar of 1764 and the treaty of Allahabad that had followed it. He recounted how the Company had not only soon reneged on its promise to pay the Emperor a tribute of 2.6 million rupees annually in lieu of the revenues of Bengal, but had also taken away the revenues of Allahabad and Kara, which had been promised to him by the treaty. He produced a series of documents, mostly from the government's own correspondence, to prove that following the capture of Delhi in 1803, the Company had once again made promises, but had gone back on them. The Company had set aside territories, literally called 'Assigned Territories', for the support of the royal family. But once the revenues from these territories rose, the increase was not paid to the Emperor and the royal family. Their repeated claim that they had treated the Emperor much better than the Marathas, was also hollow, since Mahadji Sindhia had allocated and paid 1,30,000 rupees a month to the Emperor, though that sum had admittedly fallen off in later times because of the perilous state of the finances. Thompson also referred to the assurances and promises that had been made by the Company to Shah Alam, that marks of respect, such as the presentation of nazars, would be honoured. These assurances too had been flouted.[396]

Ultimately, however, Thompson was able to achieve for Bahadur Shah no more than what Rammohan had won for Akbar II, and in 1845, Bahadur Shah acceded to the government's terms for an increase in the stipend. The government proposed the takeover of all the crown lands for management by its own officers, and the utilization of the revenues for the liquidation of the royal debts. Zafar was willing to agree to this but requested some relaxation in the terms, enabling a more gradual repayment of the debts. The government agreed to pay arrears of ten months of the stipend and a loan to help pay back the debts. The Emperor also requested that the palace be comprehensively repaired at government expense. To this the government's answer was, would it not be much better if a new palace was made for the Emperor at Mehrauli? Privately, the government was keen to move the Emperor and all of the royal family out of the Red Fort, so as to be 'rid of great inconvenience of having the Palace and its precincts exempt from the jurisdiction of our courts in the very centre of the populous city of Delhi.'[397]

Bahadur Shah's reply to the suggestion to move to Mehrauli was predictably in the negative. He pointed out that since he had been born in the fort and lived there for most of his life, he had no desire to leave it. In any case this was the only home left to him from all the properties of his forefathers. If the government could pay for the repairs (which the government's executive engineer estimated at a little over 50,000 rupees) well and good, otherwise, he would not press the point.[398]

The negotiations dragged on for several years without any final agreement. The three lakh increase in the stipend never materialized. Though in dire need, Bahadur Shah was unwilling to allow the British the degree of control over the distribution of the stipend and the general management of the royal finances that they desired. As mentioned above, one reason was that keeping the majority of the salateen within the fort under his financial and other control was considered an important prerogative by Bahadur Shah.[399] The salateen were becoming increasingly intractable, and according to Bahadur Shah, the main reason for this was the British attitude. The government listened to their complaints and asked the Emperor to defend himself against their charges. This encouraged them to forward constant petitions to the government, in one instance a document signed by more than three hundred of them. This undermined the Emperor's authority over the salateen. Thomas Metcalfe appreciated the Emperor's position to an extent, pointing out to the government that the distribution of allowances was in fact the only tool the Emperor had to control the salateen with. Some, but not all, of their complaints about mismanagement of the finances by the minister, Ahsanullah Khan, and the chief eunuch, Mahbub Ali Khan, were justified. In many cases, the withholding of their allowances was the only means of satisfying their creditors, and to which the salateen had themselves agreed. The loans in fact were only available on the guarantee of the Emperor, so he was obliged to ensure repayment.[400]

In 1849 Bahadur Shah's brothers wrote to the government claiming that he was 'revelling in debauchery' while his financial affairs were mismanaged. They went on to say, 'We ask legitimately for good and equal laws, we ask for the same protection that is extended to your meanest subjects in India and we are ready to fall under the immediate orders and protection of the Hon'ble the Lt Governor's Agent in Delhi, in all matters relating to our allowances and our property as in these we are entirely unprotected.'[401] It is worth noting that they made it clear that they were willing to put themselves under the authority of the British Government only with respect to their allowances and property, implying that they were unwilling to surrender the other privileges and immunities they enjoyed.

Helpless in the face of insubordination, Bahadur Shah had in turn begun to complain to the British authorities of the disrespectful behaviour of the salateen, as he found it increasingly difficult to maintain order among his large and unruly family. Complaints of thefts against the salateen came in, and when they were investigated, large numbers of them would crowd together and resist the Emperor's armed servants. The mufti of the royal court also complained that, in civil cases, members of the royal family frequently ignored all notices to them from the court. Finally, Bahadur Shah had to call for aid from the British commandant of the palace guard to help enforce even his most minor orders, such as the clearing of carriages from one of the main streets.[402]

26

Trouble in the Family

The British, both official and non-official, frequently painted a grim picture of the extended royal family living in the fort. They accused them of unruliness, immorality, profligacy, accused them of multiplying indiscriminately, and commented unfavourably on the general squalor of their living quarters in the fort. Ironically, the meagreness of the allowance given by the government for the support of the family was itself a major reason for some of the problems. The fact that the inside of the fort had become crowded with many mean-looking huts was simply because the salateen and their dependants did not have the money for better construction. The lack of money also often meant a lack of a good education. The unruliness was a product of the many stresses of life within the palace, in the context of financial difficulties and the complicated politics of the Emperor and princes, which was again partly at least a product of British policies.

The frequent comments on lax sexual morals reflected British notions of Indian culture, and in particular the culture of the royal family, as has been mentioned before. Now, the British were actually taking active steps for 'reform', and these frequently worked to the detriment of the female members of the royal family. One case was that of Poti Begum, the granddaughter of Bahadur Shah. She received forty rupees per month as an allowance in her own right, though she was married to a prince of the royal family. Upon her divorce from her husband, she was permitted by her grandfather to live outside the fort, in the city, and continue to receive her allowance. Simon Fraser, the Commissioner, reported to the Emperor that the lady was 'living in a disreputable manner' with a certain Muhibullah Khan, a person not of royal blood. Even if, said Fraser, the lady had contracted a *nikah*, as she claimed, according to the custom of the family, this should have been with the consent of the Emperor. There were interests within the palace working against Poti Begum. Technically, her allowance was part of the allowance of her father Dara Bakht, who had been the heir apparent before his death. If for some reason her allowance were to lapse, the sum would be added to the allowance of the new heir apparent. Not surprisingly, her petition, that she continue to receive her allowance, was rejected. The discontinuation of the allowance of course would also mean a deprivation of her independence, and she would be forced to live in the palace and, as she put it, 'submit to the indignities and dishonour which many others in like condition suffer.'[403]

The Company for many years had also been trying to bring the salateen under the jurisdiction of its court, a point that Bahadur Shah had resisted. But this position was undermined, because often members of his family themselves approached the Company's courts in internal matters. A case in point was that of Khusro Zamani Begum who was the wife of Mirza Salim, a favourite son of Akbar. The prince had been granted two gardens—the Roshanara Bagh and Sirhindi Bagh; and one *katra*, or commercial space—Katra Mazid Parcha, by his father. On the death of the prince, the widow was allowed to keep the property. Bahadur Shah also did not resume the grant immediately on his succession. Some years later, however, there was a falling out between the Begum and the Emperor, mainly, it was said, due the former's bad temper and her leaving the fort and going to live in the city. When the Emperor tried to resume the grant, the Begum took the case to the Company's courts which held in her favour. The affair finally went up to the Court of Directors.[404]

The salateen soon realized that the Company's courts were a double-edged sword. By the 1850s orders from the courts were being frequently issued to members of the royal family other than the immediate relations of the Emperor, and private property situated in the city was liable to attachment for the recovery of debts or in cases of other disputes.[405] The obligation to personally appear in the courts was considered particularly irksome. In 1852, some of the Emperor's uncles who lived in the city, wrote to the Lt Governor of the North-Western Provinces saying 'that in any suits that might arise affecting them, they wished to be freed from the obligation of appearing in person in the criminal courts and to be allowed to send wukeels to reply for them'.[406]

These cases were arising in the first place mainly because increasing numbers of the salateen were living in the city, as opposed to the palace. By the 1850s, many of the relatives of the Emperor had pragmatically begun to realize that the special status of the royal family with the Emperor at its head was not the way of the future, and an exodus from the fort was quite apparent. Several of those who had the means, which they supplemented by selling their houses within the fort, had bought property in the city and had obtained permission to live in them. By early 1857 these included many of Bahadur Shah's closest relations—four out of his eleven sons, nine of his twenty-eight grandsons, and more than a score of his cousins in the paternal line. Several women also received permission to live in the city, though the Emperor could usually call them back with the threat of discontinuing their allowance.[407] Some of the ladies, presumably those who had independent means, left even without the customary permission. One such was Sohagan Mahal Begum, the widow of Bahadur Shah's eldest son, Dara Bakht. The Emperor was casually informed one day that the lady had, together with her two sons and a teacher, Maulvi Mohammad Hasan, left the fort and the city.[408] The practice in fact had become so common that an explicit order was given by Zeenat Mahal to the servants of the palace that women wishing to go out of the fort must do so only with the Emperor's leave.[409]

Bahadur Shah was advanced in years and was not expected

to live long. Not surprisingly, those close to him wished to put themselves physically and financially out of the reach of his successor. Bahadur Shah himself advised his wives to leave the palace as soon as he died. One of his wives, Taj Mahal, was taking no chances and in fact left immediately upon hearing this! In the 1850s Zeenat Mahal too frequently spent long periods of time in her house in the city and was also reported to be transferring large amounts of moveable property from the palace to her house, located in the locality known as Lal Kuan. Similarly, the powerful chief eunuch, Mahbub Ali Khan, had bought a house in the city and was starting to move his property there.[410]

The salateens' defalcations were causing tensions with the people of the city too. Members of the royal family were chronically in debt and involved in disputes with their creditors, as a result of which the princes were often accosted by their creditors on the streets. Creditors also stood under the *jharokha*, where the palace overlooked the riverside, and clamoured before the Emperor for a settlement of their dues. On one occasion Bahadur Shah was also waylaid by some people complaining of his decision in a case where money was owed to them by one of the salateen. Towards the last years of Bahadur Shah in Delhi his chief advisor Ahsanullah Khan had begun to suggest that going too frequently out of the fort into the city 'was not suited to his dignity and that the inhabitants would not be paying the king proper respect'.[411]

The goings-on within the palace, as well as the politics of the palace were the subject of debate in the city too, and criticism of the members of the royal family was the subject of some newspaper reports. A particularly forthright though sympathetic article in the *Qiran us Sadaen* in the 1850s dealt at length with the issue of the salateen. The background was a proposal to set up some sort of educational institution for them. This had been proposed by the British authorities many years earlier also, but they had not been willing to contribute any extra money for the purpose. Evidently, the matter had now been raised again. The editor of the *Qiran us Sadaen* was of the opinion that the salateen were on the whole intelligent and capable of making quick progress. In fact, there were some among them who were educated and talented. Most, however, did not benefit from the company of learned men of good character and as a result their own conduct left much to be desired. He put himself forward as a strong supporter of measures to provide the salateen with a useful education—Urdu, Arabic, Persian, English and medicine. All that was required was that less money be wasted in the palace on kite flying, singing and dancing.[412]

This rather utilitarian solution to the problems of the salateen pointed to a growing impatience with the culture that the fort had come to represent. This was probably in large part the opinion of a section of the population that had come into direct contact with new ideas on society and education that had come in with British rule. Wider disapproval of the salateen is hinted at from time to time, particularly with regard to their lifestyle. The writer Karim ud din listed a number of poets from the royal family in his book, mentioning with veiled disapproval their fondness for breeding quails and pigeons for fighting, and for listening to music and watching dance.[413] An article in the *Dehli Urdu Akhbar* criticized the degree of polygamy practised by the princes.[414] There was also the suggestion that marriage connections with the family were not quite respectable. William Gardner had been unhappy when his Indian wife had insisted on marrying his granddaughter to a nephew of Akbar II in 1835. In this case, however, the primary reason might have been his desire to have her marry a European.[415]

By this time marriage alliances with the Mughal family were not particularly sought after by other royal families in India either. Evidently, as time went by, the social standing of the Delhi royal family among the princes of India had declined. In 1855 Sikandar Begum, the Nawab of Bhopal, was trying to arrange a marriage for her daughter, Shahjahan Begum. One of the candidates was a Mughal prince whom the young lady had seen once and been favourably impressed with. Her mother, however, was of the opinion that 'with regard to the Shahzada from Delhi his pride and pretension coupled with his want of education had made union with him impossible.' The grandmother, Qudsia Begum, was even more contemptuous: 'his head is turned already, would he ever be fit for anything, swarms of starving relatives. *Kumbukht* [wretch]'.[416]

It seemed that the wider world agreed with the British in seeing little merit in the members of the royal family. The British Government itself was contemplating an extinction of the family altogether, at least in its existing form. Simon Fraser had recommended a gradual restriction of the allowances of the salateen, by the simple expedient of restricting these to the eldest male heir alone. It was expected that slowly some of those lines would become extinct by a natural process, i.e. the failure to produce male heirs. As a result the number of pensioners would continuously fall. The government was in favour of this approach. G.F. Edmonstone, Secretary to the Government of India, wrote to the Secretary in the North-Western Provinces on the 8 May 1857, that he was in favour of the strategy suggested by Fraser, believing that it would lead eventually to the 'gradual discontinuance of political stipends and the absorption of the members of the stipendiary families in the mass of the population.'[417]

27

Two Royal Deaths

On 11 January 1849, Bahadur Shah's eldest son and heir apparent, Dara Bakht, died at the age of fifty-seven. He had been in feeble health for a while, and the British Government had contemplated the possibility that he might pre-decease his father. Less than a year earlier, the Secretary to the government of the North-Western Provinces had rather cynically noted that as 'the establishment of British supremacy over the whole course of the Indians' was complete, there was 'no reason for maintaining the empty title of sovereign, in the eldest member of a fallen dynasty'. The Lt Governor of the NWP therefore proposed, that should Dara Bakht succeed his father, he would be accorded some royal privileges, as a consideration to his age; on the other hand, if he were to die before Bahadur Shah, the next in line to the throne (by British reckoning this had to be the oldest son, though this was not Mughal tradition), the much younger Mirza Fakhr ud din, should be treated as a simple political pensioner, and accorded none of the protocols enjoyed by his father.[418]

The death of Dara Bakht therefore became the occasion for setting fresh terms before the thirty-one-year-old Fakhr ud din, as pre-conditions to recognizing him as heir apparent. Though the negotiations dragged on till 1852, he was ultimately willing to agree on all the points that were put to him, i.e. that he meet the

Governor General on equal terms, that the crown lands be made over to the management of the government, and that he and his family remove themselves from the fort. He would only receive that portion of the stipend which was for his support and that of his immediate family, who would live with him in a palace built by his grandfather at Mehrauli. The other salateen would be paid directly by the government.[419]

To Bahadur Shah, who knew what was going on, this was no less than a betrayal. For one, it was an erosion of all that the Mughal name stood for. He remarked to his courtiers 'that after his death the Royal dignity would not be upheld'.[420] The other ground for his objection was that he did not want Fakhr ud din to succeed him. Of his thirteen surviving sons, he championed the candidature of the ninth, the eleven-year-old Jawan Bakht, who was the son of his favourite wife, Zeenat Mahal. In an ironic case of history repeating itself, Zafar was now seeking to assert a prerogative to nominate an heir, a right that he had not been willing to concede to his own father. He had turned to the British for help against his father, and now Fakhr ud din entered into negotiations about the terms of his succession, quite against his father's express wishes. This led to considerable bitterness between the two, with Bahadur Shah declaring that he had disinherited Fakhr ud din, and that anyone who was a friend of the latter was his enemy.[421]

As far as the Company's government was concerned, the negotiations with Fakhr ud din were in a sense merely a formality. The government was determined to carry out its plans under any circumstance. Thomas Metcalfe anticipated a general reluctance on the part of the denizens to leave the fort on the death of Bahadur Shah, and he felt that they 'may prove refractory'. He was, however, confident that he would 'overcome their reluctance by firmness and conciliatory deportment'; in effect through a policy of carrot and stick. Though some of the ladies, such as Zeenat Mahal and Taj Mahal, owned houses in the city, arrangements would be made for the other royal ladies with the help of the eunuchs, and all the salateen who owned houses inside the fort would be compensated.[422]

Bahadur Shah too, though he continued to make representations to the government, in his heart of hearts of course knew that he would not be able to secure recognition of Jawan Bakht as his successor. In view of this, he pressed for the next best thing—securing his financial situation after his death. To this end, he sought a reconciliation with Fakhr ud din with a request that the latter should guarantee the allowances of Zeenat Mahal and Jawan Bakht after his father's death. Fakhr ud din, however, refused to give the assurance, pointing out that he had 'been appointed Heir Apparent through the generosity and kindness of the British Government', and therefore saw no reason for any gratitude towards his father and stepmother.[423] Instead, he wrote a letter to the government, complaining that Bahadur Shah was alienating a garden, which was crown property, in favour of Zeenat Mahal.[424]

The reason for Bahadur Shah's anxiety was that according to established practice within the family, he could not alienate crown properties for any period beyond his lifetime. As a result, when any Emperor died, particularly if there had been conflict during his lifetime with his successor, the financial status of his favourite consorts and sons was in jeopardy. Bahadur Shah himself had claimed the right to fix the allowances of his father's widows and children, and refused to allow one widow, Anwar Mahal Begum, Rs 500 per month as Akbar II had requested.[425] This was pointed out to him by the government, which argued that a reigning king making allowances to his favourite wife or sons to continue after his death would be contrary to the rule and practice of the family. Bahadur Shah's fears for the fate of Zeenat Mahal and Jawan Bakht after his death were sought to be allayed with the assurance that 'the British Government always administers even-handed justice to all, and it will not therefore allow the above named Begum and Prince to suffer any injustice or real injury.' [426]

Bahadur Shah's own long-standing tussle about the raise in stipend and control over the salateen was also not going anywhere. He had allowed deputies of the Agent to inspect the royal accounts, but the latter complained that their investigations into the debts of the Emperor were stalled by the machinations of palace officials, specially Ahsanullah Khan, Saligram, Debi Singh, Mahbub Ali Khan and Hafiz Daud. Bahadur Shah defended these royal officials, saying that they had loyally served him, and even loaned him money; the investigations were unjustly causing them harassment.[427] But, even though the debt question was settled, ultimately the British offer hinged also on the condition that most of the salateen should leave the fort, and become subject to British laws and courts. This was not acceptable to Bahadur Shah, who was at most willing to allow this only in the case of all those who were not descended from Shah Alam (also known as Bahadur Shah, who reigned from 1707 to 1712 and was Zafar's great-grandfather's great-grandfather) and so, the offer of the increase in stipend was formally withdrawn in 1850.[428]

Meanwhile Bahadur Shah was increasingly perceiving a lack of respect from British officials, even Thomas Metcalfe, who had been accustomed to court protocols. In 1847, the Emperor had made a large gateway in front of his palace in Mehrauli, a building that had been constructed by his father, but soon came to be called Zafar Mahal. Between this palace and a nearby audience hall lay the main road leading to Gurgaon (in modern-day Haryana). Royal protocol demanded that all would dismount as they approached the gate, and walk until they had passed it. Metcalfe refused to submit to the 'degradation' of dismounting, and demanded that the Emperor's employees who enforced the practice be handed over for punishment. Bahadur Shah on his part was willing to accommodate to the changed times. He wrote a conciliatory letter to Metcalfe saying that the royal servants who were responsible for making the officers dismount had been punished. Metcalfe himself would not be made to dismount until he actually got to the gate of the hall of audience.[429]

Bahadur Shah was also sensitive to the changed relationship with the highest officials of the government. Thus he addressed the Governor General, Lord Dalhousie, as his 'most illustrious friend', signing himself as his 'most sincere friend'.[430] Personal audiences with high British officials were by the latter years of Bahadur Shah's reign extremely rare. When the Commander-in-

Chief General Charles Napier visited Delhi and the fort in 1851, it was not to meet the Emperor but as a tourist. The Emperor himself closely supervised the cleaning of the buildings for his benefit, and gave instructions that he should be shown around. He himself stayed discreetly out of sight during the visit. Even the Agent's visits were infrequent and he certainly could not be summoned by the Emperor. The latter's officials sought to soften the blow by pointing out that this was probably 'owing to stress of public business'. In 1853, an impending visit by the Agent was evidently such an important and rare occasion that Bahadur Shah rushed around ordering repairs and redecorations.[431]

Humiliations at the hands of the British authorities were a part of everyday life. When the Agent learnt that some crown jewels were reported to have been removed from the palace, he considered it his business, and made enquiries. Bahadur Shah offered to let the jewel box be inspected and compared with the list in the record office. A munshi was accordingly sent and personally satisfied himself that the jewels were in place.[432]

Bahadur Shah tried from time to time to refer to 'traditions' and 'customs' and 'history' in support of his claims over lost privileges. He pointed out that his being denied the right to send a vakil to Calcutta or London was an infringement of the established practice of the country.[433] He also lamented the discontinuation of the nazar on behalf of the Governor General, it having been decided by the government that presents of strictly equal value would be exchanged instead. In a letter to the government he decried this as meanness, remarking bitterly that it grieved him that 'to this illustrious house of five hundred years' standing nothing was left but the bare name instead of wealth, power and country, and this only remaining privilege is also now brought under a saving'. He reiterated that the government was going back on the promises it had made to Shah Alam II.[434]

The government merely reacted to the implied charge of meanness by ordering that as the nazars had amounted to some 10,000 rupees, the Agent would pay a monthly sum of Rs 883 to the Emperor. This the Emperor was not ready to accept, since the point of the nazar was to show respect to the throne. Calling on the government to keep its pledges to his ancestors he referred to traditions of a very different sort. He mentioned that 'the Christian precepts of Holy Scriptures enjoin to [*sic*] fulfill all sacred pledges and when in power to show clemency to the weak.' Since 'the British character is pre-eminently distinguished for good faith, justice and equity...in consideration of the favours conferred by my ancestors, as may be perceived from the History of the World by William Guthrie Esq. page 751...it is incumbent on the British to protect this family'. He traced the history of the relations between Britain and the Mughals from 1600, pointing out the magnanimity with which his ancestors had treated the British. The argument cut no ice with the government. The Governor General clearly stated that 'the dignity of the British Government' did not permit the offering of nazars and the acceptance of khilats from the Mughal Emperor; and as Bahadur Shah had said that he would not accept the money if it was not presented in the form of a nazar, he would not get it at all. It was also made clear that the Emperor could only confer khilats on his own employees.[435]

In mid-1853 Bahadur Shah fell seriously ill and Fakhr ud din as well as Metcalfe began to prepare themselves for the eventuality of a succession. It was decided that on the death of the Emperor, Fakhr ud din may be allowed to stay for the customary forty day mourning period within the fort, but his coronation would only take place after the move to Mehrauli. Only the stipend due to him and his immediate family would be given to him, and the rest would be distributed by the government.[436] As it happened, however, Bahadur Shah recovered, though Thomas Metcalfe died a few weeks later, probably from the same illness from which Bahadur Shah had just recovered, and which had affected many people in the city and cantonment.[437] Ghalib wrote to a friend with regret—'*ham logon ke janne wale ek yahi sahab rah gaye the*'[438]—he was the only sahib left who was acquainted with us.

If the future of the Mughal family had looked bleak after Dara Bakht's death, an even lower point was reached when Fakhr ud din died unexpectedly on 10 July 1856 from cholera, after an acute and very brief illness. The government considered this an occasion to further pare down the expectations of a future heir. There was to be no declaration of an heir apparent. There was to be no bargaining as in the case of Fakhr ud din. No conditions were to be negotiated over; Mohammad Koeash, the eldest of Zafar's twelve surviving sons, was not even to be informed of what was intended. On the death of Zafar the new arrangements would be put into effect. The title of kingship was to be removed altogether, and Koeash would succeed as '*shahzada sadar e azeem e khandan e timuri*'—'his royal highness the prince the exalted head of the family of Taimur'. He would be allowed a stipend of 15,000 rupees a month. As for other questions of jurisdiction, stipend and residence of the salateen, these could be settled later, said Fraser, adding somewhat ominously, 'I do not anticipate difficulty if His Honor will allow me a broad discretion in carrying out the views of government'. He did, however, ask that one question be settled immediately—that 'the representative of the British Government should be allowed a seat in his interviews with the head of the family.' It was a question that affected Fraser personally and evidently was of great importance to him.[439]

Mohammad Koeash attempted to assert his claims to the throne, basing his eligibility on religiosity—he had memorized the Quran, had been on pilgrimage. His father's championing of the cause of Jawan Bakht he put down to the evil influence of Zeenat Mahal and the chief eunuch Mahbub Ali Khan, and to the Emperor's own 'weakened intellect'. He might have had an inkling of what the government had planned, for he remarked that he was 'confident that the Higher Authorities do not contemplate the extinction of this ancient dynasty'.[440]

On her part, Zeenat Mahal made a last-ditch attempt for her son Jawan Bakht. She appointed an emissary to Calcutta, in the form of one Thomas Cavendish Fenwick. The memorial (a paper outlining the facts) that was sent through Fenwick was on behalf of Zeenat Mahal and Jawan Bakht. It also included a document signed by all the other sons of Bahadur Shah, with the exception of Mirza Koeash, resigning their claims to the throne. The tone of the memorial was one to which the Governor General in Council took exception, calling it 'improper'. It had denounced the decision of the government in passing over the claims of Jawan Bakht, implying a bias against him. It called for the constitution of a 'Council or Commission [to] be appointed composed of respectable men versed in Mahomedan law to decide the claim put forth...and that such Council or Commission hold their sittings with open doors.'[441] This bold approach too had no impact on the outcome.

Eventually, neither Mirza Koeash's claims nor Zeenat Mahal's efforts on behalf of her son, were relevant. As far as the British were concerned, the Mughal dynasty was decidedly at an end. A member of the Governor General's council wrote a less than charitable epitaph—'it is necessary to march with the times, the glory of the house of Timoor has departed; the dynasty is extinguished by age and its own incapacity. The steam engine and the railroad are already at the gates of Delhie in this utilitarian age and who can stop them? They have crushed out the feebleness of an empty name.'[442]

28

The People's Emperor

No matter how much opposition Zafar faced from his own family, or from the government, he held a special place in the hearts of the people of Delhi; and this relationship continued into the 1850s, despite the Emperor's decreasing political role.

The people of course were not blind to the shortcomings of the court. For one, negative comment on the activities in the palace was frequent in the local newspapers. There was criticism in strong words of the reported financial mismanagement by officials of the court, of the alleged unsuitability, ignorance and incompetence of those appointed to responsible positions, and the injustice perpetrated by them. The poor within the fort were said to be starving because of the corruption of the officials. The Emperor himself was, however, usually exempt from direct criticism, it being said that he was kept in the dark or he would never tolerate oppression of the weak.[443] In fact, the Urdu newspapers don't seem to have referred to the Emperor with anything except respect and affection. The *Dehli Urdu Akhbar* itself spoke of how all people prayed for the long life of Bahadur Shah who was pious, wise, patient, and a patron of talent. Heartfelt wishes for his good health, and thankfulness to God at his recovery from illness, were expressed in both the *Dehli Urdu Akhbar* and the *Qiran us Sadaen*.[444]

In large measure this was the result of strong ties that the Mughal Emperors in general, and Bahadur Shah in particular, had forged with the people. Some of this was based on generosity—patronage and alms-giving. Coins were distributed to the crowds of the poor that gathered around his procession. There are instances of shopkeepers who brought goods for sale to the royal gardens having their entire stock bought up on the Emperor's account. The palace also gave patronage to a variety of artists and performers. Wrestlers, acrobats and actors frequently came into the palace and performed, and were given handsome rewards. Anyone arriving with a hard luck story—such as a stranger to the city who had been robbed on his way, was given financial assistance. The generosity extended to the occupants of various royal properties, who would often come and ask for remissions in rent and were readily granted them by the Emperor. The city kotwal was given a present of a hundred and twenty-five rupees after the wedding of Jawan Bakht in 1852, in recognition of the efficient arrangements made by that officer.[445]

Personal gestures of generosity kept alive the ties of fealty between the head of an empire that no longer existed, and the people, at least of the immediate vicinity. When Bahadur Shah went to stay in Mehrauli for a few days, the peasants would come with pots of milk and curd as a nazar, and be given presents of money in return. Relations with rural populations were not always smooth though. The Emperor's hunters had to respect local sentiments in the injunction forbidding the shooting of nilgai and peacocks; by the 1850s the peasants of certain areas were also objecting to the killing of deer and hares.[446] The Emperor's agents had also long been finding it difficult to realize revenues from the royal lands. In 1840 there was armed conflict in the pargana of Kot Qasim, in which the landlords repulsed the soldiers of the Emperor. This was the main reason why Bahadur Shah ultimately agreed to hand over the management of the royal estates to the British administration.[447]

Bahadur Shah was invariably courteous even to British officials, despite the fact that they were showing him less respect as the days passed. Direct personal interactions had decreased significantly, mainly because British officials did not consider a meeting with the Emperor important enough to submit to the necessary protocols. Nevertheless, even through the 1850s, Bahadur Shah would regularly send fruits, vegetables, game, cooked food, etc., to the Agent and the Commandant of the Palace Guard. He was always courteous towards the British officials connected with the palace, on one occasion composing a couplet in honour of the Commandant of the Palace Guard. He was also invariably extremely polite, as is evident in the following example of his concern to make his guests feel comfortable. In 1852 he sent a messenger to the Commandant of the Palace Guard 'requesting his presence with that of his friends at the entertainment given in honor of Mirza Jawan Bakht's marriage, and that he was to send his own servants in order that they might prepare what he considered would be approved by those who came'.[448]

Some of the strongest ties were those of service in the Mughal court; for unlike the impersonal rules of service in force in the Company's administration, the Emperor had a much more compassionate, if less practical approach. For instance, there was a strong concept of a hereditary right of office, and the main logic behind it was the reluctance to deprive the family of a deceased employee of his income. Quite commonly, the son would be employed in the place of his father, and a deed obtained from him by which he bound himself to support his father's family. Where giving employment was for some reason not possible, the families were at least given a substantial part of the salary the dead man had received. Ties between the Emperor and his employees continued beyond the period of service. We hear of Bahadur Shah sending money for the funeral expenses of his ex-mukhtar.[449]

The intimate personal connection between the Emperor and his employees was reinforced during marriages and births too. Bahadur Shah would ceremonially gift wedding clothes to the sons and daughters of his Hindu employees. We also hear of an instance where a Hindu clerk requested him to name his newly born son, and the Emperor obliged. On festive occasions the Emperor would also attend music and dance performances hosted by these officials.

Hindu officials were also specially received on their return from a pilgrimage, and given a ceremonial shawl in that honour. There were signs too of a more casual intimacy. Once a clerk borrowed one of the royal elephants to go to the Ram Lila. Of course, if one was the recipient of the Emperor's good wishes and generosity, this laid one open to occasional demands as well. In one instance, Bahadur Shah asked one official to present his house in Mehrauli, which was built on crown land, as a nazar.[450]

Connection with the palace—being received with honour in court, conversing with the Emperor—was still an important marker of social status in Delhi. The *mahajans* of Delhi such as Ramji Das Gurwala, were to be seen from time to time in the durbar. Mohammad Baqar, who held a government job and then was also the editor of the *Dehli Urdu Akhbar*, frequently visited Bahadur Shah and talked to him. Maulvi Mohammad Ishaq, grandson of Shah Abdul Aziz, was received with great respect and reverence in the Emperor's court. There were others who benefited directly from the connection—such as Joseph Skinner who was a farmer of the revenues of certain royal lands.[451] Despite the British discouraging the giving of khilats by the Emperor to those not in his employment, people of the city were frequently eager to receive them. This included those who were particularly close, socially and culturally, to the British. In the 1850s, one of the Skinners obtained special permission from the Agent to apply for and receive a khilat. Chiman Lal, the Calcutta trained doctor, who was posted as Sub-Assistant Surgeon in Delhi, and had converted to Christianity, used to treat Bahadur Shah. Government rules did not allow him to accept a khilat but he asked the Emperor to give him a certificate instead.[452]

Memories of connection with the Mughal court long outlived Bahadur Shah. Khwaja Farid ud din Ahmad Khan had been the mukhtar of Akbar II for a fairly short while following a long period of service with the Company's government in several capacities. However, when his grandson, Sir Syed Ahmad Khan, wrote his biography many years after his death, he referred to him in the sub-title of the book by his royal title and position. Syed Ahmad

Khan was himself referred to in that book by his hereditary royal title, though he had never been in the Emperor's service.[453]

Though the Emperor's writ did not run in administrative matters in the city, many turned to him requesting intervention, even in the 1850s. This is evident from the number and nature of petitions that were brought to him. Some of these were written applications presented in his court, some were by people addressing him from under the jharokha where the Emperor still appeared before the people, or when they were admitted to the court in person.

In 1851 the Muslim inhabitants of the Rahat ka Kuan locality wrote a petition requesting him to write to the Agent to allow cow slaughter in the city. The Emperor's intervention in the matter, however, did not yield a change in the administration's policy. The following year two hundred of the same people came in person to the Emperor's court saying that they had been warned by the Hindus against sacrificing cows, and the magistrate had put up a proclamation forbidding the slaughter of cows in that *mohalla*. Bahadur Shah replied that he could not interfere or even write to the Agent on a matter that related to the administration of the city. He also had it conveyed to them that if they would only consult the fatwas of their maulvis they would realize that the sacrifice of cows was not integral to their religion. There was in fact considerable pressure on Bahadur Shah from some members of the royal family, to support the cause of the petitioners. Hakim Ahsanullah Khan was a major mediating force, advising Bahadur Shah not to address the Agent on the issue, and that the complainants were ignorant men who were not aware that in their law cattle were to be taken to the Eidgah and sacrificed.[454]

Petitions on various subjects concerning affairs of the city, particularly Hindu-Muslim relations, continued to be brought to the Emperor. One was for the release of certain men arrested for cow sacrifice in the city; one complained against some Hindus who had placed a lock on the mosque at Nigambodh ghat. On another occasion a *kabab* seller protested against an order of the magistrate, on the complaint of certain Hindus, asking him to remove his stall from his usual place at Hauz Qazi. On the advice of Ahsanullah

Khan, Bahadur Shah ordered the man to take his case back to the magistrate.[455]

Other issues on which the Emperor was petitioned were completely non-sectarian. The *dhobis* of the city gathered under the jharokha of the fort and complained that the deputy magistrate had forbidden them to wash their clothes in the usual place, i.e. in the *nallah* from Qudsia Bagh to the Masjid ghats, and had asked them to cross the river instead. Bahadur Shah reminded them that these were matters of city administration and therefore outside his jurisdiction. They were, however, so insistent and loud in their complaints that he promised to write a letter to the Agent on the subject.[456]

29

Ties Old and New

Though the people of the city from time to time looked to Bahadur Shah for leadership, they did not forget that real power was with the East India Company, and its patronage had a very tangible and immediate significance. People were invariably eager to receive khilats from the local representatives of the British Government, and to attend their durbars. This included the Emperor's own employees, for instance the chief eunuch Mahbub Ali Khan who asked Bahadur Shah's permission to attend the Agent's durbar, and subsequently brought the khilat for the inspection of the Emperor, who was said to be very pleased.[457] It has already been mentioned that Ahsanullah Khan consistently advocated to the Emperor a policy of cooperation and compromise with the British Government, repeatedly advising him against confrontation.

The case of Ghalib, who is viewed essentially as a poet connected with Bahadur Shah's court, is a particularly interesting illustration of the relative importance of the Mughal court and British administration in Delhi. He received a hereditary pension from the British, though in his opinion, due to an injustice he did not get as much as he should have. He also had the right to be included in British durbars and be given a khilat. Nevertheless, his main source of income was the allowances he received from the Nawab of Rampur and Bahadur Shah. Initially engaged by Bahadur

Shah to write a history of the house of Timur, a few years before the revolt of 1857 he was designated the Emperor's ustad, and some of his best Urdu poetry was written in this period. Needless to say he also received the usual titles and khilats from the Emperor.

Yet, much of his time and effort was spent in attempts to win the favour of British officials, high and low. As a matter of course every new Governor General received from him a qasida or panegyric ode, as did the Lt Governor of the North-Western Provinces, important Secretaries of government, and even lesser functionaries. On the other hand he appears to have shown much less enthusiasm for writing the customary qasidas for the Mughal Emperor, claiming in a letter in 1855, that he had given up writing the qasidas at Eid and Nauroz for the last two or three years.[458] Ghalib was perceptive enough to see that the Mughal court was on its way out. The progressive erosion of the status of the Emperor, the negotiations with Fakhr ud din, made it clear that the British intended to sweep away the institution altogether. Rather cynically he distanced himself from the fort even while he earned his living from it. In a letter of 1854, he wrote that he sometimes went to the *mushairas* in the palace, and sometimes stayed away, adding, '*Aur yeh sohbat khud chand rozah hai, is ko dawam kahan? Kya maloom hai abhi na ho, ab ke ho to aindah na ho?*'[459] (This assembly is for a few more days, there is no permanence to it. Who knows if it will survive today, or if it survives today, it may go tomorrow?)

There is even more compelling evidence that at an emotional level he had transferred his loyalty to the British Government. An interesting letter to a close friend after the revolt of 1857, when his relationship with the British was under a cloud due to his possible role in the rebellion, reveals how he identified himself with the British Government. He writes: '*gorment ka bhat tha, bhati karta tha, khilat pata tha, khilat mauquf, bhati mataruk*'[460]—I was the bard of the government; I did my job and got my khilat. The khilat is suspended, and I have ceased to be a bard. This is an interesting interpretation of the relationship. By no stretch of imagination could Ghalib really have believed that the pension and other honours were patronage in reward of his poetic skills. He only wished this was the case.

There were others who perceived the hollowness of the grand titles and honours, the shabby khilats given out by the Mughal court, and recognized their futility in the changed context. The paternal ancestors of Sir Syed Ahmad Khan had been in the service of the Mughals for several generations. Though an allowance and the title continued in the family, Syed Ahmad's father increasingly stayed away from the court of both Akbar II and Bahadur Shah.[461]

But, if the British were endowed with temporal supremacy, the Emperor was attributed a quality that though intangible, was still powerful and very much alive even in his later years. This was the spiritual aura that was believed to surround him. Bahadur Shah, like some of his illustrious ancestors, had a general inclination towards debate on spiritual matters. On many occasions we see him engaging in discussions with various holy men and mendicants. Contemporary reports tell of faqirs saying prayers and breathing over the Emperor to heal him. On one occasion we find him going all the way to Dhaula Kuan to meet a certain faqir and ask for his prayers. On another, he fell into conversation with a faqir while taking an airing outside the fort walls, brought him into the palace and gave him food and gifts. Several faqirs had easy access to him, coming into the fort, being received and given charity.[462]

Spiritual qualities were attributed to Bahadur Shah himself. A certain sanctity was associated with the physical body of the Emperor, which was also believed to give him healing powers. He would breathe on water which would then be sent to the sick, used as an antidote to snake venom, or even be sprinkled around a newly dug well. When his wife Taj Mahal Begum was ill, Bahadur Shah bled her with his own hands—a medical procedure of the time, usually performed by a doctor.[463] The giving of alms on festive occasions like Diwali and Holi was also intimately linked to the physical person of the Emperor. He was weighed in different kinds of grain, precious metals, etc., that were then given in charity. This was a practice that was also followed on other occasions like eclipses of the moon.[464]

Bahadur Shah was also seen in the role of spiritual teacher, a *pir*. Many people from all walks of life came to him, gave sweets and/or a small nazar, and were given a handkerchief, a rosary or sometimes a khilat, and accepted as spiritual disciples or *murids*. Bahadur Shah also gave them a sanad, in the nature of a certificate, and containing a sequence of the spiritual line, sealed with his signet. He is then said to have given them discourses on the 'true knowledge of God'. His disciples included members of his own family, his attendants, even the most humble *darbans* and armed followers, and women. In fact this might have been an important channel of communication between him and the common people. We are told that since it was ordered that anyone who wished to become his murid must be allowed in, even poor people could enter 'the presence'.[465]

An interesting development in the 1850s was the increasing number of soldiers of the Company's army who were flocking to become murids of Bahadur Shah. Some of these were introduced by a *jamadar* in the army. By the end of 1852, this had become so noticeable that Hakim Ahsanullah Khan sounded a note of caution. He expressed the opinion that it was not proper for soldiers of the government to become the Emperor's murids, and the Agent had already instituted an enquiry in this regard. Shortly after, a message from the Agent on the subject persuaded Bahadur Shah to stop accepting as disciples those employed by the government.[466] The Emperor also began to be cautious about the several people who were coming to him expressing their intention to convert to Islam. He usually sent them to some maulvi, though on one occasion he accepted the convert as his own disciple. He was particularly circumspect when it was evident that the person concerned was an employee of the Company's government. In these cases he told them to go to the maulvis in the city, and that he would not interfere in the matter.[467]

The government was probably understandably suspicious of ties of any kind between the Emperor and those in sensitive positions, such as the soldiers of the government. It was probably equally uneasy at the information that a recently dismissed kotwal of Delhi had also become a disciple, and during his audience with Bahadur Shah, 'for a long time a conversation was carried on regarding matters of the sovereignty and their remedy'.[468] With the benefit of hindsight it is easy to see how such ties were symptoms of and in turn could keep alive sentiments of loyalty to the Mughal throne. Before the revolt of 1857, however, probably even Bahadur Shah could not have imagined that his name could become the centre of a widespread movement originating in the common soldiery.

30

Unity and Discord in the City

By 1853 the population of the walled city amounted to 1,51,000 excluding those inside the fort; a twenty-five per cent increase over the previous twenty years.[469] There was a certain pride in being Dehliwalas, and a conviction that they were culturally distinct and superior, which is evidenced by several references in the literature of the period. An ode to the city, composed in the early part of the century by Shah Abdul Aziz, the renowned religious scholar, had put Delhi above every other city in dignity and respect, excepting Mecca, Medina and Najaf. What gave Delhi its special character, according to Abdul Aziz, was essentially its people, who were superior to others in culture and disposition, and yet free of conceit. The poem then praised Delhi also for being a centre of learning and home to many grand mosques. Pride in the city and its people was evidently undiminished in later decades. Syed Ahmad Khan, writing in the 1840s, declared that the people of Delhi were unmatched in a range of good qualities, learning, piety, and etiquette. He was at pains to stress that this was an honest and objective assessment, lest people think that he was motivated by an unreasonable prejudice in favour of his home town![470]

This pride in their cultural superiority nevertheless did not make Dehliwalas insular. Even in 1835, Emma Roberts, a writer from Calcutta visiting Delhi, had remarked that nowhere else in India were people so open to adopting European fashions, and so tolerant to 'all sorts of innovations'. This openness was most evident to the visitor in the architecture, as, she noted, 'Grecian piazzas, porticos, and pediments, are not unfrequently found fronting the dwellings of the Moslem or Hindoo.' Not only were the shops 'crowded with all sorts of European products and manufactures', but many of them had signboards written in the Roman alphabet. This was a trend encouraged by no less than Badr ud din, the famous calligrapher and seal engraver.[471]

New fashions were particularly evident among the elite who had social interaction with the British. Mirza Fakhr ud din, the prince, was frequently seen in the company of British officials, who visited him in his house in the city and also in the palace.[472] Particularly in the case of the younger members of the family, this social interaction also went with a taste for European artefacts, clothing, architecture, food and drink (in some cases, particularly drink!). Many years ago, Mirza Jahangir too, during his stay in Allahabad had taken to frequently dressing in European clothes and eating with local British officials.[473] Hindu Rao, for entertaining European guests, had employed a cook from Calcutta, and imported canned exotic food, to cater to their tastes—offering on one occasion oyster pate with wine.[474] In the field of entertainment, there were now options beyond the familiar dance and music performances. A newspaper report of 1853 informed readers that a troupe of acrobats from France, consisting of six men and one woman, had performed in the Diwan e Khas, and a couple of days later, there was a repeat show in the house of the heir apparent, Mirza Fakhr ud din.[475]

The latest trends were also evident at fashionable weddings, particularly in ostentatious weddings among the mercantile class. A wedding in the house of a rich jeweller in 1841 attracted a huge crowd because of the elaborate constructions and decorations. The *iharna*, which was a royal enclosed garden with a waterfall and several pavilions at Mehrauli, had been recreated, and so had Constantia, the Lucknow palace of Claude Martin, the famous French General (the building now houses La Martiniere College, set up as per the terms of his will). A replica of the legendary jewelled peacock throne of the Mughals had been made, and the state procession of the Governor General with its elephants and carriages was also recreated![476]

While cultural assimilation came naturally to the citizens of a city that had been cosmopolitan for centuries, there were divisions too, and one of the lines of divide was religion. By the 1850s, the conflicts between Shias and Sunnis on Moharram, and between Muslims and non-Muslims over cow sacrifice on Eid, had been exacerbated. The tone of the petitions to the administration against cow sacrifice was now distinctly strident. In one such petition of 1854, the British were, ironically, credited with 'the deliverance of the Hindus from that miserable condition which they suffered long under their tyrant masters', ignoring the fact that a prohibition on cow slaughter had been lifted by the British administration in Delhi. It also claimed the existence of a conspiracy on the part of Bahadur Shah and his advisors, to persuade the Resident of Delhi to 'issue an order for the sacrifice of cows to take place in all the *bazaars* and streets of the city for three successive days at their abominable festival, Id-ul-zuha'.[477] This was in fact a gross exaggeration as Bahadur Shah, under advice from Ahsanullah Khan, had resisted lending his support to most such petitions.

As it happened, the customary sacrifices were made on the festival, but the situation did not develop into actual violence. Though Hindu shopkeepers closed their shops in protest for a day or two, they were prevailed upon by the patrolling magistrate and kotwal to finally reopen them.[478] The issue, however, did become a festering problem leading to much bitterness year after year. The Muslims would make it a point to carry out sacrifices in areas considered impermissible by the Hindus, who would then retaliate with measures such as defiling mosques.[479]

Christianity was a new contentious issue that had to be dealt with in the nineteenth century. Missionary activity was slow to grow in Delhi. The Baptist missionary, Reverend J.T. Thompson, had been stationed in Delhi in 1818 and preached there till his death in 1850, but his activities, targeted mostly at the lower castes and in surrounding rural areas, did not attract much attention. More aggressive proselytizing generally had by-passed Delhi, with the exception of the brief visit of Carl Gottlieb Pfander, a strident preacher and pamphleteer, in 1844.[480] The advent in 1852 of Midgley John Jennings, a strongly evangelical chaplain, who made no secret of his aim of widespread conversions, changed the mood somewhat.[481] The arrival of Jennings also happened to coincide with the conversion to Christianity of Ram Chander, a teacher in the government college, and Dr Chiman Lal, though it is certain that they had been contemplating the change for a while.

A more direct impact of Jennings was the establishment of the Society for the Propagation of the Gospel (SPG), which was directly concerned with conversions. By the end of 1854 an Urdu service had begun to be conducted in St James' Church for the twenty-five 'native Christians' in Delhi by Reverend Stuart Jackson, one of the two missionaries who had arrived earlier that year from England. But while these developments led to some immediate alarm among both Hindus and Muslims, no further conversions occurred, at least among the educated elite. Enrolment in the college, which had fallen due to the conversion of Ram Chander, recovered the very next year, even though it seems that some of the boys were joining Bible reading classes with Jackson a few times a week. [482]

Though there were no more prominent conversions, an intellectual ferment was in evidence. Tracts refuting some of Pfander's works challenging Muslim belief were published from Delhi, and authored by Rahmatullah Kairanawi, a theologian who had spent a significant portion of his student and working life in the city. An interesting feature of Rahmatullah's tracts was his reliance on many European works, including Biblical commentaries, works of Biblical criticism, and histories, to develop his arguments and point out the inconsistencies of the missionary position. It is evident that these books had been made available through the libraries of the government colleges at Delhi and Agra.[483]

In 1854 Rahmatullah engaged the missionaries in very public debates, though not at Delhi, but in Agra. Nevertheless, the interest was kept up in Delhi, because many of the Delhi ulema supplied fatwas, or legal opinions, on some of the doctrinal points involved. The proceedings of the debates and certain other texts as follow-ups were also published at Delhi, and were thus disseminated among the public. They all came to the conclusion that the debate had been won by the Muslim theologians. This was a conclusion that the missionaries too had to reluctantly accept, and by 1855 the confrontation had died down.[484]

Some hardening of lines in religious matters was also evident among the royal family, though traditionally they had been very eclectic in their beliefs and practices. Bahadur Shah was hurt and angry at a rumour that he had become a Shia. His physician and his prime minister Ahsanullah Khan wrote some pamphlets refuting this rumour, and posters denying the allegations were also put up in the streets and bazaars. The poet laureate, Ghalib, was ordered to write a masnavi on the subject as well. On another occasion, it was reported that both Bahadur Shah and Mirza Fakhr ud din expressed pleasure that a member of their family had converted from being a Shia to a Sunni.[485] At the same time, there was no change in the practices of the royal household and court, where diverse practices continued to be followed, and did not seem to lead to any conflict or contradiction. For instance, in 1852, the Emperor simply postponed the Dashehra durbar by a few days, as the festival itself happened to fall within the first ten days of Moharram, which was a period of mourning for Muslims.[486]

In another matter, Bahadur Shah took a clear stand against orthodoxy. This was the issue of circumcision. It was a practice not universally followed among the members of the royal family. There was an interesting reason for that. It appears that sometime in their history, the Mughal emperors decided to forego this important rite of Islam in consideration for their position as emperors of a country where the majority was not Muslim. Therefore, many Mughal males, at least those who were considered potential contenders for the throne in a future succession, were not circumcised. This soon became a well-entrenched tradition.[487] In 1851, however, one of the princes had his son, a young man, circumcised. Bahadur Shah was critical of this move, pointing out that it was a painful procedure if carried out in adulthood, and that 'the profession of the Mahommedan faith did not depend on the mere rite of circumcision'. It seems, however, that suddenly several of the young male members of the family wanted to go through the rite. Just a few days later another prince made an application to be allowed to invite some people to the fort on the occasion of the ceremony of his circumcision. This time Bahadur Shah initially refused permission, citing his objection to the performance of the ceremony, giving in later with bad grace.[488]

31

Assessing Foreign Rule

By the 1850s, most of the people alive in Delhi had been born under British rule, or at least that was the only regime they remembered having experienced. Though the Mughal Emperor remained in the fort, he was but a relic of a different regime now long past. Even those who had been damaged by the policies of the new regime, usually raised their voice against the particular policy, or against specific officials rather than against British rule per se. Among the rare ones who did was the poet Momin. He had lost his hereditary lands and hence found himself in financial straits, frequently in debt and pressured by his creditors. Not surprisingly, this made him less than favourably disposed towards British rule. He complained that under the rule of the 'unbelievers' Delhi had been ruined and the worth and prosperity of its nobility had been destroyed.[489]

Ghalib, who had also suffered from British policies, had a very different attitude. He harboured a strong sense of being unjustly treated in his pension case. At various times, particularly on his return at the end of 1829 from a fruitless visit to Calcutta, he expressed a frank criticism of individual British officials and of the colonial state's laws and institutions.[490] Yet he was not against British rule per se. When imprisoned on a charge of gambling, he expressed the view that though he had been harshly treated, he believed that rulers were appointed by God, and God cannot be argued with.[491]

In fact we come across few condemnations of colonial rule based on purely xenophobic reactions. Assessments of the colonial administration were made on the policies and actions of individuals. An article that appeared in the *Dehli Urdu Akhbar* in 1852 demonstrates some of the expectations that people held of the judicial system. The occasion was the departure of the sessions judge John P. Gubbins, who had been in Delhi seven years and had apparently endeared himself to the people of the city. A farewell meeting was held in his honour and he was presented with a letter of appreciation signed by a number of the Indian elite of the city. These included government servants, members of the nobility, merchants, the poet Zauq, Nizam ud din, the son and heir of Bahadur Shah's spiritual guide, Kale Saheb. The letter generally praised his abilities as a judge, saying, for instance, that while passing judgement he looked not merely at the letter of the law but also its spirit. More interestingly, it specifically mentioned that Gubbins had proved wrong the generally held opinion of the people, that the officials of government departments had untrammelled power. In his court he kept them in check and none but the lawyers of the parties were allowed to speak.[492]

The implication of the article was that Gubbins was an exceptional judge, notable among the vast majority of British judges. Soon after, in fact, the newspaper was arguing for a greater role for Indians, who so far occupied only subordinate positions in the judiciary. It pointed out that in the case of competent Indian judges (and here it mentioned two by name), it was fitting as well as in the public interest that they be given the same powers and responsibilities as British judges. When a British judge went away on leave of absence, the principal sadr amin was left in charge, but was not given the authority to decide the cases that were being heard by the absent judge. Not only did this lead to delays and inconvenience to the people, it was unfair on the Indian judge, who was otherwise competent to take up the responsibility. Giving able judges this power and also an increased salary to go with it would be an incentive to promote excellence and good character.[493]

Clearly then, the racial policies surrounding employment were a major grievance against the Company's government. It is, however, important to note that however critical of individual government policies, the *Dehli Urdu Akhbar* was not against colonial rule. In 1852 the local administration was carrying out searches in private homes, as well as within the Fatehpuri and Akbarabadi mosques for suspected links to the *mujahidin* (plural of jehadi, one who takes up arms to fight the enemies of Islam) in the North-Western Provinces. Commenting on this, the editor of the newspaper expressed surprise that people of the city had been helping the mujahidin against the rulers whom God had blessed with wisdom, justice and good fortune. He further pointed out that the rulers, being Christian, were 'people of the Book' and therefore had an affinity to Muslims. If Muslims wanted to prove their religious credentials, they should support the British in their fight against those in Burma and China![494]

Another Delhi newspaper, the *Sadiq ul Akhbar*, was reporting in early 1857 on the war in Iran, between Iran and Britain, which was of special interest in India because not only had troops from India been deployed, but as usual it threw up questions of the threat to India's borders through a possible alliance with Russia. While regretting that channels of news were disrupted, the editor assured his readers that when news was forthcoming, 'Please God, I shall publish it too without prejudice or bias, for our Government is a just one which does not hinder any in the free exercise of his rights, and this is the reason why its sway is daily extending, and why the arts and sciences have attained an eminence twice as great as that of former times. May the Almighty preserve this Government in the exercise of justice to the end of time.'[495]

Justification of colonial rule was sometimes explicitly expressed as a necessity in the face of Indian shortcomings. The *Dehli Urdu Akhbar*, for instance, on occasion expressed the opinion that relative peace and equality between Shias and Sunnis could only be maintained through the intervention of the British, and if there had been Indian rule, carnage would have resulted.[496] Not all newspapers were this pro-British. The *Nur e Maghribi* for instance took a critical view of race relations. It declared in March 1857 that a perusal of the Calcutta newspapers demonstrated that the '*goras*' had become very tyrannical. They picked fights and even entered homes and mosques. The reason for this clearly was that they were not adequately punished for these iniquities.[497]

In March 1857, the newspapers had a minor excitement to report, in connection with the ongoing war in Iran. Copies of a pamphlet had appeared, pasted at different localities in the city, including the Jama Masjid. It purported to be a proclamation from the ruler of Iran, and the essence of the proclamation was 'that people professing the true faith should, as a matter of duty, eschew assisting the Christians, and should as being right and proper, exert themselves to the full extent of their ability to promote the welfare of the Mussulmans; that the time is at hand when, God willing We, the King of Persia, will sit on the throne of India, and will make the king and the people of that country contented and happy. In the same measure as the English have done everything to make them destitute of even the means of subsistence, We will exert ourselves to make them rich and affluent, We use [*sic*] no interference with any man's religion.' It was also being suggested that many Iranian soldiers were secretly already in India, and many in Delhi.[498]

The *Sadiq ul Akhbar* dismissed this out of hand as an absurd falsehood and forgery, devised by 'some designing and mischievous promoter of sedition in Delhi'. It strained credulity to imagine that Indians would welcome the ruler of Iran ruling over them. Another newspaper called this so-called proclamation 'mere senseless and absurd jesting and levity'. The joint magistrate, Theophilus Metcalfe (son of Thomas Metcalfe), who ordered it to be removed from the Jama Masjid, had no doubt that the people of Delhi were convinced that it was a forgery, and that it did not 'excite much discussion or interest among the natives of Delhi'. [499]

Clearly, to the people of Delhi, the idea that the Company's government in India could be threatened by a foreign power was unthinkable. Much less could they have imagined that in a few weeks that very government would be on the brink of an overthrow by an internal force that would rise up in a sudden storm, sweeping everything before it.

PART FOUR

A World of Poetry and Education

Ram Chander

32

Languages of Culture

The more than half a century that elapsed between the advent of the East India Company in 1803, and the outbreak of the revolt of 1857 saw many changes in the political and social life of the city. Cultural and intellectual life too could not help but be affected. The change was slow to set in, however, and for a number of years things went on as they had in the past few decades. In its heyday the Mughal capital had been a centre of learning and literature, and the foundations of these strong traditions had survived even though the worst of the political upheavals of the eighteenth century had led to the drying up of patronage, and the flight of its best poets, such as Mirza Rafi 'Sauda' and Mir Taqi 'Mir'.

The basis of cultural life was a rich linguistic tradition. At the time when Shahjahanabad was established, Persian, or Farsi, had been the official language of the empire, a link language for the elite through much of the country, and a language of learning and high culture. Consequently, the study of Persian was popular, particularly among the professional and service elite. All the same, in India, Persian was practically no one's mother tongue, though this was probably what made it an acceptable, neutral, link language. This official language of the empire was referred to as *Zaban e Urdu e Mualla e Shahjahanabad*, that is, 'the language of the exalted camp of Shahjahanabad'. The 'camp' was a very specific reference, for, during the heyday of the Mughal empire, the Emperors had been frequently on the move, and the *Urdu e Mualla*, 'the exalted camp' of the Emperor was a moving capital/court in a sense. When Shahjahanabad was founded, it was not illogical that the imagery of a stationary camp was applied to it, and it came to be known as the *Urdu e Mualla e Shahjahanabad*. In this sense, the term *Zaban e Urdu e Mualla e Shahjahanabad*, during Shahjahan's time, referred to Persian, which was the language of the Mughal court.[500]

While Persian was the official language, the tongue that was widely spoken in Delhi and its surroundings was Khari Boli, more commonly called Hindi, and also, particularly in its literary form, as Rekhta. This had been developing as a literary language for some time, though its earliest literary history was associated with developments in Gujarat and the Deccan, where it was carried by emigres from Delhi. Nevertheless, the history of Hindi in the eighteenth century was dominated by the poets of Delhi—Mirza 'Mazhar' Jan e Janan, Mirza Mohammad Rafi 'Sauda', Khwaja Mir 'Dard', and Mir Taqi 'Mir' being the most prominent among them.

The ascendancy of Hindi at the Mughal court itself is dated by some scholars to the last quarter of the eighteenth century, after Shah Alam II returned to Delhi after a long exile in Allahabad. The Emperor was a literary man, with a passion for Hindi, in which he himself wrote poetry. It was under his patronage, that, even though Persian still remained the official language, Hindi began to receive patronage as a language not only for informal communication, but for literary compositions. Patronage from the Mughal court led, sometime in the late eighteenth century, to Hindi being dignified with the appellation of *Zaban e Urdu e Mualla e Shahjahanabad*, thus supplanting Persian. Soon, this unwieldy term would be shortened to '*Zaban e Urdu e Mualla*', then to '*Zaban e Urdu*', and eventually, 'Urdu', though the popular name for the language remained 'Hindi' till well into the second half of the nineteenth century.

By the beginning of the nineteenth century it not only had an established tradition of poetry, but was beginning to be used for some significant works in prose. Important steps in the direction of Hindi prose writing had been taken in the eighteenth century in North India with the production of the first *dastans*—long narrative tales. Then, in the beginning of the nineteenth century, the Fort William College at Calcutta, a school for the instruction of young East India Company officials, played a major role in the commissioning of works in simple idiomatic 'Urdu'—a word that began to be used there for the language which in Delhi was still known as Hindi. (In view of current usage, hereinafter, I will use the word Urdu for the language that was in use in Delhi.)

In Delhi, the impetus for prose writing in the language also came from religious reformers, who wanted to reach out to a wider reading public, and therefore used Urdu. In the previous century Shah Waliullah had translated the Quran from Arabic into Persian. In the early nineteenth century two of his sons translated it into Urdu. This was also the medium in which many tracts giving guidance on the tenets and everyday practice of Islam were written.[501]

Delhi intellectuals of the early nineteenth century had an especially close relationship with Urdu. In their opinion, it was *their* language in a very special sense—they practically owned it. In the first decade of the nineteenth century, Inshaallah Khan 'Insha' put forward a well-articulated theory of the origins of the language, that put the roots of Urdu very firmly in Delhi. Insha's forebears were from Delhi and though he was born in Murshidabad, he had spent some time in Delhi too. In 1808 he wrote his *Dariya e Latafat*, a work on Urdu grammar and diction. In this book, Insha held that Urdu was born in Shahjahanabad. As this city had been the Mughal capital for many years, it attracted the most talented people from all over. Urdu developed as a result of this cultural mingling, as the best words from several languages were adopted and made into a new language. By virtue of being the capital city, Delhi was seen as setting the standard for manners and trends. The language therefore naturally spread to other areas, particularly after the decline of the Mughal state, as people from Delhi scattered through the country.[502]

In *Dariya e Latafat*, Insha defined proper Urdu usage and accent very narrowly—giving examples of incorrect usage and pronunciation (invariably the uneducated tongue of non-Delhi people) alongside the correct form as understood in Delhi. He also identified it with a very few select localities within Delhi and specifically with the Muslims living there. He was at a pinch willing to extend it to those who had been born in other parts of the country, but of proper Urdu-speaking parents from Delhi—a category which included himself![503]

A different version from Insha's theory regarding the origins of Urdu was explicated by Mir Amman in *Bagh o Bahar*, just a few years before Insha. Mir Amman was originally from Delhi and was definitely the star of Fort William College. His *Bagh o Bahar* came to be considered a model of good Urdu prose and was widely read through the nineteenth century. According to Mir Amman, Urdu was born in the market of the army camp, the 'Urdu', by implication attributing to it a more plebian birth. This particular theory of the origins of Urdu was probably drawn from the hypothesis developed by the colonial scholars in charge at Fort William College, where *Bagh o Bahar* was written in 1803.[504]

Though Urdu had come into its own as a literary language, Persian held its ground till well into the nineteenth century. In the first decades of the century it was almost the exclusive medium for formal letter writing and prose compositions in particular. This status, which sprang in part from its long-held position as the language of the administration, was confirmed by the British. Persian was the language that the East India Company used in its communication with 'natives'—whether in courts of law, or in correspondence. It was the language that the lower echelons of its own bureaucracy, manned by Indians, exclusively used.

33

The World of Poetry

Urdu and Persian poetry had reached a high point in the mid-eighteenth century, and had not lost any significant momentum since then. The most popular forms of poetry in the first half of the nineteenth century were the masnavi (a narrative poem), qasida (ode), *marsiya* (a lament of grief over someone's death, usually mourning the death of Hazrat Husain at Karbala) and above all the *ghazal* (a lyric poem). The most popular poetic form was the ghazal, each composition being made up of a number of couplets, called *sher*. Each sher in fact may be considered to constitute a poem on its own, as it was complete in meaning. Individual shers were united within a ghazal only with respect to a shared rhyme scheme and metre. Not only did the shers of a ghazal not make up a single narrative, they often did not share even a common theme or spirit.

Urdu and Persian ghazal poetry was governed by fairly complex conventions and rules.[505] The language, imagery and themes that could legitimately be used, were bound by traditions that had been laid down long ago in the field of Persian ghazal-writing, on which the Urdu tradition modelled itself. This universe of the ghazal was centred around a passionate lover, expressing his longing for a mostly unattainable, indifferent, coquettish, and generally cruel, beloved. The beloved could be human or divine, and frequently, a deliberate ambiguity made it impossible to distinguish which the poet intended.

Apart from the ambiguity between a human and divine beloved, an added ambiguity was that of gender. In the Persian language, gender was not grammatically expressed, so the ambiguity was built in. Though the Urdu language did have unambiguous gender significations in its grammatical structure, the Urdu ghazal universe deliberately imported the gender neutrality of the Persian. This it did by assigning a male gender to both lover and beloved. This was a convention that was well understood and accepted by all who were participants in the world of the Urdu ghazal, and indeed this is still the case today. However strange this may appear to the outsider, for those who are intimate with this world, these ambiguities are not only acceptable but desirable. They are cherished because they allow a sher to hold multiple meanings for different people in different situations.

The basic formula of the lover and the beloved was then expanded through the use of a fairly limited set of metaphors, a very popular one being that of the beloved as a hunter, whose arrows wound the lover, or whose net ensnares him. The lover therefore, was often a wounded or captured bird. Love was often described as a fire, which consumes the lover, or leaves burns on his body. The creativity of the poet lay in the variations he could build on these basic themes, but again within certain set conventions. For instance, the beloved was often described as a 'cypress'—for being tall and slender. Using just any tree as a metaphor for the stature of the beloved was unacceptable, simply because this was a metaphor sanctioned by the original Persian ghazal universe. Within a sher, the poet created meaning out of a limited set of metaphors by interpreting them and assigning them ever new forms.

Beyond the skill of creating fresh perspectives from a set of internally well-understood and accepted metaphors, technical virtuosity involved an intimate feel for the qualities of a good sher, and the use of words to create cadence as well as meaning. The popularity of puns and wordplay was directly the result of a desire to create multiple meanings. But words could also create qualities of rhythm and of mood and emotion. Within the short poem that was the sher, each word counted, and had to be just right.

The complexity of the world of the ghazal implied that it took long years of effort and immersion to grasp its rules. This could only be achieved by an apprenticeship with an ustad, a master. The process of becoming the shagird, or pupil, of an acknowledged master in the craft, was a straightforward one. A budding poet would approach the master in question with a request to be allowed to 'show' his poetry and receive *islah* or 'correction'. The ustads were those who had mastered the many aspects of the ghazal, and whose ability had been tested and recognized by their peers.

As in other areas of learning, this relationship between the master and pupil was a flexible one. No fee was expected, but occasional gifts were given by social inferiors or equals by way of respect or friendship. Often of course the shagird was the social superior of the ustad, and in the case of a pupil of sufficient standing, a more formal patronage might be accorded to the ustad in the form of a regular stipend. The relationship between an ustad and his shagird could be a difficult one. An ustad could complain of a lack of regard or loyalty on the part of the shagird. The latter on the other hand might feel that the ustad was looking at his poetry only half-heartedly, or more seriously, passing on his themes to a rival.[506] At other times a shagird might challenge the opinion of the master and this could lead to an argument.[507]

The other major institution, on the basis of which poetry flourished, was the mushaira. This was a gathering of poets, usually organized by a patron at his house. Various poets would be invited to recite their verse, and usually a *tarah*, or verse pattern indicating a certain metre and rhyme scheme, would be set in advance, on which the poets had to compose their verses. A conventional order of precedence dictated that acknowledged masters would recite last. The order of precedence caused occasional clashes of ego, as it became an important matter of prestige for the poets concerned.

The mushaira was particularly important because it was the forum where reputations were built. Each poet's work was tested, and he faced the opinion of his peers. It was where practically every new verse was first aired, and discussed, often threadbare. The shers of even the established ustads could be challenged, and the criticism was usually a questioning of alleged inconsistencies and departures from the established bounds of language and imagery prescribed by the conventions of Urdu and Persian poetics.[508] As is to be expected, sometimes personal egos and rivalries were at work, and mushairas became the venue for sparring between two ustads. The end of a particular mushaira was also not always the end of a disputation, which sometimes led to prolonged discussions in following mushairas.

The mushaira flourished in the early decades of the nineteenth century as it had in the previous century. Apart from those organized in the palace under the aegis of the Emperor himself, mushairas were regularly held at the houses of prominent citizens, for instance, Shah Nasir, the great ustad whom many poets of the age acknowledged as their teacher, and Nawab Mustafa Khan 'Shefta', the jagirdar of Jahangirabad (in present-day Uttar Pradesh) who spent much of his time in Delhi. Another patron of mushairas was Zafaryab Khan 'Sahab', the son of Walter Reinhardt 'Sombre', who lived in Delhi till his death in 1801, and was himself a poet.[509]

The mushaira was crucial to poetry because each poem was primarily meant to be recited. The orality of poetry was reflected in the fact that the term used for composing poetry was (and still is) 'saying a verse', as opposed to writing a verse. Importance was given to the poet's style of reciting, such as, whether or not he put emotion into his voice and face.[510] Poetry recited at a mushaira or in a more casual setting was frequently written down by listeners who noted down what they enjoyed personally. From these personal notebooks, called *bayaz*, grew the *tazkiras* of poets—anthologies that recorded biographical details as well as gave samples of the verses of different poets. The many tazkiras that were written in the nineteenth century, and after, are an important source of our information about the literary world of that era. Their importance for posterity is significant if we appreciate that many of the poets that they included did not write enough to compile a *divan*—a collection that could be published. If not for the tazkiras, they would have been completely wiped from history.

34

Education

Even in the field of education things went on as before for the first several years of the Company's rule. In mid-1823, the government at Calcutta had set up a 'General Committee of Public Instruction' to investigate into the state of education in all the territories under the Bengal Presidency, and to undertake measures towards its promotion and improvement. The Committee sent out letters to local Agents, asking them to prepare reports on the state of education in the areas under their administration. The task for preparing the report for Delhi fell to J.H. Taylor, Secretary to the local Agent at Delhi, who was appointed Secretary of the Local Committee for General Education.[511]

Taylor's report of 1824 listed thirty-four institutions of education within the city, all but one of them 'Muslim'. A subsequent, more detailed report of 1827 revealed that 554 students were enrolled in thirty-one 'Hindu' schools and 933 in ninety-three 'Persian' schools.[512] By Hindu schools was probably meant all institutions where Sanskrit was taught along with the three Rs. While the students enrolled in these were fairly numerous, these were evidently geared to imparting a rather basic education. Taylor probably did not include them in his initial list as he dismissed this education with the comment that 'commerce seems to absorb the faculties and engross the attention of the Hindoo population'.[513]

Taylor therefore concentrated his attention on Persian language schools. In his opinion, it was a wonder that any sort of education should have survived at all in the context of the political upheavals of the last decades of the eighteenth century. There were schools attached to the various mosques, but the endowments associated with them had in many cases been alienated and misappropriated, leaving them devoid of means of support. Patronage from the royal court had dwindled to the support of one madrasa near the Jama Masjid. Education in fact had survived mainly due to the efforts of selfless individuals. Taylor found it remarkable that, of the educational institutions in the city, 'by far the greater portion are private schools begun and conducted by individuals of studious habits, who have made the cultivation of letters the chief occupation of their lives, and by whom the profession of learning is less followed as a means of livelihood, than undertaken as a meritorious work productive of moral and religious benefit to themselves and their fellow creatures. Few accordingly give instruction on any stipulated remuneration of a pecuniary nature, and what they may receive is both tendered and accepted in the light of an interchange of kindness and civility, between the master and his disciple'.[514]

While Taylor quite accurately analysed the basis of this education, he went on to make some assumptions that were heavily coloured by his cultural orientation—i.e. an understanding of education only in terms of the Western model. According to Taylor, the inevitable drawback of this informal education was the lack of a regular system with formal requirements of attendance and clearly laid down rules of conduct. Attendance and application were too dependent on personal interest.[515] At a fundamental level, Taylor was wrong in assuming that this somewhat 'irregular' mode of education was an anomaly, an adaptation that had arisen as a result of the decline of 'regular' education based on more formal schools. In fact, far from being an ad hoc response to circumstances, this system of education had a well-established tradition, and at its core was not the institution of a school but a very direct and personal relationship between the ustad/guru (teacher) and the shagird/*shishya* (pupil).[516]

Delhi had long been an acknowledged centre of learning. In the Persian establishments that Taylor had spoken of, teaching was based on the Arabic and Persian languages, encompassing a curriculum essentially derived from an Islamic tradition. The Quran and the sayings of the Prophet, together known as manqulat, formed an important part of this. The other category of subjects was known as ma'qulat, and included law, jurisprudence, logic, mathematics, philosophy, rhetoric, etc. Teachers frequently tended to specialize in one or the other category of subjects. In Delhi in particular, Shah Waliullah and his family had established a tradition of learning based on the manqulat, whereas teaching of the ma'qulat was a speciality of Fazl e Imam Khairabadi and his son Fazl e Haq.[517] Though traditions of scholarship did run in families, an individual had to ultimately prove his independent credentials. While the family of Shah Waliullah was highly respected for their learning, a series of tazkira writers did not hesitate to point out that Ghulam Mustafa, the son of Maulvi Rafi ud din, was not of the calibre of the rest of his family.[518]

While Taylor was making his report to the General Committee of Public Instruction, a young boy was embarking on his educational journey in exactly the kind of 'irregular' system that Taylor deplored. The boy was Syed Ahmad, who was being raised in the prosperous and respectable household of his maternal grandfather, Farid ud din Ahmad (also known as Khwaja Farid), who held important positions, both with the East India Company and in the Mughal court. Syed Ahmad, who would grow up to be the reformer and educationist we know as Sir Syed Ahmad Khan, received his earliest education at home, in the ladies' quarters, the *zanana*. His first teacher was an *ustani*, a respectable *purdah nashin* (veiled) lady employed by the family to teach the children, and the book he read first was the Quran. Thereafter he graduated to the *maktab*, which approximated more closely to a regular primary school. While boys from a more modest background may have at this stage gone to a teacher's house or maybe a school attached to a mosque, Syed Ahmad's grandfather, like many of the rich, employed teachers who taught the boys of the family at home. Syed Ahmad desultorily read some basic Persian and Arabic works, but soon became interested in mathematics. This was a subject in which his mother's family were particularly expert. He therefore studied the basic mathematical texts under his mother's brother, but here too he concentrated on what he liked best—the study of mathematical and astronomical instruments. Suddenly, he developed an interest in medicine and sought out a hakim—a doctor learned in the Yunani system of medicine, under whom he learnt some introductory texts, and even practised medicine for a short while. By the age of eighteen or nineteen years he had stopped studying.[519]

Syed Ahmad then joined the East India Company's judicial service, but he kept alive an interest in reading through his early working career, and even wrote a few texts on religious and other subjects. Then, at the age of nearly thirty, when he was posted in Delhi, he decided to go back to a systematic study of some of the schoolbooks he thought he had not paid enough attention to. This he did under three different teachers, each guiding him in the study of a different selection of books.[520]

The flexibility of such an arrangement, while it allowed a slacker to get away with very little work, gave him the opportunity to come back to studying at a later date. It encouraged the student to follow his inclinations in the choice of subjects to a remarkable extent. This freedom was of course tempered by pressures such as parental discipline over the individual child, and we see this in the case of another later educationist, Maulvi Zakaullah, somewhat younger than Syed Ahmad. His memories of his mother, for instance, reveal a woman who actively rewarded hard work at studies, and any signs of straying from the straight and narrow path of striving for academic excellence immediately drew a reprimand.[521]

Most importantly, this system of education gave a student the opportunity to approach scholars who were considered experts in certain fields and receive instruction from them. This was particularly significant because the learned, whatever their full-time occupations, often made it a point to teach students in their spare time. This was true of Syed Ahmad's grandfather Khwaja Farid, and Fazl e Imam, who was in the judicial service. It was also true of Mohammad Sadr ud din, 'Azurda', also in the judicial service, who rose to be principal sadr amin of Delhi, the highest Indian judicial official of the city. Shah Abdul Aziz and his family of course were renowned for their teaching, and the network of their students extended far beyond Delhi. All these men would also frequently extend financial help to needy students.[522]

This system of education, built into social structures rather than rigid formal institutions, had survived quite well during the eighteenth and early nineteenth centuries, despite the drying up of patronage to madrasas from royal and other rich individuals. It not only functioned but continued to produce men of learning, who made a mark around the country. The place of Delhi in the literary culture of India has been discussed earlier. Mir Amman 'Dehlvi' played a formative role in the development of the Hindi/Urdu language and literature at the Fort William College in Calcutta at the turn of the century. Well-educated Delhi men had also played important roles in the East India Company's diplomatic and exploratory forays into territories beyond the frontiers of its Indian possessions. Khwaja Farid had been on diplomatic missions in Iran as well as Ava. Another man in a very similar position was Mir Izzatullah, who had spent a number of years, from 1808 till his death in 1825, on trade, exploration and diplomatic missions to Multan, Kabul, Turkestan, Yarkand and Tibet. Part of his value as a diplomat was his descent from a politically well-connected family. His grandfather had been the governor of Lahore, and Ranjit Singh, the ruler of Punjab, showed him great respect—offering him a seat in his presence and treating 'his opinions with deference and respect'. Apart from this advantage, his proficiency in the Persian and Turki languages put him in the best position to act as an information-gatherer and mediator, as he was often trusted more than his British employers were.[523]

35

The Government College

It was within such a milieu of traditional education that the General Committee of Public Instruction decided to set up a college in Delhi. An earlier quasi-governmental effort in education had been made from the mid-1810s to mid-1820s, when William Fraser had on his own initiative set up four schools with a total of four teachers and eighty boys, in rural areas of the Delhi district. These students were children of the peasantry, who were given a basic education in reading and writing the Persian language. Through this, he hoped, they would get an introduction to the British judicial and revenue system, and thus be a conduit for the diffusion of this knowledge through the mass of the rural population. To encourage attendance, however, it was found necessary to give each student an allowance of one rupee per month and a seer of wheat flour each day.[524]

The General Committee of Public Instruction had other ideas. It flatly refused to recommend or support such a system as Fraser had initiated, believing that government efforts should be concentrated exclusively on higher education. It advised that efforts be directed towards the 'higher orders of the community', particularly those who might seek 'future employment in the Public service', to enable them to 'obtain useful and liberal knowledge'. The committee also took it for granted that this knowledge would consist primarily of the 'Sciences and Arts of Europe'.[525]

These aims found an echo in official circles in Delhi, and sanction was given for the setting up of a government college along these lines. In keeping with the government's concern at this time to make all its policies acceptable to the local population, it was decided that the choice of teachers and a principal from among the prominent learned men of the city would lend legitimacy to the institution. The name of Shah Abdul Aziz was suggested, but as he was unwilling to take up this assignment and in fact died soon after in 1824, his erstwhile pupil and a noted scholar in his own right, Maulvi Rashid ud din Khan was appointed principal. A strong reason behind such an appointment was probably the aim of strengthening the illusion of continuity with local tradition, the same motive behind housing the new institution in a pre-existing educational establishment—the madrasa of Ghazi ud din Khan.[526]

The college was set up in 1825, with twelve teachers and 300 students, out of which 120 were resident in the college. The immediate aim of its managers (a local committee made up of officials) was to provide for what were considered the main defects and lacunae in the indigenous system of education. Great stress was laid on grouping the students into appropriate classes, appointing monitors and teachers for each class, laying down fixed hours of study and leisure, and framing a well-defined body of college regulations. The aim of all this was quite clear—'the promotion of good order, strict discipline, moral conduct and studious application.'[527]

According to the government, an important aim of the curriculum was to be the introduction of modern science, to dispel the false beliefs the 'natives' generally held, 'with regard to even the most fundamental scientific principles'. This was hoped to be corrected through a study of geography, arithmetic, history, mathematics, mechanics, the use of globes, astronomy, chemistry, etc. The medium of instruction had obviously to be one that the pupils readily understood. To this end it was initially proposed that translations be made in simple Persian from suitable texts. Soon, however, the committee realized that Urdu, which was much more widely understood, would be a better choice.[528]

The problem in implementing this ideal curriculum of course was the difficulty in making the required texts available soon enough, and there was, to begin with, an almost complete lack of available translations of works from which to teach Western sciences. So, until translations were forthcoming, it was primarily the 'Oriental' subjects that were taught—for instance Islamic law. The few areas in which Western ideas were introduced, were the Copernican system of astronomy (based on the assumption that the earth orbited around the sun rather than the other way round, which had been the traditional belief), geography, and geometry. Apart from this common curriculum, the students studied one of three classical languages—Persian, Arabic and Sanskrit, in that order of popularity.[529]

The ultimate aim, however, at least according to the majority official opinion, was to be the introduction of English. In early 1827, Charles Metcalfe, then in Delhi for a second tenure, as Commissioner, declared that the institution of an English professorship would 'be more valuable than all the other arrangements of that institution', and that a familiarity with English would truly open up the stores of European literature and science to the students. Accordingly, in 1828 a class teaching English was also started.[530]

The statistics of the students enrolled in the early years (detailed reports of 1827 and 1828 exist) can perhaps best be appreciated in the form of a table:

	1827			**1828**		
	Total	*From Delhi*	*From Outside*	*Total*	*From Delhi*	*From Outside*
Arabic	50	22	28	32	5	27
Persian	147	77	70	127	43	84
Sanskrit	17	13	4	13	11	2
English				28	20	8
Total students	214	112	102	200	79	121

The tomb enclosure of Bahadur Shah I in Mehrauli, in which
Shah Alam II and Akbar II were also buried.

A view of the Red Fort from the river Yamuna. A painting by Charles Stewart Hardinge, 1847.

Diwan e Khas, as it was before the Revolt. From Charles Ball, *The History of the Indian Mutiny*, 1860.

The Mughal Emperor's procession in front of the Jama Masjid; painted by Thomas Daniell, 1780s.

Lahori Gaze of the Red Fort, with the British Commander's quarters above the entrance.

Chandni Chowk as viewed from the Red Fort; drawn by Major John Luard, 1820s.

A Mughal soldier; drawn by William Daniell, 1830s.

A temple built by Harsukh Rai in the city, popularly known as 'Naya Mandir'.

Mirza Jahangir's tomb; photograph by Samuel Bourne, 1860s.

Rammohan Roy; painted by A. Geringer, 1827.

European style houses in front of the Jama Masjid. A newspaper illustration, 1857.

Begum Samru's palace. An engraving based on a photograph by George Beresford, the manager of the Delhi Bank, which occupied the building in 1846.

St James' Church; drawn by Lt Charles Tremenheere, 1830s.

Thomas Metcalfe's house north of Shahjahanabad. Photo in the Delhi State Archives Collection.

The Kotwali; photo in the Delhi State Archives Collection.

The house of William Fraser, which was purchased by Hindu Rao, and has been a hospital since 1857.

The Qutub Minar, with the cupola on the ground, where it was placed after being removed from the top in the 1840s.

The jharokha e darshan. Photo in the Delhi State Archives Collection.

The special commemorative coin issued on the accession of Bahadur Shah II in 1837.

The interior of the Emperor's palace in the Red Fort. Photo in the Delhi State Archives Collection.

Zeenat Mahal. From Charles Ball, *The History of the Indian Mutiny*, 1860.

بعون صناع مکین و مکان و فضل خلاق زمین و زمان

کتاب حذاقت انتساب متضمن حالات تعمیرات و قلعه و باشندگان شهر دلی مسمی به

آثار الصنادید

تصنیف جواد الدوله سید احمد خان صاحب بهادر عارف جنگ سابق منصف دار الخلافه شاهجهان آباد

مطبع نامی منشی نولکشور میں طبع مزین مطبوع ہوئی

Syed Ahmad Khan's *Asar us sanadid.*

British fugitives after the outbreak of the Revolt of 1857.

The bridge of boats; photograph by Felice Beato, 1858.

Mohan Lal Kashmiri; drawn by T. Picken.

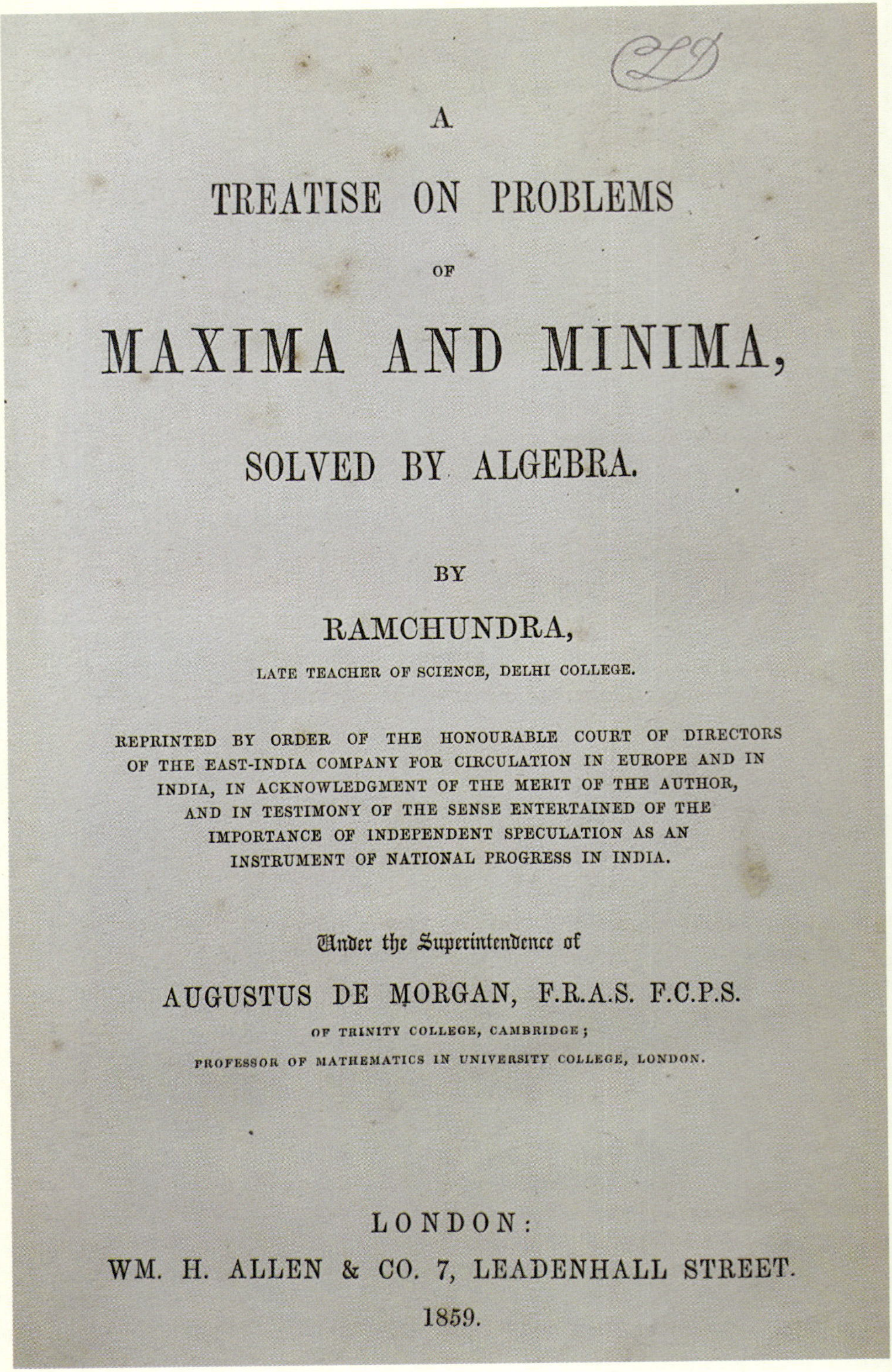

A

TREATISE ON PROBLEMS

OF

MAXIMA AND MINIMA,

SOLVED BY ALGEBRA.

BY

RAMCHUNDRA,

LATE TEACHER OF SCIENCE, DELHI COLLEGE.

REPRINTED BY ORDER OF THE HONOURABLE COURT OF DIRECTORS OF THE EAST-INDIA COMPANY FOR CIRCULATION IN EUROPE AND IN INDIA, IN ACKNOWLEDGMENT OF THE MERIT OF THE AUTHOR, AND IN TESTIMONY OF THE SENSE ENTERTAINED OF THE IMPORTANCE OF INDEPENDENT SPECULATION AS AN INSTRUMENT OF NATIONAL PROGRESS IN INDIA.

Under the Superintendence of

AUGUSTUS DE MORGAN, F.R.A.S. F.C.P.S.

OF TRINITY COLLEGE, CAMBRIDGE;

PROFESSOR OF MATHEMATICS IN UNIVERSITY COLLEGE, LONDON.

LONDON:

WM. H. ALLEN & CO. 7, LEADENHALL STREET.

1859.

Ram Chander's *Maxima and Minima*. This copy of the London edition was owned by Charles Dodgson, a.k.a. Lewis Caroll, and bears his signature.

A bust of Mirza Ghalib put up in his haveli in Gali Qasim Jan, Ballimaran. Courtesy Banswalhemant/Wikimedia Commons.

Ghalib's tomb near the shrine of Hazrat Nizam ud din. Courtesy Debashish Das/Wikimedia Commons.

The space between the fort and the Jama Masjid; before the Revolt (above), and after the demolitions that followed it (below). Engraving based on a sketch by Alexis Soltykoff, 1840s.

The flagstaff tower; photo by Bourne and Shepherd.

Kashmiri Gate damaged in the bombardment; photo by Felice Beato.

The British forces storming the city on 14 September 1857; a newspaper illustration from 1857, with later colouring.

Bahadur Shah surrenders to Hodson. Illustration in Charles Ball, *The History of the Indian Mutiny*, 1860.

Evidently there was a considerable swing in the numbers at the very inception of the college. What had happened to bring about these obvious changes in enrolment? The sharpest decline from 1827 to 1828, was in the number of students from Delhi in the Arabic and Persian departments. This was probably the result of a full realization of what the nature of the curriculum in this new government institution was. Those who wanted an education in Arabic or Persian did not seem all that receptive to what frequently amounted to heretical ideas of Western science. In Delhi, where good alternatives for a traditional education were to be had, the motive to join the government college became weaker.

Enrolment picked up in the following years but the managing committee discovered to their dismay 'that it is with very considerable difficulty that we can induce either the Professors to teach or the students to learn any European science through the medium of translations. Unless our constant vigilance is exerted, the books which relate to it are entirely neglected...'; on the other hand, remarkably, they found that 'a large portion of the students has evinced a desire to commence the study of the English language.' The Hindus in particular but also many Muslim students were keen to join the English class and were in fact eager to leave the Arabic and Persian department to do so.[531] That there was a definite interest in learning English was evidenced by the twenty students from Delhi out of a total of twenty-eight who joined the newly-opened English class in 1828.

According to the Local Committee, the answer lay in teaching Western knowledge through the medium of the English language, and in doing away with the uneasy mix of 'Oriental' and Western subjects. The logic used to justify this view was particularly convoluted. It was argued that by being taught the Arabic, Persian and Sanskrit texts, the students were given a grounding in a value system that came into conflict with the subsequent or simultaneous introduction of Western science. A boy who had never been taught Arabic or the Quran would not have his sensibilities offended, for instance, by the modern theory of the solar system.[532]

The college committee at this point consisted of the Resident,

Edward Colebrooke; the magistrate, Thomas Metcalfe; Charles Trevelyan and the Surgeon—initially Ludlow, but in 1828 replaced by his successor Dr Rankin. Trevelyan was the brother-in-law of Thomas Babington Macaulay, who, as the Law Member of the Governor General's Council, would in 1835 go on to write his famous 'minute on education'. Trevelyan's own future pronouncements on the subject of education in India were to become almost as well known as those of Macaulay. It is not unlikely that the seeds of these views, reflected in the later pronouncements of both Trevelyan and Macaulay, were sowed in the deliberations of the Local Committee at Delhi. A letter of the Committee to Calcutta in 1829 to a remarkable extent foreshadows Macaulay's Charter speech of 1833 and the Minute on Education of 1835, and thus deserves to be quoted at length:

> 'The natives in the pursuit of English Literature and English institutions, will cease to desire and seek independence after their former fashion, which they will forget, acquiring in its place a sort of national character, which may be denominated Anglo-Indian or more strictly speaking a direction of their thoughts and minds towards what is English, involving perhaps an ultimate improvement of their institutions on our model. But ages must elapse before the march of knowledge and wealth among them will reach this point and when it does it may well be questioned whether the two nations will not by that time be so much amalgamated that the change will be produced without any reaction taking place on the English interest, it will probably be conceded without even a struggle.'[533]

These views were of course by all accounts at complete variance with local public opinion. Quite clearly, even those that may have at this stage been keen to learn English purely with a view to brighter careers in the service of the government, did not want to mix it with the study of Western ideas that potentially conflicted with traditional religious and cultural values. Such a response was particularly evident among the Muslims. Early in the century Shah Abdul Aziz had pronounced a fatwa that sanctioned Western learning and a study of the English language, as long as it did not conflict with religious belief.[534] At the time, the government at Calcutta too took a fairly conservative view, though again, one that did not fully take into account local feeling. It reminded the Local Committee of its commitment to the nurturing of native languages and learning along with the dissemination of Western learning, but was willing to set up a separate English college in Delhi. Soon, therefore, the 'Delhi Institution' where English was taught, was set up as distinct from the 'Oriental College'. The former had Frederick Taylor, the son of J.H. Taylor, as its headmaster.[535]

36

The Government College: Early Years

Shortly after the establishment of the college, Nawab Fazl Ali Khan, the prime minister of the Nawab of Awadh, decided to make an endowment for the cause of higher education in Delhi, the city of his birth. To this end, he approached the government authorities at Delhi and expressed a desire to invest Rs 1,70,000 for this purpose in government funds. The government informed the Nawab that the interest on that sum would be inadequate for the setting up of an independent educational institution, but if he would allow, it might be added to the funds of the government college for the use of the Oriental section—i.e that part that taught the Indian languages. The Nawab agreed to this.

Subsequent events showed that the managing committee of the college were willing to be fairly unscrupulous in the pursuit of their agenda for the promotion of Western education. With more funds coming into the Oriental section from an external source, some of the government funds were withdrawn from it, and used to establish the Institution on an independent footing. In addition, some expenses of the English Institution were also charged to the fund meant for the Oriental section. For instance, the latter bore the entire burden, amounting to three hundred rupees, which was the salary of J.H. Taylor, who functioned as superintendent and secretary for both the sections. As a result, the funds available for the study of Persian and Arabic ended up being less than what they had been before the donation. Simultaneously, the managing committee consigned the Oriental section to a state of abject neglect. For the next several years none of the members of the Local Committee even seem to have visited it. Even Taylor did so only occasionally.[536]

As a result, the quality of education in the section suffered. The head, Maulvi Rashid ud din, died in 1833 after a period of illness,[537] and it is uncertain that he had been able to contribute very much to the college in any case. The results of an impromptu examination by W.H. McNaughten, Secretary to the Government of India in the Political Department, who accompanied the Governor General, Lord Bentinck, on a visit in 1831, showed that the standards in Arabic and Persian were particularly dismal.[538] Not surprisingly, the morale and level of motivation among the teachers was low. Two Arabic teachers, Mamluk Ali and Syed Mohammad, who had been in the college since its inception, applied in 1832 for jobs in the judicial service as sadr amins and muftis.[539] In reports to Calcutta in the following years, the Local Committee explained away the situation by the argument that Arabic and Persian had simply gone out of fashion and were not attracting many dedicated students any more.[540]

In the meanwhile, the English Institution seemed to be faring better. In 1834, Trevelyan, who was part of the managing committee, could point with pride to the fact that the number of students studying English had risen to three hundred. Of these, Trevelyan made special mention of two particularly distinguished alumni—Shahamat Ali and Mohan Lal 'Kashmiri', both of whom had been part of the first English class of the college and had continued their studies at the English Institution. Shahamat Ali had left at the end of 1832, when he was recruited to accompany a mission to Punjab. The requirement specifically was for a man 'who understood both English and Persian'. With the short tenure in the college, his knowledge of English was understandably not perfect, and he had read only a limited number of English books—

on history, mathematics, and geography. Nevertheless, he built on this foundation, and would spend the next several years on a number of diplomatic missions, as well as in positions within the territories of the Company. He would eventually rise to be the prime minister of Indore state.[541]

Mohan Lal was of a family, originally from Kashmir, that had risen in the service of the Mughal empire at Delhi in the eighteenth century. The family, however, had fallen on hard times, as a result of the resumption of their jagirs during the early years of the Company's rule.[542] A later family history attributed the troubles of the family to a bitter dispute with Nawab Ahmad Baksh Khan of Ferozepur Jhirka. Mohan Lal's father Budh Singh had eloped with a concubine of the Nawab, in revenge for which the Nawab made sure that Budh Singh's lands, which were distributed over Ferozepur Jhirka, Loharu and Jhajjar, were resumed. Budh Singh had a daughter by the concubine, who married a certain R. Hodges of mixed Indian and European blood, who was also in the Company's service.[543]

Mohan Lal had left the Institution a year before Shahamat Ali, at the age of nineteen, having been picked to accompany a mission to Afghanistan. He was evidently a charming young man, who won many hearts with what Trevelyan described as an 'amiable and gentle disposition, and unassuming deportment'. He was picked in 1831 to accompany Lieutenant Burnes, as Persian secretary, on a journey to Central Asia. Over the next few years, he had made a considerable name for himself, from the favourable impression he generally made on all he met during the course of his diplomatic interactions.[544]

Trevelyan attributed the success of both these young men almost entirely to the English Institution,[545] but in fact they were very much in the tradition of the earlier generation of literary-diplomatic figures, such as Khwaja Farid and Izzatullah, who had played a role in the advancement of British missions across frontiers. In fact, Mohan Lal's father, Rai Brahm Nath, alias Budh Singh, had played a very similar role when he accompanied Montstuart Elphinstone on a mission to Peshawar in 1808-09. Both

Shahamat Ali and Mohan Lal had a much stronger grounding in the traditional Persian education system than in English, which they had barely studied for three or four years. It was certainly their proficiency in Persian that made them suitable to act as mediators in the territories in which they travelled, though in the course of time their English language skills too would improve. One important thing that did make them stand out was that both would eventually publish English language accounts of their travels, and in the case of Mohan Lal, accounts that were often critical of British officials and policy. Their proficiency in English gave them the confidence and ability to address a new English-speaking public.[546]

It was not only the English language that this new generation of munshis was learning. Mohan Lal spent time in Calcutta learning the art of surveying from an expert, J. Rowe, in order to help him accurately record the geographical details of the places he would be visiting.[547] This was indeed a much more valuable skill to acquire than the knowledge that could be attained at the Institution. Another alumnus of the Institution, Azim ud din Hasan, who was being sent on a mission to the mouth of the Indus, in a letter to the government, said, 'I think it indispensably necessary to have some acquaintance with land survey. My knowledge of mathematics, like that of all the students of the Madrassah, consists in theories not reduced to practice....I hope I will be allowed to take lessons from Mr Rowe in the same way as Munshi Mohun Lal did.' His request was allowed.[548]

In the examination report of the college for 1828, the 'First Preparatory Class' included a fifteen-year-old boy, Chiman Lal, who later went to study in the Medical College at Calcutta, sometime after its establishment in 1835. He graduated from this institution with his medical degree in early 1841, and was posted as Sub-Assistant Surgeon in Delhi. The authorities had recommended the appointment on the grounds that 'as he is a native of that place and was educated there, his return to that situation after having obtained an excellent medical education with so respectable an appointment would tend to encourage other young men from the Upper Provinces to join the Medical College.'[549]

Those who had graduated from the college were also in demand in administrations of the independent states. For instance, in 1841 the successful and trusted prime minister of the Alwar state was an alumnus of the college.[550]

Though most of the particular success stories were from the English Institution, there were boys from among the early classes of the Oriental College who would make an impact on the city too. The report for the college in 1827 listed among those enrolled a nineteen-year-old Baqar Ali, in the 'Third Arabic Class'. This young man would soon join the staff of the college, but leave a few years later to join the revenue department as a *sheristadar*. He would continue on this post for sixteen years, and sometime in the mid-1850s, he would become the editor of the influential Urdu newspaper, the *Dehli Urdu Akhbar*.[551]

37

Upheaval and Reorganization

Despite the pride Trevelyan and others felt in the successes in the English Institution, there was no denying the fact that the Oriental branch of the college was lagging. Fazl Ali Khan had died in 1830, and soon after, his son-in-law and heir, Hamid Ali Khan, stepped in to intervene. In a series of letters to the government from 1835 to 1841, he questioned the running of the college and claimed that the terms of his father-in-law's endowment were not being fulfilled. He pointed out that the money that had been intended for the promotion of Arabic and Persian had not only been diverted from this purpose, but the functioning of the college and standards of teaching had not received any attention from the Local Committee. Finally, he bluntly declared, that a 'committee composed of Christians who are at heart the depressors of the Mahomedan faith cannot without a sacrifice of principle act with vigour, zeal and promptitude' in the promotion of Arabic and Persian education which was the foundation of Islamic learning. The neglect therefore was very deliberate. This last argument had been provoked by the induction of a Christian cleric, Reverend Everest, into the Local Committee, with the approval of the government at Calcutta. Hamid Ali demanded either a refund of the money of the endowment, or his own participation in the management of the Persian and Arabic section of the college.[552]

The government made naive attempts to placate Hamid Ali Khan by proposing that a marble slab be put into the building of the Oriental section recording the late Fazl Ali Khan's bequest, or even that it be renamed 'College of the Nuwab Itmad-ood-Dowla' (Itmad ud daulah was the title of Fazl Ali Khan).[553] Hamid Ali Khan, however, pointed out that these would be empty gestures. In fact, his motive was not even to have the money back but to see it utilized properly. To this end, he wanted a part in the management of the college, and power to inspect its accounts. So, to begin with, he was given the power to appoint a Shia maulvi, as per his wishes, since he and his father-in-law were Shia. Incidentally, one effect of the Fazl Ali bequest was that the Arabic class at the college was split into Shia and Sunni sections.[554]

Another crisis that had hit the college was the government's policy, newly inaugurated in 1836, of reducing the number and extent of scholarships. Before this, a high proportion of students in both sections of the college were given stipends, in keeping with indigenous practice. This was undoubtedly an important factor in such popularity as the institution enjoyed. The reduction of scholarships contributed to a sharp drop in enrolment, with the number of students nearly halving between 1835 and 1838, from a total of 415 to 211.[555] Both the Oriental and English sections were affected roughly in proportion.

The government was forced to take some action. Apart from Hamid Ali Khan's objections, a dissenting view had also been expressed from within the Local Committee. Lt Robinson had protested against the diversion of funds and the decline of the Oriental section.[556] In response, the government appointed J. Thomason, Secretary to the Government of the North-Western Provinces, as visitor to the college. Thomason came to Delhi in March 1841 and spent nine days carrying out a detailed inspection.

He found that by this time the number of students in the Arabic and Persian classes had fallen to seventy-five. Of this number too, many were perennially absent, others came for an hour or two a day and then went away to attend to paid jobs. Not surprisingly, standards of proficiency were low. Thomason found the advice and opinions of one individual particularly helpful in his assessment of the college. This was Mohammad Sadr ud din 'Azurda', who was by this time principal sadr amin, and was also a noted and respected scholar. Thomason respected Azurda's advice and many of the new appointments, such as that of Imam Baksh 'Sahbai' as the head Persian teacher, were made on his recommendation. The decision to take on Sahbai was an astute one for more than one reason. Apart from being a sound scholar, he was acceptable to Hamid Ali Khan, whose opinion held some weight. Both Azurda and Hamid Ali Khan were also made members of the managing committee of the college.[557]

The involvement of Azurda and Hamid Ali Khan was felt to be important for making the institution more acceptable to public opinion in Delhi. But ultimately, as Thomason pointed out, the elite continued to appoint private tutors to teach their children, except when an individual student would go to a particularly competent scholar to receive instruction. Hamid Ali Khan himself had appointed Sahbai in that capacity. The government college would always be seen as an institution for the education of those who could not afford a private education. Scholarships and allowances would therefore go a long way in attracting students.[558]

One major agenda of the college remained unchanged—the remodelling of 'traditional' education on the Western model. Even Thomason ultimately argued for bringing the Oriental and English sections closer, with a view to facilitating a greater influence of the latter on the former. A major step in this direction was the bringing of the two sections together under one roof in the erstwhile Residency building in 1844. This building had fallen vacant after the Resident had moved to quarters outside the city walls, into the mansion known as Ludlow Castle.[559]

The inspection and reorganization of the college (which came to be called the Delhi College after the unification of the Oriental and English branches) coincided with an organizational change at a higher level as well. Beginning in 1843, education in the North-Western Provinces was separated from the department in Bengal.[560] The separation from Bengal gave the institutions of the provinces, particularly the Delhi and Agra Colleges, the freedom for independent development, which would have far reaching consequences.

As part of the reform of the College, it was put under a new principal, Felix Boutros. A Frenchman, probably of Egyptian or Levantine origin, Boutros had tried his hand at a variety of occupations—as an indigo planter in Purnea, in the Company's Opium Department in Bengal, and in the Thuggee Department in Bihar. One of his qualifications for this new appointment seems to have been 'his intimate knowledge of European Literature and Sciences, together with a competent knowledge of the Oriental Languages'. More importantly, he had been developing his own ideas on the subject of education, which had been made public in 1841 as *An enquiry into the system of Education most likely to be generally popular in Behar and the Upper Province*.[561]

Though the Oriental and English sections were housed in the same building from 1844, a conceptual separation between the Oriental and English sections still remained. Within the English section, English language and literature was taught, in addition to the teaching of the other subjects through the medium of English. The Oriental section was made up of departments teaching three classical languages—Arabic, Persian and Sanskrit, from which the students could pick any one. Under this system, a student in the 'Arabic' class, for instance, would study Arabic but would spend a significant part of his time studying a variety of other subjects, which were taught through the medium of Urdu. The choice of this language was based largely on the fact that it was the language most widely understood. This combination of languages and curriculum ensured that the institution maintained its 'Oriental' character, which was very necessary in order to meet the conditions of the Fazl Ali bequest.

The Delhi College came to be known for this distinctive feature—the teaching of Western subjects in the vernacular. Those who wished to see vernacular tongues being used as a medium of instruction, pointed to this institution as a model. It was stated with pride that the students of the Oriental section were as far advanced in the study of Western science as their contemporaries in the English section.[562] This distinct feature of the Delhi College has also been looked on with pride by later commentators. C.F. Andrews remarked on the fact that though people were keen to acquire the new learning, Indian languages, including the old classical languages were not forgotten and continued to be popular.[563] Several writers and historians since then have remarked on the college as a rare example of the use of the vernacular in colonial higher education.[564]

What was special about Delhi that created the preconditions for the success of this experiment? Taking all factors together, it has to be concluded that the determining factor was probably the Fazl Ali endowment. By the early 1840s, when the affairs of the college were put in order, the government had accepted Hamid Ali Khan's argument that the fund could be used in the promotion of Oriental learning alone, and not diverted to the English section. This meant that teachers of Arabic, Persian and Sanskrit *had* to be employed, and a large number of scholarships for this section *had* to be given. The Oriental section would have probably been insignificant in the absence of this fund. The Westernization of the curriculum (which the majority of the management and pupils wanted for their own reasons—the pupils so they could get government jobs) had to be carried out within this framework, which explains the particular path taken by the institution. It is useful to compare it to a parallel institution, the Agra College, where the Oriental department retreated very much into the shadows of the English.[565]

38

A New Paradigm for Education

A major concern now was, how exactly to provide an enlightened Western education in an institution, a large part of which was avowedly Oriental. This task was taken in hand by Felix Boutros, the principal of the College from 1841 to 1845, and it was his ideas, articulated in his report of 1841, and in a note that he submitted to the government in 1844,[566] that laid the foundations for some of the most innovative experiments in the college. For Boutros, the theoretical starting point was the assumption that the aim of education was the benefit of Indians and the improvement of their 'intellectual and moral feelings', without offending their 'long cherished prejudices'. Moreover, he felt that more than language, the aim of this education needed to be the teaching of 'Grammar, Geography, History, Mathematics, Natural Philosophy, Moral and Intellectual Philosophy, Principles of Jurisprudence, Political Economy, and Law.' Though language by itself was not the main focus of learning, it was logical that the English language was the best way to acquire knowledge in these disciplines, because of the 'vast field it opens to the curious enquirer.'

Practically speaking, however, the study of language was necessarily a long process. Was the study of the European sciences to be postponed until the students had grasped enough of the language to be able to read the texts of those scientific books in

English? Given the limited number of years the average student was expected to spend in an institution of higher education, this was an impractical solution. To overcome this problem, Boutros suggested that while the students pursued the aim of proficiency in the English language, the study of the sciences could simultaneously be begun in the vernacular language. It was to be hoped that those who subsequently gained a fluency in English could go on to read further, more advanced, texts in that language, but those who left the institution before having mastered English, would still have received a basic grounding in Western subjects.

In this scheme set out by Boutros, there was no talk of teaching the classical languages—Arabic, Persian and Sanskrit, which he referred to at one point as 'foreign or dead'. However, these languages had to be an integral part of the education system to be implemented in the Delhi College, mainly due to the terms of the Fazl Ali endowment. These peculiar circumstances impelled Boutros to adapt his scheme somewhat. The solution was to keep the study of science and language separate. While continuing with the assumption that 'the elements of science shall usually be imparted in the vernacular language', he proposed 'the study of [classical] languages being kept distinct from that of the sciences, and having for its object the *literature* rather than the science [except as regards English] contained in those languages.'

There were two major implications of Boutros' ideas for the curriculum that was implemented within the college. One, a separation of the study of Indian classical languages from the knowledge systems that were contained in their texts. The other, the teaching of European knowledge through Indian vernaculars, i.e. the spoken language, which, in Delhi and other parts of North India, was Urdu. On the basis of these principles, teaching was begun in the Delhi College in various subjects, based on a 'European' curriculum—geography, history (including the history of India), arithmetic, geometry, natural philosophy, political economy, jurisprudence, algebra, trigonometry, conic sections, ancient history, English history, general history, principles of government, astronomy, and finally, Anglo-Indian law—civil, criminal, revenue, Muslim and Hindu.

In his report on the College for 1844, Boutros expressed satisfaction that rapid strides were being made in the direction of bringing the curriculum of the Oriental section as close as possible to that of the English section, in all but language. The success of this measure could be found in the quality of the exam answers, where the answers written by students in the Oriental section were found to be in no way inferior to those of the English section.[567]

Boutros realized that a major obstacle to be overcome in the teaching of these subjects in Urdu (which he called 'Hindoostanee'), was the lack of appropriate textbooks. He advised the government to play a proactive role in setting aside a fund for the production of such books (which he referred to as 'vernacular translations'). In the meanwhile, he set in motion a programme of translations within the college. Teachers and senior students of the English section were encouraged to take up the task of translating selected English works into Urdu. These translations were generally vetted and revised by the principal, headmaster or other competent teacher, and if found good, were printed. The translators were given six to twelve annas per printed page for their work. It was not merely books from English that were being translated, but also from Indian languages, mostly making popular Persian texts available in Urdu translation.[568]

The next step in the process was of course the teaching of these books in the College. Here there were limitations, mainly that there were not enough teachers who knew the subject matter well enough. To this, Boutros' solution was to recruit recent graduates from the college, in the belief that they knew enough to be able to pass on the knowledge they had, brushed up through their own careful study of the texts. With this in mind, Boutros appointed two alumni, Ram Chander and Ajodhya Prasad, each at a salary of fifty rupees a month, to the post of 'Scientific Teacher'. Both had completed their education in the English section, and were therefore in a position to teach from the Urdu translations while simultaneously referring to the English originals. Through this process of applying the translations in the classroom, the translations too were refined; 'the teachers noting in the course of their lessons all errors, obscure passages &c. which in their opinion required corrections...These corrections have been, or will be made in the second Edition; and as each successive Edition will be submitted to a similar process, it may be expected that the translation will become in the end free from all errors of any importance.'[569]

Given the relatively short period of time Boutros spent as principal, a remarkable level of progress was made with printing translations and some other books during his tenure. In a list submitted by him in April 1844, seventeen books had already been printed, another twenty-seven were listed as 'ready for printing' and a further fourteen as being 'under preparation'. Also remarkable was the fact that the preparation and printing of these books had so far been personally funded by Boutros. The government of the North-Western Provinces now acknowledged and encouraged Boutros' effort, by ordering the procurement of sixty-six copies of each of the books, for use in schools and colleges in the provinces. Also by 1844, a private organization, the 'Society for the Promotion of Knowledge through the medium of Vernacular translations' had come into being, with a promise of funding the project.[570]

Finally, another significant feature of the curriculum devised by Boutros in the Delhi College was the teaching of Urdu as a language, and not only its use as the medium of instruction for the Oriental department. This was an innovation, for thus far, the teaching of the commonly spoken mother tongues was not considered necessary in most systems of education. From 1843, the students of the English section at the Delhi College were taught Urdu, and were expected to understand and explain the subject matter of the non-language subjects in both English and Urdu. Urdu was also taught to all the students of Sanskrit. Within a year, 'Nagree' was also being taught, and thirty-six out of the 245 students of the English section, and six out of the 109 students in the Persian department, were studying it.[571]

Significantly, the aim of introducing the study of Urdu as a subject was declared to be to teach students to 'compose elegantly in that language, or to translate into it idiomatically.' The need for educated young men to be able to 'compose elegantly' in Urdu was definitely related to one development that had taken place within the administrative structure. This was the replacement of Persian by Urdu as the official language of correspondence and business in the North-Western Provinces in the mid-1830s. Though Urdu was the widely spoken language, proficiency in the written form could not be taken for granted. One report of 1846 pointed out that students of the Oriental section were not adept at translating texts into Urdu. Graduates of the Delhi College, many of whom aspired to jobs in the administration, would no doubt need to cultivate the writing of Urdu more formally, just as they once did with Persian.[572]

It is likely that at least one motivation behind making the students of the English section proficient in Urdu was to further the translation programme and the teaching of the sciences within the Oriental section through the medium of Urdu. The declaration that one of the aims of instruction was to enable students to 'translate idiomatically' into Urdu, is a hint in that direction. Under Boutros, the graduates and senior students of the English section had not only undertaken translation projects, the more competent of them, such as Ram Chander and Ajodhya Prasad, were also found to be the best teachers for the 'European' subjects through the medium of Urdu. A logical step from this was to ensure that these students wrote and otherwise expressed themselves well in that language.

For Boutros, the education system put in place in an institution such as the Delhi College had immense potential for social change. In his note of 1841, he had remarked, 'It is expected that the benefit of the instruction afforded in the Government Schools will not be confined to those who actually receive it in those schools, but that the latter will, by original works or translations, communicate their knowledge to their countrymen through the medium of the Vernacular language.'[573]

To this end, Boutros made another innovative suggestion in his note of 1844 towards the general education of Indian students and others. This was that the government might support the publication of 'a Hindoostanee Periodical of four quarto pages published every week...it would contain 1st News, 2nd Translations of good Editorials from Anglo Indian papers, or translations from English periodicals of articles or parts of articles of any peculiar interest to India, 3rd Original articles.' This periodical would be for circulation in schools, colleges and government offices. This, according to Boutros, would fill an important lacuna in the intellectual development of Indians, which was, a 'Knowledge of the world acquired from...the perusal of Newspapers and Periodicals.'

Having laid this crucial foundation of an innovative pedagogical system at the Delhi College, Boutros departed for Europe in 1845, for reasons of deteriorating health. Before leaving he could see the fruits of his work in the college. Concrete proof of the rising credibility of the college among the people of Delhi was the enrolment of what the college report called 'two youths of noble families'—one the brother of the Nawab of Jhajjar, and the other the son of Raja Sohan Lal, who had been the mukhtar of Akbar II. The success of the scientific education within the college was evident in the placement of one of the students, Pitamber, under the guidance of Lt Baird Smith, an army engineer, for training as a civil engineer. The cause of scientific education was furthered, when the college acquired a good collection of scientific equipment from England, for the setting up of well-equipped laboratories.[574]

39

The Translation Project, and its Limitations

Boutros was succeeded as principal by Aloys Sprenger, an Austrian, who had arrived in India in 1843 as a medical doctor in the East India Company's army. He was a very competent Oriental scholar as well, and was therefore found suitable to replace Boutros as the principal of the Delhi College in March 1845.[575] Broadly speaking, Sprenger, and James Cargill, who succeeded him in 1850, built on the foundations laid by Boutros, continuing to oversee the publishing of books in a system that coordinated the efforts of the Delhi College and the Vernacular Translation Society.

The publication programme expanded prodigiously, and over the course of just a few years, a large number of books were printed at the in-house press, the Mataba ul ulum. It is interesting to analyse the categories of books published by the Vernacular Translation Society. Within the tenure of Boutros, thirty-seven books were printed, and of these, the largest number, eleven, were on law, five were on history and political economy, six on mathematics, one each on the science of surveying, physics and natural science, and eleven were on literature and language, with an emphasis on the learning of Urdu grammar and idiom. This trend would continue in the following years, with additions on more subjects, such as medicine and geography, being made to the list.[576]

The Vernacular Translation Society, however, faced some particular challenges. The aim, when it came to producing translations, was of course to encourage their use outside the school as well. It soon realized, however, that books that were specifically aimed at increasing 'Western knowledge', such as scientific works, were not in demand among the general public, and were for most part bought by the government for use within its own institutions. The exception to this were works seen as having a practical benefit, and this was mostly to gain proficiency in an area that guaranteed employment, such as law, or Urdu language composition and translation. The latter was important because Urdu had become the language of official business. The books that sold most copies among the public were Urdu translations of popular Persian works, mostly literature, such as the Gulistan, and Alif Laila, as well as law books. It was the publication of these books that made the society's work commercially viable. For the same reason, i.e. they sold well, texts other than translations were also printed, such as works of literature, particularly poetry.[577]

The limited popular appeal of translations of scientific and other 'educational' books, was brought home not only to the Vernacular Translation Society, but to the few private presses that ventured in this direction. For instance, Karim ud din, an alumnus of the Delhi College who had been associated with the translation programme of the College as well, had set up a press too. In this press, rather idealistically named *Rifa e Am* or 'Public Welfare', Karim ud din hoped to print inexpensive copies of translations of books for the spread of knowledge among his fellow countrymen. This aim was evidently not shared by his partners, who seem to have dispossessed him of the press altogether. Karim ud din then moved to the Agra College and made valuable contributions to the translation programme there.[578]

An evaluation of the translation project came a little more than a decade after its inception, in the form of an official committee that was set up in 1854 to evaluate the books in use in schools and colleges in the North-Western Provinces. Its report, submitted in March 1855, dealt largely with the publications coming out of the Delhi College and the Vernacular Translation Society. The works listed numbered just over fifty, suggesting that not too many new works had been taken up after the thirty-seven which had been printed during the initial years. The official verdict on their quality was mostly negative. Members of the committee were unanimous that the majority of the publications were unsuitable for educational purposes, and few were considered worthy of being used in institutions even after modifications.[579]

The problem lay partly in the selection of the texts. Works such as Plutarch's *Life of Alexander* and *Life of Cicero*, were originally written for Europeans, and were unintelligible to a readership that was not familiar with the cultural context of the originals, i.e. 'Greek politics, manners, customs, mythology, and ancient geography.' A few explanations were given in the form of notes, but were completely inadequate for a subject that really demanded very extensive explanation. Experts on the committee questioned the benefit of such works for Indian students at all, much less in the form of a straight translation. The lack of familiarity with the subject was compounded by peculiarities of orthography, such as the transliteration of proper names as detached syllables, e.g. 'Oc-ta-vi-us', instead of 'Octavius'.[580]

The poor choice of original texts was also evident in the case of works such as *History of Mahommedanism*, a history of Islam. In this book, though the subject was an 'Oriental' one, the text had been translated from an indifferent European work on the subject. As such, it contained many inaccuracies, which ironically, would be immediately obvious to the Indian reader, who could be counted upon to have better knowledge from original works in Indian languages. There were other works which were deemed unsuitable for use as school textbooks, because they were on subjects too esoteric, or too specialized and detailed.

The other criticism related to the quality of the translations, which in many cases was literal and unidiomatic. In the case of scientific and technical works, often the translators were unfamiliar with technical terms that already existed in Urdu or Persian, and where they did not exist, made no attempt at formulating appropriate ones. The usual practice was to simply use the English word, and the committee was divided on this point. Though some members of the committee were in favour of the use of English technical terminology, others suggested the systematic development of a technical vocabulary based on the indigenous languages. In this respect, at least one book, *Arnott's Physics*, translated by Sheo Narain and Saroop Narain, two senior scholars, came in for praise for adopting this system successfully. Another criticism directed at scientific works was that there had been no attempt at adaptation to cultural context. For instance, the illustrative examples used in a series of works introducing mechanics, hydrostatics, etc., to beginners, included many objects that were familiar to European students but not to the Indian—'pokers, snuffers, grates, chimneys,' etc.

The sum total of these observations was that the members of the Committee were 'unanimous in their views as to the general unsuitability of the Dehli publications in their present form for educational purposes', and regretted that 'the laudable and spirited undertaking of the Delhi Society has resulted in failure.' The lesson to be learnt was that just 'because a student has an imperfect acquaintance with English, and can compose in bald Oordoo, he is not necessarily competent to the translation of a scientific work.' The committee also put their finger on the root of the problem, i.e. that students had been employed to make the translations, which were then not subjected to any rigorous revision. Often they were ignorant of the subjects they were dealing with, and imperfectly fluent in the languages they were translating from and into. There had been an undue haste in executing the project. Part of the eagerness to produce a large number of books quickly had been the result of a pecuniary motive, since students were paid per page for their translation work.

It was not just the committee appointed in 1854 that realized the inadequacy of the translations. A report by the principal of the Delhi College at the same time contained the startling revelation that few of the books had actually been used for teaching purposes in the college. Some that had been introduced, had been discontinued after just a few years. This was probably the reason why the program, begun so enthusiastically under Boutros, had lost momentum very soon.

One view that had been expressed in the committee's report was that while Urdu was suitable for introductory studies of a 'Western' education, in the long run, especially for higher education, English was the only answer. This was not a view unheard of within the Delhi College. Even a supposed 'Orientalist' like Boutros expressed satisfaction that one consequence of introducing Western subjects to the students of the Oriental section was that they were now eager to learn English. Many had begun to do so on their own initiative in their free time, and intended to try and get scholarships for the English section. The desire on the part of many students of the Oriental section to find a place in the English class is in fact a recurring motif in the reports of the college.

A large number of students were prevented from migrating from the Oriental section to the English only because they would lose their valuable scholarships, paid out of the Itmad ud daulah fund. Despite this, the number of students in the English section was consistently higher than those in the Oriental, and the proportion continually grew. So, whereas in 1843-44 there were 13 per cent more students in the English institution, a decade later that figure had risen to 72 per cent. Even within the Oriental section, as early as 1845, pupils were reported to be pursuing the study of the English language in their leisure hours. In the report of 1846, principal Sprenger reported that the popularity of English was growing. It was presumably on this ground that he and the Local Committee suggested that students of the Arabic class who had no talent for higher Mathematics, be allowed to study English instead; and the government of the North-Western Provinces agreed to this suggestion.[581] In this manner, English was introduced into the Oriental section almost through the back door.

Boutros of course had misread the situation, in that it was not really the exposure to Western knowledge that prompted the eagerness to learn English. For the vast majority of students, and certainly for their parents, the purpose of studying in the government college, and of learning English, was to get a good job, preferably in government service. A letter written to the *Dehli Urdu Akhbar* in 1841 expressed the hope that the syllabus would include the study of the language used in documents in courts of law! This was not such a far-fetched idea, as some of the earliest books translated in the college and advertised in the *Dehli Urdu Akhbar* in the same year, were works concerned with the laws administered in the Company's courts. These included The Sadar Board of Revenue's Circular No.3, William McNaughten's 'Principles of Dharmashastra', and Princeps' 'Abstract of the Civil Judicial Regulations'.[582] In the following years as well, many of the works translated into Urdu were concerned with the laws and regulations of the government.[583]

If the English section was filled with those who were interested in knowledge that would help them get good jobs, the Oriental department fell between two stools. It could not develop a robust new 'Western knowledge' curriculum based on translations, as had been hoped, nor did it sustain its 'Oriental' character by standards of other institutions of the time in Delhi. The curriculum had been reorganized so that only 'useful' subjects would be taught—arithmetic, geometry, algebra, natural philosophy, geography, political economy, history, jurisprudence. Subjects that were part of a classical education system, such as advanced Arabic syntax and logic, authorities on *fiqh* (Islamic jurisprudence) and hadis, were relegated to 'free lectures'. The teaching of Sanskrit and Hindi too was in a bad state.[584]

In Delhi, the Oriental section of the college was probably an object of contempt. The poet Hali, who joined a traditional madrasa in the 1850s, found that people in that institution were of the opinion that the students of the Delhi College were profoundly ignorant.[585] Essentially, in the field of Arabic and Persian education, the Delhi College was unable to effectively challenge the traditional institutions of education. Its own teachers, such as Imam Baksh Sahbai and Mamluk Ali, heads of the Persian and Arabic departments respectively, seem to have maintained their scholarly integrity with the traditional system, though they contributed to the translation program. On more than one occasion the principal Sprenger complained of their stubborn adherence to old ways. Another form of dissension was the teaching of students outside the framework of the college, in the traditional ustad-shagird mode. At least Mamluk Ali seems to have taught several students privately in this manner.[586]

Another sign of a lack of confidence in the institution even among some individuals closely associated with it, was in the setting up of an alternate school by Sadr ud din Azurda, who was on the managing committee of the college. Around the same time as the reorganized curriculum based on new translated texts was taking off in the early 1840s, Azurda renovated the buildings of an institution that dated from Shahjahan's time, but had fallen into disuse. This was the Dar ul Baqa, just south of the Jama Masjid. The institution was financed entirely by Azurda and closely supervised by him. The students were given stipends, and competent teachers were appointed to teach them. We unfortunately know nothing of the nature of the teaching and organization in this school, but it is likely that the curriculum was a traditional one. The Lt Governor of the North-Western Provinces at any rate felt it necessary to remind Azurda that the government college had first claim on his loyalties and time.[587]

Despite these limitations, the government college flourished in the 1840s and 1850s. The fact that graduates of the college generally succeeded in getting jobs in the government, in the Indian principalities or in private teaching, must have contributed to the popularity of the institution.[588] The restoration of scholarships was an important factor in restoring enrolment, but the introduction of fees in 1845-46 did not substantially affect the numbers. One notable feature of the statistics is the proportion of Muslims among the students. There were always fewer Muslims than Hindus in the college and the proportion steadily declined. In 1835-36 there were 201 Hindus, 158 Muslims and five Christian students. By 1854-55, there were 243 Hindus, ninety-seven Muslims and ten Christians.[589] The reason for this is not very clear. It may have been that misgivings about the college were felt more by the Muslim population, and increased as time went by.

Though most students and their parents may have been motivated by the prospect of good jobs, there were a significant few on whom the scientific teaching and experiments carried out in the college left a profound impact. Mohammad Zakaullah, who was a student in the college, and went on to become a teacher, would recall many years later of himself and his friends at the college, who 'used to go back to their homes—their minds and imaginations overflowing with startling ideas—to dream at night about the marvellous things they had seen and heard during the day.'[590]

In the attention that the Delhi College has received, it is easy to forget that it was only one of several avenues of education that were available in Delhi. A report of 1850 revealed some remarkable statistics as regards 'indigenous education'. Between 1826 and 1850, the number of 'Persian schools' within the city had increased from ninety-three to 242, and the number of 'Hindee schools' from thirty-one to thirty-seven. Moreover, the census of 1845 had listed six girls' schools as well, run by Punjabi Muslim women. There was a total of forty-six pupils in these. Admittedly, the average number of students per institution was much smaller than the Delhi College, probably less than ten, and these included primary level schools as well.[591]

Education was thriving even outside the Delhi College. In fact, those without means and without connections had a good chance of acquiring a reasonable education if they were determined. The poet, Altaf Husain 'Hali', a native of Panipat, ran away from home in 1854 at the age of seventeen because his enthusiasm for studying was not supported by his family. Arriving penniless in Delhi, he nevertheless managed to join a well-known madrasa where he got the education he wanted.[592] Another person who was to go on to become a major literary figure, Nazir Ahmad, came to Delhi as a child. Though there is some controversy about precise biographical details, he was from a poor family and consequently the time he spent studying under the learned maulvi at the Aurangabadi mosque was difficult.[593] Karim ud din, another resident of Panipat, came to Delhi and was fortunate enough to be taught by Azurda.[594]

Both Nazir Ahmad and Karim ud din eventually joined the Delhi College.

The impact of the Delhi College was limited to mainstream higher education, and in this too many alternatives existed. There were other areas of education where the impact of the colonial culture appears to have been much less evident. Teaching in a variety of professions and skills, not all associated with earning a living, continued to be based on the ustad-shagird relationship. These included medicine, calligraphy, swimming, archery, astrology, and poetry.

40

Master Ram Chander and the Advancement of Learning

To find the greater significance of the Delhi College, and its long-term impact, one has to look not in the field of translation, but of original work. One of its stars was clearly Ram Chander. Apart from his active involvement in the translation project, he produced original work in his particular field of interest—mathematics. His first and best-known book on mathematics, *A Treatise on Problems of Maxima and Minima Solved by Algebra*, was published in 1850. It sought to apply the methods of algebra, which was a field in which Indians were traditionally considered strong, to the solution of elementary problems of calculus.

The Indian mathematical tradition, from ancient times, had been based on algebra rather than geometry, as evident in the twelfth century text, *Bija Ganita*, by Bhaskara. Ram Chander sought therefore to make the new concept of calculus intelligible to Indians according to principles which they understood better, i.e. algebra rather than geometry. In a way, this project of Ram Chander's was not very distant from his commitment to the translation project, with one important difference. This was translation not so much in a linguistic sense, but in the sense of pedagogy—the practice of learning. It was based on the understanding that new concepts, imported from and grounded in a different knowledge system, could be better understood in the receiving culture if they could be adapted and made intelligible in the conceptual systems and 'language' of that culture.[595]

Ram Chander's achievement in mathematics was not the result of any particularly high quality of mathematics education he had received at the college, and much of his study of the subject was done at home through the books he managed to procure. What he owed to the college was a familiarity with the English language, not only because it gave him access to the storehouse of knowledge in that language, but because it eventually gave him access to the wider academic world. The recognition was slow to come, however,. Initial copies of the book were published in Calcutta at the author's own expense, and the work received bad reviews. Not only that, Ram Chander was 'subjected to kind rebukes from some of the best friends of native education in the North-West Provinces, for his ambition in publishing his work in *English*.' He did, however, present a number of copies of his book to the government at Calcutta, which ordered that he be rewarded with honours and money. Several copies of the book were also forwarded to England, and one of these found its way into the hands of Augustus de Morgan, Professor of Mathematics at University College, London. He was sufficiently impressed with it to have it published in 1859 in England, where it was well received.[596]

Ram Chander also spearheaded a movement, with help from some of the senior students of the Delhi College, to form 'a society for the diffusion of knowledge among our countrymen.'[597] They aimed to do this through the medium of periodical journals in Urdu. The suggestion made by Boutros for the publication of a periodical through the college had been achieved during the tenure of Sprenger, in the form of the weekly *Qiran us Sadaen*, which was founded in 1845 and issued from the college. The name of the journal was a reference to the planetary conjunction of Jupiter and Venus, and, in this context, it referred to the interaction between Eastern and Western cultures at the college. It was helmed by various teachers at the college from time to time, and contained articles of current news—much of it local, including happenings in the palace, as well as book reviews, translations of scientific and literary articles, etc.[598]

While Ram Chander contributed articles to *Qiran us Sadaen*, he soon founded two other journals, which he felt would more closely serve the aims of the society. One, *Fawaid un Nazirin*, was a fortnightly priced at four annas and started in 1846, and the other, *Muhibb e Hind* a monthly priced at one rupee, which started in September 1847. Both carried articles on science and technology, world history, natural history, social practices and beliefs, etc., most of which seem to have been contributed by the editor himself.[599] The language was a very simple Urdu, without literary flourishes.

The committee of 1854, going through issues of *Muhibb e Hind*, found that it contained 'excellent articles'.[600] The topics covered were varied, and the aim seems to have been to inform and entertain readers, but also to encourage them to question long-held views. Readers were educated about famous personalities—Demosthenes, Confucius, Shah Abbas of Iran. One article, on the principles of government in Britain, explained the idea behind the separation of powers. The January 1849 issue of the newspaper carried an article on the life of Tipu Sultan. The following issue carried an addendum to this article, which said that a certain Dr P. Roland had informed Ram Chander on reading his article, that Tipu Sultan was highly intolerant to Hindus, and on one occasion had ordered the castration of two thousand Brahmins on their refusing to accept conversion to Islam. This information Ram Chander duly passed on to the readers of the newspaper, though with the proviso that he had not found this in the histories he had consulted.

Scientific articles included those on the telescope and on astronomy, the physics of sound, light, the planet Mars, comets, the barometer, steamboats, the circulation of blood, the diving bell, the 'divisibility of matter', the work of Isaac Newton, and the relationship between the human mind and body. An article on education expressed Ram Chander's strongly held belief that the future of education in India lay in the spread of Western knowledge through the medium of the Urdu language.[601]

Ram Chander on several occasions spoke out on controversial subjects too. An article in the June 1849 issue of *Muhibb e Hind* denounced Hindu scriptures and traditions for patently unscientific explanations of the natural world. The issue of January 1850 directly took on the system of education and the tradition of learning of the Muslims of India. Ram Chander was highly critical of the 'Farsi walas'—the scholars of the Persian tradition, who according to him, had not contributed to any useful branches of knowledge, and that which they had acquired from the Greeks and the Arabs, they had obscured through their abstruse commentaries and their love for philosophy and logic.[602]

These journals proved to be less popular than Ram Chander would have hoped. *Muhibb e Hind* folded up in 1851, due to falling circulation rates—which had fallen from their highest level of 52, to 33. Though the numbers seem small, they should not be underestimated. The relatively high price meant that many would have borrowed copies rather than bought them. All the same, circulation was falling, and particularly among the Indian readers. Part of the problem may have been the esotericism of the topics dealt with. For instance, the lengthy and detailed discussion on agriculture and horticulture that occupied a major part of the total column space in *Muhibb e Hind* over a period of several months in 1849 could hardly be expected to have riveted the interest of a largely urban Delhi population. Even the other topics that featured—on scientific, political and cultural subjects, which were intended to educate the readers about modern developments in Europe, at the same time attacking all that Ram Chander saw as regressive in Indian society—were probably not entirely to the taste of the average Delhi readership.[603] There were also active fears that the arguments for science and the outspoken stance of Ram Chander against traditional learning and beliefs, was a challenge to religion. The resistance to the new learning was exemplified by no less than the future educationist Syed Ahmad Khan, who in 1848 wrote a tract refuting the Copernican understanding of the universe, that the earth revolved around the sun.[604]

The problem of popularity was one Ram Chander seems to

have been aware of. Every issue of *Muhibb e Hind* printed some Urdu poetry, frequently by the Emperor, Bahadur Shah 'Zafar'. Since there is no evidence that Ram Chander took any interest in Urdu poetry, this was clearly a marketing exercise, one which was adopted by many others, such as the *Dehli Urdu Akhbar*.[605] It was a concession to a perceived public demand, as Zafar was not only held in regard as Emperor, but was a very popular poet; his songs, ghazals and thumris were sung all over North India by *qawwals* and courtesans.[606] The reason that the *Qiran us Sadaen* lasted longer, was probably because it published more material that was of interest to the public—such as local news, including the goings-on in the palace.[607]

Fawaid un Nazirin initially did reasonably well, though the circulation fluctuated wildly. While in 1849 it was 140, it fell to 52 the year after. In 1851 its circulation again increased to 84, probably as the discontinuation of the *Muhibb e Hind* in 1851 removed a competitor. The subscribers to this periodical were usually roughly equally divided between Europeans and Indians. The relative popularity among the Indian readership was probably because of the more accessible price, of four annas a fortnight, compared to *Muhibb e Hind*. Nevertheless, there was an abrupt drop in circulation in 1852, down to 62, and it closed the following year.[608]

Its troubles were due to the fact that in the middle of 1852, its editor, Ram Chander, converted to Christianity. He was baptized in a ceremony at St James' Church on 11 July, along with another prominent citizen of Delhi—Dr Chiman Lal, who, like Ram Chander, was of the Kayastha caste, and had also been an alumnus of the college. The incident caused a sensation in the city. The newspapers reported the baptism—the *Delhi Gazette* expressing satisfaction, the *Dehli Urdu Akhbar* with studied caution.[609] Master Ram Chander agreed to take on a *pandit* who had arrived from Banaras, in a public debate on the relative merits of Hinduism and Christianity.[610] Not surprisingly both Ram Chander and Chiman Lal suffered ostracism from their community and a general unfriendliness in the city, a fact that seems to have bothered Chiman Lal in particular. A notice was published in the *Dehli Urdu Akhbar* some four months later to the effect that Dr Chiman Lal, who had for thirteen years been treating individuals not in government service free of charge, and even making house calls, would now do so only upon payment of his usual fee, authorized by the government, of four rupees per consultation.[611] On another occasion he also declared that he thought it unfair that he had been cast out by the Kayasthas despite the fact that 'though he had professed the Christian faith still he had not eaten with any of the Europeans'.[612]

Ram Chander's move came as a surprise to those who knew him. He had thus far been a steadfast rationalist, a strong critic of all religions, which he charged with promoting irrational beliefs and practices. He himself claimed that his decision came after he had studied the religious books of Hindus and Muslims, along with the Bible, and had thereupon been convinced of the truth of the latter. Be that as it may, his acceptance of Christianity seemed to justify every fear of those who saw the onward march of Western learning as the thin edge of the wedge that would lead to a belief in the Western religion, i.e. Christianity. Enrolment at the Delhi College dropped, though it would soon pick up again.[613]

41

Print and Journalism

The books and journals issuing from the Delhi College were made possible by the growing use of newly popularized lithographic print technology, and its use was not limited to the college. Islamic reformers of the 1820s first used print to spread their teachings[614] and this, combined with the increasing use of Urdu, both in original writing and in the translations of religious and other texts, had important implications for the way knowledge was transmitted. Printed books, though still expensive, were more readily available than manuscripts, and when in Urdu, could be understood by a larger public. In theory at least this gave an individual much greater freedom to explore a text on his own, without the mediation of a teacher. While we have little evidence of whether and how exactly this had an impact on indigenous education in the first half of the nineteenth century, there were some who had begun to see a change. Translations, whether of religious works or academic texts, according to them had one drawback. Syed Ahmad Khan regretted that the tradition of discipleship had been eroded in his time, as people trusted in their own imperfect abilities, and based on their study of translated texts, had come to consider themselves experts.[615]

The print revolution, however, was an irreversible process, and particularly by the 1840s and 50s, there was a proliferation of printing presses churning out all manner of publications from divans (collections of poetry by individual poets), tazkiras, to works of literature like Mir Amman's *Bagh o Bahar*, and the *Shahnama* in Urdu verse, various literary commentaries, an Urdu translation of the history titled *Sair ul Mutakherin*, dictionaries, translations of the Quran, etc. Some were clearly aimed at students—such as the book which was advertised in the *Dehli Urdu Akhbar* in May 1853 as being a work of prose and poetry in simple and idiomatic Urdu, suitable for students.[616]

By 1846 there were said to be some six or seven presses in Delhi,[617] and by the mid-1850s there were so many that according to one writer, it was difficult to count them.[618] More seriously, competition between them was causing a crisis in the industry. Even an established press like that of the Mataba ul ulum, attached to the Delhi College, went through a difficult time when the manager complained that business was being ruined by cut-throat competition from newly sprung presses that were churning out substandard books cheaply. Many of the shareholders of the press had sold out their shares, some at a loss. The Mataba ul ulum was lucky to be rescued by the surviving shareholders who also replaced the manager.[619] Karim ud din's Rifa e Am press had already shut down by then. The evidence we have is inadequate for a definite conclusion, but it is worth speculating whether the problems both these presses faced was a result of their orientation towards translations of 'useful knowledge' for which there may not have been as much of a demand as they had hoped.

Often proprietors of presses took measures to try and ensure beforehand that their books would sell. This was done through advance subscriptions. The Mataba Sultani published Ghalib's Urdu divan in 1841, but the publication of the Persian divan and collection of Persian letters was held up for a while as it was dependent on the receipt of a sufficient number of subscriptions.[620] Incidentally, this also suggests that even in the case of a writer and poet as renowned as Ghalib, Urdu works were clearly more in demand than Persian ones. Similarly, in 1841, an advertisement was carried in the *Dehli Urdu Akhbar*, for an almanac, costing a rupee for those subscribing in advance, and a rupee and a half for later buyers. It was later decided not to publish the almanac because not enough subscriptions had been received.[621]

The market for books was quite limited, and partly the reason was that they were still relatively expensive. Many more people read books than actually bought them. For instance, there was a flourishing business in book lending. There were people who loaned books out on a charge for others to read. Ghalib relied heavily on this system, and is said never to have bought a book.[622]

One of the results of the proliferation of printing was the appearance in the 1830s of the first modern newspapers. The first printed newspaper in Delhi was an English one—the *Delhi Gazette*, established in 1833. As was to be expected from an English language newspaper, it had a primarily British readership. The first Persian newspapers published in Calcutta had a reasonable circulation in Delhi, and then very soon Urdu and Persian newspapers were started in Delhi. While the use of print technology was a new development, the concept of the newspaper was not a new one in India. There had long been a variety of handwritten Persian newspapers, akhbars, fairly widely circulated through North India. Most had been written with a view to gathering information, particularly news of developments in important centres of political power or economic influence. The client base was that of political and business patrons, who were likely to be affected by decisions and developments emanating from such centres. In Delhi, for instance, many of the rulers of neighbouring principalities stationed news writers at the Mughal court, as well as at the office of the Resident, to gather information which might be of interest or use to them.[623]

Printed newspapers had rather modest circulations in Delhi, with one of the more successful ones, *Dehli Urdu Akhbar*, never exceeding eighty.[624] One of the problems was undoubtedly the expense. The weekly *Dehli Urdu Akhbar* was priced at two rupees for a month's issues; while those subscribing for six months paid eleven rupees, and those for the year, twenty rupees. The practice of subscribing to and reading a newspaper was slow to catch on even among the educated elite. In the 1830s Ghalib was unsuccessful in persuading his wealthy friends to subscribe to a newspaper published by a friend in Calcutta—*Aina e Sikandar*. Ghalib blamed this lack of interest on the low journalistic standards of some newspapers, and as an example he mentioned a rival Calcutta newspaper, the *Jam e Jamshed*, which had made it a habit to print news that could not be relied upon.[625]

The reach of these limited numbers, however, should not be underestimated. Apart from the fact that a single copy would often be shared among a number of families, there were other modes of circulation, even among people who could not read. For instance, there were people like Chunni Lal, who wrote a daily paper which, he said, 'used to contain articles on all subjects of general interest and all information that I could glean from printed papers....I wrote it daily, and took the manuscript round and read it to my subscribers'. This practice, which had been reported in the first decade of the century, had survived till 1857.[626]

The content of the printed newspapers was in some respects very close to the pattern of the handwritten ones. There was news from the Emperor's court as well as that of the Resident, and important government orders emanating from Calcutta or Agra. One remarkable feature was the amount of column space, usually at least half of the total paper, that was devoted to news from outside Delhi. For example, just one fairly typical issue of the *Dehli Urdu Akhbar* carried news from Afghanistan, Herat, Peshawar, Ludhiana, Jodhpur, Hugli, France, Gwalior, Lucknow, Berar, Bharatpur, Russia, Agra, and Nagpur![627] This had been a typical feature of the older akhbars as well.

There were new elements too, modelled more closely on the English language newspapers. There were advertisements, including those for books published by the press that published the newspaper, and notices of sales and auctions. There were also government advertisements—orders, circulars and gazette notifications. An advertisement of 2 May 1841, called for applications for three posts of teachers of the Urdu language to the Delhi College. Finally, of course, local news, including crime, weather reports, letters to the editor, were included.[628]

It was not just new technology that characterized the newspapers, but a growing consciousness of the role of a journalist as fulfilling an important social responsibility that was beyond the profit made by the newspaper. The most well-articulated stance in this regard was that of the *Dehli Urdu Akhbar*. The newspaper changed hands frequently and in 1853, came into the hands of Mohammad Baqar. Mohammad Baqar was an alumnus of the Delhi College, and had taught for a while at the college too, then held a government job for a number of years. He came to be associated with the *Dehli Urdu Akhbar* in 1853, when he purchased the press that published the newspaper. From then on, Mohammad Baqar featured on the paper as its *muhtamim* (manager) and Mohammad Husain 'Azad', his son, as 'printer and publisher'.[629]

The first issue after this takeover also featured an editorial which explained the idea of journalistic responsibility:

> 'The main object of producing and publishing a newspaper… is the teaching and preaching of subjects, which are useful for the human beings and the common welfare. The intention is that the common people should imbibe virtues and shun vices. They should feel ashamed of their bad conduct when they read the newspaper and as a result fight to give it up. Therefore, the manager of the newspaper should first himself strive for laudable manners and agreeable qualities. If he wants to teach something to the common people, he should practice it himself. As far as possible, therefore, he should acquire knowledge of the arts and sciences, and ponder over questions of morality…and never indulge in satire and foolish prater. This should also be the attitude he should encourage in his correspondents….As far as possible, the manager of a newspaper should investigate whether the reports of the correspondents are true or false. Otherwise, the standard of the paper will be brought down and it will lose its reputation. The readers will then begin to cast doubts even on the true news.'[630]

The editorial went on to praise the British for the introduction of the printing press, which had made newspapers flourish in India. Ram Chander too praised the advent of the modern newspaper.

The wonders of Western science, technology and learning, he believed, were not the only things to be learnt from the British. In a newspaper article in 1847, he commented:

> 'Besides several good and useful principles in vogue in England, the one deserving special mention is the freedom of speech and publication. And if one disagrees with a particular royal decree one can without invoking any punishment publish his views in a newspaper giving reasons for disagreement. In such a situation one may hold opinions contrary to that of the king and the ministers.'[631]

In fact, the Delhi newspapers were not at all hesitant to criticize the government either. By the second quarter of the nineteenth century the Indian language newspapers had become an important forum for the discussion of various government policies. The *Dehli Urdu Akhbar* was one of these, and its pages reflected the opinions of the reading public of Delhi. Typically, government employment, taxation, and law and order were frequently topics of discussion. In 1840, a letter from a writer in Agra who complained that he had lost his government job simply because a new collector wanted to appoint his own nominee, prompted the editor to comment on the service conditions of Indians in government service. Poor service conditions, he said, were often to blame for the bribe-taking and general lack of probity that Indian functionaries were accused of. It was pointed out that if Indians enjoyed the same salaries as the English and protection against arbitrary dismissals, they would display the same zeal and honesty which was attributed to the latter.[632]

The editor of the *Dehli Urdu Akhbar* saw the newspaper as a means of putting public opinion across to the government when the latter's policies were unpopular. The increase in *chowkidari* tax and its rigorous realization in 1841 led the newspaper to come out in strong criticism. It alleged that the functionaries of the bakshi responsible for collecting the tax were going to the extent of seizing personal belongings of the poor who had been unable to pay the tax. It warned that in the context of unemployment and high prices, the implementation of this high tax would ruin more than half the city and crime rates would rise. Pointing out that the consent of the people was essential for a policy that affected them, it expressed hope that the government would not wish to force anything on the people.[633] Criticism of the government's failure to fix prices of grain in times of scarcity was also voiced in the newspaper on more than one occasion. It also repeatedly criticized the police, for instance in its failure to check crime.[634]

The *Dehli Urdu Akhbar* did not simply criticize. It was quick to give praise to the government where it was due. In the early 1840s it praised the police arrangements during the major festivals, and the consequent avoidance of the anticipated disturbances—such as the disputes between Shias and Sunnis during Moharram. It also praised the success of the kotwal in solving crimes.[635] In late 1840 it lauded the attempts of the magistrate to involve the public in police arrangements. A proclamation had been issued by the magistrate's office saying that the people were called upon to nominate one person per thana to convey their collective complaints to the administration. Action would be taken against local thanadars based on enquiries into such complaints, and if found to be justified the erring thanadar could be transferred or dismissed. The newspaper went further to praise the system of Justices of Peace in Bombay and Surat. It lamented the lack of public-mindedness in the people of the city, who would not see beyond narrow personal interests, which precluded the institution of such a system in Delhi.[636]

Finally, newspapers were also becoming a forum for the discussion of religious as well as social issues. One subject that was taken up in the *Dehli Urdu Akhbar* in 1841 was that of widow remarriage among Hindus. Articles in the newspaper as well as letters to the editor discussed the pros and cons of the practice. One of the letters expressed the opinion that this was a matter of faith for Hindus for whom such marriages were prohibited, and that these were topics which should not be discussed in the newspapers at all, but should be confined to purely religious forums.[637]

Another newspaper, the *Qiran us Sadaen*, envisaged an active government role in social change, suggesting that the magistrate and other functionaries consult with the elite of the city to stop the practice of wasteful expenditure during weddings.[638]

42

The Changing World of Poetry

Print technology was also having an impact on an important area of intellectual and cultural life—literature, particularly poetry. In the age of print, a poet was closer to a wider audience than he had ever been before. Around the late 1830s or early 1840s newspapers had begun to carry the latest poetry of well-known poets to readers across the country.[639] About the same time, divans and tazkiras had begun to be printed, making them available in a reasonably large volume for the first time. Ghalib's works, for instance, started being published in the early 1840s. Even before this of course there was a demand for his verse and letters, and Ghalib himself had obliged friends and patrons by sending them manuscript copies made by a paid scribe, but such copies were necessarily expensive to produce and hence made in smaller numbers. With the advent of print, the use of a scribe became much less common. Around 1850 or so the Nawab of Banda requested Ghalib for copies of his works. Ghalib no longer offered to have them written out, but instead promised to institute a search for printed copies, which had by this time become hard to find.[640]

Printing also brought with it a new set of problems. In this era before copyright, poets were often faced with a lack of control over how their works would be disseminated. Printing magnified this problem. When Ahsanullah Khan asked Momin for a copy of his poetry, it was not for a purely personal enjoyment, but with the intention of publishing it. Momin, prevented by politeness from refusing outright, put forward elaborate excuses, saying that he never really wrote down his own poetry, that which had been written down by others had been misplaced, and that he was not really writing any more.[641] Ghalib found himself in a similar position. His friends decided to publish collections of his letters, because of their literary merit, but he was not happy about it. Eventually, he was not able to prevent the publication.[642]

One of the most innovative uses of print in relation to poetry was made in 1845, by Karim ud din, the alumnus of Delhi College who had gone into the publishing business. Karim ud din was trying to make a success of his newly acquired printing press, and hit upon the idea that poetry was a safe avenue that could ensure sales of any newspaper or book. He decided to organize a series of mushairas—at a frequency of two a month—and decided that the verses recited at them would be published at similar intervals by his press. The result would be a kind of serial tazkira.

He realized that he was a bit of an upstart in the field, a young man who was neither a noble patron, nor a poet himself. So he sought out and succeeded in enlisting the patronage and active help of Zain ul abidin Khan 'Arif', a close relative of Ghalib by marriage, and definitely among the elite of the city. At least some sessions of the mushaira were also graced by the presence of Imam Baksh 'Sahbai', and verses sent by the prince, Mirza Fakhr ud din, were read out. The majority of the poets, however, were not particularly well known. Ghalib, Zauq, and Momin stayed away. Even otherwise, the flavour of the mushaira was rather different from the descriptions we have of earlier mushairas, as fairly intimate gatherings where each individual was known, and his style and verse was familiar to others, who would be ready to comment on his latest offerings. In Karim ud din's mushairas, verses were recited by people whom later Karim ud din himself could not recall. There were some who participated in the mushaira by post, and their verses were included in the paper that was printed. The mushaira as an assembly of poets where verses were first aired in public had in fact been appropriated in this case by the medium of the newspaper. In any event the project was aborted after a few months due to Karim ud din's problems with the management of the press.[643]

Interestingly, participation by large numbers of poets in mushairas was a feature of the later mushairas held in the Red Fort too. In Ghalib's description of a mushaira in the palace, which was probably held around 1852, the venue was packed and people had to sit cheek by jowl. The royal mushairas were evidently no longer exclusive affairs as they used to be, and now had to be held in the spacious Diwan e Am.[644]

The medium of print—whether it was used to print larger numbers and copies of divans and tazkiras, or to publish poetry in the newer periodical journals, or special issues like Karim ud din's fortnightly series—played an important role in popularizing poetry, and even democratizing it. This broadening of the base of poetry is very evident in some of the later tazkiras as well. One of the last to be written before 1857, was that of Qadir Baksh 'Sabir' a poet and a member of the royal family. He decided to base his tazkira of 1855 exclusively on more or less contemporary poets, and that too focusing primarily on those of Delhi. He listed as many as 540. At least fifty were from the royal family alone.[645]

Sabir's tazkira had another telling characteristic. It began with a long introduction, and an important part of this was the discussion on theoretical aspects of poetry—an analysis of correct and incorrect language, different genres of poetry, rules of metre and rhyme, etc. Sabir also told his readers the purpose behind this exercise, which was to provide guidance to budding poets. Clearly, this was an attempt at least to supplement if not entirely replace the personal guidance of the ustad. In fact Sabir himself mentioned in his tazkira some poets who did not have ustads.[646]

If the centrality of the ustad-shagird relationship to the practice of poetry had diminished, even where it had survived, its nature had changed in some respects. Long-distance master-pupil relationships were now common. This is attested to by Ghalib's later years, when many shagirds scattered around the country sent him their poetry by post. Many of these relationships had been initiated through letters alone. Finally, Ghalib was so burdened with letters and poetry sent to him for correction that he actually got a notice published in a newspaper in 1867 asking people to excuse him from replying to each.[647] These long-distance relationships are quite likely to have been a very diluted form of the traditional ustad-shagird relationship, the personal day-to-day instruction received by a novice from a master.

It has been speculated that Sabir's tazkira may have been ghostwritten by Imam Baksh Sahbai, who was not only a renowned poet and scholar, but taught at the Delhi College. This puts a very different complexion to this work, tying it to developments that were taking place within the College. Sahbai himself had written a book in 1844, called *Intikhab e Davavin,* commissioned by the principal, Boutros, as a textbook for the college. The book was an anthology of Urdu poetry, and at first glance it fell somewhere between the traditional bayaz, which was an informal and completely personal selection of poetry from diverse sources, and the tazkira, which also contained short biographical notes. But Sahbai's work sought to go further, to educate rather than just inform and entertain. To this end, it had an introduction which included some account of various genres of poetry. The anthology was arranged chronologically, to enable an analysis of trends in the development of Urdu poetry.[648]

Karim ud din had also written a tazkira that was produced under the auspices of the Delhi College. It claimed to be a translation, jointly authored by F. Fallon, of the French Indologist Garcin de Tassy's history of Urdu. As it happened, Karim ud din's original contribution to the work was considerable, but the connection with Western scholarship is undeniable, particularly in its attempt to arrange the poets in different categories chronologically, thereby analysing the development of Urdu poetry. These developments were taking place at the same time as the college was introducing a study of the Urdu language to those who already knew it as a mother tongue. Traditionally, people had imbibed a taste for Urdu poetry because they grew up surrounded by it, and those who became poets learnt its intricacies through personal instruction from a master. Now, they were being encouraged to see it as an academic subject, to be analysed critically and historically. Some attempt was also made to bring the practice of poetry into the Delhi College, when a series of mushairas was started at the college under the initiative of Faiz 'Parsa', a mathematics teacher.[649]

On the whole, however, poetry remained in the world outside the College, and here too, important changes were taking place. For one, it appears that by the mid to late 1840s the mushaira had declined in Delhi. Shah Nasir had gone away to the Deccan where he died in 1838, and Nawab Mustafa Khan 'Shefta' too had shifted residence from Delhi by the mid-1840s, and so, the mushairas that had been held in their homes necessarily ended. The Delhi College mushairas too did not last long. No tazkira, and they are our major source of information for mushairas, mentions mushairas taking place anywhere other than the fort from the late 1840s onwards. Even in Ghalib's letters, our other major source of information for the period, after about 1843 there is no mention of his attending any mushairas except at the palace.[650]

By the early 1850s we have more positive evidence about the decline of the mushaira. 'Zahir' Dehlvi, who wrote his memoirs much later, tells us that he attended his first mushaira around 1849. He then writes, 'After this there were one or two other mushairas in the city, but I did not attend those.'[651] In 1854 Ghalib wrote to a friend saying unequivocally that there were no longer any mushairas in the city. The people of the palace got together from time to time and held gatherings, but Ghalib said in so many words that these were hardly of any significance. His own interest in them was minimal. He sometimes attended, and that too probably because of his connection to the Emperor, and at other times stayed away.[652] In these later mushairas there is also no reference to the kind of discussions and disputations that had been a hallmark of the earlier mushairas. Certainly, Ghalib's descriptions of them suggest a fairly tame recitation of poetry by one poet after another, where he excused himself from time to time and stepped out just to relieve the tedium.[653]

43

New Worlds in Language

The new print culture was also beginning to have an impact on the evolution of language. Urdu was, even till the mid-nineteenth century, very much an evolving language. In spellings, for instance, in the pre-print or early print era, there was a fair amount of laxity, i.e. a variety of different ways of spelling the same word were used and considered equally acceptable. Ghalib's letters are characteristic of this transition period. While on the one hand he stressed the importance of correct spelling in letters to his shagirds, his own writing is not entirely consistent and he also often used spellings that would not be recognizable today.[654] A process of standardization was, however, underway, helped along at quite a fast pace by the widespread use of the printing press and the relatively high volume of books and tracts this made possible.

There was also a growing interest in the study of the Urdu language, not only within colonial institutions such as the Delhi College, and the Fort William College earlier in the century, but also outside them. For instance, Ghalib, who was a particularly influential literary figure of the period, also from time to time expressed his views on what good Urdu was and where one was to look for reliable standards for the language.

One very important area for debate was that of vocabulary. Urdu tended to include a more or less large number of 'foreign', mostly Persian, words, on its essential base of Khari Boli. The language in literary usage could contain an admixture of words from different sources in varying proportion, depending upon the personal inclinations of the author. The question of vocabulary eventually turned on personal taste. Ghalib's own inclination often took him in the direction of a rather Persianized style. In his Urdu prose he often used Persian verb forms and grammatical structures.[655] In his poetry, he used a vocabulary that was disproportionately rich in Persian words. But the language could go in a diametrically opposite direction and still technically be Urdu. For instance, Inshaallah Khan 'Insha' had written *Rani Ketaki ki Kahani* in 1803 as a linguistic exercise, in Urdu, but using no Persian or Arabic words.[656]

On the whole, the trend was towards the increasing use of a simple everyday Urdu, free of too many Persian words. One reason for this was that an education in Persian was slowly getting rarer, even among the cultural elite. One group that was particularly affected was the royal family. Any high degree of formal learning was unusual within the palace. Partly, this was a result of lack of opportunity and means. For the lesser salateen, many of whom subsisted on very meagre allowances, the only chance of an education was being allowed to participate at the fringes during lessons organized for others. Moreover, for those who were never expected to turn their education to a means of earning a living, learning depended largely on individual inclination. While Zafar was reasonably well educated, his younger brother Jahangir was apparently unable to read and write Persian.[657]

It is likely that the vast majority of the salateen might have had a basic sort of education, but not one that extended to any great knowledge of Persian. In this context, the taste for Urdu as a vehicle for creative expression, as opposed to Persian, becomes quite understandable, and particularly the inclination was towards a form of Urdu free of too many unfamiliar foreign words. Sabir, who was a poet and one of the salateen, wrote about how he came to choose Urdu over Persian for writing poetry. He attributed it to the advice of sensible friends, who pointed out that Persian 'was the stock in trade of a foreigner's shop and the merchandise of an alien's trade'. To attain proficiency in it needed a very long time. A simple and idiomatic Urdu on the other hand could put Persian to shame, and it was a language that was his own.[658]

Thus, there were good practical reasons favouring the use of Urdu over Persian, and encouraging a polishing of the language so it could become an appropriate medium for poetry and prose. As far as the Mughals went, these factors had probably been in operation even in the eighteenth century, coinciding with the decline in the fortunes of the royal family. Furthermore, even after political influence had faded away, the royal family continued to influence culture and tastes in poetry and literature. Observers in the last quarter of the eighteenth century noticed that the taste for Persian poetry had to a significant extent been superseded by Urdu poetry.[659] This trend continued in the nineteenth century. Bahadur Shah was a poet himself and a patron of poets. Regular mushairas were organized in the palace, and in keeping with the prevailing taste, he encouraged poets, particularly his current ustad (for most of his reign Zauq, followed after Zauq's death in 1854 by Ghalib) to recite primarily in Urdu. Ghalib thus wrote much of his superlative Urdu poetry at the instance of the Emperor.[660]

Outside the fort, too, the virtues of a simple Urdu that could be understood by those who did not know Persian, were being appreciated by the literate public. This trend was further encouraged by an important change in government policy. A decision of the government in 1837 had replaced Persian in the lower rungs of the administration with local languages, which, in the North-Western Provinces, meant Urdu. Now, those seeking government employment did not need to know Persian. Further, it was understood that the government promoted the use of 'simple' Urdu, the definition of which becomes clear in an advertisement that appeared in 1840 in the *Dehli Urdu Akhbar*. This was for an Urdu translation of a circular of the Sadar Board of Revenue, and it specifically mentioned that the work was in simple, easy to understand language, and that Persian and Arabic words had been used only when a 'Hindi' equivalent of the English word could not be found.[661]

Even for Ghalib, who was quite comfortable in Persian, the main benefit of Urdu prose was the informality of an everyday conversational style that could be adopted through its medium. Later in life, in a letter to the publisher Naval Kishore in 1860, he confessed that he could not be bothered to make the effort to write his letters in Persian any more. When he had something to say to his friends he pretended he was speaking to them face to face and wrote in simple Urdu. In Urdu in any case it was not customary to use flowery language and to show off.[662]

Thus, Urdu was seen as an easy, convenient alternative to Persian. It did not demand the effort required in acquiring Persian and then using it effectively. Yet, at least in a literary milieu, a certain amount of exclusivity could be maintained by limiting the idiom, vocabulary and pronunciation to the prevailing usage among a narrow class of elite. In this manner Urdu could be used as well as Persian to establish one's status. For instance, for the inhabitants of the fort, language was an important marker of identity. Great emphasis was laid on teaching children correct pronunciation, and they were made to practise on a large variety of tongue-twisters and sayings that were supposed to improve their diction. The language of the fort was also somewhat different from that of the city, for instance, the children of the palace used a more refined 'tum' instead of the 'tu' more common outside the walls of the fort.[663]

Despite all this, there was an underlying sense that Persian had greater cachet, so to speak. Imam Baksh 'Sahbai', Mustafa Khan 'Shefta', and even Ghalib, wrote more in Persian and were more proud of their Persian poetry. This was a view that was even internalized by Sabir to an extent. He wrote of a certain poet, Maulvi Abdullah Khan 'Alavi', that though it was beneath the dignity of a man of his abilities to make any effort in Rekhta, (another name for Urdu, particularly in the context of poetry), he did occasionally say a few couplets.[664]

In Ghalib's opinion too, at times the sheer ease of composition in simple Urdu was almost a defect. When asked by Henry Stuart Reid (Visitor General of Schools in the North-Western Provinces) to produce a sample of his Urdu prose, Ghalib was very reluctant to do so. He complained to a friend—'How can I show my brilliance in Urdu? Where is the scope of embellishment of style in this language? At most my Urdu will be more polished than that of others.'[665]

In the Persian-Urdu equation, another factor that had been introduced in the nineteenth century was English. In Ghalib's opinion the beginning of the influence of English coincided exactly with the advent of British rule—from about 1760 in Bengal and forty years later in the North-Western Provinces. Ghalib's letters, which incidentally reveal an influence of English letter-writing practice in the inscription of the date on each letter and the use of paragraphs, contain a fair sprinkling of English words. These often had modified pronunciations—some of which persist even today in the Urdu language. As expected, most of these were related to concepts for which exact words did not exist in Urdu, such as—registered letter (*rajistari*), secretary (*sakartar*), barrack (*barak*), and stamp (*astamp*). There were others for which an Urdu word could more easily have been substituted—such as box (*baks*), report (*riport*), deputy (*dipti*), and number (*lambar*, such as of a newspaper). Ghalib often used Urdu words creatively to describe new concepts—*tar barqi* (telegraph), *aine ki tasvir* (photograph), *jarnaili bandobast* (martial law), *hakim e akbar* (Governor General), *bunk ghar* (bank).[666] The words in the last category have of course fallen completely out of use and we are in fact not sure how general was their usage even in Ghalib's time. They do represent an alternative scheme of translating imported concepts into an indigenous language, one that maybe did not survive due to a lack of official patronage.

English and Anglo-Indian words and idioms were used by Ghalib often in a humorous context, as when he spoke of himself, his wife and their adopted sons as '*sahab aur mem aur baba log*'. In fact such words had also by now entered Urdu poetry, again in humourous situations. Imam Baksh 'Nasikh' thus wrote about the 'miss' and '*mem sahib*'. Ghalib encouraged his disciples to use words like *kapi* (copy) and *chapi* (chappie?), saying that in these times the use of English words in poetry was valid.[667]

On the whole, however, even among the educated elite, knowledge of English was very limited. Hindu Rao probably could not say more than the 'how do you do' he sought to impress Fanny Parks with.[668] Furthermore, it was one thing to use stray English words in conversation and poetry, and quite another to make it the primary medium of communication in important matters. And yet, though that level of knowledge of the language was very rare in Delhi, it was increasingly felt that a petition to the government, particularly to Calcutta, might carry more weight if it were written in English. Ghalib by 1830 had decided that it was a good strategy to send such petitions in English.[669] Some members of the royal family had also by now taken to having all the letters which they addressed to the government in Calcutta, translated into English.[670] In 1829, Mirza Salim decided to take one step further, to learn the English language himself, for which he engaged the Surgeon, Dr Rankin, to instruct him.[671]

The suspicion that English was taken more seriously in government departments was in fact not without foundation. In 1830, W.B. Martin, the Resident, had announced that from now on, he would conduct official work in English.[672] By 1833, intimation was received from Calcutta by those who routinely corresponded with the government there (i.e primarily rulers of the principalities under British suzerainty) that the Governor General wished that in future such correspondence would be carried out in English rather than Persian. This caused some amount of disquiet among those affected. The Nawabs of Jhajjar and Ferozepur who were connected to the Delhi Agency, pointed out that neither they nor any of their trusted employees were familiar with that language. While they could always locate a person who could make translations, an unreasonable degree of dependence would have to be placed on the integrity and competence of this person. So, since they were eager to please the Governor General they would fall in with his wishes, but would take the precaution of enclosing the Persian version with each English letter.[673] The Raja of Alwar, Vinay Singh, expressed the same sentiments, adding, 'Persian is a language which is in use from of old among the people of Hindoostan, and every business is transacted in this country in that language which seems to give full confidence to the people of this quarter.'[674] Bahadur Shah, while heir apparent and then again as Emperor, regularly wrote his letters to the higher government authorities in English, though probably always with an attached Persian letter.[675]

One major pitfall in the use of English was that the potential correspondent was forced to more or less implicitly trust the translator. Since most such letters were on subjects of great importance to their senders—usually petitions for the redressal of grievances—such trust did not come easily. Those in the upper echelons, such as rulers of principalities and the Emperor himself, employed clerks proficient in English, usually of European or Eurasian descent.[676] Others went to great trouble to find a trustworthy translator as and when required. In 1858, when Ghalib learnt that a publisher friend in Agra, Shiv Narain 'Aram', knew English, he was very pleased, saying that when next he had to have a letter written in English he would send the Urdu version to Agra where Aram could translate it and send it back.[677]

The use of English in correspondence and other official business was a potential source of erosion of confidence in the working of the state. Language was an important source of distrust in the highly charged Fraser murder trial. The representatives of Shams ud din Khan accused the magistrate of altering the statements of the witnesses while writing them down in English.[678]

Language was in fact seen as a significant divide between the rulers and the ruled. A firsthand familiarity with the local language of business or of ordinary conversation could not be taken for granted, even in old India hands. Ochterlony, the epitome of the 'white Mughal' did not understand Persian, the language which in his time was exclusively used in official correspondence with Indians.[679] Yet Indians seem to have valued a familiarity with their language among their rulers. Apparently, one important quality of a very popular judge, Gubbins, was that he knew enough Persian to be able to write letters in it himself and that his Urdu was excellent.[680]

Too often, when members of the ruling race took the trouble to learn Indian languages at all, it was, in the eyes of their educated Indian subjects at least, at a superficial level. There is an interesting story, recounted by Mohammad Husain Azad in a much later work, of a chance encounter between his ustad Zauq, and an English scholar. The Englishman proudly asserts that he has learnt Arabic, Persian and Urdu since he came to India, and is contemptuous of Zauq's ignorance of English. For all his arrogance, however, he speaks all the while in ungrammatical Urdu, which, the story suggests, is the typical English approach.[681]

The story is no doubt apocryphal and its significance is complex. The moral victory in the story lies with Zauq who says to himself that this man may claim to know three Indian languages but his proficiency in them is contemptible. Yet, even a person of Zauq's generation could see that the inequality of the colonial relationship was manifest in the sphere of language too. The Englishman had the tools, if he so wished, to learn many Indian languages. But ultimately, even a lack of such knowledge did not matter much, because the English could call upon translators where needed and even decide to use their own language for higher administration. It was the Indian elite who felt inadequate, because clearly English did have a privileged position. That the excellence of their command over their own language was one to which only an exceptional foreigner could aspire, was small consolation.

44

Questioning the Heritage of the Literary Tradition

It was not only language that was the subject of discussion and questioning. In the field of literature, content was becoming a contentious issue. For instance, contemporary tazkiras suggest that a more puritanical stance had set in. Certainly by the second quarter of the nineteenth century, authors of these tazkiras were adopting a slightly disapproving tone with regard to what was considered indecent language or themes. For instance, in his tazkira, Shefta dismissed the well-known poet 'Nazir' Akbarabadi entirely on the ground that his poetry was vulgar. Shefta's allusion was probably to the sexuality and particularly the homoeroticism in Nazir's verse. Sabir too, while acknowledging the immense popularity enjoyed by Nazir, found his poetry lacking in decency. He followed Shefta in giving a very brief and bowdlerized selection of Nazir's poetry. Karim ud din's tazkira was more explicit about what exactly was objectionable in Nazir's poetry—the fact that he not only wrote verses on homoerotic themes, but was himself homosexual.[682]

We see here a shifting of position from a very relaxed and flexible attitude to individual sexual preferences. In the previous century Mir Taqi 'Mir' and Shah Mubarak 'Abru' had written verses that had clear references to homosexuality, without inviting criticism of their poetry on that count. The gender ambiguity in Urdu verse had in fact provided a convenient space for such expression. Frequently, there were no clues to the actual gender of the beloved, though sometimes references to an article of clothing or physical feature may give 'him' away as being a woman or, somewhat less frequently, a man. The use of homosexual themes and references moreover were not automatically interpreted as a literal indication of the poet's own inclinations, unless there were references in other sources, such as tazkiras, to suggest it—as was the case with both Mir and Abru.[683]

By the nineteenth century references to an unequivocally male beloved, however, did become much more restrained.[684] Ghalib, for instance, has no more than a handful of such verses and they are by no means sexually explicit. The example chosen here is one of those exceptions. It also illustrates a love that transcends the bounds of creed as well as gender, the sacred thread being a symbol of a Hindu upper caste man:

> *mar jaun na kyun rashk se jab voh tan e nazuk*
> *aghosh e kham e halqah e zunnar mein ave*

> Why would I not die of jealousy when that delicate body
> is encircled within the embrace of the coil of the sacred thread?[685]

This poetry was composed in the context of a society that was traditionally comfortable with same-sex love. Actual instances of homosexuality were probably fairly limited. Where such relationships did exist, however, they were not looked at with absolute disapproval. Two of Ghalib's friends—Mir Mehdi 'Majruh' and Miran were in a relationship which was treated quite matter-of-factly by their circle of friends. Occasional jokes by Ghalib in his letters to Majruh were well-meaning and totally without malice.[686] Despite this open attitude, however, not only were homosexual relationships fairly rare, but the basic premises of society were based on stable heterosexual relationships. Strong family and social expectations worked on an individual to get married at the appropriate stage in life and to produce a family. Homosexual relationships were to that extent socially disruptive. Miran's marriage suffered because of his relationship with Majruh, his wife complaining of being neglected. Majruh did not get married at all till he was in his forties.[687]

More generally, it was a society that was not uncomfortable with the idea of men forming close bonds, and this included feelings that were strongly emotional if not actually sexual. This was reflected in the language of relationships. We frequently come across references to friendships that were strong enough to border on *ishq* or love.[688] Ghalib wrote of close male friends as *mashuq* or 'lovers' without implying any actual sexual context, and we know enough about Ghalib at least to say with some certainty that he had no homosexual relationships.[689] The beauty of young men and the appreciation of it by their male admirers was written of quite unselfconsciously. Even late tazkiras such as that of Sabir contain many such references.[690]

While references to male homosexuality in poetry were becoming muted, other kinds of sexually explicit poetry continued to have a popular appeal. One genre that had become very popular in the late eighteenth and early nineteenth centuries was '*rekhti*'. Composed by men, it purported to express a feminine voice—using language and expressions supposedly exclusive to women, depicting the everyday concerns and relationships of women. Women did in fact speak in an idiom that was distinct, known as '*begumati zaban*'. The rekhti poetry, however, was a caricature of this, containing a marked sexual content, including lesbianism. The appeal of the rekhti lay in the titillation and general entertainment it provided to an all-male audience. This factor was underlined during recitation by the poets affecting feminine mannerisms, and maybe using a *dupatta* to cover their heads. As if to underline the status of rekhti as a non-serious genre, in mushairas rekhti poets said their verses at the very beginning, together with humorous poets.[691]

While most closely associated with non-Delhi poets like Insha, Rangin and Jan Sahib, rekhti was popular in Delhi. The opinion of the tazkira writers on the subject was ambivalent. Shefta was critical of the genre and did not include selections from, say, Rangin's rekhti verses in his tazkira. Sabir on the other hand was full of praise for his contemporary rekhti poet 'Naznin'. Karim ud din pointed to the fact that such verses were popular mainly among young people who enjoyed lascivious subjects, and as such, the popularity enjoyed by poets who composed chiefly in rekhti was somehow spurious.[692] There are indications that even among rekhti poets, there was a certain alteration in subject matter by the second quarter of the nineteenth century. Among the verse of later poets like Jan Sahib, references to lesbianism are relatively insignificant.[693]

It is a complex picture that we are presented with. Social norms had probably not changed very much from the previous century. The culture was one where strong bonds often existed between men, which were expressed in the language of 'love' without being necessarily translated into actual sexual relationships. Sexually explicit poetry, particularly that depicting women in all manner of sexual contexts was a popular genre, composed by men for the entertainment of men. And yet there was a formal disavowal of homosexual themes to a greater, and sexual themes generally to a lesser extent, especially among the tazkira writers who were commenting on the poetry of their contemporaries.

So where did these literary critics get their insights, if not from the prevailing cultural milieu and the traditions of their literature? Maybe we should look for an explanation in the role of work done under the auspices of colonial institutions in assessing a traditional culture against an alien value system. The interest that British scholar-officials took in the literature of the Indians, and their efforts to compile, translate and interpret, was bound to have an impact on that literature. The work of institutions like the Fort William College and the Delhi College, as described above, is very visible. As already mentioned, Karim ud din's and Sahbai's tazkiras were produced at the Delhi College.

That the new value judgement on poetry was inspired by an external source is the probable explanation of why tazkira writers were sometimes drawn into rather conflicting and inconsistent positions with regard to 'indecent' verse. Shefta, for instance, included several verses with sexual overtones, justifying their inclusion on the ground that the lusty young men in his readership may have no complaint.[694]

A more fundamental questioning of the literary tradition itself was also evident, say, in some of the writing that was emanating from the Delhi College. Karim ud din explained his own disinclination to write poetry as an objection on principle. According to him, poetry writing was not an occupation that befitted the learned. It was the frivolous pastime of those who did not have to earn a living. Such people used poetry as an outlet for their emotions.[695] Ram Chander too, made it clear that he did not take this literature seriously. In his article denouncing indigenous learning, he also attacked the 'Farsi walas' of being preoccupied with flowery language and poetry, to the extent that the substance of their writing was obscured by exaggeration and superfluity. Pages were wasted at the beginning of books on eulogies to Emperors, praise of God and of the Prophet, frequently in works where such references were totally unsuitable. Time was wasted on frivolous literary exercises such as *muammas* or word puzzles.[696]

A more reasoned critique of the poetry of the time can be found in a letter published in 1846 in Ram Chander's magazine, *Fawaid un Nazirin*. The writer, on the authority of unspecified 'European thinkers', started off by characterizing poetry as that thing which could stir up human emotions—anger, courage, love, compassion, patriotism, etc. From this it followed that poetry could be considered good or bad depending on the particular emotions, good or bad, that it aroused in the listener. It was obvious that the kind of themes that were typical of Urdu-Persian poetry only served to stir up an inclination for frivolities, and a disinclination towards beneficial knowledge and skills. Moreover, this kind of poetry gave rise to a lassitude, and a weakening of the qualities of courage and manhood. This kind of poetry was only fit for the dissolute and lecherous. As for those who wrote this poetry, if only they applied their skills to the writing of poetry that stirred up proper passions, the state of the people of India would be considerably improved.[697] The writer, applying a utilitarian approach to literature, was attributing the purported weaknesses in Indian character to defects in the literary tradition.

Though these ideas were still stray comments, and we cannot

say if they had any direct impact on the more far-reaching criticism of the tradition that was to come later in the century, there were signs that something was amiss in the world of classical poetry. Pre-1857 Delhi has frequently been described as the site of a literary and cultural efflorescence, and this assessment is in large part based on the poetry of the period. The era of Company rule coincided neatly with the lifetimes of some notable figures in Urdu and Persian poetry—Asadullah Khan 'Ghalib', Momin Khan 'Momin', Mohammad Ibrahim 'Zauq', Bahadur Shah 'Zafar', and some lesser known to us but almost equally respected in their own time—Mohammad Sadr ud din Khan 'Azurda', Mustafa Khan 'Shefta', Imam Baksh 'Sahbai', etc. This does not take away from the fact that by the middle of the century, even as the popular base of Urdu poetry was growing, there were some signs of a faltering among its most sophisticated and cerebral practitioners.

Momin had given up writing poetry by the mid-1840s.[698] In his tazkira of 1835, Shefta said that he himself had practically given up writing poetry.[699] If we examine the output of Ghalib, based on various editions of his divan, two-thirds of his Urdu ghazals (and he did not write that many) were written before 1834.[700] If we take into account the further fact that much of his later ghazal writing was part of his job description as the ustad of Bahadur Shah, we are looking at a serious disinclination to write poetry. Even if we account for the fact that Ghalib continued to write, and in fact, Shefta is also said to have written, though avowedly under pressure from his friends and shagirds, at the very least there was a tendency to decry poetry writing or to make out that one was not really interested in it. If this is read together with the decline of the mushaira, we are looking at a crisis of confidence in the very tradition of poetry that is seen by many as a defining feature of pre-1857 Delhi culture. It is more than a coincidence that many of the intellectual elite who reached manhood in the couple of decades before 1857 did not write much poetry in those years of youth—Syed Ahmad Khan, Karim ud din, Ram Chander, Nazir Ahmad, Zakaullah, Mohammad Husain 'Azad', and even Altaf Husain 'Hali'.[701]

45

New Preoccupations

One reason for the slowing of interest in poetry, particularly as a full-time avocation, may have been the lack of patronage, though this could not have been the entire story. Though the British were not interested in patronizing poets, and the Mughal royal family had very limited means, there were others—landed magnates, and rulers of independent states, who still had the means and presumably the inclination to do so. The real reason probably was that the new generation of the educated elite had other interests, which centred at least to some extent around the new knowledge being disseminated by the institutions sponsored by the colonial state.

The Delhi College was one such institution. The work of Master Ram Chander has already been mentioned, and the fact that his most original work was sparked by his own interest rather than sponsored by the College, though undoubtedly it grew out of the education he had received there. The same was the case with Karim ud din. This dynamic man, who participated in the translation programme, ran a printing press and also came up with the innovative idea of the public/print mushaira, also wrote a manual in Urdu for the education of women.

No copies have survived and we have no way of knowing how many were circulated, but this work was probably a part of his project for which he had set up his printing press—aimed at printing books that would educate and uplift the public. Entitled *Talim un Nissa*, this manual covered eight areas that were considered of relevance to women, particularly Muslim women. Of these some were oriented towards an understanding of the fundamentals of religious belief and practice; others were of a secular nature, dealing with subjects that would help women in their everyday lives. Women were to be instructed in the knowledge of God and the Prophet, an understanding of Islam and the duties enjoined by it, on the laws pertaining to conjugality, menstruation and childbirth. They would also be given practical advice for the efficient management of their homes, which included being cautious where servants were concerned and exercising integrity when dealing with goods, and knowledge of tried and tested remedies and measures for the preservation of physical health.[702]

This was a work that was clearly not sponsored by the College. Neither do we have any way of knowing if and how familiar Karim ud din was with similar English domestic manuals aimed at making women more efficient managers of their homes. In any event, in the Indian context it was definitely pathbreaking, since it presaged the popular domestic manuals that were to emerge only in the 1880s in Bengal, and in Urdu only in 1905, when Maulana Ashraf Ali Thanawi's *Bihishti Zewar* was published.

While looking at the intellectual and literary contributions of Ram Chander and Karim ud din, one must put the role of the Delhi College in perspective. It is true that Ram Chander was introduced to the Western mathematical tradition there, but it was his ability to relate that to his foundation in the Indian system, that formed the basis of his original work. Karim ud din studied in the Oriental section, and his exposure to works in English would necessarily have been limited. Much of what they both did, though inspired and made possible by new intellectual spaces that were opening up, would have been equally impossible without a grounding in the strong intellectual traditions they grew up in.

Another institution that was providing a new intellectual space was the Archaeological Society of Delhi, set up in 1847. A resolution passed at its inaugural session declared that the Society's object would, 'in the first place, be the investigation, by means of plans, drawings and elevations, by inscriptional, traditional and historical researches, and, if possible, by publications of the ancient remains, both Hindoo and Mahomedan, in and around Delhi; and in the second, the institution of similar researches, in other parts of the North-West Provinces'. The Archaeological Society bore a strongly official character. Its patron was the Lt Governor of the North-Western Provinces, and it received some government grants for specific purposes. Its meetings were held on the first Monday of each month at venues such as the Residency and the Delhi College, and its members included several British officials, including its first president, the Commissioner, Thomas Metcalfe. Membership was fixed at a rupee a month, and office bearers were elected from among these members. Non-paying 'honorary members' could also be inducted, provided they had 'distinguished themselves in Indo-Archaeological Researches'.[703]

The Archaeological Society undertook a variety of activities. One of its first acts after its foundation in 1847, was the setting up of a committee to carry out archaeological investigations into the Jama Masjid within Feroze Shah Kotla. A sum of 250 rupees was sanctioned by the Lt Governor of the North-Western Provinces for the purpose.[704] It also carried out repairs in the Jantar Mantar observatory, for which the Raja of Jaipur had given 600 rupees.

The membership of the society by 1850 had swelled to eighty-seven. Its members were mostly British civil and military officers, from all over North India, including Punjab, Bundelkhand, Rajputana, Central India, Agra, Lucknow, Calcutta, Darjeeling, and of course Delhi. Initially, there were few Indian members, probably because the subscription of a rupee a month was beyond the means of most. There were only three, and of these, two had reached fairly high levels in the British administrative machinery. One of these was Pir Ibrahim Khan—from a noble family of Punjab, who was posted as the 'Native Agent' at the court of the ruler at Bahawalpur.[705]

The other was Mohan Lal, the Delhi man. Mohan Lal's career had seen considerable ups and downs since he had left the Delhi

College nearly two decades earlier. The high point had been reached when he had been an energetic and successful agent for the British in Afghanistan during the first Afghan War (1839-42), with a salary of 1,000 rupees a month. Unfortunately, he fell victim to the British bungling in that country. He barely escaped alive, and was abandoned by his British employers, who refused to honour the financial commitments and agreements he had entered into on their behalf. He received little reward for his work, and was posted in relatively minor positions on a much reduced salary of 320 rupees.[706] He visited Britain in 1844-46, largely with a view to laying his case, for restitution for the injustices done to him, before the Court of Directors of the East India Company. His stay in England was interspersed with travels in Scotland, Ireland and Europe, where he took in everything from church services to the opera. In Prussia he dined with King Fredrick William IV. In Scotland his portrait was painted by the famous painter, William Allan, and he was photographed by David Octavius Hill and Robert Adamson, early practitioners of the photographic process. He thus became probably the first Indian to be photographed.[707]

In Britain he made a distinct impact—being received in audience by Queen Victoria, being invited to a royal ball, and being entertained by Members of Parliament. Details of his visit were covered by the local newspapers. The Directors and Chairman of the Company received him and he was granted a one-time payment of 15,000 rupees and a pension of 6,000 rupees annually. A payment of 20,404 rupees was awarded to him against certain claims he had put forward, short of the 24,404 rupees he had claimed. While in Britain he also re-published his memoirs and published another book, *Life of Amir Dost Mohammad Khan of Kabul*, in which he was candid in his criticism of British actions in Afghanistan.[708]

The considerable attention he received in Britain was not enough for Mohan Lal to gain justice back in India. His claims were rejected by the government and he never got another government job, in spite of several applications. In 1850 he was living in Ludhiana. His membership of the Archaeological Society no doubt stemmed from his own interest in antiquities. His observations and sketches of shrines and mausolea he had visited in the historic Uch Sharif in Punjab had been published a number of years earlier by the Asiatic Society of Bengal in its journal.[709]

The third Indian member in 1850 was not a public servant, but a member of the nobility—Zia ud din Ahmad Khan, the son of Ahmad Baksh Khan and half-brother of Shams ud din Ahmad Khan. Though he had inherited the principality of Loharu jointly with his older brother, Amin ud din Ahmad Khan, in 1848 the British recognized Amin ud din as the ruler of the state, providing an allowance of 11,000 rupees a year to the younger brother. From that date, Zia ud din came to reside permanently in Delhi. Zia ud din had had no connection with the Delhi College but had studied at the feet of noted scholars in Delhi—Abdul Qadir, Sadr ud din Azurda, and Fazl e Haq Khairabadi. He was also a noted poet, writing in both Persian and Urdu.[710]

Zia ud din had a keen interest in history and contributed materially to the work of the Society. For instance, he analysed and commented on several coins presented to the society. He also helped to identify the older cities of Delhi, particularly those whose locations had been in some doubt, such as Siri, Jahan Panah, and Ferozabad, on the basis of old records. This helped in the creation of a map of historic sites, which was published in the journal of the Society. The Archaeological Society was starting to realize that it could benefit greatly from the contributions of learned Indians, who may have been excluded at least partly due to the high membership fee. In 1850 it was resolved, 'that in order more fully to take advantage of the position held by the Society in this part of India... it is proposed to invite native gentlemen to become contributors to the objects of our Institution, not in the shape of any money donation, but in the communication of such information their local, linguistic, or other knowledge may enable them to supply with greater readiness and accuracy than our Western Orientalists usually arrive at.'[711]

In the following couple of years several Indian members entered the society. These included Roy Ramsaran Das (Deputy Collector of Delhi), Sadr ud din Azurda, Dr Chiman Lal, Pundit Ram Chandra

Shastri and Pundit Ghasi Ram (both of the last were teachers in the Delhi College) and Syed Ahmad Khan.

Syed Ahmad would prove to be a real asset to the Society. Shortly after he joined, in 1852, he presented an interesting paper on different kinds of bricks from historical sites, and how a study of bricks could help archaeologists to date sites. He presented to the society a couple of bricks he had obtained from Hastinapur. He also presented a somewhat controversial paper on the Qutub Minar, in which he claimed that the lower storey of the minar was a construction dating from before the Ghurid conquest.[712] This was a claim hotly contested by Zia ud din Ahmad Khan, who presented a detailed paper on the Qutub Minar, the mosque and other buildings adjoining it, based on inscriptions found on the buildings, as well as textual sources. This was accompanied by a plan of the complex and the area around it.

The scholarship of Zia ud din Ahmad Khan and Syed Ahmad Khan was much appreciated within the Society. Syed Ahmad's study of bricks and his conclusion that 'it is highly probable that wherever bricks of the same kind are found, these places are of the same age' was acknowledged as being profound. The Secretary of the society noted that 'I am not aware whether any such remark has been made before with regard to the archaeological remains of this country; and, if not, the Moonsiff deserves the highest praise for his acuteness. In genuine ability few Mohammedans are equal to the Moonsiff, or to Nawab Zea-ood-deen, both members of this Society.' To us today, looking at the records of the Society that have survived, it certainly seems that no members, Muslim or otherwise, were equal to these two.

Syed Ahmad Khan's forays into the archaeology of Delhi predated not only his membership of the Archaeological Society, but even its founding. Syed Ahmad had joined the Company's judicial service as a munsif in 1840, and on the death of his brother, Syed Mohammad, in 1846, sought a posting in his place of birth, Delhi, in order to be with his mother. Soon after his arrival he appears to have embarked on a work titled *Asar us sanadid*, which was published in 1847.[713] The subject matter included a brief history of Delhi, a fairly extensive listing of the monuments of the city with painstaking reproduction of their inscriptions, and finally a long chapter which dealt with the climate, language, and people. It was written in a flowery style of Urdu which was in fact still the style that was current in the majority of writing in the 1840s.

Shortly after its first publication the book was brought to the notice of the Royal Asiatic Society, which commended the work and suggested its translation into English. For various reasons, which were beyond the control of Syed Ahmad, the translation did not materialize. A second edition of the work, however, was produced in 1854, and it included major amendments and 'corrections'. The language had been made free of 'Asiatic hyperbole and conventions', the chapter on the people of Delhi, which was an account of a number of the important scholars, hakims, Sufis, musicians, etc., of Delhi had been left out altogether. It is likely that these changes were the result of Syed Ahmad's participation in the activities of the Archaeological Society. It led to the book becoming an impersonal work, more in the nature of an archaeology report, without the cultural details that had been included in the earlier version.[714]

Syed Ahmad was inspired by Western scholarship in more than the *Asar us sanadid*. In the early 1850s he also spent considerable time and energy working on an edition of the *Ain e Akbari*, a history of the reign of Akbar, written by the sixteenth century historian, Abul Fazl. His translation was based on a painstaking study and comparison of extant manuscript copies. Far from being a symptom of his attachment to a Mughal past, the project appears to be a contribution to the interest Western Orientalist scholars were taking in the text at the time. Syed Ahmad's friend and biographer Altaf Husain Hali specifically mentions that Syed Ahmad also referred to certain Western editions/translations of the text.[715]

Incidentally, Syed Ahmad requested Ghalib to write a foreword to the book, hoping that the endorsement would help in adding credibility to the work. Rather unexpectedly, Ghalib's foreword, in Persian verse, practically castigated Syed Ahmad for wasting his time on an outdated document, at a time when new advances in knowledge were being introduced by the British, India's new rulers.[716] Clearly, it was not just the new generation that was receptive to the new influences in intellectual life.

PART FIVE

1857 and Its Aftermath

Fighting in the city, September 1857

46

11 May 1857

On the night of 10 May 1857, the people of Delhi went to sleep unaware of the momentous events that had occurred that day at Meerut, where the Indian troops had mutinied. Though there were several reasons for discontent among the armies of the Company, the proximate cause was the introduction of the new Enfield rifle. These rifles had to be loaded with cartridges that were rumoured to be greased with pork and cow fat. Since beef and pork products were abhorrent to Hindus and Muslims respectively, the soldiers strongly objected to the new cartridge, particularly because it had to be torn open by mouth. The British officers were equally adamant about forcing the soldiers to accept them, thus triggering the mutiny. The Meerut troops had killed many of their officers and their families, and had set out for Delhi.

News started trickling into Delhi only after 7 o'clock, when, in keeping with the summer schedule, the morning's work was well under way.[717] The first information, received from the darogha in charge of the bridge of boats, said that a group of mounted soldiers from Meerut had come over the bridge of boats, and had looted and set fire to the customs house. The news caused consternation, and the magistrate, John Hutchinson, who had received the news in his courthouse near Kashmiri Gate, rushed off to the house of the Commissioner, Simon Fraser, to inform him. In fact, the previous night, a soldier had come from Meerut with a letter for Fraser, bringing him news of the outbreak there. The latter, who was already asleep in his chair, barely woke up enough to slip the letter, unread, into his pocket. The urgent news, therefore, had not registered.

One of the soldiers showed up at the Lahori Gate of the fort, where he told Douglas, the Captain of the palace guard, that he and his companions had come from Meerut, after having mutinied. Douglas had barely given the order for the man to be arrested, that he received a summons from the palace. This was a message informing him that the rest of the soldiers had gathered under the jharokha, asking to be let in and to speak to the Emperor. Bahadur Shah, as soon as he heard the news, had sent for Douglas, who joined him at the jharokha. Douglas wanted to go down to the river's bank to speak to the soldiers, but the Emperor advised him against it, and also told him to ensure that the city gates be closed. Bahadur Shah also ordered the dispatch of some palanquins to convey the ladies of Douglas' family to the royal zanana, the ladies' quarters, to ensure their safety.

The soldiers, finding that the doors would not be opened to them, went off, looking for other ways of entering the city. They found the Calcutta Gate, nearest to the bridge of boats, also closed. This had been closed soon after the first information had arrived, under orders from Fraser, who had taken up a position on the gate to see what was happening outside. He was joined at the gate by Hutchinson and Douglas, and scarcely had he begun to give orders that a small group of troopers galloped up to them from the southwards, and shot at them. These horsemen were a part of the troop of soldiers, who had made their way from the jharokha southwards, and had managed to enter the city through the gate close to the Zeenat ul Masajid, located south of the fort.[718] This initial troop was but the advance guard, and by nine o'clock two regiments of infantry and one of cavalry could be seen crossing the bridge en route from Meerut into Delhi.

At the Calcutta Gate, Fraser and his companions had managed to escape from the attacking soldiers and to reach the Lahori Gate of the fort, where they were let in. They had obviously assumed that the fort, with a guard of the government's soldiers stationed at the gate itself, was safe, though they would soon realize that their confidence had been misplaced. While Hutchinson and Douglas, both of whom were wounded, were helped by their attendant orderlies to go up the stairs to Douglas' quarters, which were located above the gate, Fraser, unhurt, headed up the chhatta bazar, or covered market, towards the interior of the fort. By the time he was halfway down, he found himself face to face with a threatening crowd of some of the fort's inhabitants, men and boys, who had gathered there, and seeing him, began to clap in a show of belligerence. Fraser turned back, but at the foot of the stairs leading to Douglas' quarters, he received a serious cut from a sword wielded by a gem cutter called Haji, who had a shop in the chhatta bazar. The *havildar* commanding the Company's troops, who by this time had also joined the crowd, did nothing to stop him, and Fraser received further mortal blows by two or three other armed men, members of the chief eunuch Mahbub Ali Khan's guard. These men, followed by more who were part of the crowd, then entered Douglas' flat, where they soon killed not only Douglas and Hutchinson, but also Pastor Jennings and his daughter, and a Miss Clifford who was visiting them. All this had happened before ten o'clock.[719]

All resistance at the Lahori Gate having been overcome, the mutineers entered the fort and quickly rode into the courtyard in front of the Diwan e Khas, ignoring the etiquette which required all to dismount before they entered it. They also fired their weapons in the air, the noise prompting Bahadur Shah to come into the hall to demand an explanation from the officers at the head of the troops. On again hearing that they had mutinied and had come to Delhi for his protection, he castigated them, saying that they had behaved unwisely. Hearing this, over a hundred of the soldiers walked into the hall, saying that since they had burnt their boats by mutinying, their only hope now lay in the Emperor joining their cause. This was a situation with which at one level Bahadur Shah may have sympathized, while on the other he may have feared the repercussions, should the British overcome this mutiny and hold him to account for his actions. As things stood, however, in the face of the adamant soldiers surrounding him, he had no choice but to seat himself on the throne and place his hands on their heads as they came up to him one by one, for his blessings. Once this was over, the soldiers took over not only the courtyard, where they kept their horses, but the hall of audience itself, laying their bedding in it. There was not much Bahadur Shah could do, but his chief minister and physician, Ahsanullah Khan, who had all this while been advising his master to exercise caution, secretly dispatched a letter to the Lt Governor at Agra on his behalf, informing him of the occurrences.

In the afternoon the leaders of the soldiers again presented themselves before Bahadur Shah, and proclaimed their intention to set up an administration with members of the royal family at the head. The *Siraj ul Akhbar*, the palace newspaper, reported that the Emperor was very uncomfortable with these developments, but ultimately agreed to the nomination of some princes at the head of the administration simply because he realized that the immediate concern was to maintain order in the city, and for that, the city had to be protected against the excesses of the out-of-town soldiers.[720]

In the meanwhile, orders were already being issued by the soldiers in the name of the Emperor, with the active support of the Emperor's own confidants and troops. One of their first actions was to try and secure the stores of arms and ammunition that were in the magazine, north of the fort. The British officers, however, had been quick to react, and led by Lt Willoughby and Assistant Commissary Forrest, had locked the gates against all comers. They refused to open them to the Emperor's troops who arrived saying that the Emperor had ordered that the stores of the magazine be handed over to them. As a matter of fact, it was highly unlikely that this order came from the Emperor, because at this time, before ten a.m., Bahadur Shah was still very ambivalent about his position on the developments that had taken place. When the few British staff in the magazine refused to open the gates, the Meerut soldiers brought ladders and began to scale the walls of the magazine. By three-thirty in the afternoon, when the takeover of the magazine by the rebels was imminent, its British custodians lit a charge to blow up the magazine with all the ammunition in it. It killed not only the many Indians around the magazine, but also most of the British staff as well as many European women and children who had taken shelter in what they had seen as a safehouse.

The staff of the magazine had received no backup, simply because, if the city's civil administration was in disarray, the military leadership had been even slower to respond. Most of the troops were located in the cantonment beyond the Ridge, to the north-west of the city, with a small contingent at the Kashmiri Gate. It was nine o'clock before the officers in the cantonment had begun to make some preparations to respond to the news that large bodies of mutinous troops were arriving from Meerut. It took them even longer to get some troops organized to go down to the city. By then it was too late. Not only had the mutineers from Meerut entered the city, but one after the other, each of the three infantry regiments stationed at Delhi, as they were sent down from the cantonment to the city, began to fall in with the mutineers. It had not taken long for the Delhi troops to mutiny, because they too had been affected by the discontent that was spreading through the country among the soldiers, including the fears of the greased cartridges. Some witnesses later even claimed that information of the impending mutiny at Meerut had been available to the soldiers in Delhi in the days leading up to the outbreak.[721]

Now, many refused to take orders from their British officers, and some actually turned their arms against them. This led to a rout at Kashmiri Gate, with surviving officers and some of the women and children who lived in the bungalows in this quarter, barely managing to escape with their lives. This group, together with Europeans from the cantonment, regrouped at the Flagstaff tower, a lookout point on the Ridge. Here, by the end of the day, the decision was taken for a retreat to Karnal.

Among the group that had gathered at the Flagstaff tower, and who later in the day tried to get away from the scene of the disturbances, was the Wagentreiber family. Elizabeth Wagentreiber was the youngest daughter of James Skinner. George Wagentreiber, the editor of the magazine called the *Delhi Sketch Book*, was her second husband. This brave woman put her two children and husband in a carriage, while she herself harnessed the horses and drove them. On the way they met several groups of Jats and Gujars who attacked them, but managed to escape them through George's use of his firearms and her furious and expert driving. They arrived safely two days later in Karnal, their escape at least in part due to help from an old soldier they met on the way, who had served under 'Sikandar sahib', and felt he owed the old colonel's daughter something.[722]

Within the city there was chaos too. Soon after their arrival the mutineers had set free the prisoners in the Kotwali. These, as also what many eyewitnesses would later describe as 'common people', '*badmash*', i.e. the poor and/or the criminals, took an active part in directing the soldiers to the houses and shops of Europeans. The soldiers were eager to eliminate these Europeans, as they were seen as a potential source of opposition. In Dariyaganj itself, where the soldiers had entered the city, there were the houses of many Europeans, particularly the lower officials and non-officials, and these became the target of attack. Christian Indians were also seen with suspicion, on the assumption that their loyalties lay with the British. Dr Chiman Lal, who was at the dispensary, was pointed out by a *bhishti* (water carrier) saying that he was a Christian, and was immediately killed. Some cavalrymen went to the house of the Skinners and brought George, the son of Joseph Skinner, to the Kotwali, were he was killed.

The lives of some Indian Christians were spared. A preacher's wife and children were defended and helped by friends and neighbours. Master Ram Chander was also in the city and, for a while at least, walked in the streets unmolested. Later he was to put his own interpretation to this circumstance, saying, 'Many of the Hindoos and Mohammedans passing by knew that I was a Christian, but God shut their mouths, and they did not say to the mutineers that I was a Christian.' These were exceptional cases, and even Ram Chander soon found it prudent to leave the city altogether.[723]

While the soldiers were focused on their main aim of neutralizing the British, the mob had other motivations too. There was some amount of pure vindictiveness against symbols of colonial rule and culture. Mohammad Baqar, who had left home out of a sense of journalistic responsibility, to see for himself what was happening in the city, saw with horror the scene at the Delhi College, his alma mater. He noted that not only the furniture, but thousands of rupees worth of books and laboratory equipment was being looted or destroyed.[724] Another eyewitness saw a large group of *pahalwans*, wrestlers, on the street, and one of them, breaking a street lamp (being public property, seen as a symbol of the administration), exclaimed, 'there goes another kafir'.

Plunder and loot was another strong motivation. Besides damaging government property, many also tried to break open locks on shops. An officer of the police force saw that 'On every side the scum of the population was hurrying to and fro, laden with the plunder of European houses'.[725] Not only did the mob point out the houses of Europeans, but also of wealthy Indians, often on the pretext that they were hiding Europeans. The house of Saligram was plundered by the mutineers and the mob, its heavy gates giving way after much effort only at midnight.[726] An attack on the Delhi Bank, located in what had once been the palace of Begum Samru, was motivated both by the desire to lay hands on the money stored in it, and also to deal with the European manager Beresford, and his family, who had taken refuge in one of the buildings in the compound of the bank. They were all killed, though not before putting up a brave fight. Mrs Beresford herself killed one of the attackers with a spear.[727] The bank was then looted and set on fire.

Loot seemed to have been a major motivation at least for some of the soldiers too. Just four days after the outbreak it was reported that some 200 soldiers had accumulated loot from the people of the city, deserted and headed to their homes. Of course what they had not reckoned with, were the Gujars that inhabited the villages around Delhi, who relieved them of their spoils before they had gone very far. In the next few days, soldiers usually tried to exchange their loot for gold which was easy to carry, but in this too they were often duped by con men in the city.[728]

47

Suspicion and Terror

Disorder was the hallmark of the days that followed. The first priority of the soldiers was to find potential enemies, which meant hunting down those Europeans who remained. Though most Europeans had been killed or had escaped, some were sheltered by their Indian friends, neighbours and colleagues, often at great risk to themselves. One case was that of Mrs Aldwell and her children, who were in turn hidden in the house of a grandson of Bahadur Shah, whose wife and sister were known to them; then in the house of a tailor named Nathu. The latter had also hidden some other Europeans in his house, and when this was discovered, his house was set afire.[729]

The Aldwells had also been told that Nawab Hamid Ali Khan's was a safe house for Europeans, but did not go there, for by then he too was under suspicion. The Emperor's grandson, Abu Bakr, arrived at his house, looted it and arrested him. No Europeans were found in his house, and ultimately at the insistence of Bahadur Shah himself, his property was restored.[730] Part of the problem was that the informants, usually those of the mob, were activated by the desire to loot, and used the pretext of searching for hidden Europeans to break into houses. The house of Ram Charan Das, the Deputy Collector, was broken into and looted on the same suspicion.[731] Informers also led the soldiers to the house of Mohan

Lal, accusing him of being a Christian. His life was spared, as Shah Nizam ud din (the son of Bahadur Shah's spiritual guide, Kale Sahab) testified to his being a Muslim. This was in fact true, because by this time he had converted to Islam. His house, however, was still plundered, as were those of several others accused of being 'friendly' to the British. Mohan Lal soon escaped from the city.[732]

No one, no matter how influential, was immune. One informer pointed the finger at Shah Nizam ud din himself, saying that he was hiding Europeans in his house. In response, soldiers arrived at his house as well, but were turned back by the righteous rage of Nizam ud din. Mahbub Ali Khan, the trusted chief eunuch of the palace, also had to swear on the Quran that he was not in collusion with the British. Things came to a crisis on 16 May,[733] when a letter, bearing the seals of Mahbub Ali Khan and Ahsanullah Khan, was intercepted at the Delhi Gate of the city. It was addressed to the British authorities, and offered terms of negotiation—i.e. if the British were willing to accept Jawan Bakht as Bahadur Shah's heir apparent, they on their part were willing to help seize and hand over all the mutinous soldiers. The two officials accused stoutly denied having authored the letter, and claimed that it was a forgery.

The soldiers, however, were still very distrustful. With drawn swords they confronted Ahsanullah Khan, accusing him of colluding with the British. Why else, they demanded, were the European prisoners in the fort still allowed to live, if not so that they could be handed over to the British authorities? The prisoners they referred to were all the Europeans that had been found in the city and not immediately killed—mostly women and children. The soldiers had brought them into the fort, where they themselves had taken up their residence. According to other sources, some of them had been rounded up on the orders of Bahadur Shah from Dariyaganj, to protect them from the massacre taking place there. By this time there were some fifty in all, confined in a building that had once been a kitchen, not far from the Diwan e Khas.

The soldiers now asked for the execution of these prisoners. Bahadur Shah was loath to give his assent, but now, on the backfoot, and under pressure to prove the anti-British sentiments of himself and those close to him, gave in. The prisoners were led out into the large forecourt in front of the naqqar khana, where they were executed with swords. Those who participated in the massacre included the soldiers as well as the Emperor's own troops. The bodies were thrown into the river. Among the Europeans who had been imprisoned was Mrs Aldwell and her children, and remarkably, they were spared. According to her own explanation, it was because she had written a petition to the Emperor representing that they were Muslims, and when asked, all of them could recite the Kalima, the expression of faith.

Bahadur Shah was not able to prevent the massacre on the 16th, but continued to shelter some other European women who were being held prisoner in the fort. When asked by the soldiers to hand them over, he produced a fatwa, or legal opinion, to the effect that the killing of women was unlawful according to Islamic law.[734] There were others who took the support of law to stand up for the lives of Europeans and Christians who were under attack. John Everett, a man of mixed blood, was among a large group that had been imprisoned in the Kotwali, and would later give his evidence during the trial of Bahadur Shah once the Revolt had been defeated. He described how he and about forty other Christians (presumably mixed race or Indians) were finally 'all released in consequence of a Moulvie by the name of Mohammed Ismail giving evidence that we were all Mahommedans, and that if there were any Christians that they would become Mahommedans and that it was not lawful to kill such as turn Mahommedan of their own accord.'[735]

Europeans continued to be discovered in the city till at least the end of May. The *Dehli Urdu Akhbar* reported that one or two were turned up every day.[736] This evidently suggested that there were people in the city who did not want to be complicit in the taking of lives, even if it meant dire consequences for themselves. There also seems to have been a general awareness among the city people that the Emperor disapproved of violence, particularly against women and children. A spy sent into Delhi by the British on 18 June reported seeing a European woman and her two children being dragged along by some soldiers. He noted that 'the people remonstrated and said it was against the King's order to harm helpless women and children.'[737]

The suddenness of the Revolt took the people of Delhi by surprise. It was hard to believe that a government that had seemed so well entrenched could be uprooted overnight. The *Dehli Urdu Akhbar* of 24 May carried on its front page a poem that articulated these feelings. It was written by Mohammad Husain 'Azad', the son of Mohammad Baqar, the editor. Azad, like his father, was an alumnus of the Delhi College, having graduated from the Oriental section some three years previously. He was also a poet, a shagird of 'Zauq', the Emperor's own ustad.

The poem was titled *Tarikh e inqilab e ibrat afza*, 'A history of instructive revolutions'. Though subsequently it has generally been interpreted as being in support of the rebellion, it managed to say much without taking any sides. It began in a contemplative mood, meditating on the fleeting nature of temporal power. It recalled that the great and powerful rulers and conquerors of history had been consigned to the dust of time:

ko milk e sulaiman, o kuja hukm e sikandar
shahan e ulu'la'zam, salateen e jahandar
ko satwat e hujjaj, kuja saulat e changez
ko shan e halaku, kuja nadir e khunkhar
na shaukat o hashmat hai, na wo hukm na hasil
kis ja hai jahan aur kuja hain jahandar
ko rustam o sohrab, kuja sam e nariman
is ma'rake mein, kand hai har ek ki talwar

Where is the kingdom of Solomon, and where the authority of Alexander?
Where the kings of masterful resolution, the world-possessing rulers?
Where the awfulness of Hujjaj,[738] where the ferocity of Chengiz?
Where is the glory of Halaku, where is the blood-thirsty Nadir?
Neither pomp nor splendour remains, neither authority nor resources,
Where is the world and where are the world-possessors?
Where are Rustam and Sohrab, where is Sam Nariman?
In this battle-field, each one's sword is blunt...

It related in wonder how:

hai kal ka hi zikr ke jo qaum e nasari
thi sahib e iqbal o jahan baksh o jahandar
thi sahib e ilm o hunar o hikmat o fitrat
thi sahib e jah o hashm o lashkar e jarrar
allah hi allah hai! jis waqt ko nikle
afaq mein tegh e ghazab e hazrat e qahhar
sab jauhar e aql unki rahi taq par rakhi
sab nakhun e tadbir o khird ho gaye bekar
kam ayi na ilm o hunar o hikmat o fitrat
purab ke tilangon ne liya sabko yahin mar.

It was only yesterday that this race of Christians,
Was possessed of fortune, world-bestowing, world-upholding,
Was the master of learning, skill, wisdom and sagacity,
Was possessed of dignity, retinues, and a powerful army.
God alone is everlasting! For when there emerged
Over the horizon, the raging sword of the vengeful lord,
All the jewels of wisdom they possessed were of no avail.
All their clever plans and contrivances came to naught.
Their learning, skill, wisdom, and sagacity, were of no use,
All were destroyed by the Telingas of the East.

If the Telingas (the name used for European trained Indian soldiers) were the tools of providence come to teach the Christians a lesson, it was a capricious and even mischievous providence:

yeh saneh woh hai ke na dekha na suna tha
hai gardish e gardun bhi ajab gardish e dawwar
nairang pe ghaur iske jo kije to a'yan hai
har sha'bdah tazah mein sadd bazi e ayyar

This is an occurrence such as was not seen or heard before
Strange are the vicissitudes of the revolution of the heavens
If one contemplates the wonders of fate, there is evident,
In every fresh sleight of hand, a hundred tricks of a knave.

The lesson Azad took from this was a sobering one:

haan, didah e ibrat ko zara khol to ghafil
hain band yahan ahl e zabaan ke lab e guftaar

ankhein hon to sab khul gayi duniya ki haqiqat
mat kijo dil iska bharosa kabhi, zinhar!
ibrat ke liye khalq mein yeh saneh bas hai
go deve khuda aql e saleem o dil e hushiyar
kya kahen ke dum marne ki ja nahin hai
hairan hain sab aina-sifat, pusht e ba-deewar
hukkam e nasair ka badin danish o beenish
mit jaye nishan khalq mein is tarah yak bar

Open your eyes and take heed, O unmindful one!
For the lips of the eloquent have been sealed
If you have eyes, see! For the truth of the world has been revealed
Beware, O heart! Never trust in it again.
This event serves as a warning in this world
If God has given you a sound mind and a vigilant heart.
What can one say? For there is no scope to breathe a syllable
All are astounded, like mirrors with their backs to the wall,
That, despite their wisdom and vision, the Christian rulers' mark
Should be erased in this manner from the world.[739]

48

The New Regime

Bahadur Shah had given his blessings reluctantly to the rebel soldiers on the 11th. He was not certain if it was wise to ally himself with those who had taken up arms against the Company, but neither was he able to refuse the insistent and indeed rather aggressive soldiers who invaded his palace. He was also genuinely distressed by the murder of British officers. He ordered that the bodies of Fraser and Douglas be given a respectful burial in the graveyard.[740] He also instituted an enquiry into the fate of Theophilus John Metcalfe, the son of Thomas Metcalfe. Theophilus, who was the joint magistrate at Delhi, had managed to escape from the city on the 11th, but for a long time it was not known if he had survived.[741]

Drawn willy-nilly into leadership, Bahadur Shah soon proved that he was more than a merely symbolic leader. Faced with the disorder that was visited on the city by the unexpected arrival of the soldiers, he rose to the occasion, and took the lead in directing the administration. The restoration of some semblance of order and normalcy in the city was an immediate concern. The very next day after the outbreak, an order had been proclaimed by the beat of the drum, announcing that the Emperor's authority had been established, and directing the opening of shops. Following the looting that had occurred, merchants and shopkeepers were understandably reluctant to open their establishments. A couple of days later, as a further measure to instil confidence in the people, Bahadur Shah himself went out in a ceremonial procession into the city, down the main street, up to Chandni Chowk, with a salute of twenty-one guns being fired on his departure from and return to the palace. Soon after, he summoned the grain dealers of the city and asked them to ensure the availability of grain at reasonable rates.[742]

Bahadur Shah was alive to the fact that to the soldiers he was a mere figurehead, whose name and influence could serve to lend legitimacy to their authority. All orders of the administration were to be in his name, and at times of crisis he could be called upon to issue a special proclamation, or even address the people directly. Yet the soldiers do not seem to have treated him as being personally worthy of any particular respect, and for the most part were probably ignorant of the protocols that surrounded his royal person. In their attitude to him, there was a manifest lack of the customary deference, even reverence, with which he was treated by the high and low in the city. They had scant regard for court etiquette, walking into the Diwan e Khas and standing on the carpets with their shoes on.[743] On the very first day, his attempt to remonstrate with the troops killing British officials received the reply, 'It appears you are in league with the Christians—you will see what will happen'.[744] According to Jivan Lal, one of the main contemporary chroniclers of that period, some of the officers addressed Bahadur Shah as '*arre Badshah*' or '*arre buddha*' and took the ultimate liberty of touching his hand and beard.[745]

The soldiers hoped to concentrate actual power in their own hands and use Bahadur Shah as a puppet king, but it soon became evident to them that he was not willing to a be mere tool in their hands. He was also less supportive of the soldiers' actions than other members of his family. For instance, he repeatedly upbraided them for their oppression of the city people, questioned the wisdom of their mutiny, and had made his displeasure and distress at the massacre of the Europeans quite obvious. There was, however, no denying that the Emperor was a figure who could wield a strong symbolic influence, and more importantly, one that could unite diverse elements of the population. Soon after the arrival of the mutineers and the wiping out of the British administration, the people of the city had started to turn almost instinctively to the Emperor with their petitions, usually complaining against the excesses of the soldiers and their associates. One way out was to replace a recalcitrant Emperor with a more amenable one, and indeed, by 17 May, there was some talk that the soldiers were considering deposing Bahadur Shah and placing on the throne Abu Bakr, his grandson.[746]

To find a way out of this situation, Bahadur Shah turned to the time-honoured Mughal technique of deploying court ceremonial. A special durbar was held on 18 May in the Diwan e Khas, where Bahadur Shah took his seat upon the royal silver throne. This had been lying disused for many years, and was now dusted off and put in use again. The ceremonial followed on this occasion demonstrated once again the creative use that the Mughals could make of symbols, to draw in and bind seemingly alien and incompatible groups and institutions, through ties of loyalty to the throne. At the durbar English military music was played by the bands of the five regiments. The Emperor conferred khilats on his sons, who were formally given high positions in the army, an army which was previously the Company's, but was now symbolically allying itself to the Emperor. The nomenclature of the positions conferred on the princes served as a bridge between royal traditions and the military institutions the soldiers had been trained in. Thus, the Emperor's son, Mirza Zahur ud din, alias Mirza Mughal, was appointed 'Commander-in-Chief'. Other sons (Mirza Kuchak, Mirza Khizr Sultan, Mirza Mendu) and a grandson (Abu Bakr) also received military ranks as generals and colonels.[747] The next day, coins were issued in the name of Bahadur Shah, reinforcing his sovereign status.[748]

There was a limit to how much symbols could achieve. Bahadur Shah intended to use the office of Commander-in-Chief to bring the soldiers more firmly under his authority, but the power equations were not so simple. Mirza Mughal and the other princes had joined the rebels quite readily from the day they arrived. As they saw it, under British rule the writing was already on the wall as far as their special position in Indian politics was concerned. In contrast, the Revolt, with its promise of the revival of Mughal sovereignty, was an attractive proposition, worth taking risks for. Yet they lacked any practical experience in administration or in the command of troops. Unlike Bahadur Shah, who at least commanded some personal respect among the population of the city, the princes were also unable to exert any charismatic leadership. There were frequent allegations against them of misappropriation of money intended for the payment of troops, of looting, oppressing the people and generally behaving irresponsibly.[749] The soldiers too were often unwilling to accept the princes as their commanders, and there were frequent eruptions of a power tussle between them. Moreover, they too were a collection of disparate groups, from different regiments, and, in the sudden absence of their British officers, lacking their customary command structure.

In an attempt to reconcile these disparate forces, an innovative mechanism was worked out sometime around late June or early July. This was the setting up of a 'Court of Administration' (*court e administration* in the original), the scope of which was formally stated in a document that laid down the constitution of the court and its rules and regulations. Its aim was 'better administration of the army and the government'.[750] It envisaged the setting up of a court, or committee, consisting of ten members—four civilians and six military, out of which one '*President*' and one '*Vice-President*' would be picked unanimously. Both would be assisted by a '*Secretary*' each, and more secretaries and functionaries would be appointed as needed. The members of the court would take office after swearing an oath that they would work 'with sincerity and devotion and without any prejudice or laxity' and seek to 'strengthen the government and benefit the public'. The Court's decisions would require a quorum of five, and its deliberations would be secret until deemed fit to be made public. Rules for orderly debate, discussion, and voting were also laid out in some detail.

The decisions of the Court would in the first instance be presented to the Heir Apparent (it is not entirely clear who occupied this position at the time, but probably Jawan Bakht) and the Commander-in-Chief (Mirza Mughal). On their assent it would be forwarded to the Emperor, whose decision would be final. The mode of appointing members of the committee was laid out, but only in the case of the military members. Persons with 'long service', ability and intelligence, would be elected by a majority; two from the infantry platoons, two from the cavalry, and two from the artillery. How the civilian members would be chosen was left vague, i.e. saying that they too would be 'elected/appointed like this'. This was a remarkable document, seeking to put in place a government that was monarchical but assisted and to some extent bound by an elected decision-making body that was part civilian and part military.

Eventually, the court did not take shape entirely as envisaged. It seems that the civilian members were never elected, probably because it was not clear what the constituency was from which they would be elected. In practice, therefore, the court became entirely a military court. It did, however, work reasonably well in providing a mechanism for giving an organized body of soldiers a voice in the decision-making process. The court regularly addressed the Emperor and he addressed them, and at times Bahadur Shah expressly asked them to make recommendations.

There were important challenges before the administration, and one was to provide an adequate and reliable source of revenue. The *Dehli Urdu Akhbar* in its 24 May issue commented on the breakdown of the revenue administration system and advised that it may be useful to turn to the officials of the old regime for their expertise.[751] Summons were issued to the landholders of independent territories, asking them to bring order to their territories as well as those towns and villages that had been till recently under the control of the British. Nevertheless, by early July the problem was still not solved, and the Emperor turned to the Court for suggestions. Their suggestions basically amounted to proclaiming the sovereignty of Bahadur Shah in the countryside, establishing contact with the landholders and leaders of village communities, sending out soldiers to collect the revenue but controlling their tendency to loot.[752] These were practical suggestions, though not particularly different from what was already being implemented. Transporting the revenue collected to Delhi was also not an easy task, as these convoys were often attacked and looted. Besides the city, there were many in the countryside too who looked to turn the sudden breakdown of the entrenched administration to their own advantage.[753] Ultimately, it was difficult to establish a working system in a state of war, and the collection of revenue remained a major challenge.

It was also imperative to bring order to the city. Though the worst of the violence by the soldiers and looting by the mob had taken place in the day or two after the outbreak, things were far from settling down. Bahadur Shah had to direct the kotwal and other administrative officials to prevent incidents of looting that were still taking place many days later. The presence of a large number of armed soldiers roaming the city was also causing unease among the citizens, and the Emperor passed an order that nobody may go about the streets of the city with a drawn sword.[754]

Bahadur Shah continued to play an important part in the day-to-day administration of the city. One aspect of that was his direct supervision of the police. All the reports of the kotwal and the thanadars used to be presented and dealt with in his own office.[755] He also received and addressed a slew of petitions often on very mundane matters. For instance, measures to suppress gambling seem to have got a surprising amount of attention from the kotwal and thanadars, and the matter came right up to the Emperor. In one case a man whose washerman had been arrested for some reason, and then released again, wrote to the Emperor, requesting that his clothes be recovered from the man. The deputy kotwal complained that new badges issued to the barqandazes (armed men) of the Kotwali were too small, and requested that larger ones be issued.[756]

While all proclamations and many administrative orders issued bore the seal of the Emperor, he was far from being in full control. His orders were frequently flouted, and at one point it was remarked that his seal was used by whichever of those around him pleased. We frequently find him between May and September denying letters and orders that purported to have come from him.[757]

49

War

The government set up in May 1857 in Delhi was above all a war-time government, and its most urgent aim was to win the war against the British. Though the British may have been vanquished in Delhi, the country needed to be won, and this required the gathering together of a large army, at the same time neutralizing the enemy's forces. In a sense, these two aims were simply two sides of the same coin, i.e. to induce more and more soldiers to desert from the Company's army and gather under the Emperor's banner. To encourage this, one of the first things Bahadur Shah, under the advice of the rebel soldiers, did was to send out letters to regiments stationed far and wide, exhorting them to come and join the Emperor's forces at Delhi, promising that they would be paid and supported. The response to this was good, and thousands of soldiers began to pour into Delhi.[758]

The British army was thrown into disarray as more and more of the Indian soldiers began to mutiny and desert throughout North India. Nevertheless, the European troops soon began to re-group, marching from Simla and Punjab, where they had mostly been stationed. With them were such Indian troops as had not mutinied, notably the Gurkhas and the Sikhs. Their intention was to march on Delhi, because they realized that Delhi, with the Emperor as a magnet, was the centre of the Revolt. Uppermost in the minds of both the civilian and military personnel was the thought that they 'must take Delhi, or the empire is lost'.[759]

Closer home, there was a body of European troops at Meerut too. The Emperor repeatedly urged the soldiers to go out and deal with this threat, but there were delays in putting this into effect. The troops were disorganized and their royal commanders were inexperienced. Another problem was a lack of gunpowder, which had all been blown up in the explosion of the magazine at Kashmiri Gate, or looted by the Gujars from the magazine outside the city, at Wazirabad. Manufacture was begun but it was not till late in May that supplies really started coming in. Finally, on 30 May a body of troops under Mirza Abu Bakr set out for Meerut. At the Hindon river, close to Ghaziuddinnagar (now called Ghaziabad) they met the British force, which had in the meanwhile been advancing from Meerut towards Delhi. It was a battle which went against the Indian troops and they were forced to retreat; but they came back the following day to fiercely attack the British position again. Though no real breakthrough was made and they had to retreat, the British were too exhausted to follow. The retreat of the Indian forces into the city caused consternation in the Emperor's court. Some of the people of the city, who had suffered at the hands of the rebel soldiers in the last few days, now took a perverse pleasure in their plight. In the ranks of the soldiers there was some demoralization, and it was reported that large numbers of them deserted and left for their homes.[760]

The British forces advancing from the north had been delayed, through the lack of guns and transportation, and the sudden death of their Commander-in-Chief, George Anson, at Amballa on 27 May, due to cholera. Finally, on 7 June, what had become known as the Delhi Field Force, marching from Karnal under the command of Major General Henry Barnard, met up with the troop from Meerut at Alipur. The next day, as they advanced towards Delhi, they found the rebel force waiting for them at Badli ki Sarai, some eight kilometres north-west of Delhi on the Grand Trunk Road. The battle was hard fought, with both sides numbering some 3,000 men, but the rebel force ultimately had to retreat to their second line of defence on the Ridge, from the Flagstaff tower to Hindu Rao's house. This too had to be surrendered quite soon to the British, who then settled down in their old cantonment to the west of this defensive line.[761]

The events of 8 June began what has been called the siege of Delhi, though at no point did the British forces actually encircle and besiege the city. For the next three months, the two sides would face off against each other, the Indian troops from the city and the British from the Ridge. The city and the fort frequently received damaging bombardment, in which many lives were lost, and which caused panic. Over the next weeks and months there were regular engagements, the Indian troops making attacks on the British position but being repulsed with reasonably heavy casualties. The British were not in a position to advance either, as they did not feel confident that, given their limited numbers and firepower, they could successfully take the city.[762]

The reverses on the field disheartened the soldiers; they also made their critics in the city more vocal. It had been several weeks since the outbreak of the Revolt, and people were feeling the strain. In the early days shopkeepers were more or less forced to open their shops, which were also often plundered or the goods confiscated on slight pretexts—on suspicions of hoarding, selling at raised prices, or supplying the enemy. Jivan Lal reported that 'several respectable men were seized and made to carry burdens to intimidate them and extort money'. As the days went by, money was regularly extorted by the soldiers and the princes from traders and shopkeepers who then appealed to the Emperor in protest. Most of the soldiers had been stationed outside the city walls, to the west and south of the city, in the localities like Jaisinghpura, Paharganj, Pahari Dhiraj and Teliwara, and the residents of these suffered the most. They complained that soldiers took goods from shops without payment, and even entered houses to forcibly take away household goods, fuel, etc., and used violence on anyone who resisted. Daily life was seriously affected. Even the cultivators outside the city walls suffered, as the soldiers and their animals caused damage to standing crops.[763]

The soldiers disrupted life inside the city too. People complained on a regular basis that the soldiers broke up houses and carried away the woodwork—doors, door-frames and beams from roofs. The royal property too was not immune. Ratan Chand, the superintendent of the Sahibabad garden and the adjoining royal estate, which included the main square, Chandni Chowk, reported that some soldiers had stationed their horses in the square. This understandably created a nuisance, as a result of which many of the tenants of the shops were leaving, which would lead to a loss of revenues for the Emperor. In fact the palace was not immune to encroachments either. Bahadur Shah regularly complained, to no avail, of the soldiers who were camping in his gardens within the fort.[764] Shops as well as houses and public buildings such as the Delhi College and the courthouse were forcibly evacuated for use as barracks by the soldiers.[765] Much of this so-called oppression was of course not deliberate. The soldiers needed lodging, food, fuel, construction supplies for military works, etc., and their attempts to procure these led to many of the 'excesses' they were accused of.

An atmosphere of fear and suspicion hung in the air, as anyone suspected of sabotage, or of helping the British, was killed. The leading men of the city attended the Emperor's durbar, to deliberate on the events. Even Bahadur Shah seemed to be losing his nerve. He upbraided the soldiers, putting the blame on the mutineers who had put them in this situation, and were now not being able defeat the English. He saw before him the end of his dynasty, which had lasted five hundred years, and he wished them to leave.[766]

It was in this time of low morale that news arrived of the approach of the Bareilly brigade—led by Mohammad Bakht Khan. At his first audience with the Emperor in a full durbar he was unmindful of court etiquette, he and his companions striding through without the customary salutations and obeisance, and saluting the Emperor as an equal. At any other time Bahadur Shah would have been offended, but now, he 'grasped his hands in token of friendship', for Bakht Khan's reputation preceded him. In his sixties, he had been in the Company's army for some forty years. His distinguished service record, particularly in the Anglo-

Afghan war, had led to his promotion as *subahdar* in the artillery. At the time of the outbreak he was posted in Bareilly, and was soon persuaded to join the mutiny. By the time of his arrival in Delhi on 1 July, he had amassed a considerable body of troops around him, comprising seven hundred cavalrymen with three hundred spare horse, over three thousand infantrymen, fourteen elephants, several artillery guns, and a hundred '*jehadis*'. He also carried treasure amounting to four lakh rupees. Bakht Khan was a charismatic leader with considerable military experience, and just what the Emperor was looking for in his time of need. He gratefully and readily agreed to the suggestion, put forward by Bakht Khan himself, to appoint him Commander-in-Chief, and give him far-reaching powers to discipline the forces, lead the war, and bring order to the city. He was put in charge of the police, revenue and civil administration of the city. The Emperor also presented him a sword, a shield and the rank of General. Proclamations were made in the city and in the army that all must follow the orders of Bakht Khan.[767]

Bakht Khan's measures to bring order to the city were draconian. The princes were informed that if they plundered the city their ears and noses would be cut off. Any soldier caught plundering would be arrested, and his arm severed. For good measure the kotwal was informed that if there was any more plundering he would be hanged. The residents of the city were ordered to arm themselves. At the same time he did try to raise the morale of the troops. A general parade was held shortly after his investiture where he 'spoke kindly to the men and comforted them; every regiment received a message from the King, that each man who went out to the battlefield, and each man who distinguished himself, would receive a grant of five bighas of land, and receive honorary posts.'[768]

These developments did not go unquestioned. Prominent citizens complained that peremptory orders were being issued to them through the police. The princes were resentful of this newcomer, on whose insistence they had been divested of all military functions. Abu Bakr had even been arrested after an intoxicated looting spree in one of the city's neighbourhoods. The other officers of the army, led by Taleyar Khan and Sidhara Singh, were dissatisfied too, that Bakht Khan had unceremoniously been put in command over their heads. Necessity brought these two groups together, and Bahadur Shah was given a petition by Mirza Mughal on behalf of the officers, that they wanted the Court (which had apparently been envisaged but not set up yet) to be established, so that the affairs of the army could be managed through it. They also gave a list of the members that had been picked by them.[769]

As to the military face-off, it had settled into a stalemate. The repeated attacks from the city exhausted the British forces on the Ridge and prevented them making a decisive onslaught on the city. By 18 July, Brigadier General Wilson, commanding the Delhi Field Force, was admitting that unless reinforcements were sent, he would have to order a retreat to Karnal. The report of 27 July stated that effective British force (i.e. excluding those ill or wounded) consisted of 171 officers, 3,450 European men, and 3,135 Indian men. In reply Wilson was informed that reinforcements were on their way from various locations, but could not be expected to reach Delhi except in batches between the middle and end of August.[770]

50

A City Divided

If the rebel army was to win the war, it needed money and supplies. The soldiers who had left their previous masters and had gathered under the banner of the Mughal Emperor, needed to be supported. This money was proving to be very difficult to procure, given the disordered state of the revenue collection mechanism. Very soon, the expedient of extracting money from the rich people of the city was resorted to. Several traders, bankers and shopkeepers were asked on a regular basis to contribute towards the support of troops, and they were generally extremely reluctant, even on the understanding that anything advanced in cash or kind would be treated strictly as a loan.[771]

To be fair to the commercial class, the burden was a heavy one. Soldiers and other freelance rebels had been arriving constantly in Delhi since the outbreak. The numbers fluctuated as some left from time to time to engage the enemy in different areas, but at their peak in late July they numbered over 50,000, and by some reports, even 80,000 by August.[772] At the same time, the traders struggled to function in a climate of severe disruption caused by war. Trade with the outside world was affected as the passage of goods and even letters past the city walls was looked on with suspicion by the rebels. As a result, availability of essential goods suffered and prices skyrocketed. On the other hand, if they sold goods at a higher price, they and their shops were attacked. Some of them sold some supplies to the British, probably just to keep afloat, rather than from any deep-seated treachery to the Indian cause.[773]

It was even more difficult to get money out of the non-commercial wealthy class—the landed and service elite. Bahadur Shah was very aware that the support of the rich and influential in the city was essential, so this was a class he was even less willing to alienate. He repeatedly remonstrated with the soldiers not to harass such individuals. For instance, it was at his insistence that goods looted from the house of Hamid Ali Khan, who had been his mukhtar in earlier years, were restored once the soldiers had satisfied themselves that no Europeans were being sheltered there. He then summoned Hamid Ali Khan, and advised him to attend his court every day. It was too late. If Hamid Ali Khan had any sympathies with the rebels, this incident was enough to push him to the other side. By mid-June certainly he was in touch with the British, telling a spy that the people of the city just wanted to be rid of the 'tumultuous' mutineers, and that he would extend all help to the British. Hamid Ali Khan was not alone among the elite of the city to distance himself from the new dispensation. When similar summons were sent to Amin ud din and Zia ud din Ahmad Khan, they came and paid their respects to the Emperor. When he ordered them to attend the durbar every day, however, they pleaded ill-health. Sadr ud din Khan Azurda had already refused to take up his erstwhile judicial responsibilities.[774]

There were other members of the educated elite who were more sympathetic to the cause. One such was Mohammad Baqar. Early in the Revolt he put himself at the service of the Emperor, and was given responsibilities. On 17 May, he was directed to go with two companies of infantry and one troop of cavalry to deal with three hundred Gujars and Mewatis who were attacking a treasure of several lakhs of rupees, the revenue of Gurgaon, which was being brought to Delhi under an armed escort.[775]

All the same, there was evidence that enemies lurked within the city walls, most clearly manifest in the form of sabotage. In two separate instances towards the end of May, guns mounted on the bastions of the city's defences were found to have been rendered useless by being filled with stones, gravel, iron nails and string. This led to an uproar and trading of accusations. Ahsanullah Khan and Mahbub Ali Khan were again the prime targets of the soldiers' wrath, and swords were drawn against them. Bahadur Shah had to step in to protect them, asking in turn for an explanation as to how guns which were manned by the soldiers themselves could have been sabotaged by someone else. It was a situation that created high tension and mutual suspicions, and accusations were also hurled at Abu Bakr, the Emperor's grandson. Abu Bakr was also accused of being involved in the smuggling of gunpowder hidden in cartloads of grain.[776]

Ahsanullah Khan and Mahbub Ali Khan were repeatedly accused by the soldiers of colluding with the British, and sending them information clandestinely. The soldiers went to the extent of placing guards on Ahsanullah Khan to monitor his activities, even when he was in attendance on the Emperor. At the same time, the real network of spies that was operating efficiently to provide information to the British, escaped detection. One of their most reliable informants was Jivan Lal. Jivan Lal's forbear was Raja Raghunath, the prime minister of Emperor Aurangzeb. His father, Girdhari Lal, had worked as a writer with David Ochterlony and Charles Metcalfe. Jivan Lal himself had been in the service of the Company from the start of his career in 1827. At the time the Revolt broke out, he was the mir munshi, or head clerk, of the Residency office in Delhi. In this position, he interacted on a daily basis with both the administration and the palace. For instance, he was in charge of the distribution of the pensions paid by the administration to various members of the royal family which made him privy to the affairs of the royal family. Jivan Lal remained loyal to his masters when the Revolt broke out. He stayed within the city walls during the course of the Revolt and employed four men to bring him information which he could then pass on to the British.[777]

The other potential source of discord within the city was sectarian strife, but this remained by and large controlled, through the direct intervention of the Emperor. On 19 May, Bahadur Shah was informed that a 'banner of jehad', armed struggle for Islam, had been raised in the Jama Masjid. While Jivan Lal had been told that this was done by some residents of Dharampura (a locality near the Jama Masjid) and some 'low characters of the city', Chunni Lal, a news writer, attributed it to some ulema, or Islamic theologians and some other Muslims. The Emperor was outraged at this, and demanded to know what was the meaning of this jehad, when the enemy had already been eradicated from the city? Making it out to be a religious war was bound to antagonize the Hindus, which included the majority of the soldiers. He immediately sent Azurda to the mosque, to have the banner taken down. The next day one of the ulema responsible, Mohammad Syed, visited Bahadur Shah, and when it was put to him, admitted that the jehad had been declared against the Hindus too. To this Bahadur Shah replied firmly that he absolutely forbad this jehad, and to him Hindus and Muslims were the same. Moreover, particularly at a delicate time like this, 'it was fitting that sympathy should exist among all classes.' Along the same lines he reassured the deputation of soldiers that had come to complain about the issue.[778]

It was close to the end of the holy month of Ramzan, and Eid ul Fitr was approaching, which made it even more imperative that peace be maintained. The *Dehli Urdu Akhbar* noted that on 22 May, which was the last Friday in Ramzan, and an important day in the Islamic calendar, the crowd at the Jama Masjid was thin. The Emperor and the princes did not turn up at all, according to Mohammad Baqar, because they were too busy and distracted. The Emperor did, however, order it to be proclaimed throughout the city by beat of drum that Hindus and Muslims must keep the peace. Eid came and went peacefully, and Bahadur Shah went with his sons to pray in the Jama Masjid.[779]

Things remained quiet till 8 July, when some butchers were caught trying to smuggle meat out to the British and in consequence, five of them were killed by the soldiers. This was not an occurrence that was in itself so unusual. Harsh deterrent measures were being taken against those who were caught helping the enemy. For instance, in mid-June, thirteen bakers had been killed for supplying bread to the British.[780] But there was a history of contention over cow slaughter in the city, and the butchers in question were Muslims and the soldiers Hindus. At once rumours of cow slaughter started circulating; the soldiers over-reacted and various butchers and at least one completely innocent kabab-seller were arrested.

The butchers as a group complained to the Emperor. They were joined by some other Muslims who on principle declared that they would kill a cow on the approaching Eid uz Zuha, and would defend their right by force of arms if need be. It appears that it was the mujahidin who were at the forefront of this demand. On their part the Sikh and Hindu soldiers made it an issue too, saying that they would not fight if cattle were killed. Bakht Khan was at the time out on a sortie against the British, so Bahadur Shah directed Mirza Mughal to make enquiries. The order that was issued as a result, showed that the Emperor's main aim was to prevent sectarian violence. A ban on the slaughter of cattle was proclaimed, punishable by death; at the same time it was decreed that anyone objecting to the killing of a goat would be punished. This was the most balanced solution that could probably have been arrived at under the circumstances.

The kotwal of the city was ordered to keep a close watch on all Muslims who owned cows, to make sure they were not killed. The apprehension that someone might defy the ban and nevertheless kill a cow was so great, that an order was issued to the effect that cows belonging to Muslims of the city be rounded up by the kotwal and kept under his custody until Eid was safely over! The poor kotwal, horrified at the thought of scores of cattle swarming the Kotwali, represented to the Emperor that for one he did not have the space to accommodate all the animals, and it would also be a measure that would highly inconvenience all the owners of cows. He suggested instead that bonds be taken from the concerned individuals, to the effect that they would respect the law. In any event the festival passed off peacefully.[781]

Finally, one major, damaging form of division within the rebel camp was the intense rivalries amongst the different regiments of the soldiers. As early as 28 May, when it was proving difficult to pay the soldiers their salaries, there was grumbling among the Delhi regiments, that this was all the Meerut soldiers' fault. Regret was expressed that when these mutinous troops arrived in Delhi, they had been welcomed rather than arrested and punished for their mutiny.[782] As time passed, this discord only got worse, and would ultimately have a very negative effect on the military response to the British who were slowly but surely strengthening their position.

51

A Cause to Fight For

On the very first day of the outbreak of the Revolt in Delhi, the soldiers coming from Meerut had been asked to explain themselves, and had tried to articulate the motivation behind their mutiny. While addressing Douglas from beneath the jharokha, they had said, 'We have mutinied at Meerut and have come here for justice.'[783] A little later, when they addressed Bahadur Shah in the Diwan e Khas, they told him, 'we have come to fight for our religion and to pay our respect [*sic*] to His Majesty.'[784] Over the next few months, religion was frequently invoked, as the motivating factor for the war against the British—in the soldiers' petitions to the Emperor, in various official proclamations, and even in individual cases, such as the lone soldier who had travelled all the way from Amritsar, and petitioned the Emperor saying, 'your slave has presented himself, solely to fight for the faith.'[785] In these articulations, the enemy was invariably identified in terms of religious belief, i.e. 'kafir' (infidel), or 'nasrani' (Nazarene, e.g. Christian).

In British histories of the Revolt that were written after 1858, this reference to religion was specifically linked to the greased cartridge question, and the uprising was attributed to this particular grievance. In fact, the greased cartridge was probably a triggering factor, but was far from being the only or even the most important one. The evidence is to be found in the proclamations of the rebel government itself, exhorting others to rise up, and come and join the cause. One of these, issued in mid-June, went out on behalf of 'the Hindoos and Muslims assembled at Dehli' to 'all the inhabitants, Hindoos and Mussulman, and others of Hindostan'. It laid out a list of grievances against the British rulers. One, they had 'exacted as revenue Rs 300 where only Rs 200 was due'. Two, they had 'doubled and quadrupled and raised tenfold the Choukeedaree Tax'. Three, there was a loss of jobs, particularly those of respectable and learned men; and people were deterred from travelling in search of employment because of the heavy toll taxes. Having outlined these grievances, it went on—'Gradually matters arrived at such a pitch that the Government had determined to subvert everyone's religion. Therefore the whole army of Hindostan, both Hindoo and Mussulman, from Calcutta to Peshawur, has risen.' It exhorted the people of the country to rise up in revolt—'Let no Hindoo or Mussulman be alarmed; let them watch their opportunity and kill the enemies of their religion. Trust in God and let not your resolution waver. It is a great thing to trust in the Almighty. Remember Him always. With His aid you will be victorious.'[786]

This proclamation was enclosed in a letter addressed specifically by the rebel soldiers to their brother soldiers in Punjab. The letter talked more specifically of the threat to religion. 'Assalamualaikum and Ram Ram' it began, and appealed to the soldiers to stand up in defence of their faith. It promised them a welcome at Delhi, where they would get food and pay, and the chance to fight for their faith. If they died, Muslims would be martyrs, and Hindus 'Bycoonth-Bashees' (literally, dwellers in the abode of Vishnu). It urged the soldiers to widely disseminate the main proclamation.[787] Proclamations issued from the Emperor too frequently referred to 'faith', and again this was meant to include Hindus and Muslims both. A typical proclamation was addressed 'To all Hindoos and Mahomedans who wish the advancement of religion', and spoke of the soldiers who had gathered in Delhi 'in the cause of the faith and of religion'[788] (the words 'faith' and 'religion' are British renderings of *din* and *dharam*). In a similar vein, most of the other proclamations and the letters exchanged among the rebels, referred to Hindus and Muslims 'fighting for their faith', but in very generic terms, without reference to specific grievances, about how exactly the British had tried to destroy their faith.

One very vocal ideologue of the Revolt was Mohammad Baqar, whose *Dehli Urdu Akhbar* continued to report through the course of the Revolt. Before the Revolt the newspaper had been generally pro-British, though critical of specific government policies. The first issue of the weekly newspaper to come out after the outbreak of rebellion in Delhi, that of 17 May, was neutral in tone. Mohammad Baqar reported on the events in the city and palace, for the most part being careful not to reveal his own opinions except in one case. He spoke of the Principal of the Delhi College with a fair degree of venom. Mohammad Baqar told his readers that Fredrick Taylor was killed on the 12th, and added details about him that were not creditable to the dead man, saying that he was a great miser and now all that hoarded wealth was gone, that he used to mislead the ignorant to convert them to Christianity. But here too Mohammad Baqar's bitterness had a very concrete cause. He said of Taylor that the blood of Chiman Lal was on his head, implying of course that Chiman Lal was killed because he was a Christian and he was a Christian because of the teaching of Taylor.[789]

Only by the end of May, i.e. the issue of the 31st, did the *Dehli Urdu Akhbar* come out strongly against the British. Probably it took this much time for Baqar to decide that the British were really gone, and that the Emperor had thrown in his lot with the rebels. That his paper had not spoken out against British rule for so many years, did not seem an incongruity in Baqar's eyes. On 5 July 1857 he wrote, that for long under British rule, the people had been oppressed, but were helpless. Now that the armies had united against the British, the people could all rise against them. From the following issue the title of the newspaper was changed to *Akhbar ul Zafar*, a play on words, since 'zafar' was the word for victory as well as being the title of the Emperor.[790] Apart from this turnaround in political opinion, Mohammad Baqar's approach to the writing and editing of his newspaper did not change much. He was critical of the shortcomings of the administration, yet he tried to inspire his readers to support the Emperor and his cause.

Mohammad Baqar clearly tried to use religion as a strong psychological instrument, to persuade people to join the cause of the Revolt. He was concerned that many of the people of the city were still not convinced of the wisdom of the Revolt, and were perhaps afraid that the British would come back and exact revenge. He reassured them with the thought that the sudden wiping out of British rule was in fact a sign that God was not on the side of the Christians. God was on the side of the Emperor and his subjects; this was evident because He had after all taken power away from the British. History proved that when this happened, as it had many times before, even the weak could overcome the strong. One of the examples he gave was when Ram, with a relatively small army, had defeated the mighty Ravan, and Krishna had put down the tyrant Kans. He exhorted the people of the city, both Hindus and Muslims, not to lose hope because the British appeared to be winning some of the battles. Instead, they must follow and swear loyalty to the Emperor, who was the *zill e subhani*, 'the shadow of God'. One who failed in this was failing in his duty to God, and would be punished in this world and the next.[791]

It was easy to appeal to faith, because religious belief was an important part of both public and private life. For instance the fighting men, whether Muslims or Hindus, frequently and publicly swore on their respective religious scriptures. There were also pandits who went about exhorting Hindus to go out and fight against the *malechh* (foreigners), and in so doing achieve heaven even without requirements of any last rites.[792] There was also a shared complex of ritual and superstition that the soldiers subscribed to. For instance, the justification given by subahdars Taley Yar Khan and Ram Baksh, on behalf of their respective regiments, for not immediately following the royal command to advance on the enemy was, that 'this is a day of the week on which it is unpropitious to proceed towards the East. We shall accordingly leave at a propitious hour.'[793]

Religious belief and ritual could serve as a powerful morale booster. Hence, a certain Pandit Hari Chander not only gave prescriptions of auspicious times and strategies for battle, but predicted a comprehensive victory for the rebel forces in a battle, which he said, would be 'like the Mahabharat'. With the same aim, Maulvis gave speeches in mosques, exhorting people to jehad, and on the tenth day of Moharram, additional operations were planned, apparently because, as one spy reported to the British, 'Muslims are hoping to attain martyrdom on that day.[794] Many military morale boosting exercises had a distinct flavour of religious ritual. Jivan Lal in his diary entry of 23 June said, 'A gun constructed in the reign of Shah Jahan was taken, and mounted. When ready, a he-goat was tied to the mouth, and twenty-five seers of sweetmeats placed inside, and a necklace of flowers hung around the muzzle. Several Brahmins and astrologers were summoned, and directed to consult their almanacs as to whether the mutineers would be victorious."[795] This was clearly a typical mix of symbols and practice. The gun was associated with a great Mughal Emperor, and the sacrifice was a ritual sanctifying the war.

A fatwa, or opinion by Islamic jurists, could also be used as an instrument to pressurize Muslims to join the war effort. Towards the end of July Bakht Khan managed to obtain a fatwa sanctioning jehad against the British and making it encumbent on Muslims (though the language of the fatwa spoke only of the 'people of Delhi', the fatwa by its very nature was directed towards Muslims) of Delhi to support it. The aim of the fatwa was undoubtedly to inspire Muslims to greater support of the anti-British war. The text of the document, as printed in the *Sadiq ul Akhbar* of 27 July, made no suggestion of any animosity towards Hindus. Nevertheless, Bakht Khan had found great difficulty in obtaining the signatures of the prominent religious jurists of the city to sign it. When he requested Bahadur Shah to direct ulemas such as Sadr ud din Khan Azurda and Mahbub Ali to sign it, Bahadur Shah in fact refused. Their signatures, in addition to several others, did finally appear on the fatwa as printed in the newspaper (the original was never found), but Azurda would later claim that he had been coerced into it. Even more significantly, there were some, such as Maulvi Abdul Qadir, and Maulvi Nazir Husain, who refused to sign it, despite coercion.[796]

The appeal to faith was at all necessary because this was an era that pre-dated modern nationalism. Since the idea of the nation was not well developed, the concept of colonial rule as the rule of one nation over another was not entirely understood either. Racial distinctions were recognized of course, particularly because racism from British officials was quite common. Mohammad Baqar reminded his readers: '*sau baras ke istiqlal e saltanat se khalq e khuda ko haqir aur tumhare bhai bandon ko "kala admi", "kala admi" kah kar zalil o khwar karte the'*, i.e. '[the British] during an unbroken rule of a hundred years referred to creatures of God as "vile" and to your brothers and kin as "black man", "black man" and thus dishonoured and disgraced them'.[797] In the rhetoric against the British, race was conflated with a religious category, i.e. Christians, within which all members of the ruling race could conveniently be fitted, and in which few Indians fell. Categorizing the enemy by religion rather than race was an effective device, simply because the Revolt was projected as a war for 'the faith'. Hence the terms 'kafir' and 'Nasrani' were used more frequently than 'gora', i.e. 'white man'.

While the ideas of nationalism and colonialism had not taken coherent form, the nascent signs certainly existed. The *Dehli Urdu Akhbar* expressed the idea of a common identity in the terms '*hamare mulk wale*' or '*ahl e watan*' (countrymen).[798] A proclamation issued in the name of the Emperor on 6 September, illustrates the fact that the Revolt sought to unite people on a basis that transcended religion and ethnicity. It read: 'This is a religious war, and is being prosecuted on account of the faith and that it behoves all Hindoos and Mussulman residents of the Imperial city, whether they be men of the Eastern Provinces or Seikhs [Sikhs] or foreigners [it is likely that the original here was *wilayati*, commonly used for Afghans] or natives of the Himalaya hills or Nepaulese… whenever they come over to this side…they will be allowed to continue in their own creed and religions.'[799]

The idea of colonial exploitation at a national level was also being grasped. The *Dehli Urdu Akhbar* on 31 May spoke of the looting of the equipment and powder of the magazine, which 'the

English had in a smooth and easy manner, by cutting and burning the throats and hearts of the people, produced and gathered'. In another issue, the newspaper spoke of the resumed landed estates or jagirdaris, and livelihoods of many which had been taken away by the British. On 21 June it reminded its readers that during their rule the British had given all higher government jobs, worth hundreds of rupees a month, to people of their own colour. Besides this, they spent money very carefully and lived frugally. As a result, they saved thousands and lakhs of rupees and took this money to their country. Thus their wealth did not spread in our country and their gold and property did not bring any benefits to our people.[800] The idea that the wealth of an entire nation was transferred by alien rulers to their own country, was in fact a revolutionary idea. This idea would some years later be further developed by the nationalist leader Dadabhai Naoroji, and articulated as the 'drain of wealth'.

The rebels had many reasons to wish to be rid of British rule, but what was the alternative before them? For more than three centuries the Mughal name had been associated with sovereignty over the area that was now affected by the Revolt. This was a memory that still persisted, even though the Emperor had been reduced to less than a cipher. There was no better proof of this than the soldiers who almost instinctively converged on Delhi from all corners. Several soldiers of the Company's army stationed in Delhi had begun to approach him in the mid-1850s to become his spiritual disciples, until stopped by government order. So there were at least some to whom he was a charismatic figure. The *Dehli Urdu Akhbar* more clearly expressed the idea that the Mughal dynasty, in contrast to the British, had been more sympathetic to the people, and that this was justification for Revolt in its name. In the issue dated 14 June, a long article that began 'a certain elder was saying' (which was probably a euphemism for the views of Mohammad Baqar himself) reminded his 'fellow countrymen' that the Mughal dynasty had not discriminated between its subjects on the basis of religion, and had allowed all to follow their own inclinations.[801]

Yet, it was not a mere revival of the old empire, no matter how glorious or how just and benevolent, that the new situation called for. Times had changed and even the Emperor sought to adapt to these changed circumstances. On 27 July, the deputy kotwal addressed all the thanadars to the effect that they had so far been addressing the Emperor as '*hazrat jahan panah salamat*' (your exalted majesty). Henceforth, they were to address him as '*gharib parvar salamat*' (protector of the poor).[802] The Revolt had opened up the possibilities of a changed worldview, of a world in which a ruler's right to rule would be tested on his ability and willingness to support the downtrodden.

52

A World Turned Upside Down

In these disturbed times, it was not clear which of the Emperor's subjects needed the most protection. The burden of the war fell on all of course, but there were some to whom it provided new opportunities as well. On the very first day of the uprising in Delhi, observers had noticed that the 'mob' had played a big part in the violence and looting. This mob contained criminals, such as pickpockets and thieves, who had been released by the soldiers from the jail. It also comprised many of the non-criminal labouring poor—wrestlers, tanners, carriers of night soil, washermen, water carriers, butchers, greengrocers, and weavers.[803] The loot that was collected was considerable, particularly in the early days, when shops and the Delhi Bank were attacked. Once the British forces arrived outside the walls of the city, and the war began in earnest, this throng also took to following closely behind troops as they went out of the city walls to attack enemy troops, hoping to mop up plunder from the latter's camp. Their role was not entirely negative either. It was said that it was the city badmashes who constantly exhorted the soldiers to get down to the task of defeating the enemy, chaffing them on signs of hesitance and accusing them of cowardice.[804]

Many of those who indulged in loot were those who ordinarily lived outside the city walls. On their way to Delhi the mutineers had collected around them convicts from Meerut jail and people from the villages surrounding Delhi, mostly Gujars from the villages of Chandrawal and Wazirabad. They looted and burned the houses of the cantonment, and the grand mansion built by Thomas Metcalfe. They also carried away all the furniture in Ludlow Castle, and burnt all records of the Commissioner and Agent to the Lt Governor, which were stored there. The Gujars plundered shops in localities outside the city walls, such as Subzi Mandi, Teliwara, Rajpur, Pahari Dhiraj; and their villages were burnt in retaliation. The Mewatis of Jaisinghpura were also responsible for plunder, and the soldiers were ready to go and destroy Jaisinghpura as punishment. This was prevented by a petition to the Emperor from the agent of the Raja of Jaipur, who owned the land of Jaisinghpura—the area adjoining the Jantar Mantar observatory, which had been the property of the kingdom since early Mughal times. [805]

Those indulging in looting within the city soon found that if they donned the uniforms of soldiers, it was even easier to loot or extract money by force, since people were more readily intimidated by soldiers. In the following days, many such cases came to light, of men carrying out looting in the guise of soldiers.[806] But it was not just looting that they were interested in. The looting had led to a forcible redistribution of wealth and provided its receivers a chance for upward mobility. At least some of these newly-liberated labouring poor and criminal classes of the city got themselves horses, uniforms and arms. They were probably major buyers in the arms market that was held every evening around the Jama Masjid. They also probably provided much of the business for tailoring and sword sharpening establishments, which flourished while many other kinds of shops were often closed.[807]

The arming of this population, whether it was the poor of the city or those of the rural areas, was a matter of concern for the 'respectable' city-folk. When the stores within the munitions magazine at Wazirabad were carried off by 'peasants and Gujars', the *Dehli Urdu Akhbar* feared that they might be selling them to the British. But the thought that they would use the arms themselves was equally worrying.[808] The taking up of arms by these groups went against the traditional caste configurations in Indian armies. In the Company's Bengal Army too, the Hindus were mostly Brahmins and Rajputs, and the Muslims, Syeds and Pathans.[809] For this reason the authorities, when they caught men impersonating soldiers, felt it was worth recording and reporting that they were 'weavers', Jats, Ahirs, Chamars, etc.[810] It was no wonder then, that when Bahadur Shah directed Hamid Ali Khan to raise a troop of 500, he specifically remarked that these should be of the '*sharif qaum*', i.e. upper castes such as Syeds, Pathans and Mughals, and not '*neech qaum*' or lower castes.[811]

Denied space in the regular armed contingents, the latter began to go out on sorties against the British in an organized body, under a flag of their own. A spy reporting in mid-June on the forces going out to give battle to the British, said, 'they had 3 standards—1 for the Regular Cavalry, 1 for the Lucknow Irregulars, and 1 for the riff-raff of Delhee.'[812] Not able to prevent them arming themselves, the Emperor tried to give them legitimacy in the hope that through this they would be amenable to control. Hence, one of the spies reported to the British camp that 'the King has given kettle drums and flags to the Goojurs with orders to plunder and kill the Europeans forces, about 1000 of them have collected'.[813]

In the eyes of those who had long enjoyed social and economic privilege, the implications of this upturning of the social order were serious. In a letter to the kotwal, the thanadar of Bhojla Pahari reported, 'today in execution of your order, four barqandazes of this thana had been sent to requisition a hundred coolies and diggers. Afzal Beg, the notorious badmash, confronted the barqandazes and stated that you take people from here without my orders, we will stand up to you and use force too…the coolies and diggers who had been conscripted were freed by him and he said if you are armed, we too are armed.'[814] Even when not armed, the poor were liberated by the newfound wealth they accumulated through plunder. Many stopped carrying out menial jobs. The *Dehli Urdu Akhbar* reported that the water carriers had stopped filling water in the houses. The sweepers and cleaners had all disappeared and as a result many areas had not been cleaned for days and there was a real danger of some epidemic starting up.[815]

This defiance by the underclasses, and their refusal to conform to their socially ordained roles, led to an unease among the well off. There was a pervasive feeling that respectable people's hold on their dignity had become tenuous. Bahadur Shah, giving permission to an individual to set up a newspaper, exhorted him to 'observe great care, that false intelligence or that statements by which the characters of respectable of the city may be aspersed, directly or by implication, be not inserted.'[816]

The category of the newly armed men from marginalized communities overlapped with one other category of person that was an active participant in the Revolt. These were the '*ghazis*', a word meaning a soldier, often but not exclusively implying one who fights against infidels. The term jehadi, specifically alluding to a Muslim who wages a war in defence of his religion, was also sometimes applied.[817] In the context of Delhi in 1857, these terms were applied to a sort of freelance soldier, usually a Muslim. They often came from outside—for instance Tonk and Amroha, accompanying the rebel soldiers. Many of them, dressed in blue clothes, were men of the north-west frontier. The largest contingent was from Tonk, which had a history of supporting Afghan cavalrymen. Later memoirs, as well as spies reporting to the British, mentioned more than once that a small section of people actually from Delhi—predictably the 'badmashes'—were a part of these ghazis who numbered several thousand.[818]

The ghazis, or jehadis, began to arrive in numbers in Delhi from about end-June, a large group arriving with Bakht Khan's Bareilly brigade. Various groups of jehadis had leaders of their own; for instance Sarfaraz Ali, a Maulvi, was the leader of the group that had accompanied Bakht Khan, and Liaqat Ali was the head of the jehadis of Allahabad. They constituted themselves as an auxiliary army, and frequently represented themselves as one body in various petitions to the Emperor. They took an active part in the fighting, but that was not their only role. They were vocal in their attempts at mobilizing the people, by one account marching along Chandni Chowk shouting 'citizens, citizens, all who would be martyrs for the faith, come, follow us'. They were also part of the mob that after a repulsed British attack, triumphantly carried heads of British soldiers on poles into the city.[819]

Contemporary observers, for instance the informers carrying news to British officers, saw the ghazis as Muslim 'fanatics' preaching a holy war, distinct from the rebel soldiers and from the population at large.[820] An unknown spy reporting in mid-July wrote, 'The ghazis, of which many are convicts released from jails, have gathered in the mosque under the leadership of one Talib Ali. Gulzar Ali of Amroha is in the city with ten thousand badmashes. Apart from some badmashes, none of the city people are a part of these ghazis.'[821]

The Emperor, the court, and the city people had mixed feelings about these freelance soldiers. Bahadur Shah initially gave them some funds for subsistence, but many felt they were a burden on the city. A petition to the Emperor by a number of Muslim merchants complained that apart from other exactions, they were being made to pay for the support of 1,200 mujahidin, which was a great burden for them. In the latter part of July, when another large group of jehadis arrived, Bahadur Shah bluntly said that he had no money to give them. Many of the people in the city were also generally rather wary of groups claiming to be ghazis or jehadis. There were rumours circulating that this guise was being used as a cloak by those who intended either to dupe and loot the city, or betray it to the enemy. The regular soldiers too did not give them any military support when they went out to battle, about which the ghazis complained bitterly.[822]

The rise of marginal groups was not the only threat to the established social order. These extraordinary times put a strain on family ties too. The administration was frequently called upon to intervene in marital disputes and elopements, with many of these petitions reaching the highest levels, i.e. the Commander-in-Chief. Some of these no doubt took place because of a large number of men from outside who were billeted in the city. There were some complaints of women eloping with the newly arrived soldiers, and others of soldiers' wives eloping while they were out fighting. The soldiers were also sometimes used as brawn to settle scores, as in the case of a certain Surajbali, who used the help of some soldiers to bring back his ex-wife, after beating her and her family.[823]

The state of war suggested new avenues for empowerment to some women. In early August, one of the Indian soldiers on horseback who was captured by the British, turned out to be a woman. On 8 September, the leader of a platoon reported to the Commander-in-Chief—'at twelve o'clock at night, a woman dressed like a man and armed attempted to go out of the city gate.' This attempt at breaking out of gender roles, however, did not lead very far, as she was arrested and released with a caution, and the remark that 'I hope that nobody else should do anything like this and whoever does so will be punished'.[824]

53

Nerves and Resources Stretched Thin

On 1 August, Eid, the Indian side attacked the British with renewed vigour, but with disastrous results. Not only did they fail to make any headway, they suffered casualties amounting to some 2,000-3,000 men. The enemy's loss on the other hand was less than fifty. The only reason the hopelessly outnumbered British had survived on the Ridge all this while was that though the Indian side had more numerous troops (by this time some 60,000), their attacks were rather disorganized. The lack of an effective battle plan was not surprising, given the fact that there were few officers of a high enough rank on the Indian side. Indians had never risen to higher ranks in the service of the British. Despite the rank of 'General' bestowed on him by the Emperor, Bakht Khan's experience was that of a subahdar, and he was not accepted as a leader by many of the other officers, and neither by the princes, and therefore he could not rely on the cooperation of all the regiments for a coordinated plan. Also, by the end of July they were very short of gunpowder. The only advantage the Indians had was in numbers, but the high casualty rate was demoralizing. Many soldiers had begun to desert and leave the city.[825]

Bahadur Shah had begun to realize quite soon that Bakht Khan held no magic bullet, and could be a divisive figure too. Bakht

Khan had himself admitted that the other officers did not obey his commands. So, with his consent, he restored the command of all the regiments to their own officers, leaving only the Bareilly regiment under Bakht Khan. As a consolation of sorts, he was given the rank and title of 'Governor'. The Emperor had also realized that an outsider like Bakht Khan could not be effective in running the civil administration of the city. He therefore turned to the old and influential residents, and a committee was formed, superintended by Mirza Mughal, to coordinate the very important task of collecting contributions from the wealthy. This proved to be a successful measure, and some money started coming in.[826]

It was, however, never enough, and as the days went by and the need grew greater, coercive methods were used. Prominent bankers were frequently arrested, in order to put pressure on them to pay up.[827] Pressure was also being put on other rich citizens, who decided to protect themselves through the use of hired guards, in fact drawn from the same amorphous 'jehadi' category. Thus, there had been a guard on the houses of Hamid Ali Khan and Azurda since shortly after the outbreak.[828] On 9 August when tensions and suspicions were running high, Jivan Lal wrote, 'The house of Moulvie Sadar-u-din Khan was attacked today by fifty soldiers; but, seeing that there were seventy Jehadis ready to oppose them, they retreated.' A request had been sent out on behalf of Azurda just the day before, asking one of the leaders of the mujahidin to send him a hundred men. A group of two hundred men went the next day to the house of the Nawab of Loharu, Amin ud din Ahmad Khan to demand money, but he too managed to successfully resist because he had an armed contingent on the ready. As Amin ud din and his brother Zia ud din continued to resist these demands for money, the princes complained that it was because they were sympathetic to the British cause.[829]

By the second half of August the bankers and the nobility were joining hands to oppose the extortions of money, and this was a tactic that worked. Jivan Lal wrote in his diary, 'Mirza Zia u din Khan and Mirza Amin u-din Khan called a meeting, and addressing it, said: "If there were any persons present who preferred death to being plundered by the Sepoys, let them bind themselves to resist further exactions." The bankers of Lal Koti (Kuan?) and Chandi (Chandni) Chouk were called on to sign a document to the same effect. When the Sepoys heard of this they determined to kill the originators, but finding the whole city was against them, they thought better of them.'[830] There were also constant accusations of misappropriation of money, particularly that the princes collected money but did not pass it on to the army, which was in dire need. To tackle this problem, the kotwal was informed that no one except the Court was allowed to demand money from any bankers.[831]

As September set in, things had come to such a pass that in desperation the soldiers threatened to divide the city between themselves and plunder it if they were not paid or fed. Bahadur Shah could do nothing but offer up the royal jewels, as he had on occasion in the past too, when pressed too hard. This embarrassed the elite of the city as well as other members of the royal family into promising to raise some of the money required. By then the soldiers were going so far as to imprison some of the *ashraf* (the elite) of the city as well, so some concrete promises had to be made. In the beginning of September, Azurda and Lala Mukund Lal agreed to collect one lakh rupees from the Muslims and Hindus respectively. They promised to have the money ready within fifteen days, estimating quite accurately as it turned out, that by then Delhi would be in British hands.[832]

The fates conspired to frustrate the rebel cause. An explosion in the gunpowder factory in the old mansion of Begum Samru in Churiwalan on 7 August killed nearly five hundred people. Bahadur Shah stepped in with a proclamation that dependants of those who died would be given financial help by the state, but apart from the loss of life, this created a shortage of gunpowder. This was probably simply an accident, but in the atmosphere of suspicion that prevailed, there was a strong rumour that it was sabotage engineered by Ahsanullah Khan. His house was looted and set on fire, he was arrested and narrowly escaped with his life only because Bahadur Shah swore that he would kill himself if his minister was harmed.[833]

Unknown to Ahsanullah Khan, the suspicions were being fuelled by Rajab Ali, one of the informers of the British, who was working with Hodson, a subaltern in the British camp. Rajab Ali was evidently not only sending out information, but working actively inside the city to foment dissentions.[834] Accusations now were even being made against Zeenat Mahal, who was suspected to be a traitor, and by 18 August even the British informants in the city believed that she was in favour of the British. This was not an unfounded suspicion either, for the British camp had received an emissary from her, offering her cooperation in return for safety. The British, however, were not willing to make any terms with her.[835] Zeenat Mahal's motives were understandable. Before the outbreak, the single aim of her exertions had been to secure the succession for her son Jawan Bakht. The Revolt had pushed the other princes, notably Mirza Mughal, to the forefront. Understandably, she felt that the success of the Revolt would put paid to her ambitions for Jawan Bakht. On the other hand, if the revolt in Delhi was put down with assistance from her, the other princes being implicated in the uprising, Jawan Bakht's position would be secure. For the same reason, she had all along kept Jawan Bakht aloof from participation, and prevented him from accepting any military position, such as the other princes had received.[836]

There was a feeling of desperation in the court. There were those, like Maulvi Fazl e Haq who felt that it was imperative to win the war quickly. If not, the British would soon overcome the city, and then 'not only would the House of Taimur but all the Musalmans also be exterminated.' Fazl e Haq had arrived in Delhi on 18 August, and had been given important responsibilities in the realization of revenues.[837]

But that was easier said than done. The explosion in the powder manufactory was a setback and had caused shortages of firepower. In the meanwhile, the British forces had strengthened their position alarmingly. By mid-August their long-awaited reinforcements had begun to arrive, and on 21 August they managed to advance down the Ridge, to capture the Indian positions and guns in Ludlow Castle and Qudsia Bagh, a garden just outside the city walls, near

Kashmiri Gate. By advancing their batteries to this position, the British brought their firepower much closer to the city. From here their bombardment on the city could be used to deadly effect. There was also news of the approach of a siege train with heavy guns which would enable the British to finally break through the city's defences. A force was sent out from the city to intercept this, but suffered a crushing defeat on the 25th.[838]

The Emperor by now had lost confidence in Bakht Khan. There were strong rumours, being spread by the general's rivals in the army, that he too was secretly in league with the British and therefore his Bareilly troop was lukewarm in their campaign. On 23 August Bahadur Shah ordered that he be denied entry to the palace. He also ordered a re-constitution of the Court, with six members appointed by him and six by the army, to conduct future military operations. Bahadur Shah himself frequently visited Salimgarh, to direct the operation of the guns that were directed at the British position.[839]

These shortages of ammunition, delays in pay, the frequent disagreements and rivalry between the regiments and their officers, mutual suspicions of betrayal to the enemy, continued, and led eventually to a breakdown of morale. Soon, not only were the Indian soldiers facing repeated defeats, many were reluctant to go out and fight at all.[840] A bitter letter addressed by the officers to Bahadur Shah in late August complained that the people of the city appeared to be conspiring with the British, the soldiers were short of money and food and if conditions did not improve soon, they were ready to leave Delhi.[841] One of the British officers posted on the Ridge wrote to his father—'Delhi now goes by the name Pandy-monium'. Pandy was a corruption of Pandey, and a popular British shorthand for the predominantly high caste Hindu soldiers.[842]

And yet by then probably everyone realized what the consequences of defeat would be. This added to the feeling of resentment against the soldiers. Every time they came back the worse for an encounter with the enemy troops, they were taunted by the people of the city and castigated by Bahadur Shah. The latter frequently complained bitterly, saying that the mutineers had come uninvited and taken over the city, had made him an enemy of the British and were now going to lose and thus ensure the destruction Delhi and of his own life. He threatened now and then to go out to talk to the British authorities to try and make peace. On other occasions he attempted to boost the soldiers' morale with rousing speeches in his durbar, expressing confidence in imminent victory. Every small victory against the British was rewarded by the Emperor who distributed money for celebratory feasts.[843]

Nevertheless, the possibility of defeat was a real one, and many of the soldiers and ghazis had begun to leave the city even in the beginning of August. At the end of August less than five thousand rebel soldiers were estimated to be left. The others were ready for flight, busy selling bulky items of plunder to make their wealth more portable. Not all of them were moving on to new fronts against the enemy. Some clearly wanted to just go home, anxious that their villages were being destroyed by the enemy and demoralized due to the lack of provision in Delhi and bleak outlook in the war. Many of the people of the city were also leaving, eager to escape the impending takeover of the city by the British. At the end of August and in September some last-ditch efforts were made by the soldiers to go out and fight the British forces seriously, and in this they were joined by several of the princes. But if defeating the British had been a difficult task earlier, it was now impossible. By 7 September the British forces had swelled to 14,000.[844]

Bahadur Shah, who had refused to leave the city with the rebel soldiers, rallied the remaining soldiers and the people of the city, calling on every person of the city to go out and fight, and having Hindus and Muslims swear on their respective scriptures. But by 12 September a breach had appeared in the wall near Kashmiri Gate and the people of the city, Hindus and Muslims, rich and poor were moving southwards to Dariyaganj. Some had already begun leaving the city altogether. On the 14th the British entered the city and the Revolt in Delhi was practically over.[845]

54

A City Destroyed

The British troops entered the city from Kashmiri Gate sometime after 3 o'clock in the morning of 14 September, but encountered stiff resistance as they tried to make their way into the main streets, and along the perimeter of the city walls. Many of the remaining people of the city as well as the rebel troops started leaving from the southern gates of the city in increasing numbers, anticipating a bloodbath. Their departure and the simultaneous takeover by the British was spread over a few days. Bahadur Shah too left the fort and the city, but some of the townspeople, together with such soldiers as had not left, hung on in the fort and managed to defend it for a few days. Though much depleted in numbers they also fought hard to hold out in the streets of the city for a while, even fighting from rooftop terraces; until on the 20th, the entire city and the fort had been overcome. Some soldiers and ghazis continued to hide in Dariyaganj, but they too left by the 24th.[846]

The fierce fighting that lasted a week left dead bodies piled up in the streets, causing a horrific stench of decomposition. When the British forces entered the fort, they found that the Diwan e Khas was being used as a hospital, and they immediately killed all the wounded men in their beds. One of the officers among those who then took up their quarters in the palace wrote home—'It was all very fine living in marble halls, but the old King left his palace in a very dirty state—the stench of dead bodies has quite done me up and I feel very seedy'.[847] As a result cholera soon broke out. The authorities at Delhi were instructed—'Collect and burn your dead in convenient places—abundance of timber from old houses and fuel will be found in the city. It will purify the air.' The convalescent soldiers were ordered to be sent to Mehrauli.[848]

There were some who had remained in the city when the British entered, believing that the innocent would come to no harm, but were soon proved wrong. The spirit of the British soldiers and officers was one of revenge and a thirst for blood, and they looted and killed even the unarmed and innocent without discrimination. The most horrific of these incidents was that of Kucha Chelan. According to the Commissioner of Delhi, Saunders, a group of European soldiers entered this locality 'on a plundering expedition and being opposed by a few of its inhabitants, seized all the Mahomedan portion of its population and shot them down'. Among these men who were taken down to the sands of the Yamuna where they faced a firing squad, was Imam Baksh 'Sahbai', the respected teacher in the Delhi College, and his two sons. According to Zakaullah, twenty-one of those killed in the locality were from Sahbai's family alone. Neither Sahbai nor any of his family had given any support to the rebels. Ram Chander, who made enquiries reported that Sahbai 'always accused the Mutineers and the ghazees of the highest folly'.[849]

Most of the remaining population was driven out. The motive of the army for evacuating the city was strategic. They could not otherwise be sure of holding the city in case of a flare up of resistance from within.[850] One of those who did not leave was Ghalib, who remained in his house at Ballimaran, relatively unmolested because his neighbours were the hakims of the Sharif Khani family. The family had a history of service with the Raja of Patiala, and since this chief was an ally of the British, his own troops guarded the neighbourhood. Nevertheless, the inhabitants, though safe within their houses, suffered from lack of food and water.[851] Some of the other people of the city remained because they were simply too weak and helpless to even organize an escape in the interests of self-preservation. One of these was the mother of Syed Ahmad Khan. She was thrown out of her house which was then looted, and spent eight to ten miserable days hiding in a shack; hungry, thirsty and fearful, until Syed Ahmad came looking for her. She never recovered from the trauma and died soon after.[852]

The theme of violated women figured prominently in the rhetoric of revenge. The 'fanatics' had to be pursued and wiped out because 'relics of our countrywomen are upon them'. British public opinion was inflamed by rumours supported by newspaper reports claiming that many Englishwomen had been raped before being killed. An official enquiry was specifically carried out in the case of Miss Jennings and Miss Clifford, who had been killed on 11 May in the Red Fort. It confirmed the trend of the rest of the country affected by the Revolt, i.e. that the women had in fact been killed outright.[853] Nevertheless, some of the English soldiers entering the city took what they perceived as a very direct revenge, and there were instances of women of the city being subjected to sexual violence. Some women were also actually killed by their own menfolk, to prevent them falling into the hands of the invaders.[854] Many of the women of the palace were indeed abducted by the invading troops and subsequently had to fall back on prostitution to support themselves.[855]

The fleeing people had abandoned their homes and property, on a scale described by the British army officials as 'immense'. The wealthy, who had been reluctant to give their wealth to the rebel government, were now not even around to see it all fall into the hands of the invading army. A large quantity of wines and spirits was found in shops by the soldiers, and the invading force soon lost all discipline. They got drunk and concentrated their energies on breaking open shops and plundering them. British officials at the time laid the entire blame at the door of their 'native' troops—'new levies raised from among tribes who have been brought up in habits of plunder.' Later they were to acknowledge that soldiers of the English regiments were equally to blame, often taking jewellery even from the bodies of the slain, which the streets were strewn with.[856] Apart from a desire to possess themselves of valuables there was also a spirit of destruction that filled the invading soldiery in the first few days of the takeover. Whole libraries of Persian and Arabic books for instance were deliberately destroyed.[857] Many private individuals participated in these treasure hunts too, guided by city folk. Among those who found some treasures were the Wagentreibers, who were 'more than repaid' for their material losses of 11 May, when their house had been looted.[858]

Soon after, official Prize Agents were appointed by the army to appropriate enemy property in a more systematic manner. One of their first acts was the seizing of the crown jewels, which Bahadur Shah was induced to hand over. The plunder of the city continued for many months, and John Lawrence, the Chief Commissioner of Punjab, under whose charge Delhi had been placed, commented that 'all classes, whether friends or foes were despoiled with equal impartiality.' For a long time no real rules were laid down, though it was suggested in passing that the property of people innocent of rebellion should not be included in the 'prize'. Even those bankers and merchants who could prove that they had not taken an active part in the rebellion had to pay a tenth of the estimated value of their immoveable property as a 'ransom'. Many did get their property back but not before it had been completely pillaged. Though Lawrence had given orders on 15 December stopping all further search of private property in the city, the army had other ideas. Orders of April 1858 directed that Prize Agents would be left free to search the houses of all rebels and appropriate movable property within them.[859]

If official orders were unclear and contradictory, the situation on the ground was even more arbitrary. Many parties of soldiers went out searching for property without any authority from the Prize Agent at all, confident that no one would stop to ask any questions.[860] The methods of the Prize Agents themselves were oppressive. Often they would enter a house without discrimination as to whether the owner had been loyal or disloyal to the British. They would put a gun to the head of the occupant and demand all valuables. A large part in this search for treasure was played by informers. Bricklayers sought out the Prize Agents and pointed out hoards bricked up and buried in houses, receiving a share in the booty recovered. The search for treasure went on for a full two years after the Revolt had been suppressed. Some property arbitrarily appropriated by the Prize Agents was given back, but the procedure for claiming it was not easy. The claimant had to prove ownership of the article, and to prove that he had been faithful to the British cause.[861]

The civil authorities were to an extent more mindful of public opinion. Petitions were coming in from various people, some of them considered influential, complaining of the severity and arbitrariness of the confiscation of all sorts of property. William Muir, Secretary in the Government at Agra, on the basis of information received from Saunders, the Commissioner at Delhi, regretted that 'The policy of the military authorities has, it is evident, occasioned vast amount of misery and distress indiscriminately among the innocent, even among those who suffered bitterly from the mutineer reign at Delhie.'[862] John Lawrence was also against prolonging the sufferings of its inhabitants. While some of them were undoubtedly guilty of rebellion, he said, it could not be denied 'by any impartial person, that the majority were not connected with the late insurrection, and that a large section would have sided with us, had they possessed the power. They were, however, as is well known, in the hands of a merciless lawless soldiery. They have suffered prodigiously, and it would appear therefore good policy to allow those that have survived to return to their houses.'[863]

55

Leader of a 'Muslim Conspiracy'

When the British operations to take over the city had been underway, Hodson, who had by then been promoted to the rank of Lieutenant, had opened up negotiations to secure the person of the Emperor. The fear among the military was that he would leave Delhi with the rebel soldiers, and continue to be the rallying point of the Revolt from a centre other than Delhi. At the same time, the complete conquest of Delhi could not be put off, so forces could not be spared in pursuit of the rebel party. Hodson therefore asked his confidant Rajab Ali to offer such terms of surrender as would be acceptable. The latter opened up negotiations for surrender through Ilahi Baksh Khan, the father-in-law of Mirza Fakhr ud din, who in turn negotiated with Zeenat Mahal and her father, Ahmad Quli Khan. The terms finally agreed to, were that they would surrender on the condition that the lives of the Emperor, Jawan Bakht, Zeenat Mahal, and her father Ahmad Quli Khan, be spared. The Emperor also asked for assurance that he would not be submitted to *be-izzati*, 'insult', by the *gore log*, white men. Under this assurance the Emperor, with some of his family and a large accompanying group of fugitives from the palace, surrendered on 22 September at Humayun's Tomb, where they had taken shelter.[864]

Among the members of the royal family who had been captured by Hodson in Humayun's tomb, were Mirza Mughal, Khizr Sultan and Abu Bakr, who seemed to have been under the impression that the guarantee of life had included them. Not only was this not the case, they would not have the benefit of a trial either. As they approached the city under escort of the guard under Hodson, a crowd gathered, probably out of curiosity. This was a trigger for Hodson; as he recalled later, 'I rode in among them at a gallop, and in a few words I appealed to the crowd, saying that these were the butchers who had murdered and brutally used helpless women and children, and that the Government had now sent their punishment: seizing a carbine from one of my men, I deliberately shot them one after another. I then ordered the bodies to be taken into the city, and thrown out on the "Chiboutra", in front of the Kotwalie.' Hodson's act was endorsed by his colonel, who described it in a report prefaced with the remark, 'All going wonderfully well at Delhie.'[865]

Two princes who had survived and had been captured, Mirza Bakhtawar Shah and Mirza Mendu were speedily tried, and executed by firing squad. It had been decided not to try Jawan Bakht, mainly because little evidence against him could be gathered. Against Bahadur Shah on the other hand, there was plenty. Much of it consisted of the documents of the administration that had been run in Delhi under his name from May to September. All these papers had to be collated and translated into English. Numerous witnesses had to be gathered and their statements taken, and charges framed against the accused. All of this took time, and a final reason for delay was the poor health of Bahadur Shah, as the Civil Surgeon certified that he was seriously ill, and may not recover.[866]

He did recover, however, and the trial was held in the Diwan e Khas between 27 January and 9 March 1858. The prisoner was charged with aiding and abetting mutiny and war against the state, with having 'proclaimed and declared himself the reigning king' despite being a 'subject of the British Government in India', and finally, having allowed the murder of a large group of Europeans and mixed European persons in the fort. The defendant was assisted by a lawyer, Ghulam Abbas.[867] Many documents, including those that had been seized from the palace, were used to build up the case. Jivan Lal, the mir munshi, was now given the task of sifting through this mass of documents and putting up for consideration all that were relevant to the trial not only of Bahadur Shah, but of many others who were tried in Delhi.[868]

The documentary record was supplemented by many oral testimonies. Among the many who appeared as witnesses, there were those who had been in the service of the British administration, and also those who had been employees of the Emperor. Prominent among the latter was Ahsanullah Khan, whose life had been guaranteed on the condition that he 'answer satisfactorily' all questions put to him. His testimony, though balanced and honestly given, tended to implicate Zafar fully in the Revolt, but not in the violence. More damning was the testimony of Mukund Lal, who had been the secretary of Bahadur Shah. He claimed that the latter had been for a couple of years conspiring against the British, had entered into correspondence with the ruler of Persia, and had also, by making disciples of them, established a relationship with the soldiers of the Company's army. Mukund Lal also claimed that it was the Muslim citizens of Delhi who had welcomed and joined the mutinous soldiers.[869]

The proceedings of the trial helped the authorities to piece together the main events of the Revolt in Delhi. As to the verdict, the mind of the court was made up even before the trial began. Official opinion on the line to be taken with the Emperor and the royal family had been laid down quite early during the Revolt. As early as June, the instructions from the government at Calcutta were that no promises or agreements were to be made with them, and when Delhi fell, the palace should be searched for all incriminating documents and these were to be preserved. In the following weeks all their overtures to the British forces were therefore turned down.[870] Though he did not know it, it was decided quite early that Bahadur Shah was not to be given a chance to come over to the British side, and the ground was already being laid for him being made the scapegoat for the insurrection.

This was a deliberate and cold-blooded move, certainly not

born of a misunderstanding as to the real nature of Bahadur Shah's role in the Revolt. The Emperor had at best been a reluctant leader of the Revolt, and in fact messages from the palace had clandestinely been despatched from time to time to the British camp on the Ridge, offering terms for a truce. The British government, however, had decided not to accede to them. This is clear from a letter addressed by J.R. Colvin, Lt Governor of the North-Western Provinces, to Edmonstone, the Secretary to the government in Calcutta in July 1857. He spoke of the latest overtures from the Emperor with the remark that though one was not supposed to take any notice of this, 'it would have been a great point to have shewn the world it is a mere Pandees war' (i.e. mainly a mutiny by the predominantly high caste Hindu soldiers). The government clearly understood that Bahadur Shah was not wholeheartedly behind the movement, and their spies in Delhi constantly told them this throughout the period from mid-May to mid-September.[871]

A similar policy was followed during the trial of Bahadur Shah as well. The latter, in his statement, protested his innocence of the murder of Europeans, the most grievous, or at any rate the most emotionally loaded, charge that had been brought against him. He declared that he had not ordered the murder, had in fact opposed it, and if his bodyguard were implicated, it was certainly in opposition to his wishes.[872] This was a fact that was corroborated by other, relatively independent witnesses. He argued that he had been at many times helpless to prevent the activities of the soldiers and even his own family and employees. This the court chose to ignore, even though the spies of the British throughout the course of the Revolt had brought reports to that effect from the palace. The court found the Emperor, acting 'through his troops', guilty. As for his leadership of the rebellion it was sufficient to say that he 'has ever been looked upon by Mohammedan fanaticism as the head and culminating star of its faith. In him have still been centred the hopes and aspirations of millions. They have looked up to him as the source of honour, and, more than this, he has proved the rallying point not only to Mahomedans, but to *thousands of others with whom it was supposed no bond of fanatical union could possibly be established*' (emphasis added).[873]

In the official British narrative, the fact that Hindus could have joined the Revolt was a source of surprise because the British insisted on interpreting the Revolt as a religious war against the Christians by Muslims under their 'spiritual leader', Bahadur Shah. The rebels had used religion as a rhetorical rallying point for their movement, and the British narrative accepted this at face value. This was certainly the conclusion arrived at by the commission that tried the Emperor. All the evidence that could not be reconciled with this view, was simply put aside as something inexplicable. The Judge Advocate General, summing up at the end of the trial remarked with surprise on 'the suddenness with which elements, *hitherto deemed utterly discordant on the score of religion*, have united themselves in a common crusade against a faith' (i.e. Christianity).[874] The prosecution perceptively pointed out how the continuous reference to the 'greased cartridge' was in fact a red herring. It was never made much of in the everyday internal correspondence of the mutineers, which was not meant to be subjected to British scrutiny. Clearly, even the greased cartridge was more an emotive symbol than a substantial grievance. And yet the British would not extend this argument to explain the other components of the rhetoric—particularly the 'war for the faith', which was equally a rallying cry rather than an actual motivating factor.[875]

The Emperor became a symbol of the Revolt to the British as much as he had been for the rebels. The desire to see him 'hanged on the highest pinnacle in Delhi' was wished by many as an 'atonement for the massacre of our unfortunate countrymen and countrywomen and children.'[876] But, as it happened, the life of Bahadur Shah had been publicly guaranteed, and so it was decided that he, Zeenat Mahal, Jawan Bakht and Shah Abbas, another son, would be exiled to Rangoon. Ahmad Quli Khan, whose life had also been guaranteed had died in the meanwhile. Various attendants and close relations decided to accompany them. Soon, however, maybe when it became clear that in Rangoon they would be kept under close surveillance, and not be allowed to communicate freely with people around them, many of these changed their minds. Thus,

Taj Mahal, the wife of the Emperor, Jawan Bakht's mother-in-law and sister-in-law, and a cousin of Bahadur Shah decided to turn back from Allahabad.[877]

The truncated royal party arrived at their destination at the end of 1858. Here, in Rangoon, Bahadur Shah would die on 7 December 1862 at the advanced age of eighty-seven years. The much younger Zeenat Mahal survived him by twenty years, during which she lived in penury. Jawan Bakht, who had become an alcoholic, died in 1884, aged only forty-two. The exact location of the grave of the last Mughal Emperor was soon forgotten. Though a memorial now exists, it is only approximately where the grave is believed to be located.[878]

The trials of those considered to have taken a part in the rebellion were speedily held.

Several princes were tried in the beginning of October, found guilty and shot. It was decided that other male members of the royal family, however remotely related to the Emperor, and wherever resident, had to be exiled 'to some distant place of security' where they could not become leaders of any form of anti-British revolt. Culpability was not the criterion to be used. In the event, most of the men of the family were exiled to farflung places—mostly in Burma and to Karachi. Most were ultimately granted measly pensions of Rs 5 or less each per month.[879]

Many were tried and executed. Mohammad Baqar paid with his life for the *Dehli Urdu Akhbar*'s support for the rebellion, and it was said, for failing to do enough to protect Taylor, the principal of the Delhi College. Taylor apparently had hidden in his house briefly, but then, trying to escape in disguise, was caught and killed.[880] According to one official report some five hundred men were 'disposed of summarily' in the early months after the capture of Delhi. Another 1,500 or so were awaiting trial and their numbers were increasing as more arrests were made. By the end of 1857, several hundred had been hanged in Delhi. The British soldiers 'bribed the executioner to keep them a long time hanging, as they liked to see the criminals dance a "Pandies's hornpipe", as they termed the dying struggles of the wretches'.[881] The Gujars of the villages around Delhi also felt the brunt of British vengeance. When a village near Mehrauli, in the neighbourhood of Delhi, displayed a 'refractory spirit', it was subdued, and ninety villagers were arrested and later shot without a trial.[882]

The reminders of the immediate horrors stayed in Delhi for months—the two gallows in Chandni Chowk, the pervading nauseous smell, and the ruined houses. And yet amidst this desolation, the main street of Chandni Chowk was an incongruous spectacle of bustle, and brisk business in all manner of goods, a large portion of it likely to be loot. It was all for the benefit of the many British soldiers, officers and their families who were now living in the better houses in the city and in the fort, and also to some extent for the Sikh and Gurkha soldiers now stationed at or passing through Delhi.[883]

It was only in March 1858 that John Lawrence expressed the opinion 'that the time has now arrived when the Delhi Prisoners should have a trial more deliberate and formal than could have been afforded in the days when the disturbances and excitement of the contest had scarce subsided. It will now be necessary to discriminate with some accuracy between different shades of guilt.'[884]

Accordingly, the punishments of the subsequent months were somewhat less severe. Fazl e Haq had been an active participant in the rebellion, continuing to operate even after the fall of Delhi. He was finally caught, tried and exiled to the Andaman Islands where he died later.[885] Over time, his grave in Port Blair became a dargah, a popularly revered shrine. Also brought to trial were those who were not believed to be guilty of any active participation in the rebellion, but simply that they had not been active in helping the British, or had been in the presence and company of the Emperor and the rebel leaders during the rebellion. Sadr ud din 'Azurda' was imprisoned and tried on this charge, and as punishment, dismissed from government service and deprived of all his property. Only later, after an appeal to Lawrence, half of his property was returned, to enable him to maintain himself and his family.[886] Hamid Ali Khan was sentenced to imprisonment, together with a confiscation of his property.[887]

Ghalib escaped relatively unscathed. He had kept a low profile through the Revolt, despite his close association with the court. He seems to have gone to the fort from time to time, though Bahadur Shah at the time probably had little time or inclination for poetry. According to a later memorialist, on 11 August 1857, he had also presented an ode, or qasida to the Emperor, and been presented with a khilat. Though later no specific documentary or other evidence could be found against him, a shadow remained against him for a while. His pension, as well as honours, such as khilats that he used to receive from the government, were suspended. The pension was finally restored in May 1860.[888]

Amin ud din and Zia ud din Khan spent some days under surveillance in the fort until a variety of evidence in their favour was forthcoming—that they had communicated with the British to send them information, had saved several members of the Skinner family by hiding them in their house, and finally even that Amin ud din Khan was 'always looked upon by the local officers as an adherent of the English, as a boy he was brought up and educated by Lady Colebrooke, and has always more or less affected English society and manners.'[889]

Many humanitarian gestures had been exhibited by those within the city towards Europeans in trouble, but only some of these were recognized. Brown of the *Delhi Gazette Press* was helped over several days by a number of people, workers in the press, the darogha of the Kashmiri Gate police station, and finally the qazi of a mosque who gave him the *kurta* and *pajama* in which he got away from the city.[890] Even a certain army surgeon was helped by one of the ironsmiths employed in the ammunition magazine.[891] The kotwal of the city at the time of the rebellion, Sharf ul Haq, had tried to save the life of his superior British officers, but his failure to do so was held against him.[892]

One instance where the saving of a life had its reward was in the incident of Mrs Leeson and Maulvi Abdul Qadir. The latter had come upon the wounded lady late at night in a street. For the next several weeks he and his family hid her in their house at considerable risk to their own lives, and nursed her to good health.

According to Rashid ul Khairi, the well-known writer and grandson of Abdul Qadir, the story had a dramatic climax. Mrs Leeson was assisted out of the city and subsequently the British troops entered it. Abdul Qadir was implicated in the rebellion and almost at the very instant that he was due to be hanged, Mrs Leeson appeared and rescued him. Happily, this was the beginning of a long and intimate friendship between the two families.[893]

Amidst the punishment being meted out to the guilty, the loyal had to be rewarded, and succour had to be provided to the victims. Those who had supplied information from the city, like the government clerks Nathmal and Gauri Shankar, were given life pensions and jagirs.[894] Mirza Ilahi Baksh, a kinsman of the Emperor and a close confidant, had constantly tried to influence him in favour of the British and had finally been instrumental in the surrender of the Emperor. He expected to be rewarded handsomely. However, his claims for the restoration of certain lapsed jagirs, and for compensation for the loss of his property in Delhi were turned down. All that was allowed was a continuation of the original pension of him and his family.[895]

Master Ram Chander, who had escaped the rebellion with his life, put in a word for the two widows of Chiman Lal—Sarah, whom he had lived with, and Martha whom he had not lived with since his conversion, but continued to support. He particularly made out a strong case for Sarah, who had gone to live with her parents after Chiman Lal's death but had resisted their attempts to reconvert her to Hinduism. A pension was accordingly sanctioned to her, but not to Martha.[896]

56

The City Transformed

Ram Chander himself found that he had a lot to do. After his escape from the city during the Revolt he had soon arrived at the British camp. Here his proficiency in English proved useful, as he was set the task of translating into English the intelligence reports that came in from the network of spies in the city.[897] Now he was officially employed by the Prize Agency and given a variety of jobs. He was set the task of collecting and arranging any books found in the city, including those of the Delhi College, that had been plundered and sold. He was also translating papers for the trials of rebels being held before the special military commission set up for the purpose.[898] But he found that his life in Delhi had become unbearable. In November he wrote a letter to his superior officer with the details. He mentioned an incident when he came across British officers standing at a parapet in a mosque hitting passing Indians with slingshot. When he told them that he was a Christian, 'that only seemed to exasperate them more'. Then the British officials living in the house across the street from his started throwing stones at his door and through his windows.

Finally, one day he was walking to some place in the fort and, he wrote, 'I received a heavy blow on the head from an English officer on horseback…and after inflicting this blow with his stick this officer turned around and required me to make him a salaam. I made many salaams instead of one, and cried I was a Christian sir! ...and after this he proceeded towards the Diwan e Khas abusing me and saying that I was black as a jet.' When Ram Chander then sat down to recover from the shock, the officer came back and hit him some more. Ram Chander ended his letter by saying, 'This my appeal is not only for native Christians exclusively, for they are very few in Delhi, but for Hindus and Mahommedans who are allowed to live in the city but are exposed to danger from the English soldiers and particularly English officers.' Shortly afterwards, Ram Chander received the offer of a 'native' Head Mastership at Thomason College, in Roorkee, and decided to leave Delhi altogether.[899]

Meanwhile most of the people of the city were still outside the walls. From being a security measure, after a while the policy of keeping the people out of the city became more simply a punitive one. It was decided that a few 'useful tradespeople' were to be let in with special licenses, but the policy discriminated on the basis of religion. By the end of 1857 Ghalib reported to his friends that some Hindus were coming back to their houses though Muslims were still kept out. In the beginning of 1858, Hindus generally were given permission to return.[900] Muslims were kept out for much longer. They were given passes to enter the city for specific purposes, but could not reoccupy their houses or otherwise take up residence in the city till late in 1859.[901]

The physical map of the city was affected in the immediate aftermath of the suppression of the Revolt. The immediate imperative was a military one. The sections of the city walls immediately adjoining the gates were demolished to render them useless for defence, while still leaving enough of the rest of the wall to protect the city from the plundering population of the surrounding area. Though in the early days, in the heat of the moment there had been talk of demolishing the Jama Masjid, at this point the order from Calcutta was explicitly to spare 'places of worship, tombs and all ancient buildings of interest.'[902] In Delhi itself, the highest army officers saw the laying in ruin of a large portion of the city as a just retribution, and expressed satisfaction that the city was 'a perfect picture of desolation.'[903]

The taking over of the royal palaces after the conquest of the city was a triumphal act of the victorious, and Queen Victoria's health was drunk in the Diwan e Khas. Soon this hall of audience was to become the venue for Church services, and it was also here, between 27 January and 9 March 1858, that Bahadur Shah's trial had been held. The Moti Masjid nearby was turned into living quarters for officers.[904] The palace had suffered in the preceding months due to the large number of soldiers that had camped in its courtyards and gardens. It was also wilfully damaged by the British soldiers who occupied it. One wrote home—'It was then a general belief that the Palace would be blown in the air to mark our abhorrence of the massacres committed there, and wishing to save a flower made of different coloured precious stones from the ornamented walls and pillars I tried to scoop one off with my knife, but it went to pieces in the doing, so I tried no more.'[905] In the event, a few of the most beautiful marble buildings in the fort were saved, but all of the others were destroyed. To make the task easier, since many of the buildings were made of stone, explosives were used.[906]

Many buildings of the city were demolished as well. This was justified on the grounds of security requirements, i.e. that an area five hundred yards in width, shooting distance, be cleared around the fort. Many important localities and buildings were sacrificed to this policy. There was a significant turnover in ownership of property too. A large amount of property, belonging to those found guilty of rebellion, had been confiscated. A part of this was gifted to those who had served the British loyally during the Revolt.[907] A more substantial portion was given as compensation to those whose property was demolished to make way for the railway line which was driven through the heart of the city soon after. The complicated transactions involved led to major speculations in property and a resulting concentration in very few hands.[908]

An important part of the punishment meted out to the Muslims of the city specifically was the occupation of the Eidgah and Jama Masjid, both considered to be intimately connected with the Emperor. The latter was also seen by many as the heart of the 'fanaticism' that had purportedly fuelled the Revolt. In early 1860, when the issue of restoring the mosque to the Muslims of the city was raised, Philip Henry Egerton, the Deputy Commissioner, was against it. Incredibly, he felt this would be an example for the populace of Delhi, on which no notable punishment had been inflicted as yet![909] The government, however, did not agree with this view. Finally, at the end of 1862, the mosque was handed over to a committee 'elected by the majority of the Mussulman inhabitants' which included Mirza Ilahi Baksh, Azurda, and Syed Ahmad Khan. They were made to sign an agreement which among other duties, required them to report any use of seditious language. The rules to be enforced in the mosque were also set down by the government, and included the clause that 'European officers and gentlemen civil and military can enter without restriction as to shoes.'[910]

Observers noticed in the months and years after the Revolt that the character of the city appeared to have changed. Ghalib complained in 1864 that the city was a camp—no palace, no nobility, no chiefs of the surrounding principalities. What in effect he was mourning was the passing of the elite of the city that he knew. What was even more noticeable was the absence of the Muslim elite. The government particularly picked out the Muslims for punishment. Irrespective of individual involvement in the Revolt, as a class they were treated more harshly. Ghalib could see this around him and wrote to a shagird thus in 1862: '[Delhi] is a military camp. The Muslims are either tradesmen or craftsmen, or the servants of the officials. The rest are all Hindus. Those of the Emperor's people [the royal family] who have survived, receive five rupees each per month. Of the women, those who are old are procuresses, and the young are prostitutes.' He went on to list a large number of Muslim friends and acquaintances who were either killed or had become destitute. Many had left the city for other places like Lahore.[911]

It was not simply that there were fewer Muslims around. For many there was a deeper implication here—the people who now occupied their place were of a culturally different sort. A couple of years after the Revolt Ghalib related an anecdote involving an ignorant postman, who, misreading a word on an envelope addressed to Ghalib, had concluded that the latter had been appointed 'Captain' by the British Government. Ghalib, relating this amusing incident to a friend, mentioned that the 'postman these days is a certain [newly?] literate *baniya*, some Nath or Das or other.' The implication was that under the circumstances, such a mistake was not to be wondered at. The people of Delhi who were the arbiters of taste in Urdu were no longer to be found. The people of Delhi were now, Ghalib pointed out, either Hindus, or tradesmen, or soldiers or Punjabis or the British. Which of these could really speak Urdu?[912] This was true only to some extent. There had in fact always been Hindus who had spoken the kind of elegant Urdu Ghalib was referring to. Among them was a close friend and fellow-poet, Hargopal 'Tafta'. For the moment, however, Ghalib disregarded that.

The fact was that for several years after the Revolt, not only Ghalib, but Delhi Muslims in general felt that they were being discriminated against. When it was decided that an area five hundred yards wide would be cleared around the fort in the interests of security, the only exceptions made were temples of the Jains and Hindus, and Dariba, where many Hindu and Jain merchants had shops and homes.[913] Ghalib, describing the scene of the demolition of Kucha Qabil Attar and the Akbarabadi Masjid, noted the distinction: 'Allah! The domes of the mosques are razed and the pennants on the temples of the Hindus flutter'.[914]

The circumstances of the Revolt and its suppression had driven a wedge between the Hindus and Muslims. There were prejudices that fed off each other. Many Hindus had taken advantage of the British determination to see Bahadur Shah as the head of a Muslim religious war, in order to argue that Hindus as a body had not supported the Revolt. Given the atmosphere of revenge, this was an understandable strategy. One witness at the trial of Bahadur Shah after the defeat of the rebels by the British, was Jat Mal, who was a news writer in the pay of the British from before 11 May. He testified regarding the non-military opinion within the city, that

'The Mahommedans as a body were all pleased at the overthrow of the British Government, while the merchants and respectable tradesmen among the Hindoos regretted it.' Beyond this, he could give no concrete instances to back up his view.[915] Many others, such as Jivan Lal, expressed similar views.

It was clear that the situation in Delhi in the following years was by all accounts much worse than other cities that had been affected by the Revolt. According to Ghalib a major source of the problems in Delhi was that firstly it was under martial law and then no longer part of the North-Western Provinces, but of Punjab. Ghalib explained to his friends that in contrast to Lucknow and other towns in the North-Western Provinces such as Agra and Meerut, here there were no regulations and no laws. Every official did as he pleased. Further, all decisions of the administration were a divine decree against which there was no appeal. As a result, properties in the form of houses and shops were arbitrarily confiscated and demolished, pensions were suspended and people were arrested. Orders were passed according to one's destiny, i.e. arbitrarily, and not according to any law. No citing of precedents or sophisticated argument could do any good.[916]

For Ghalib, and probably for most of the elite, while there was grief at the violence that the royal family had been subjected to, no deep regrets at the passing of the Mughal court were expressed. The expectations of the future were related entirely to bringing the relationship with the government back on an even keel. Ghalib, who had had such a close relationship with the Mughal court, seldom spoke of the Emperor in his voluminous letters to his friends in the following years. He noted the death in exile in 1862 of Bahadur Shah with a brief epitaph: 'On Friday, the 7th of November, Abu Zafar Siraj ud din Bahadur Shah was freed from the prison of the British and the prison of the body'.[917]

In the months and years following the Revolt all his hopes and fears revolved around the government. His situation was precarious as his role in the rebel administration at the palace was being investigated, and in the meanwhile, his pension was suspended. In March 1859 he wrote with joy of the letter written to him by the Lt Governor of Punjab (as John Lawrence's position was now designated), in acknowledgement of the presentation copy of his own latest book. What seemed to make him happiest were the old signs of favour—'the same paper sprinkled with gold dust, the same honorific address of old...words of kindness'. And when in 1863 Lawrence called him and announced the restoration of his khilat, his cup of joy was very nearly full. As he told Hargopal 'Tafta', his closest friend, it was as if 'a corpse had come to life.'[918]

57

The Lament

The book through which Ghalib had opened channels of communication with the authorities was *Dastambu*, a 'diary' of the Revolt. Not strictly speaking a diary, it was a brief chronological account of the period between May 1857 and July 1858. Ghalib wrote it in ancient Persian without the use of any Arabic words, and soon conceived the idea of publishing it and presenting it formally to the highest representatives of the British state, from Queen Victoria downwards. He also included in it an ode to Queen Victoria and a prayer for the restoration, in that order, of his title and khilat which had been marks of honour from the government, and his pension which he had not received since May 1857.[919]

There were few who were prepared to write about their experiences yet. The period of the revolt and its brutal suppression thereafter had been a traumatic episode in the life of the city. Many of its inhabitants were at best reluctant participants in the rebellion, and unfairly and harshly punished by the returning British. While cases of implication in the revolt were still being tried, to express any opinion at all was dangerous. Even Ghalib wrote repeatedly in letters to his friends, even in early 1858, that he had a lot to say but was afraid to write.[920] Under the circumstances, Ghalib had to make sure to edit *Dastambu* so that there were no passages that might give offence. He admitted as much to a friend, saying,

'I have used the utmost care and circumspection in everything I have written'.[921]

One member of the Delhi elite whose loyalist credentials were not in doubt was Syed Ahmad Khan. Posted in Bijnor when the Revolt broke out, he had displayed bravery and initiative in saving British lives and helping to restore peace to the area. He therefore had no reason to be less than forthright in expressing his opinion. In fact he felt that as a loyal subject it was his duty to make the rulers of India aware of where they had gone wrong. He chose to do so in a pamphlet entitled *Asbab e Baghavat e Hind* (Causes of the Indian Rebellion), published in 1858, but only for the consumption of government circles in India and Britain.[922]

If *Dastambu* and *Asbab e Baghavat e Hind* were the work of two individuals who were basically pro-British, a more heterogeneous group was the many poets who composed the *shahar ashob* poetry that was written in the immediate aftermath of the suppression of the Revolt. Their verses were elegies to the city, often full of detail about the calamity that had befallen it. They were not intended for an official readership, and they were eventually published in 1862, by which time the more extreme persecution of those suspected to have been implicated in the rebellion had died down. Against this background, the poets could express their views reasonably freely, and their work therefore can tell us much about how the people of Delhi saw the Revolt.[923]

Some placed blame specifically on the royal family, such as Azurda:

afat is shahr pe qile ki badaulat ai
wan ke a'mal se dilli ki bhi shamat ai
roz e mau'ud se pehle hi qiyamat ai
kale merath se kya aye ke afat ai.[924]

Misfortune befell this city due to the fort;
It was the evil deeds of that place that invited punishment on Delhi.
Doomsday dawned before the appointed day
When the black men came from Meerut, misfortune arrived.

In contrast, Ghalib in *Dastambu* portrayed the Emperor as a helpless puppet in the hands of the soldiers, a full moon that had been temporarily eclipsed.[925] Some of the poems too saw the Revolt purely as an act of the alien soldiers, absolving both the palace as well as the people of any complicity:

tamam shahron ki pusht o panah thi dehli
gunahgar hui be gunah thi dehli
...
raha na koi hasin aur na koi waris e takht
mitane takht ko aya tha bakht khan kambakht[926]

Of all cities, Delhi was the protector and asylum,
It was held guilty though it was innocent
...
None of the beautiful people [of the palace] are left, nor any heir to the throne
The accursed Bakht Khan had come to destroy the throne.

Bakht Khan in fact had to suffer more than one pun on his name (bakht literally meant fortune):

badbakht tu hi kah ke tujhe is mein kya mila
ham ko jo tune khak mein aisa mila diya[927]

O ill-fated one, tell us what you achieved
By having us ground into the dust in this manner

The condemnation of the mutinous soldiers and their supporters took many forms. The typical *Dehliwala*'s cultural chauvinism came to the fore in many descriptions. The rebels were described as 'peasants', '*purabias*' (by which was meant the people of the eastern Doab), even speaking a tongue that was unfamiliar.

Mirza Khan 'Dagh' wrote:

jagah jagah the zamindar dar ki surat
chadhe hi ate the sar par bukhar ki surat
bala se kam na thi ek ek ganwar ki surat

Everywhere there were peasants like gibbets [death]
They were irrepressible, like a fever
Each rustic had the face of evil

ghazab mein koi jo raiyat, bala mein shahar aya
yeh purbi nahin aye, khuda ka kahar aya[928]

The raging peasants entered the city as an evil
The wrath of God arrived in the form of these Purabias

Qurban Ali Beg 'Salik' wrote in a similar vein:

daraz dasti e dehatiyan e bad anjam
khuda dikhaye na surat, kabhi sunaye na nam
kisi tarah se samajh me na awe un ka kalam
gurez pa jo nikal kar gaye, lute woh tamam[929]

Oh the oppression of the evil villagers!
May God never show us their faces or let us hear their names.
Never could one understand their speech
Even those fleeing were plundered.

The very appearance of the outsiders set them apart. They were frequently described as being 'black', in words such as *kale* and *rusiyah*. This was an allusion perhaps to darker complexions which in a pre-industrial society were associated with the rural labouring classes. Black also became a convenient double metaphor for the supposed blackness of their deeds and their opposition to the 'white' British.[930]

As the appearance and deeds of the rebels was condemned, so was their rhetoric:

zaban se kehte hue 'din! din!' aye layeen
jo matadin that koi to koi gangadin
yeh jante na the cheez kya hai din matin
kiye hain qatl zan o bachhe kaise kaise hasin
rawa na tha kisi mazhab mein jo woh kam kiya
gharz woh kam kiya, kam hi tamam kiya[931]

These accursed men came chanting 'Faith! Faith!'
One was a Matadin and another Gangadin,
They did not know what is true faith,
Such beautiful women and children they have killed.
They did what was not permitted in any religion
What they did was murder.

There is an ambiguous comment here on the religious ideology of the rebels. Their slogan was '*din*' or 'faith', but they were not jehadis, simply because most of them were not Muslims but Hindus. 'Matadin' was in fact a term for the mutinous soldiers, often used by the Sikh soldiers allied with the British, just as the British used 'Pandie'.[932]

Ghalib wrote in *Dastambu* that it was members of the lower classes who supported the rebel soldiers and saw the Revolt as an opportunity to oppress their respectable neighbours.[933] This aspect of the Revolt finds prominence in the shahar ashob too, such as in these lines from the *musaddas* of Mohammad Taqi Khan 'Sozan':

yahan ke jitney the aubash mil ke un ke sath
kya bataein tumhein zar ke hath ane ki bat
...
jo ghar koi takte to us par chadh jate
firangi is mein hai yeh kah ke ghar woh lutwate[934]

All the ruffians of this place joined them [the soldiers]
What can one say about the gold that came into their hands
Any house they eyed, they would at once attack
Saying 'There is a *firangi* inside!' they would plunder it.

A strong sense of an upturning of the social order is evident in some of the poetry. Mohammad Zahur 'Zahur' wrote—

sada tanur jhonke tha jo ladka nanbai ka
bhara hai is ke sar mein ab to sauda mirzai ka
qaroli bandh kar nikle hai ab ladka qasai ka
amiron ke barabar baithe hai farzand dai ka[935]

The street cook's lad who did nothing but stoke the fire,
Now he fancies himself a *mirza*
The son of the butcher goes abroad wearing a hunting knife
The son of the midwife sits on level with noblemen.

If the rebel soldiers had been responsible for the creation of a situation of social upheaval, where the distinction between the high-born and the base had been blurred, the British did not restore the familiar order immediately. And some of the angst about a world turned upside down that is to be found in the shahar ashob, no doubt relates equally to the period after September 1857. Zahur more directly blamed those he considered low-born ruffians for the further calamities that befell the high-born—i.e their persecution by the British when they re-captured Delhi:

na main hi balke alam badmashon se hirasan hai
yeh shahid jhute lawein bas yeh in ka din o iman hai[936]

Not I alone, the whole world lives in dread of these badmashes
To give false evidence is their only creed and faith.

Nevertheless, some of the shahr ashobs, such as that of Syed Zahir ud din 'Zahir' Dehlvi, explicitly celebrate the return of the British:

hazar shukr ke dauran e daur cooper hai
zamana ahd mein is ke taraqiyyon par hai
who asman e karam ka mah e munavvar hai
sunh o sarwar o zi jah dad gustar hai[937]

A thousand thanks that it is now the era of Cooper [Frederick Cooper, who had succeeded Egerton as Deputy Commissioner]
In his time the world is on the path of progress and improvement
He is a brilliant moon on the munificent sky
He is a blessing after a misfortune, a master, and a dispenser of justice

In fact, the victors of course were in many ways worse for the city than the rebel army had been. Ghalib, a supporter of the British, wrote in *Dastambu* of the arrival of the British army into the city: 'The enraged lions on entering the city saw fit to kill the helpless and burn houses. Yes, the inhabitants of any city that is conquered have to suffer such oppression. The faces of the people turned white when they saw this fury and revenge.'[938] Even though Ghalib was trying hard to ingratiate himself with the authorities, he could not help mentioning the terror that was unleashed in the city, and the fear Muslims in particular lived in immediately after 14 September (Ghalib himself staying hidden in his house). He expressed his feelings in verse to his shagird and kinsman Ala ud din Ahmad Khan of Loharu:

bas ke fa'al mayrid hai aaj
har silahshor inglistan ka
ghar se bazaar mein nikalte hue
zohra hota hai aab insan ka
chowk jis ko kahen who maqtal hai
ghar bana hai namuna zindan ka
shahar dehli ka zarra zarra khak
tashna e khun hai har musalman ka[939]

Since every English soldier today
Has a sovereign will
Just to go from one's home to the market
Is enough to turn one's courage to water.
That which was known as the chowk is now a place of death,
The home is now a prison,
Each particle of the dust of the city
Thirsts for the blood of the Muslim.

At other times, however, he spoke of the destruction of the city and its people as if it were the rebel soldiers that were solely and directly responsible for it. He mourned the death of friends thus in mid-1858, glossing over the fact that the Indians he mentioned among those dead were killed by the British:

> 'Of the English race that were murdered by those with black faces and black deeds, some were my patrons, some my sympathizers, some my friends, some my companions, and some my shagirds. Of the Hindustanis, some who were dear to me, some friends, some shagirds, some lovers; all have been ground into the dust.'[940]

There were others who struggled to reconcile their horror at the destruction with their support for the British who were directly responsible for it. Shahab ud din Ahmad Khan 'Saqib', son of Zia ud din Ahmad Khan, pictured a scenario that is actually quite deceptive, the destruction of the city being laid at the door of the rebels and its reconstruction being credited to the British without qualification:

ahl e dehli na karen bakht ka shikwa kyon kar
bakht khan ji hue jab baj satan e dehli

hakim adil dana ko khuda ne bheja
tab yeh abad hue chand makan e dehli[941]

Why should the people of Delhi not bemoan their misfortune
When Bakht Khan is the tribute collector of Delhi
[Then] God sent the just and wise ruler [Cooper]
Only then did some of the houses of Delhi become inhabited again

Memoirs such as Ghalib's or the shahar ashob were the work of survivors, the relatively lucky ones. There were many who were dead. Ghalib described those hanged in Delhi as 'countless'.[942] Many were in prison, or like Fazl e Haq, had been transported to the Andamans. Much of the immediate post-1857 writing was thus also a medium for paying tribute to friends who had suffered in the Revolt's aftermath. Such references also show that some poets were not afraid to comment on the atrocities of the British, however cautiously they did it. Azurda wrote of his friends Shefta, who had been imprisoned, and Sahbai, who had been executed:

tukde hota hai jigar, jan pe ban ati hai
mustafa khan ki mulaqat jo yad ati hai
kyonkar azurda nikal jaye na saudai ho
qatal is tarh se be jurm jo sahbai ho[943]

My courage crumbles, I feel I could die
When I remember the times spent with Mustafa Khan
Why should Azurda not be driven insane
When the innocent Sahbai is thus murdered?

The physical desolation and destruction of the city left a strong visual and psychological impact that is frequently repeated in the shahar ashobs, as in this couplet by Sabir:

bas ke bedad se tute hain makan e dehli
ho raqam khat e shikastah se bayan e dehli[944]

So unjustly have the buildings been razed in Delhi,
It is fitting to inscribe in the *shikastah* [literally, 'broken'] script,
the account of Delhi.

As the city was slowly rebuilt but along new lines, Dagh wrote a ghazal that contains a highly ironical account of the new British order in the city, particularly the building of new barracks in the fort to house the soldiers who were now stationed inside it:

muzhda ai bakht, ke phir aye yahan sahib log
zeb e dehli hai koi, koi hai shan e dehli
de diye fauj ko hukkam ne inam mein sab
ganj e qaroon se fuzun ganj e nihan e dehli
qile mein barakein lohe ki bani hain kya khub
nahin kalkatta ab gharz to basan dehli[945]

Glad tidings, O fortune! The sahibs are back;
One is the ornament, one is the glory of Delhi.
The authorities have given them all to the army as a prize,
The hoarded, hidden, treasures of Delhi.
What wonderful concrete barracks in the fort!
Now Calcutta is not a patch on Delhi.

One aspect of the shahar ashobs was a loving description of the city as it was before the Revolt. Its physical structures, its people, and even its language were idealized in this poetry. This idealization was a conventional hyperbole, meant to evoke images that contrasted sharply with the equally heightened descriptions of the 'evil purabias' and the only too real destruction of the city after its fall.[946] As Dagh summed it up:

ye shahar woh hai ke har jins o jan ka dil tha
ye shahar woh hai ke har qadardan ka dil tha
ye shahar who hai ke hindustan ka dil tha
ye shahar who hai ke sare jahan ka dil tha[947]

This is the city that was the heart of every human being
This is the city that was the heart of every benefactor
This is the city that was the heart of Hindustan
This is the city that was the heart of the whole world.

Many came to the conclusion that Delhi had been the most perfect city in the world, but the trauma of 1857 had destroyed it.

Epilogue

Though the city was slowly re-built, its character after 1857 was perceptibly different. Hard as the loss of life and material possessions was, the cultural loss had a more long-lasting impact in the minds of many. The expropriation and exile of the royal family; the execution, exile or ruin of many of the educated elite, the closure of the Delhi College for a long period, created a cultural vacuum. Mohammad Husain 'Azad' wrote of his ustad, Zauq:

> 'So there is now no hope at all of another such
> Master of poetry being born in India
> For he was the nightingale of a garden
> That has been destroyed'[948]

Azad had suffered great personal loss. His father had been executed, his home destroyed. Azad himself, under a shadow of suspicion, had laid low, only to surface again in Lahore in 1864. This was the year of the opening of the Lahore College, where Azad joined the 'Anjuman e Punjab', a literary society, and soon became its secretary. The Anjuman e Punjab's declared objects were 'the revival of ancient Oriental learning, the advancement of popular knowledge through vernaculars, the discussion of social, literary, scientific, and political questions of interest, and the association of the learned and influential classes with the officers of the government.'[949] This was a project that was very close in spirit to all that the Delhi College, Azad's alma mater, had stood for. In 1870 Azad was joined at Lahore College by Altaf Husain 'Hali', who had also been a part of Delhi's cultural milieu as a student, though he never studied at the Delhi College.

At the Lahore College, Azad and Hali soon emerged at the forefront of a movement to reform Urdu poetry, to free it of its traditional subservience to classical Persian forms, which were alleged to be devoted to exaggerations, pre-occupation with themes of love, obscure language and literary verbiage. This powerful criticism gave rise in 1874 to a series of mushairas on a new pattern, which encouraged new themes that were supposedly closer to nature and human experiences—'The Rainy Season', 'Hope', 'Justice', 'Patriotism', 'Peace', 'Compassion', 'Contentment', 'Civilization', and so on. Both Azad and Hali would go on to write powerful critiques of classical Urdu literature. This was a project that would have appealed to Ram Chander of the Delhi College, who had made exactly the same criticism of the traditional literature of the 'Farsi-walas'. Ram Chander himself had come back and taught for a few years as a mathematics teacher in a district school in Delhi, before retiring in 1866, due to indifferent health.[950]

There was another alumnus of the Delhi College who was putting into practice the lessons learnt at the Delhi College. Karim ud din, who had also been critical of the 'frivolity' of Indian literature, particularly poetry, in 1862 published a work that has been referred to as the 'first novel in Urdu'. Though Karim ud din did not use the word novel, he certainly admitted that he had deliberately set out to write a new style of *qissa*, departing from the traditional 'Asiatic' style, and instead writing on realistic themes. As he put it, the old style qissas dealt with well-worn themes of kings, faqirs and love. The authors felt that gross exaggeration, fantastic beings and supernatural phenomena would add to the popularity of their works. They felt that the only purpose of writing was to entertain, and this of course, was wrong. In his age, however, Karim ud din pointed out, people had realized that there must be a utilitarian purpose behind the telling of stories. They had come to understand that these stories worked in subtle ways on the minds of impressionable readers, who subconsciously internalized the lessons in them. It had now become clear that the style of those old stories was not good, and they were particularly inappropriate for the young. Karim ud din's work was careful not to use any indecent words, so that women as well as men could read his qissa. The theme of love had been introduced into it reluctantly, simply because it was a concession that had to be made if anyone with Asiatic tastes was to be induced to read the book at all.[951]

The Delhi College, which had been destroyed in 1857, re-opened in 1864, but was a shadow of its former self, simply preparing students for the exams of the Calcutta University, to which it was affiliated. Then, in 1877 it was closed altogether, and its students asked to shift to the Lahore College. Some of the spirit of the old college, however, could be found in the work of Syed Ahmad Khan, who had never studied in the college but was undoubtedly familiar with its working. He would eventually set up the Muhammadan Anglo-Oriental College in Aligarh in 1875, to impart to young Muslim men a modern education which was at the same time rooted in their faith. Syed Ahmad also set up a Scientific Society in 1864, dedicated to the promotion of scientific thinking, in large part through translations of Western works, and the publication of basic text books.[952]

Two other members of the Delhi diaspora took steps in education of a different sort. Mohammad Qasim and Rashid Ahmad, though they belonged to small towns in the upper Doab, both had studied for four-five years in Delhi. Their education in Delhi in the 1840s was under Mamluk Ali, who was the head of the Arabic Department in the Delhi College, but also taught a more traditional curriculum to students privately. They also had an opportunity to learn from other noted scholars, such as Sadr ud din Azurda. In 1867 these two men became the founders of Dar ul ulum, a madrasa, in Deoband, which became a centre for Islamic reform and revival, one not looking to the West for inspiration.[953]

The spirit of another dead institution of Delhi found a new life under Alexander Cunningham, who had been a member of the Archaeological Society of Delhi. In 1861, Cunningham proposed to the Viceroy, Lord Canning, the institution of an 'Archaeological Survey', to carry out an investigation into the archaeological remains of 'Upper India'. Arguing for a more proactive approach towards documentation and preservation of this heritage, Cunningham wrote in a memorandum: 'All that has hitherto to been done towards the illustration of ancient Indian history has been due to the unaided efforts of private individuals. These researches consequently have always been desultory and unconnected and frequently incomplete....' The writer, who had been a member of the Archaeological Society of Delhi, had adopted a deliberate amnesia with regard to the systematic investigations, reports and conservation that had been carried out by that body. The Archaeological Survey of India was set up the following year with Cunningham at its head, and in time was to become the main state manager of India's historic monuments. One of Cunningham's early reports was on Delhi, but in this too, while writing on the location of the historic cities of Delhi, or the Qutub Minar complex, he failed to acknowledge the researches of Zia ud din Ahmad Khan, who had presented detailed papers and sketch plans to the Society; or to mention the excavation and conservation work that had been undertaken at Feroze Shah Kotla by the Society.[954]

The seeds that had been sown in the favourable soil of Delhi, and had been fertilized with the vibrant cultural and intellectual life of the city before the Revolt, were now bearing fruit. The reluctance to acknowledge those roots probably had a lot to do with the traumatic episode of the Revolt. For the British, who Cunningham represented, the Delhi of an earlier period, and particularly the collaboration between the Indian and British intellectual elite had been tainted by what came after. Once Zia ud din Ahmad had been under suspicion, could he ever be seen in the same way?

For the Indians, particularly those from Delhi, like Azad and Hali, the problem was even more complex. There was a general silence that had descended on the subject of Delhi. The trauma of the violence, and the continued fear of reprisals created an atmosphere in which it was not wise to even mention Bahadur Shah, or other members of the royal family, or others of the elite who had been implicated in the Revolt. By extension, discussions or appraisals of the culture of the period could not be made.

Almost three decades passed before the first memoirs of this period in Delhi's history began to be written by those who had lived through those times, or a younger generation who had heard their reminiscences. They sought to capture for posterity the memories of the Mughal court and a culture that had now gone forever. They looked at the past with rose-tinted glasses, and painted a picture of an idyllic world where old values and culture flourished, and even the advent of British rule had made a minimal cultural impact. There was no space here for doubts or questions about the significance of the royal family, about the soundness of the literary tradition. The intellectual and cultural ferment of the period was completely glossed over.

There were reasons for this collective amnesia, and for why 1857 came to acquire this significance as a cultural watershed. At a very simple level the trauma of the Revolt came to dominate the lives of those who had lived through it, and their perspectives of the past. For the people of Delhi, there was life before 1857, and life after it. Moreover, for many who had survived 1857, the period before the Revolt was a beautiful age simply because it contained family, friends, homes and jobs. For precisely the same reason the Revolt was a sharp break, because for most of them it meant a sudden loss of these coordinates of everyday life. These personal tragedies, through the passage of time came to be seen as sudden cultural losses, leading to the common assumption that 1857 was a major cultural watershed.

In actual fact, for the cultural and intellectual history of Delhi, 1857 represents a disruptive episode, rather than a turning point. A dispersal of a large portion of its Muslim population, the appropriation of important places of worship and the disappearance of the Mughal court caused an abrupt interruption of the institutions on which the culture was based. But ultimately Muslims did return to the city, the mosques were restored to them, education and literature revived. An important source of patronage for poetry had become much reduced, with the breaking up of the Mughal court and the dis-appropriation of many of the principalities. But there were other deeper reasons why the old style mushairas were no longer held, and the era of the great ustads seemed to have passed.

To that extent some of the lamentations of a loss of people and culture are misleading. Ghalib wrote in 1861 of the passing of the poetic culture of the city: 'where is Nizam ud din "Mamnun", where is Zauq, where is Momin? Azurda is there but he is silent. Ghalib is there but he is not in his senses.'[955] The requiem was couched in terms that related the loss to the calamity of 1857. But of course the three poets mentioned first had died some years before the Revolt. Azurda never did write a lot of poetry, and Ghalib himself, despite an advanced age continued to play an influential role in the world of poetry even after 1857. If, as he added, there was no longer anyone to really write or appreciate good poetry, surely this was a malaise that had set in earlier. Was that not why he could not name any but poets of his own generation?

*

I first became interested in research into the 'Company period' in Delhi's history because I was intrigued and puzzled by what I read. Paradoxically, it was a period much written about and yet relatively unknown to readers of history. Its cultural and intellectual life had been written about in clichés that were as contradictory as they were simplistic: it was simultaneously viewed as a cultural high point and an age of decay. It was characterized sometimes as a period of 'twilight', at others as a 'renaissance'; and as if to somehow reconcile the two, as the last bright flicker of a candle before it goes out.[956]

A closer study revealed the complexities that characterize this period. Behind the clichés was a vibrant and dynamic culture embarking on a process of far-reaching changes, at least some of them impelled by the interaction between Western education and thought, on the one hand, and a strong tradition of language, literature and learning on the other. Some of them were the product of a lived reality of contest between a once powerful dynasty and a newly rampant political order. And finally, some were the result of social change, brought about by changing class and community balances.

It was not that the revolt of 1857 and its brutal suppression destroyed an old order. The old order had already in many ways passed. The true impact of 1857 was varied. It resulted in a sharpening of sectarian divides, though not because of the Revolt per se but through its suppression. The British projected the uprising as a 'Muslim conspiracy', in part because they may have genuinely believed it, but also because through this they could comprehensively implicate the Mughal Emperor and get rid of him for good, without having to answer any uncomfortable questions about any valid grievances. The resultant discriminatory treatment of the Muslims helped to drive a broader wedge between Muslims and others. In times to come the colonial government would find that an exploitation of this divide served as a useful means of dividing opposition to it.

But the Revolt also highlighted the articulation by Indians of ideas that were precursors to new concepts like nationalism and anti-colonialism. The suppression of the Revolt pushed down these ideas for a while, but they would soon rise again in the form of the national movement. Even budding new ideas in the literary world survived the disjuncture, and achieved their full flower soon enough. There were, however, other developments that did not survive. One of them was the promise, manifested in the Delhi College, of a new higher education system that would be based on strong foundations of the mother tongue.

A study of Delhi during this period can tell us much about how some Indians negotiated political, social and cultural changes brought about by colonial rule, adopting a modernity that was to an extent shaped by Western ideas and institutions, but rooted strongly in indigenous systems of thought and learning too. The Revolt of 1857 not only seriously disrupted this trajectory of change, it also politically relegated Delhi to a marginal position, from which it would not recover till well into the twentieth century, when the British decided to make it their capital in India.

Acknowledgements

This study of Delhi began when I enrolled in a PhD programme at Jamia Millia Islamia in 2000. During the seven years that it took me to submit my thesis and in its later re-working into a book, I have incurred many debts. Prof Narayani Gupta's work was the inspiration behind the decision to study this subject, and to do my PhD at Jamia. Her comments, advice and encouragement have played no small role in the shape the study took. My two supervisors, Prof Azizuddin Husain and Mukul Kesavan, helped me not only to think more deeply about the material and develop my arguments more rigorously, but also to navigate the requirements of an academic programme. The academic and administrative staff at Jamia made my time there a uniformly pleasant one.

The work has benefited from comments by Prof Gail Minault and Prof Amar Farooqui, and conversations with Margrit Pernau. It would also not have been possible without the benefit of the large body of work that has been done by many outstanding scholars. I have tried to list some of these in a select bibliography.

The research for this book was done at various libraries and archives. I am grateful to their staff, who gave helpful advice in locating material in their collections and made it readily available. The list includes, at Delhi, the National Archives of India, Delhi State Archives, Nehru Memorial Museum and Library, the Ghalib Institute library, the Ghalib Academy library, the library at the Anjuman Taraqqi Urdu (Hind); the British Library in London, the Centre for South Asian Studies at Cambridge University; and in

Hyderabad, the Osmania University Library, and the Salar Jung Museum Library.

I thank Speaking Tiger, specially Ravi Singh and Renuka Chatterjee, for agreeing to publish yet another book written by me. I specially thank my editors Renuka Chatterjee and Nazeef Mollah who have taken pains over a complex text. Any errors that remain are entirely my responsibility. Maithili Doshi as before has done a stellar job in giving this book its beautiful cover. Thanks are due to her and Devashish Verma, as well as to Rajinder Ganju for the page layouts.

Neeti and Deb have grown up with this book, and Gourab Banerji has learnt quite a bit about Delhi's history over the years. I am grateful for their support. To many other members of the family, friends, and readers, this study has been a part of what I am. With them I share my joy at the culmination of this journey.

Endnotes

1 For a reasonably detailed account of the politics of north India in the late eighteenth century, see Percival Spear, *Twilight of the Mughals*, Oxford University Press, New Delhi, 2002

2 William Dalrymple; 'Transculturation, assimilation and its limits: The rise and fall of the Delhi White Mughals 1805-57', in Margrit Pernau ed. *The Delhi College: Traditional elites, the colonial state and education before 1857*, Oxford University Press, New Delhi, 2006, pp 63-4

3 Foreign Department, Political Proceeding, National Archives of India, New Delhi, (henceforth FP) 7.12.1807 no.23

4 FP 5.10.1807 no.41A; 9.11.1807 nos.29-31;11.1.1808 no.19; Sangin Beg, *Sair-ul-Manazil*, Nausheen Jaffery trans, Tulika Books, New Delhi, 2017, p 168

5 George Thompson, *Debate at the India House, December 18th 1844, on the claims of the Royal Family of Delhi*, William Congreve, London, 1845, passim

6 Stewart Gordon ed. *Robes of Honour: Khil'at in Pre-Colonial and Colonial India*, Oxford University Press, New Delhi, 2003

7 FP 21.9.1807 no.51

8 FP 12.3.1807, no.55; 18.8.1807 no.52; 30.4.1807 no.32; 5.10.1810 no.202

9 FP 4.10.1811 no.46; 8.9.1807 no.13

10 FP 21.5.1807 no.39

11 FP 7.12.1807 nos.25-26; 6.5.1820 no.20-1

12 FP 29.11.1811 no.14-15

13 FP 16.4.1807 no.1; 21.5.1807 no.39; 13.3.1812 nos.35-6

14 FP 16.4.1807 no.1; 5.3.1807 no.92A

15 FP 19.3.1807 no.44; 5.3.1807 no.110A

16 FP 16.4.1807 no.1; 7.5.1807 no.68

17 FP 29.2.1808 no.49; 2.5.1808 no.39

18 FP 28.12.1810 no.80

19 FP 25.2.1814 no.14

20 The evidence of C.B. Saunders in the 'Trial of Mahomed Bahadoor Shah, Ex-King of Delhy', Foreign Department Miscellaneous Documents, National Archives of India (henceforth FMisc), vol 376

21 Margrit Pernau and Yunus Jaffery eds, *Information and the Public Sphere: Persian Newsletters from Mughal Delhi*, Oxford University Press, New Delhi, 2009, pp 58, 60, passim; FP 3.6.1848 no.70; 'Precis of palace intelligence: January 1851-January 1854' FMisc vol 361, 1.2.1851; *Dehli Urdu Akhbar* 17.5.1840; 2.8.1840; 1.11.1840; 10.1.1841

22 Palace diary, FMisc vol 361, 16.4.1851

23 Pernau and Jaffery, *Persian Newsletters*, passim

24 FP 5.2.1807 no.89

25 FP 15.7.1809 no.52

26 FP 12.9.1809, no.54

27 FP 12.9.1809 no.54; Letters from Lt. John Anthony Hodgson (1777-1848), Bengal Army 1800-48, to his family, 1806-1815, British Library, London, Mss Eur D1200, letter to his father dated 15.11.1806

28 FP 19.12.1809 no.4; 17.10.1809 no.19; 15.7.1809 no.52; 12.9.1809 no.54

29 FP 12.2.1807 no.98

30 Jatindra Kumar Majumdar, ed., *Raja Rammohun Roy and the last Moghuls: A*

selection from official records (1803-1859), Art Press, Calcutta, 1939, pp 65, 74, 109; Thompson, *Debate at the India House,* p 27

31 Pernau and Jaffery, *Persian Newsletters*, pp 39, 62, passim

32 Ibid., p 76

33 FP 21.5.1807 no.9; 4.6.1807 nos.23-24; 21.9.1807 no.51

34 FP 27.3.1810 no.4

35 Pernau and Jaffery, *Persian Newsletters*, pp 66, 71

36 FP 7.5.1807 no.69

37 FP 28.5.1807 no.51

38 FP 19.6.1807 no.47

39 FP 21.9.1807 nos.51-53

40 FP 16.11.1807 no.18

41 FP 23.11.1807 nos.20-22

42 FP 13.6.1808 no.51; Majumdar, *Raja Rammohun Roy*, p 98

43 FP18.7.1808 nos.63-6

44 FP 17.4.1810 nos.45-6; 4.6.1813 no.19

45 FP 7.4.1814 no.8; A.A.D. Seymour 'The least known Lord High: A note of James Stewart Mackenzie', in Anthony Hirst and Patric Sammon eds. *The Ionian Islands: Aspects of their history and culture*, Cambridge Scholars Publishing, Newcastle upon Tyne, 2014, p 147

46 FP 13.4.1811 no.63; 26.6.1818 no.102; 10.7.1818 no.6

47 FP 9.11.1807 no.24; 30.11.1807 no.51; 26.12.1808 no.6; 27.3.1809, no.12; 27.5.1809 no.22; 16.8.1810 no.48; 28.7.1810 no.43; 30.8.1811 no.33; 21.12.1811 no.67; 3.6.1814 no.25; 26.4.1817 no.4; 13.6.1823 no.45

48 Translation of a fatwa, or legal opinion, in Barbara Daly Metcalf, *Islamic Revival in British India; Deoband 1860-1900*, Oxford, University Press, New Delhi, 2002, p 46

49 Ibid., pp 46-52; Margrit Pernau, 'Multiple Identities and Communities; Re-contextualizing Religion', in Jamal Malik and Helmut Reifeld eds *Religious Pluralism in South Asia and Europe*, Oxford University Press, New Delhi, 2005, especially p 154

50 Margrit Pernau, 'Preparing a Meeting-Ground: C.F.Andrews, St. Stephen's, and the Delhi College' in C.F.Andrews, *Zaka Ullah of Delhi*, Oxford University Press, New Delhi 2003, pp lxiv-lxv

51 Ibid. p lxv

52 Swapna Liddle 'Azurda: Scholar, Poet, and Judge', in Pernau ed. *The Delhi College*, pp 143-4

53 James Baillie Fraser, *Military Memoir of Lt Col James Skinner*, Smith, Elder & Co., London, 1851, vol 1, pp 279-87, 291-93; *Mr Dyce Sombre's refutation of the charge of lunacy brought against him in the Court of Chancery*; Published by Mr. Dyce Sombre, Paris, 1849

54 Jonathan Gil Harris, *The First Firangis*, Aleph Book Company, New Delhi, 2015, p 173; Jean-Marie and Rehana Lafont, *The French and Delhi, Agra, Aligarh and Sardhana*, India Research Press, New Delhi, 2010, p 100. FP 18.12.1806, nos.20,24; 28.5.1807, no.77

55 FP 5.3.1807, no.90; 28.7.1807, no.5

56 FP 28.7.1807, nos.3-4; 31.7.1812, no.30; 25.9.1812, no.48

57 James Baillie Fraser, *Military Memoir of Lt Col James Skinner*, vol 1, pp 105, 108, 166, 188

58 Ibid. pp 250-54, 258, 276-77

59 Ibid. vol 2 pp 35-36

60 Ibid. vol 2 pp 98-101

61 FP 24.7.1812 no.41

62 Fraser, *Military Memoir of Lt Col. James Skinner*, pp 102-03, 109, 155, 159-60, 192, 196, 199
63 Jyoti Prasad Jain, *Pramukh Eitihasik Jain Purush aur Mahilayen*, Bhartiya Gyanpeeth, pp 373-74
64 FP 5.6.1810, nos.50-52
65 FP 1.1.1807, no.36
66 FP 21.5.1807 no.12
67 *Delhi Jain Directory*, Jain Sabha, New Delhi, 1961, p 29
68 FP 21.5.1807 no.9; FP 28.12.1810 no.109
69 FP 21.5.1807 no.9-12; 4.6.1807, no.17-19
70 FP 4.6.1807 no.18
71 FP 16.7.1807 no.26
72 FP 28.9.1807 nos.18-19
73 FP 16.7.1807 no.26
74 FP 29.8.1808 nos.25-26; 12.9.1809, nos. 59-62; 27.3.1810, no.4
75 FP 5.12.1809, no.107
76 FP 19.6.1807, no.28
77 FP 25.6.1807 no.39
78 FP 19.6.1807, no.29
79 A description of the prince by Sleeman seems to have set the tone for later accounts. W.H. Sleeman, *Rambles and Recollections of an Indian Official*, Hatchard and Son, London, 1844, vol II p 269; Spear, *Twilight of the Mughals*, pp 63-64
80 Spear, *Twilight of the Mughals*, p 50
81 Foreign Department, Secret and Separate Proceeding, National Archives of India, New Delhi, (henceforth FS&S) 8.8.1809 no.1
82 FS&S 8.8.1809, no.5
83 FS&S 8.8.1809, nos.2,13,16
84 FS&S 15.8.1809 nos.49-50, 52, 56; FP 17.9.1832 no.67
85 FP 14.11.1809 no.14
86 FP17.10.1809 no.8
87 FP 30.6.1810 no.43
88 FS&S 15.8.1809 no.50
89 FS&S 15.8.1809 no.50; 15.8.1809 no.52
90 FS&S 15.8.1809 no.50
91 FP 26.9.1809 no.54; 10.10.1809 no.14; FS&S 15.8.1809 no.55
92 FP 12.12.1809 no.72; 9.1.1810 nos.54-56
93 FP 26.7.1811 no.115
94 FP 26.7.1811 nos.105-15; 2.8.1811 nos.85-6
95 FP 13.2.1810 nos.54-5
96 FP 6.3.1810 no.61
97 FP 6.8.1810 no.88
98 FP 5.10.1810 nos.149,152
99 FP 30.1.1810 nos.49; 6.2.1810 no.4; 20.2.1810 no.21; 29.5.1810 no.78; 6.8.1810 no.85; 7.12.1810 nos.19,21
100 Munshi Faiz ud din, *Bazm e Akhir*, Urdu Academy, Delhi 1992, pp 94-5; Palace diary, FMisc vol 361, 2.8.1851; 28.8.1851; 19.8.1852; 21.9.1853; 2.8.1852; 7.9.1853; *Dehli Urdu Akhbar* 5.7.1840; 9.8.1840; 30.8.1840; 15.8.1852
101 D.N. Panigrahi, *Charles Metcalfe in India; Ideas and administration 1806-1835*, Munshiram Manoharlal, New Delhi, 1968, p 32
102 John William Kaye, *The life and correspondence of Charles, Lord Metcalfe*, Richard Bentley, London, 1854, vol 1, p 224
103 FP 31.5.1811 no.62
104 FP 14.8.1806 no.22

105 FP 12.7.1811 no.83
106 FP 2.8.1811 no.85
107 FP 20.9.1811 no.44
108 FP 10.1.1812 no.87
109 FP 10.1.1812 no.88
110 FP 29.5.1812 nos.14-15
111 FP 11.2.1813 nos.8A-13; 5.3.1813 no.41, 44
112 FP 11.2.1813 nos.8A-9; 12.3.1813 no.13,16
113 FP 12.3.1813 nos.18,20
114 FP 15.4.1813 no.24; 7.5.1813 nos.28,30,33; 16.7.1813 no.45
115 FP 12.3.1813 no.21; 5.10.1816, no.32
116 FP 30.4.1813 no.4
117 Ibid
118 FP 30.4.1813 no.5; 4.6.1813 no.20; 16.7.1813 no.46
119 FP 7.5.1813 no.28, 30; 16.7.1813, nos.45
120 FP 7.5.1813 no.31; 15.10.1813 no.52; 5.11.1813 nos.11-12; 26.10.1816 nos.66-7; 5.6.1818 nos.20-1; 10.7.1818 no.78; 31.7.1818 no.3; 27.2.1819 nos.26-7
121 FP 16.7.1813, nos.42-43
122 FP 16.6.1821 nos.44-5; 28.7.1821 nos.50, 53
123 Faiz ud din, *Bazm e Akhir*, pp 46-9; Palace diary, FMisc vol 361, 18.1.1851; 27.8.1852; William Dalrymple, *The Last Mughal: The fall of a dynasty, Delhi, 1857*, Penguin/Viking, New Delhi, 2006, pp 27-29
124 FP 5.11.1813, no.11
125 FP 16.11.1810 no.27
126 Lady Maria Nugent, *A journal from the year 1811 till the year 1815, including a voyage to and residence in India, with a tour to the North-Western parts of the British possessions in that country, under the Bengal Government*, London, T and W Boone (printer), 1839, vol 1 pp 413-14
127 Correspondence of Resident of Delhi with the Persian Department of the government at Calcutta, FMisc vol 123, letters dated 14.7.1809; 17.2.1811; FP 25.4.1808 nos.41-42; 17.5.1811 nos.106-7; 24.5.1811 no.70; 19.7.1811 no.98; 26.7.1811 no.86; 11.12.1812 no.38; 11.2.1813 nos.83-4; 30.5.1815 no.32
128 FP 10.10. 1809, nos.12-13; 28.11.1809, no.15; 23.11.1810 no.75; 9.3.1811 no.45
129 Syed Ahmad Khan, *Asarussanadid*, Urdu Academy, Delhi, 2000, pp 100,132; FP 9.3.1811 no.45
130 FP 13.3.1809 no.102; 24.10.1823 no.42; 28.11.1823 no.20; 19.10.1827 no.99
131 FP 29.8.1808 no.25-27; 12.9.1809 nos.59-62
132 Palace diary, FMisc vol 361, 25.7.1851; 24.10.1852; 4.11.1851; 11.8.1853; 4.7.1852; *Dehli Urdu Akhbar* 6.12.1840; Letter from Seton, dated 20.11.1806, in Majumdar, *Raja Rammohun Roy*, p 50
133 Khan, *Asarussanadid* pp 273-4; FP 7.10.1831 no.16; 21.3.1828 no.22
134 FP 25.6.1807 no.39; 11.7.1808 nos.16-17; 26.6.1809 no.6
135 FP 22.2.1808 nos.18,19
136 FP 29.7.1809 no.58; 28.12.1810 no.109; 26.1.1811 no.27; 29.6.1816 no.14; 29.11.1811 no.14; 18.3.1814 no.26; 1.4.1814 no.60
137 FP 28.11.1808 nos.54-5
138 FP 6.6.1828 no.23
139 FP 27.2.1809 no.21
140 FP 29.10.1813 no.8
141 Pernau and Jaffery, *Persian Newsletters*, pp 38-39, 43, 45, 46, 52, 64, *passim.*; A Dean, *A Tour through the Upper Provinces of Hindostan; comprising a period between the years 1804 and 1814*, C & J Rivington, London, 1823, pp 150-59

142 FMisc vol 123, 29.3.1814
143 FP 20.11.1806, nos.3-4; 7.12.1807 no.23
144 Ratish Nanda, Narayani Gupta, *Delhi, The Built Heritage: A Listing*, vol I, Intach Delhi Chapter, New Delhi, 1999, vol 2 pp 77, 72. For the history of its renovation also see FP 18.10.1811 no.28-30; 22.5.1812 no.17
145 FP 5.10.1807, no.41A, 9.11.1807, nos.29, 31
146 Nugent, *Journal*, vol 1 p 417
147 Sangin Beg, *Sair-ul-Manazil*, pp 66, 70; FP 13.9.1828 no.20; for the location and extent of both see the large map of Shahjahanabad in Eckart Ehlers and Thomas Krafft eds. *Shahjahanabad/Old Delhi*, Manohar, New Delhi, 2003
148 FP 29.8.1823 no.12; 24.6.1825 nos.25-6
149 Kaye, *The Golden Calm*, pp 14-5
150 Pernau and Jaffery, *Persian Newsletters*, Akhbarat of 1810
151 Nugent, *Journal*, vol 1 p 410
152 Thompson, *The life of Charles Metcalfe*, p 180
153 A Dean, *A Tour through the Upper Provinces,* pp 159-60
154 Pernau and Jaffery, *Persian Newsletters,* p 61
155 William Francklin, *Military Memoirs of George Thomas*, John Stockdale, London, 1805, p 92
156 A Dean, *A Tour through the Upper Provinces,* p 149
157 Sangin Beg, *Sair-ul-Manazil*, pp 74-75, 78; Kaye, *The Golden Calm*, p 181
158 FP 15.10.1813, no.29
159 Kaye, *The Golden Calm* p 174; Lucy Peck, *Delhi: A Thousand Years of Building*, Roli, New Delhi 2005, p 251
160 Pernau and Jaffery, *Persian Newsletters*, pp 126-27
161 FP 21.3.1828, nos.19-22
162 Sangin Beg, *Sair-ul-Manazil*, p 71
163 *Dehli Urdu Akhbar* 15.11.1840
164 Fraser, *Military Memoir of Lt Col. James Skinner*, vol 1, pp 105-6
165 Fanny Parks, *Wanderings of a Pilgrim in Search of the Picturesque*, Pelham Richardson, London, 1850, vol I, pp 378-97; Letter of William Gardner to his aunt. 25.5.1815, Gardner Papers, Cambridge Centre for South Asian Studies; Narindar Saroop, *Gardner of Gardner's Horse*, Palit and Palit, New Delhi, 1983, pp 22-23; FP 12.6.1812, no.83
166 Memoir of Emily Bayley, daughter of Thomas Metcalfe, in M.M.Kaye ed. *The Golden Calm*, Webb & Bower, Exeter, 1980, p 166
167 *Dehli Urdu Akhbar* 22.3.1840;19.4.1840; 10.5.1840; Qadir Baksh Sabir, *Gulistan e Sukhan*, Uttar Pradesh Urdu Akademi, Lucknow, 1982, p 205
168 For a biography of Skinner, see Dennis Holman, *Sikander Sahib The life of Colonel James Skinner, 1778-1841*, Heinemann, London, 1961
169 Letter dated around 1803, quoted in Dalrymple, *White Mughals*, p 382
170 *The annual biography and obituary for the year 1827,* Longman, Rees, Orme, Brown and Green, London, 1827, p 15
171 Dalrymple, *White Mughals*, pp xx, 120-21, 183; Parks, *Wanderings of a Pilgrim*, vol I, p 415. The account of how William Gardner's marriage came about, shorn of its romantic embellishment, also certainly suggests a strongly political context.
172 Kaye, *The Golden Calm*, pp 142-3
173 Thompson, *The life of Charles Metcalf*, pp 178-79, 234
174 FP 28.7.1821, nos.24-25
175 Letters of William Linnaeus Gardner to Edward Gardner, British Library, Mss Eur C 304, letter dated 18.8.1820
176 Parks, *Wanderings of a Pilgrim*, vol I, pp 415, 421; *Dehli Urdu Akhbar*, 29.11.1840, 6.12.1840, 25.12.1840, 24.1.1841

177 Spear, *Twilight of the Mughals*, pp 101-2, 108, 164; Panigrahi, *Charles Metcalfe in India*, pp 44-70
178 Figures from *The Asiatic Journal and Monthly Register Jan-Apr 1834*, Asiatic Intelligence, p 8
179 Panigrahi, *Charles Metcalfe in India*, p 71
180 FP 9.3.1811 nos.54-55
181 By way of example see; FP 12.1.1820 nos.53-4
182 FP 29.6.1816, no.14
183 FP 10.2.1821, nos.19-20
184 FP 7.11.1818, nos.65-66; 5.3.1832 no.21
185 FP 31.5.1817, nos.107-108; 22.8.1817, nos.31-32
186 FP 7.11.1818, nos.65-66, 68, 71
187 Thomas Fortescue's report on the Delhi Jageerdars, 4.12.1819, Mss Eur F88/383: 1819, British Library
188 John Adam's letter to C.T.Metcalfe, dated 7.11.1818, Mss Eur F259/4: 1818, British Library
189 FP 17.4.1819 no.35
190 FP 5.9.1808 no.1
191 'Management of mal, wakf, lawaris, zubt and taiul lands in Delhi—1821-22' in *Records of the Delhi Residency and Agency*, Sang-e-Meel Publications, Lahore 2006, p 215
192 FP 29.12.1821 no.28
193 FP 25.6.1824 nos.85-6
194 FP 3.1.1822 no.18
195 FP 12.11.1832 nos.12-13
196 FP 1.7.1820 no.8; 21.6.1822 no.30-1; 5.7.1822 no.57; 9.8.1822 no.15; 5.2.1830 nos.13-4
197 Godfrey Charles Mundy, *Pen and pencil sketches: Being the journal of a tour in India*, John Murray, London, 1832, pp 66-67
198 FP 6.2.1819 no.1
199 FP 8.4.1819, no.145
200 FP 24.11.1821, no.27; 26.1.1822, no.26; 2.2.1822, no.13
201 FP 17.3.1821 nos.73-4
202 FP 4.12.1812 no.13; 15.5.1813; 9.7.1813 no.13
203 FP 9.7.1813 no.13
204 FP 13.3.1819 no.36
205 FP 13.8.1813 no.18; 13.3.1819 no.38
206 FP 9.7.1824 no.40
207 FP 27.4.1826 nos.2-5
208 FP 9.8.1822 no.16
209 FP 7.11.1823 no.21
210 FP 11.4.1828 no.14
211 FP 6.6.1836 no.69
212 FP 20.3.1822 no.41
213 FP 16.10.1834 no.22; Majumdar, *Raja Rammohun Roy*, pp 224-27
214 Major Ross of Bladensburg, *The Marquess of Hastings, K.G.*, Clarendon Press, Oxford, 1900, pp 191-92
215 'Ceremonial observed on the occasion of the visit of the Governor General (Lord Amherst) to His Majesty the King of Delhi in 1827', *Records of the Delhi Residency and Agency*, pp 337-38
216 FP 15.6.1827 no.6
217 FP 15.6.1827 no.6
218 FP 27.7.1827 no.7

219 FP 19.6.1829 no.106
220 Gardner letters, Mss Eur C 304 10.3.1827
221 FP 18.2.1814, no.32
222 FP 10.11.1815, no.18; 16.4.1830, no.140; Syed Ahmad Khan, *Sirat e Faridiya*, Mataba Mufeed e Aam, Agra, 1896, pp 25-27
223 FP 12.12.1814 no.20
224 FP 25.2.1814 nos.13-15
225 FP 11.4.1822 nos.66-7
226 FP 17.10.1828 no.13-15
227 FP 6.2.1819 no.1
228 FP 25.9.1812, no.20; 13.11.1812, nos.12, 14; 26.2.1813, nos.5-6; 12.3.1813, nos.46-47
229 FP 29.8.1828 nos.13-14; 31.12.1828 nos.4-6; 17.1.1829 no.5
230 FP 27.11.1829 no.17
231 FP 11.7.1833 no.194; 18.7.1833 nos.32-3; 7.1.1835 no.132
232 FP 3.10.1823 nos.46-51
233 FP 5.2.1830 no.16
234 FP 6.6.1833 no.30; 25.7.1833 no.22
235 FP 10.12.1832 no.24; 31.12.1832 no.46
236 Pernau and Jaffery, *Persian Newsletters,* pp 88, 223
237 Akhbar of 1.1.1825, Pernau and Jaffery, *Persian Newsletters,* p 88
238 FP 20.2.1832 nos.4-6
239 FP 2.9.1834 no.20
240 FP 31.12.1832 no.51; 4.2.1833 no.41
241 FP 23.12.1820 nos.60-2
242 FP 2.7.1807 no.12; 23.7.1830 no.98; 7.10.1820, nos.5-7; Khan, *Asarussanadid*, p 709
243 Majumdar, *Raja Rammohun Roy*, p 203
244 FP 13.3.1829 no.20
245 FP 22.1.1830 nos.51-2; Majumdar, *Raja Rammohun Roy*, p 206-7; *The Asiatic Journal and Monthly Register, Jan-Apr 1834*, pp 55-57
246 Majumdar, *Raja Rammohun Roy*, pp 203, 207-10
247 FP 23.7.1830 no.98
248 FP 23.7.1830 nos.98-99; 21.1.1831 nos.16,49
249 Majumdar, *Raja Rammohun Roy*, pp 227-28
250 FP 21.6.1833 no.1; 2.8.1833 no.13; 24.10.1836 nos.13-15
251 FP 21.6.1833, no.1
252 FP 16.10.1834 nos.22-3; 28.1.1835 nos.13-14; 24.10.1836 no.13; North Western Provinces Papers, Abstract of Proceedings of Charles Metcalfe, National Archives of India, (henceforth NWPAbs) 18.2.1837 no.5
253 Majumdar, *Raja Rammohun Roy*, pp 248-51
254 FP 27.7.1835 nos.40-1
255 FP 8.6.1835 no.10; 29.6.1835, no.2
256 FP 9.3.1811 no.49; 26.7.1811 no.56
257 Pernau and Jafferey, *Persian Newsletters*, pp 326, 334
258 FP 3.6.1814 nos.27-8; 22.2.1817 no.155; 19.4.1817 no.24; 24.5.1817 no.37
259 Ochterlony to Charles Metcalfe, dated 3.6.1820, FP 8.7.1820 nos.7-8
260 FP 22.7.1820 no.6; Gardner letters, Mss Eur C 304 14.7.1820
261 FP 29.8. 1823, no.12; 24.6.1825 nos.25-6
262 FP 23.11.1807 no.19; 31.5.1817 nos.107-8; 22.8.1817 nos.31-2
263 FP 11.1.1822 no.7
264 FP 23.5.1823, no.96; 12.9.1823, no.46
265 FP 23.1.1835 no.159; and Sangin Beg, *Sair-ul-Manazil*, p 50

266 FP 1.1.1820, nos.101-02
267 Lieut. W. Franklin, 'An account of the present state of Delhi', *Asiatick Researches, Vol 4*, Vernor and Hood, London, 1799, p 436; FP 5.6.1829 no.83
268 FP 12.9.1823 nos.46-7; 17.9.1824 no.16; 11.11.1825 no.10; 5.6.1829 no.84; Khan, *Asarussanadid*, p 132
269 Khan, *Asarussanadid*, pp 491-4
270 Pernau and Jafferey, *Persian Newsletters*, p 94
271 Zahir Ahmad Siddiqui, *Momin, Shaqsiyat aur Fan*, New Delhi, 1995, p 77; there were others who wrote in favour of Syed Ahmad, for instance Shah Nasir. Muhammad Husain Azad, *Ab-e hayat: shaping the canon of Urdu poetry*, edited and translated by Frances W. Pritchett in collaboration with Shamsur Rahman Faruqi, Oxford University Press, New Delhi, 2001, p 326
272 Siddiqui, *Momin, Shaqsiyat aur Fan*, pp 20-1
273 Metcalf, *Islamic Revival in British India*, pp 61-2; FP 22.6.1827 no.38
274 The radicalism attributed to the Waliyullahi school did not pre-date Syed Ahmad's movement, and in fact the latter was only one of the trends to grow out of the reform movement. For a clarification of this point see Marc Gaborieau, 'A Nineteenth—Century Indian 'Wahhabi' Tract Against the Cult of Muslim Saints: *Al-Balagh al-Mubin*', in Christian W. Troll ed. *Muslim Shrines in India*, Oxford University Press, New Delhi 2003, p 198
275 Khan, *Asarussanadid*, pp 552-3
276 Mukhtaruddin Ahmad, 'Mufti Sadr ud din Azurda ki Kuchh Nayab o Kamyab Tahrirein' in Nazir Ahmad ed. *Tahqiqat: Intekhab Maqalat Ghalib Nama*, Ghalib Institute, New Delhi 1997, pp 109-10; Abdurahman Parwaz Aslahi, *Mufti Sadr ud din Azurdah*, Maktaba Jamia, New Delhi 1977, p 69-71
277 Palace diary, FMisc vol 361, 27.6.1851
278 Metcalf, *Islamic Revival in British India*, pp 55-9
279 *Akhbar* of 28.6.1830, Pernau and Jafferey, *Persian Newsletters*, p 295; *Dehli Urdu Akhbar* 15.3.1840; 22.3.1840; 11.7.52; 31.10.52; 7.11.52
280 Metcalf, *Islamic Revival in British India*, pp 55-9. Marc Gaborieau makes a very similar argument in, 'A Nineteenth-Century Indian 'Wahhabi' Tract'; Margrit Pernau, *Ashraf into Middle Classes*, Oxford University Press, New Delhi, 2013, pp 43-47
281 *Dehli Urdu Akhbar* 15.3.1840
282 Khan, *Asarussanadid*, pp 502-3
283 Mohammad Zakaullah, *Intekhab e Zakaullah*, edited by Asghar Abbas, Uttar Pradesh Urdu Academy, Lucknow, 1983, p 77; *Dehli Urdu Akhbar*, 11.10.1840
284 FP 27.9.1822 no.29
285 FP 21.5.1807 no.12
286 Khan, *Asarussanadid*, pp 339, 343-47; Also see Nanda and Gupta, *Delhi, The Built Heritage: A Listing*, vol I. For lists of places of worship built in different phases see Shama Mitra Chenoy, *Shahjahanabad: A City of Delhi 1638-1857*, Munshiram Manoharlal, New Delhi 1998, Appendices A, B and C
287 FP 27.9.1822 nos.29-30; 15.1.1823 nos.74-76
288 Pernau and Jafferey, *Persian Newsletters*, pp 111-12, 262, 296
289 Ibid., p 126
290 Ibid., p 322; Faiz ud din, *Bazm e Akhir*, pp 82-84
291 *Akhbar* of 15.8.1830, Pernau and Jafferey, *Persian Newsletters*, pp 327-28
292 Wazir Hasan Dehlavi, *Dilli ka akhiri deedar*, Urdu Academy, Delhi, 1999, p 65
293 These are landmarks of Mehrauli—the Andheria Bagh, and the Shamsi Talab
294 Literally, 'maze' but in this case the popular name for another Mehrauli landmark, the sixteenth century tomb of Adham Khan
295 The pen name of Abu Zafar

296 Thompson, *Life of Charles Metcalfe*, pp 149-50
297 Pernau and Jafferey, *Persian Newsletters*, p 128
298 Ibid., p 329
299 Kaye, *The Golden Calm*, pp 146-8, 200
300 Khan, *Asarussanadid*, pp 169; FP 25.4.1829 no.16-19. Some of this construction can still be seen on the building.
301 FP 25.4.1829 no. 20
302 FP 25.4.1829 no.20, 22; 4.9.1829 no.22; Khan, *Asarussanadid*, pp 169
303 FP 21.6.1810 nos.40-1; FP 24.11.1821 no.30
304 FP 28.12.1810 no.109; FP 26.1.1811 nos.25-6; 1.7.1820 no.50
305 FP 24.11.1821 no.30; 15.1.1823 nos.78-9; Pernau and Jafferey, *Persian Newsletters*, pp 91, 92, 100, 130-32, 136, 191, 192, 242-43, 260, 318, 386, 412-13
306 Pernau and Jafferey, *Persian Newsletters*, pp 414-15; FP 21.4.1849 no.157-8; India Office Records, Board's Collections volumes, British Library, IOR/F/4/1863/79-096
307 FP 25.4.1846 no.299-302; 25.5.1855 no.69; 23.1.1857 no.158
308 FP 3.4.1830 no.63; 28.5.1830 no.8-9
309 For the Colebrooke case see Spear, *Twilight of the Mughals*, p 167 onwards. For the role of Bakhtawar Singh also see FP 4.10 1822 no.25; 17.7.1829 no.19; 18.9.1829 no.23; 11.3.1831 no.69; 2.4.1831 nos.31-2; 27.5.1831 nos.32-4
310 *Papers transmitted from India by C.E.Trevelyan, Esq.*, Printed by J.L.Cox, London, 1830
311 Ibid
312 FP 2.4.1831 no.32
313 FP 6.1.1832 nos.6-7
314 Palace diary, FMisc vol 361, 16.1.1851
315 Gardner letters, Mss Eur C 304 n.d.; 16.9.1820; 10.8.1821; 16.8.1821
316 FP 16.4.1822 no.15; 15.1.1823 nos.78-9; 21.11.1823 nos.25-6; Pernau and Jafferey, *Persian Newsletters*, pp 106, 122
317 FP 18.6.1830 no.25
318 Gardner letters, Mss Eur C 304, 21.8.1821; 22.8.1821; 22.11.1821
319 Ibid., 10.8.1821
320 Khan, *Sirat e Faridiya*, p 29
321 Azad, *Ab-e hayat*, pp 350-1
322 Akhbar of 3.2.1830, and 5.2.1820, Pernau and Jafferey, *Persian Newsletters*, pp 177, 180-81
323 *Papers transmitted from India by C.E.Trevelyan*, pp 130-34
324 Akhbar of 8.2.1830, Pernau and Jafferey, *Persian Newsletters*, p 185
325 FP 5.3.1832 nos.21-4
326 FP 23.7.1832 nos.36-7
327 FP 31.7.1819, no.41; *Gazetteer of the Gurgaon District 1883*, n.d., p 28
328 FP 19.12.1829 no.21
329 FP 23.4.1830 no.64
330 FP 1.6.1840 no.85; 27.7.1840 no.30
331 Asadullah Khan Ghalib, *Auraq e Ma'ani: Ghalib ke Farsi Khutut, Urdu Tarjuma*, translated and edited by Tanvir Ahmad Alavi, Urdu Academy, Delhi, 2001, pp 138-9
332 *Dehli Urdu Akhbar* 6.12.1840
333 Asadullah Khan Ghalib, *Ghalib ke Khutut*, edited by Khaliq Anjum, Ghalib Institute, New Delhi, 2000, vol 2 pp 705, 766; vol 1 p 310
334 FP 2.9.1834, no.21
335 FP 18.5.1835 no.21
336 Ibid

337 FP 27.4.1835, no.30; 1.6.1835, no.109; Pernau and Jaffery, *Persian Newsletters*, pp 222, 240, 254 258, 287
338 Ralph Russell and Khurshidul Islam, *Ghalib: Life, Letters and Ghazals*, Oxford University Press, 2003, pp 32, 52-3
339 FP 28.5.1830, no.12
340 FP 20.8.1830 nos.35-38
341 Ghalib, *Auraq e Ma'ani*, pp 51, 79, 97-98, 106, 123
342 Ibid., pp 146-47; Russell and Islam, *Ghalib*, p 53
343 Ghalib, *Auraq e Ma'ani*, pp 146-7
344 FP 1.6.1835 no.109
345 FP 18.5.1835, no.21; 1.6.1835 nos.111-12
346 FP 14.9.1835 nos.65-7; 19.10.1835 no.122
347 FP 21.9.1835 nos.31-2
348 Thomas Bacon, *First Impressions and Studies from Nature in Hindostan*, W.H.Allen, London, 1837, vol II, pp 267-75
349 FP 26.10.1835, no.11
350 FP 24.12.1834, no.84
351 Spear, *Twilight of the Mughals*, pp 187-8; FP 26.10 1835 nos.12-3
352 Debate at the East India House—Grant to the estate of Mr. W Fraser, *The Asiatic Journal and Monthly Miscellany*, W.H. Allen, London, 1838, pp 170-84, 191-95
353 FP 29.6.1835 no.124
354 FP 15.2.1836 no.99; 21.3.1836 nos.8-9; 16.5.1836 nos.17-8,91; 23.1.1837 nos.19-21; NWPAbs, 7.10.1837 no.27; 25.10.37 no.11; 8.11.1837 no.4
355 Russell and Islam, *Ghalib*, p 54
356 Momin Khan 'Momin', *Insha e Momin*, edited and translated by Zahir Ahmad Siddiqi, Ghalib Academy, New Delhi, 1977, p 225
357 FP 16.10.1837, no.66; NWPAbs, 6.5.1837, no.4; Nasir Nazir, *Lal Qile ki ek Jhalak*, Urdu Academy, Delhi, 2001, pp 33-4
358 Frances Pritchett, *Nets of Awareness*, University of California Press, Berkeley, 1994, p 5
359 Faiz ud din, *Bazm e Akhir*, p 45; Palace diary, FMisc vol 361, 2.2.1851; 4.12.1852; 7.12.1852
360 FP 23.6.1849 nos.13-15; *Dehli Urdu Akhbar* 24.1.1841; 17.1.1841; Palace diary, FMisc vol 361, 11.7.1851; 26.3.1853; 23.6.1853
361 *Dehli Urdu Akhbar*, 19.4.1840, 10.5.1840
362 *Dehli Urdu Akhbar*, 17.1.1841, 19.4.1840, 7.6.1840, 14.6.1840, 24.1.1841
363 *Dehli Urdu Akhbar*, 22.3.1840;19.4.1840; 10.5.1840, 13.12.1840; Sabir, *Gulistan e Sukhan*, p 205
364 Pernau and Jafferey, *Persian Newsletters*, Akhbarat of 1825, passim. *Dehli Urdu Akhbar* 1.3.1840; 29.11.1840;13.12.1840; Palace diary, FMisc vol 361, 16.8.1851; 30.9.1851; 2.10.1851; 17.4.1853
365 *Dehli Urdu Akhbar*, 17.1.1841, 24.1.1841, 13.6.1841
366 *Dehli Urdu Akhbar*, 23.2.1840, 22.11.1840, 13.12.1840, 14.2.1841, 28.3.1841
367 Vidya Rao, 'The Dilli Gharana' in Mala Dayal ed. *Celebrating Delhi*, Ravi Dayal, New Delhi, 2010
368 Azad, *Ab-e Hayat*, pp 338-90
369 FP 16.10.1837 no.66; 14.3.1838 no.115; NWPAbs 15.11.1837 no.9; Thompson, *Debate at the India House*
370 NWPAbs 15.11.1837 no.10
371 NWPAbs 6.5.1837 no.4; 10.5.1837 no.3
372 FP 21.2.1838 nos.66-7
373 FP 22.3.1843 nos.81,93
374 NWPAbs 29.11.1837; FP 22.3.1843 no.117; 29.10.1843 no.185

375 FP 22.3.1843 nos.81,93
376 FP 16.10.1837 no.66; 14.3.1838 no.115; NWPAbs 15.11.1837 no.9; Thompson, *Debate at the India House*
377 FP 31.10.1838 nos.2,4
378 FP 15.6.1835 no.81; 29.6.1835 no.2; 8.6.1835 no.10; 14.9.1835.
379 *Dehli Urdu Akhbar*, 21.2.1841, 23.5.1841
380 FP 31.10.1838 no.4
381 For instance, see issues of *Dehli Urdu Akhbar*, 18.4.1841, 25.4.1841, 23.5.1842; 15.8.1841
382 FP 15.6.1827 no.10; 23.7.1832 no.34; 5.7.1841 no.79; NWPAbs 28.1.1837 no.9
383 FP 10.10.1838 nos.46,48; 17.10.1838 no.92
384 FP 16.8.1841 no.17
385 FP 16.8.1841 no.19
386 FP 16.8.1841 no.17
387 FP 31.10.1838 no.2
388 FP 31.10.1838 no.4
389 Taimuri, *Qila e Moalla ki Jhalkiyan*, pp 25-6
390 FP 1.8.1828 no.16; Parks, *Wanderings of a Pilgrim*, vol 1, pp 192-4, 381-2; *Dehli Urdu Akhbar* 25.12.1840; 24.1.1841, 14.2.1841, 21.2.1841
391 FP 16.8.1841 no.17
392 FP 24.5.1843 no.10
393 *British India: the duty and interest of Great Britain, to consider the condition and claims of her possessions in the East*, Clark and Baldwin, London, 1839, p 1
394 FP 10.2.1844 no.30
395 FP 23.9.1843 nos.21,23
396 Thompson, *Debate at the India House,* passim
397 FP 13.12.1845 nos.125-6
398 FP 17.10.1846, nos.32-35
399 FP 16.6.1849, no.23; 23.6.1849, nos.13-15; 11.10.1850 nos.199-202; 24.9.1852 nos.253-61; 23.12.1853 no.70; 24.9.1852 no.257
400 FP 3.6.1848 nos.70-77, 154-55
401 FP 31.3.1849 nos.26-7; see also 7.12.1835 no.14 and 3.6.1848 no.154
402 FP 24.5.1843 no.10; Palace diary, FMisc vol 361, 8.6.1851; 2.7.1851; 11.7.1851; 3.3.1853; 18.3.1853
403 FP 14.3.1856 nos.105-12
404 FP 6.5.1848 nos.33-49
405 Palace diary, FMisc vol 361, 18.1.51; 27.3.1851
406 Palace diary, FMisc vol 361, 17.6.1852
407 FP 2.12.1831 no.135; 31.3.1849 no.26; 13.2.1857 no.220; Palace diary, FMisc vol 361, 1.5.1851; 27.8.1851; 13.9.1852
408 Palace diary, FMisc vol 361, 5.10.1852
409 Ibid., 3.12.1852
410 Ibid., 31.5.1852; 23.6.1852; 25.9.1852
411 Ibid., 7.11.1853; 18.12.1853; 8.1.1853; 19.6.1852; 2.4.1852; *Dehli Urdu Akhbar* 10.5.1840; 17.5.1840; 24.5.1840; FP 26.9.1828 no.18
412 *Qiran us Sadaen* pp 551-2
413 Karim ud din, *Tabqat Shoara e Hind*, Uttar Pradesh Urdu Academy, Lucknow 1983, pp 416-17, 424
414 *Dehli Urdu Akhbar* 28.11.1841
415 Parks, *Wanderings of a Pilgrim*, vol I pp 421-22
416 FP 19.1.1855 no.62
417 FP 8.5.1857, nos.17-18

418 FP 24.2.1849 no.20
419 FP 24.2.1849 nos.21-25; 31.3.1849 nos.22-25; 11.10.1850 no.199; 27.2.1852 nos.53-58
420 Palace diary, FMisc vol 361, 27.3.1851
421 Ibid., 31.1.1852; 9.3.1851
422 FP 23.12.1853 nos.68-69
423 Palace diary, FMisc vol 361, 20-21.9.1852
424 *Qiran us Sadaen*, p 238
425 FP 24.9.1852 no.255-6
426 FP 24.9.1852 no.257; 10.6.1853 no.161
427 FP 23.6.1849, nos.14-15
428 FP 11.10.1850, nos.199-202
429 FP 7.10.1848 nos.53-7
430 FP 21.4.1849 no.155
431 Palace diary, FMisc vol 361 24.2.1851; 5.3.1851; 1.3.1851; 6.3.1851, 19.2.1851, 21.12.1853
432 Ibid., 14.3.1851
433 FP 22.10.1852 no.16
434 FP 29.10.1852 nos.183-8
435 FP 29.10.1852, nos.185, 188, 195
436 FP 23.12.1853, nos.65-71
437 *Dehli Urdu Akhbar*, undated, 2.10.1853, 13.11.1853
438 *Ghalib ke Khutut* vol 3 p 1138
439 FP 29.8.1856 no.183,189; Political Despatches to Court of Directors, National Archives of India 8.9.1856, no.96
440 FP 29.8 1856 no.188; 12.9.1856 nos.83-4
441 FP 5.12.1856, no.112
442 FP 29.8.1856 no.191
443 *Dehli Urdu Akhbar* 10.5.1840; 18.4.1841; 25.4.1841; 2.5.1841; 9.5.1841; 23.5.1841; 6.6.1841; 15.8.1841
444 *Dehli Urdu Akhbar*, undated, 1852; 2.10.53; *Qiran us Sadaen* undated 1853
445 Palace diary, FMisc vol 361, 11.3.1853; 6.2.1852; 14.10.1851; 7.4.1852
446 Ibid., 10.2.1851, 20.8.1852
447 *Dehli Urdu Akhbar* 7.6.1840; 19.4.1840; 14.6.1840
448 Palace diary, FMisc vol 361, 30.3.1852; 6.1.18 51; 19.1.1851; 3.6.1852; 21.10.1852
449 FP 10.4.1812 no.20; Palace diary, FMisc vol 361, 15.2.1851; 21.2.1851; 8.7.1853; 29.12.1853; *Dehli Urdu Akhbar* 14.6.1840; 18.10.1840; 25.10.1840
450 Palace diary, FMisc vol 361, 25.1.1853; 21,23-4.2.1853; 5.3.1851; 9.10.1853; 7.8.1851; 11.6.1851; *Dehli Urdu Akhbar* 12.7.1840
451 *Dehli Urdu Akhbar* 13.12.1840; Palace diary, FMisc vol 361, 10-12.3.1851; 11.12.1852; 1.2.1853; 3.5.1853; 24.6.1853; *Qiran us Sadaen* May 1853
452 Palace diary, FMisc vol 361, 8.1.1853; 17.1.1853, 28.6.1852
453 Khan, *Sirat e Faridiya*
454 Palace diary, FMisc vol 361, 13.11.1851; 19-20,22.9.1852
455 Ibid., 23.6.1852; 27.11.1852; 12.10.1852
456 Ibid., 8-9.10.1852
457 Palace diary, FMisc vol 361, 3.2.1851; 4.7.1853
458 *Ghalib ke Khutut*, vol II, p 705; vol III pp 1161;1163;1167
459 Ibid., vol IV p 1490
460 Ibid., vol I p 366
461 Altaf Husain Hali, *Hayat e Javed*, Qaumi Council Barae Farogh e Urdu Zaban, New Delhi, 1999, pp 33

462 Palace diary, FMisc vol 361, 21.3.1851; 25.3.1851; 8.5.1851; 22.12.1851; 14.4.1852; 18.9.1852; 9.2.1853
463 Ibid., 7.10.1851; 19.10.1851; 1.8.1852; 20.12.1852
464 Faiz ud din, *Bazm e Akhir*, p 83; *Dehli Urdu Akhbar* 1.11.1840; Palace diary, FMisc vol 361, 6.3.1852; 18.1.51; 30.6.1852
465 *Dehli Urdu Akhbar* 7.6.1840; 13.12.1840; *Qiran us Sadaen* Feb-Mar 1853; Palace diary, FMisc vol 361, 5.3.1851; 13.3.1851; 15.12.1852; 26.12.1852; 24.4.1851; Nazir, *Lal Qile ki ek Jhalak*, p 39
466 Palace diary, FMisc vol 361, 15.5.1851; 5.12.1852; 18.12.1852; 20.12.1852; The evidence of Jat Mall, in the Trial of Bahadur Shah, FMisc vol 376
467 Palace diary, FMisc vol 361 16.6.1851; 18.1.1853; 12.3.1853;1.5.1852; 28.10.1853
468 Ibid., 30.1.1853
469 Narayani Gupta, *Delhi Between Two Empires, 1803-1931: Society, Government and Urban Growth*, Oxford University Press, New Delhi, 1998, pp 4-5
470 Khan, *Asarussanadid*, pp 459-60, 522
471 Emma Roberts, *Scenes and Characteristics of Hindostan*, W.H. Allen, London, 1835, vol 3, p 167, 171
472 Palace diary, FMisc vol 361, 14.8.1852; 30.9.1852; 27.1.1853
473 FP 12.12.1809 no.72; 9.1.1810 no.56; 10.1.1812 no.87
474 Thomas Bacon, *First Impressions*, vol II, p 276, 291
475 *Qiran us Sadaen*, Jan/Feb 1853
476 *Dehli Urdu Akhbar* 5.12.1841; also very elaborate was the wedding in the house of Ramji Das Gurwala, see *Dehli Urdu Akhbar* 15.2.52
477 Spear, *Twilight of the Mughals*, p 196
478 *Ghalib ke Khutut* vol 3 p 1151-2
479 *Dehli Urdu Akhbar* 31.10.1852
480 Avril A.Powell, *Muslims and Missionaries in Pre-Mutiny India*, Routledge, London 1989, pp 203-5
481 For a detailed background of Jennings, his opinions and activities, see Dalrymple, *The Last Mughal*, especially pp 58-61
482 Frederick James Western, *The Early History of the Cambridge Mission to Dehli*, (for limited circulation), SPCK, London, 1950, pp 25-26
483 Powell, *Muslims and Missionaries,* pp 221-25, 230-34
484 Ibid., pp 242-62
485 FP 1.8.1828 no.16; Palace diary, FMisc vol 361, 7.10.1853; 21.12.1853; 19.3.1851; Hali, *Yadgar e Ghalib*, pp 77-8
486 Palace diary, FMisc vol 361, 21.10.1852
487 Syed Ahmad Dehlavi, writing in 1905, gave this explanation for this departure from Islamic law on the part of the Mughal royal family. Maulvi Syed Ahmad Dehlavi, *Rusum e Dehli*, Urdu Academy, Delhi, 1986, p 60
488 Palace diary, FMisc vol 361 4.2.1851, 12.2.1851; 15.2.1851; 9.3.1851
489 *Insha e Momin*, p 312, 337, 342
490 Ghalib, *Auraq e Ma'ani,* pp 97-8, 105, 120-21, 279-80, Russell and Islam, *Ghalib*, p 51
491 Hali, *Yadgar e Ghalib*, p 30
492 *Dehli Urdu Akhbar* 7.3.52; 14.3.52
493 *Dehli Urdu Akhbar* 26.12.52
494 *Dehli Urdu Akhbar* 29.8.52
495 Extract from *Sadiq ul Akhbar*, 11 May 1857, in Trial of Bahadur Shah, FMisc vol 376
496 *Dehli Urdu Akhbar* 7.3.1841; 7.11.52
497 Salim Qureshi and Syed Ashur Kazmi ed. and trans. *1857 ke Ghaddaron ke Khutut*, Anjuman Taraqqi Urdu (Hind), New Delhi 2001, p 31

498 Extract from Sadiq ul Akhbar, 19 March 1857, in Trial of Bahadur Shah, FMisc vol 376
499 The evidence of Theophilus Metcalfe, and extracts from various newspapers, in Trial of Bahadur Shah, FMisc vol 376
500 This and the following synopsis of the development of Urdu is based on Shamsur Rahman Faruqi, 'A Long History of Urdu Literary Culture, Part 1', in Sheldon Pollock ed. *Literary Cultures in History: Reconstructions from South Asia*, Oxford University Press, New Delhi, 2004, pp 805 onwards
501 Metcalf, *Islamic Revival in British India*, pp 38, 48, 67-8; Syed Zamir Hasan Dehlavi, *Dehlavi Urdu*, Urdu Academy, New Delhi, 2000, details the development of Urdu prose in Delhi specifically, though he subscribes rather uncritically to the Delhi chauvinism of the nineteenth century tazkira writers
502 Mir Inshaallah Khan 'Insha', *Dariya e Latafat*, Anjuman Taraqqi Urdu (Hind), New Delhi 1988, pp 27-8
503 Ibid., pp 28-31, 40, 47
504 Shamsur Rahman Faruqi, 'Unpriviledged Power: The Strange Case of Persian (and Urdu) in Nineteenth-Century India', *Annual of Urdu Studies*, vol 13, pp 15-16
505 For an excellent explanation of the world of Urdu poetry, especially the *ghazal*, see Pritchett, *Nets of Awareness,* pp 77-122
506 See for instance Azad's recounting of Zauq's conflict with his *ustad*, Azad, *Ab-e hayat*, pp 340-42
507 Abdul Ghafur Nasakh, *Sukhan Shoara*, Uttar Pradesh Urdu Akademi, Lucknow 1982, p 218
508 For a a brief but informative account of *mushairas* and other institutions of Urdu poetry see Pritchett, 'A Long History of Urdu Literary Culture, Part 2: Histories, Performances and Masters', in Pollock ed. *Literary Cultures in History*, p 864 onwards, and also Pritchett, *Nets of Awareness*; and Haneef Naqvi, *Shoara e Urdu ke Tazkire, Nikat ush Shoara se Gulshan e Be Khar tak*, Uttar Pradesh Urdu Akademi, Lucknow, 1998, p 157
509 Karim ud din, *Tabqat Shoara e Hind*, pp 219, 329, 331, 340; Qutubuddin Batin, *Gulistan e Bekhizan*, Uttar Pradesh Urdu Akademi, Lucknow, 1982, p 281; Nasakh, *Sukhan Shoara*, p 46-7; Sabir, *Gulistan e Sukhan*, p 161-3; Azad, *Ab-e hayat*, pp 375-6
510 Syed Md.Miyan, *Ulema e Hind ka Shandar Mazi*, Maktaba Burhan, Delhi 1963, vol 4, p 254
511 'Government Resolution and Correspondence for the establishment of a Genereal Committee of Public Instruction for the purpose of ascertaining the stage of public education under the Presidency of Fort William', FMisc vol 178; FP 5.6.1829, no.83
512 FP 5.6.1829, no.87
513 J.H Taylor to H.H. Wilson 7.1.1824, FP 5.6.1829 no.83
514 FP 5.6.1829 no.83
515 Ibid
516 For brief discussions of this form of education see Lelyveld, *Aligarh's First Generation*, pp 50-55; and Gail Minault and Christian W. Troll, 'Introduction' in Ian Henderson Douglas, *Abul Kalam Azad: An Intellectual and Religious Biography*, Oxford University Press, Bombay 1988, pp 12-3
517 Metcalf, *Islamic Revival in British India*, p 38; Khan, *Asarussanadid*, pp 560-2
518 Karim ud din, *Tabqat Shoara e Hind*, p 360; Batin, *Gulistan e Bekhizan*, p 53; Nasakh, *Sukhan Shoara*, p 83
519 David Lelyveld, *Aligarh's First Generation: Muslim solidarity in British India*, Oxford University Press, New Delhi, 2003, pp 39-40, 53-54
520 Hali, *Hayat e Javed*, pp 54-6, 62-4

521 Andrews, *Zaka Ullah of Delhi*, p 53
522 Khan, *Asarussanadid*, pp 518, 560-2, 582; and *Sirat e Faridiya*, p 33; Aslahi, *Mufti Sadr ud din Azurda*, p 27
523 FP 3.3.1826 no.14. Pernau and Jafferey, *Persian Newsletters*, p 131; Horace Hayman Wilson, *Travels in the Himalayan Provinces of Hindustan and the Panjab; in Ladakh and Kashmir; in Peshawar, Kabul, Kunduz, and Bokhara, by Mr. William Moorcroft and Mr. George Trebeck from 1819 to 1825*, John Murray, London, 1841
524 FP 5.6.1829 no.83; FMisc vol 178
525 Ibid
526 FP 5.6.1829 nos.83-84
527 FP 5.6.1829 nos.83, 86
528 FP 5.6.1829 no.86
529 FP 5.6.1829 no.89
530 FP 5.6.1829 no.87
531 FP 3.7.1829 no.82
532 Ibid
533 FP 3.7.1829 no.103; for the development of the Liberal opinion on the question of education in India see Eric Stokes, *The English Utilitarians and India*, New Delhi, 1992, especially pp 45-47
534 Pernau, 'Preparing a Meeting Ground', p lxv
535 FP 3.7.1829 no.107
536 An account of these developments is to be found in the notes and correspondence at Home Department, Public Proceedings, National Archives of India (henceforth HPub) 15.7.1840, nos.7-14
537 Khan, *Asarussanadid*, p 541
538 Abdul Haq, *Marhum Dehli Kalij*, Anjuman Taraqqi Urdu (Hind), New Delhi 1989, p 38
539 FP 25.6.1832 no.106
540 Haq, *Marhum Dehli Kalij*, p 39
541 C.E. Trevelyan, 'Memoir of Mohan Lal', in Munshi Mohan Lal, *Journal of a tour through the Panjab, Afghanistan, Turkistan, Khorasan, and part of Persia in Company with Lieut. Burnes and Dr. Gerard*, Baptist Mission Press, Calcutta, 1834, pp ix-xii; Shahamat Ali, *The Sikhs and the Afghans, in Connexion with India and Persia, immediately before and after the death of Ranjeet Singh*, John Murray, London, 1847, pp v-xiii; Hari Ram Gupta, *Life and Work of Mohan Lal Kashmiri 1812-1877*, Minerva Book Shop, Lahore, 1943, p 8
542 Mohan Lal, 'Preface' in *Journal of a tour*, p iii
543 Gupta, *Life and Work of Mohan Lal Kashmiri*, pp 3-4
544 Trevelyan, 'Memoir of Mohan Lal', pp xii-xvii
545 Ibid., p xviii
546 Michael Fisher, *Counterflows to Colonialism: Indian Travellers and Settlers in Britain 1600-1857*, Permanent Black, Delhi, 2004, pp 351-66
547 Munshi Mohan Lal, *Journal of a tour*, pp vi-vii
548 FP 28.1.1835, no.54
549 FP 3.7.1829, no.81; Home Department Public Proceedings, National Archives of India, 10.2.1841, no.11
550 *Dehli Urdu Akhbar*, 28.11.1841
551 FP 5.6.1829, no.89; Margrit Pernau, 'The *Dehli Urdu Akhbar*: Between Persian Akhbarat and English Newspapers', in *The Annual of Urdu Studies*, vol 18, 2003, p 120- 21
552 FP 5.3.1835 no.22; HPub 20.10.1841 no.11; 15.7.1840, no.9
553 FP 3.8.1835, no.83; HPub 15.7.1840, no.12

554 FP 26.10.1835 no.5; HPub 20.10.1841 no.11; 30.6.1841, no.19; *General Report on Public Instruction in the North Western Provinces of the Bengal Presidency for 1843-44*, Agra Ukhbar Press, Agra, p 60
555 Haq, *Marhum Dehli Kalij*, pp 106-7
556 HPub 20.10.1841, no.11
557 HPub 30.6.1841, no.19
558 HPub 30.6.1841, no.19
559 HPub 30.6.1841, no.19; FP 4.5.1844 no.28
560 *General Report on Public Instruction, 1843-44*, pp 1-3
561 Ikram Chaghatai, 'Dr. Aloys Sprenger and the Delhi College' in Pernau ed. *The Delhi College*, p 108; J.A. Richey, *Selections from Educational Records, Part II 1840-1859*, Bureau of Education, India, Calcutta, 1922, pp 5-10
562 Haq, *Marhum Dehli Kalij*, pp 34-7
563 Andrews, *Zaka Ullah of Delhi*, p 46
564 See for instance Gail Minault, 'Delhi College and Urdu' in *The Annual of Urdu Studies*, vol 14, 1999, p 119; and also Minault, 'The Perils of Cultural Mediation: master Ram Chandra and Academic Journalism at Delhi College' in Pernau ed. *The Delhi College*, pp 192-3
565 Powell, *Muslims and Missionaries*, p 197
566 'Minute' Appendix N, *General Report on Public, 1843-44*; Richey, *Selections from Educational Records*, pp 5-10
567 *General Report on Public Instruction, 1843-44*, p 61, Appendix O
568 *General Report on Public Instruction 1843-44*, Appendix R
569 *General Report on Public Instruction 1843-44*, p 55, Appendix R
570 *General Report on Public Instruction 1843-44*, Appendix R
571 *General Report on Public 1843-44*, Appendix R; *General Report on Public Instruction 1844-45*, pp 6, 70
572 *General Report on Public Instruction 1846-47*, p 86
573 Richey, *Selections from Educational Records*, p 5
574 *General Report on Public Instruction 1844-45*, pp 75-76, Appendix M
575 Chaghatai, 'Dr. Aloys Sprenger', pp 111-12
576 *General Report on Public Instruction 1844-45*, Appendix A; *1845-46*, Appendix G; *1846-47*, Appendix C
577 *General Report on Public Instruction 1843-44*, Appendix R, *1846-47*, p 3
578 Maulvi Karim ud din, *Guldasta e Nazninan*, Azimushshan Book Depot, Patna 1972, pp 6-8; *Tabqat Shoara e Hind*, introduction, pp 400, 415, 468-9
579 'Report on Educational books in the Vernacular', in *Selections from the records of the Government of the North-Western Provinces*, Government Press, Allahabad, 1867, vol 3, pp 395 onwards
580 Notes by W. Muir and G.J Christian, ibid. pp 398-401
581 Haq, *Marhum Dehli Kalij*, pp 43-44, 119-20; *General Report on Public Instruction 1844-45*, pp 74-75, *1845-46*, p 69
582 *Dehli Urdu Akhbar* 5.12.1841, 14.11.1841
583 Karim ud din lists a number of teachers and senior students of the college with the compilations and translations to their credit. Karim ud din, *Tabqat Shoara e Hind*, pp 462-73
584 Haq, *Marhum Dehli Kalij*, pp 40, 46-47; *General Report on Public Instruction 1846-47*, p 86
585 Malik Ram, *Qadim Dehli Kalij*, Delhi, Maktaba Jamia Limited, 1976, p.27
586 Pernau, 'Introduction' in Pernau ed. *The Delhi College*, pp 22-3; Ram, *Qadim Dehli Kalij*, p 51; Metcalf, *Islamic Revival in British India*, p 77
587 Khan, *Asarussanadid*, p 283; Secretary to Agent, 8.3.1845, North Western Provinces Proceedings, 8.3.1845, nos.19-21

588 *Qiran us Sadaen* Aug/Sept 1853; p 209-10; *Dehli Urdu Akhbar* 2.8.1840; 28.11.1841
589 Haq, *Marhum Dehli Kalij*, pp 110-20
590 Andrews, *Zaka Ullah of Delhi*, p 46
591 *Memoir on the statistics of indigenous education within the North Western Provinces of the Bengal Presidency*, Baptist Mission Press, Calcutta, 1850, pp 24-26
592 Pritchett, *Nets of Awareness*, p 14
593 Farhatullah Beg, *Daktar Nazir Ahmad ki Kahani, Kuch Meri aur Kuchh un ki Zabani*, Anjuman Taraqqi Urdu (Hind), Delhi 1992, p 42; Christina Osterheld, 'Deputy Nazir Ahmad and the Delhi College' in Pernau ed. *The Delhi College*, p 301
594 Karim ud din, *Guldasta e Nazninan*, p 7
595 Raina and Habib, *Domesticating Modern Science* pp 24-38; Gail Minault, 'The Perils of Cultural Mediation', pp 194-200
596 Ramchundra, *A Treatise on Problems of Maxima and Minima Solved by Algebra*, W.H.Allen & Co., London, 1859
597 Ibid., p xvi
598 *Qiran us Sadaen*, issues of 1853-54, in Osmania University Library, Hyderabad; Minault, 'The Perils of Cultural Mediation', p 194
599 Minault, 'The Perils of Cultural Mediation'
600 'Report on Educational books in the Vernacular', pp, 397, 405-06
601 Gail Minault, 'The Perils of Cultural Mediation', pp 197-200; for a sample of the topics that figured in both newspapers see Raina and Habib, *Domesticating Modern Science*, pp 16-19; *Muhibb e Hind*
602 *Muhibb e Hind*
603 Gail Minault, 'The Perils of Cultural Mediation', pp 197-200; 'Note on native presses in the North-Western Provinces' for the years 1850, in *Selections from the Records of the North-Western Provinces vol iv*, pp 51, 72
604 Hali, *Hayat e Javed*, p 69
605 *Dehli Urdu Akhbar* 24.10.1841; 22.8.52; 8.8.52, and *Muhibb e Hind*
606 Karim ud din, *Tabqat Shoara e Hind*, p 434
607 *Qiran us Sadaen*
608 'Note on native presses in the North-Western Provinces' for the years 1850, 1851, 1852, 1853, in *Selections from the Records of the North-Western Provinces vol iv*, pp 51, 59, 72, 105, 141
609 *Dehli Urdu Akhbar* 18.7.52
610 Palace diary, FMisc vol 361 9.7.1852
611 *Dehli Urdu Akhbar* 21.11.52
612 Palace diary, FMisc vol 361 4.12.1852
613 Ramchundra, *A Treatise*, pp xx-xxi
614 For a discussion of the impact of print see Francis Robinson, *Islam and Muslim History in South Asia*, New Delhi 2006, pp 66-77
615 Khan, *Asarussanadid*, pp 518
616 For references to such works, often with the press where they were printed, see, Karim ud din,*Tabqat Shoara e Hind*, p 236, 251, 370-1, 415,439, 471-73; *Dehli Urdu Akhbar* 26.1.1840, 3.10.52; 17.10.52; 29.5.53; *Qiran us Sadaen* May 53
617 *General Report on Public Instruction 1846-47*, p 3
618 Sabir, *Gulistan e Sukhan*, p 169
619 *Dehli Urdu Akhbar* 12.9.52; 19.9.52
620 Ghalib, *Auraq e Ma'ani*, pp 213, 359
621 *Dehli Urdu Akhbar* 28.2.1841, 11.4.1841
622 Hali, *Yadgar e Ghalib*, p 18

623 Pernau, 'The *Dehli Urdu Akhbar*, Between Persian Akhbarat and English Newspapers', pp 105, 116; and Gail Minault, 'From Akhbar to News: The Development of the Urdu Press in Early Nineteenth Century Delhi' in Kathryn Hansen and David Lelyveld eds *A Wilderness of Possibilities, Urdu Studies in Transnational Perspective*, Oxford University Press, New Delhi, 2005, pp 101-117
624 Gail Minault, 'From *Akhbar* to News', p 111
625 Ghalib, *Auraq e Ma'ani* pp 140-1
626 Evidence of Chunni Lal, in Trial of Bahadur Shah, FMisc vol 376
627 See the several issues from 1841, in Professor Irtiza Karim, edited, *Dehli Urdu Akhbar, 1841*, Qaumi Council Barae Farogh e Urdu Zaban, Delhi, 2010
628 *Dehli Urdu Akhbar*, issues of 1841; 10.5.1840
629 'Note on native presses in the North-Western Provinces', for the years 1848, 1849, 1850, 1853, in *Selections from the Records of the North-Western Provinces,* Govt. Press N.W.P., Allahabad, 1867, vol iv, pp 8, 24, 49, 138; *Dehli Urdu Akhbar* 7.8.53
630 *Dehli Urdu Akhbar* 7.8.53; English translation from Pernau, 'The *Dehli Urdu Akhbar;* Between Persian Akhbarat and English Newspapers', pp 121-22
631 *Fawaid ul Nazirin*, 5.11.1847, quoted in translation in Dhruv Raina and S. Irfan Habib, *Domesticating Modern Science: A Social History of Science and Culture in Colonial India*, Tulika Books, New Delhi 2004, p 5
632 *Dehli Urdu Akhbar* 28.6.1840
633 Ibid., 15.8.1841
634 Ibid., 1.2.52; 2.10.53, 26.1.1840
635 Ibid., 22.3.1840; 21.2.1841;14.3.1841; 31.10.52, 4.4.1841
636 Ibid., 1.11.1840
637 Ibid., 21.11.1841, 28.11.1841
638 *Qiran us Sadaen* May 1853
639 Ghalib, *Auraq e Ma'ani* p 214
640 Ibid., pp 37-38, 212, 269
641 *Insha e Momin* p 228-9
642 *Ghalib ke Khutut* vol 1 p 303; vol 3 p 1062
643 Karim ud din, *Tabqat Shoara e Hind*, pp 400-1, 406, 409-10, 415- 417; This idea of linking a *mushaira* to a newspaper was followed some years later in Lahore; Pritchett, *Nets of Awareness*, pp 69-70
644 Ghalib, *Auraq e Ma'ani* p 223; Ali Jawad Zaidi, *Tarikh e Mushaira*, Shan e Hind Publications, Delhi 1992, pp 106-7
645 Pritchett, *Nets of Awareness*, p 10
646 Sabir, *Gulistan e Sukhan*, introduction, especially p 15, and p 182
647 Nasakh, *Sukhan Shoara*, p 191-2; *Ghalib ke Khutut* vol 2 p 574
648 C.M.Naim, 'Shaikh Imam Bakhsh Sahbai'i: Teacher, Scholar, Poet, and Puzzle-master', in Pernau, *Delhi College*, pp 145-85
649 Azad, *Ab-e* hayat, pp 375-6
650 Ghalib, *Auraq e Ma'ani* pp 165-6, 169
651 Syed Zahiruddin 'Zahir' Dehlavi, *1857 ke chashmdeed halaat, almaruf Dastan e Ghadar* Adib Publications, New Delhi, 2008, p 23
652 *Ghalib ke Khutut* vol 4 p 1490
653 Ghalib, *Auraq e Ma'ani* pp 223-4
654 *Ghalib ke Khutut* vol 1 p 61-63
655 Ibid., p 79
656 Azad, *Ab-e hayat*, p 231
657 FP 16.8.1810, no.52; 5.3.1813, no.44
658 Sabir, *Gulistan e Sukhan*, p 9
659 Naqvi, *Shoara e Urdu ke Tazkire*, p 133
660 Ghalib, *Auraq e Ma'ani* p 269-70

661 *Dehli Urdu Akhbar* 2.8.1840
662 Ghalib, *Auraq e Ma'ani* p 317
663 Nazir, *Lal Qile ki ek Jhalak*, pp, 41-3
664 Sabir, *Gulistan e Sukhan*, p 364
665 *Ghalib ke Khutut* vol 3 p 1064;1067
666 *Ghalib ke Khutut* vol 2 p 804, vol 1 pp 20, 90-92, 268, 278, 290; vol 3 pp 1021, 1055, 1242; vol 4 p 1423
667 *Ghalib ke Khutut* vol 1 p 399, vol 4 p 1435
668 Parks, *Wanderings of a Pilgrim*, vol II p 222
669 FP 20.8.1830 nos.35-38; Ghalib, *Auraq e Ma'ani* p 107, 280
670 FP 2.12.1831 no.135
671 FP 12.6.1829, no.22
672 Akhbar of 12.12.1830, Pernau and Jafferey, *Persian Newsletters*, p 403
673 FP 6.6.1833 nos.9-11; 16.8.1833 nos.19-20
674 FP 6.6.1833, no.9
675 FP 14.9.1835 no.18; NWPAbs 8.4.1837 no.7; Palace diary, FMisc vol 361, 2.12.1851
676 FP 13.4.1842, no.20
677 *Ghalib ke Khutut* vol 3 p 1060
678 FP 1.6.1835 nos.109-12; 27.7.1835 no.135
679 FP 31.7.1819
680 *Dehli Urdu Akhbar* 14.3.52
681 Pritchett, *Nets of Awareness*, pp 141-43
682 Naqvi, *Shoara e Urdu ke Tazkire*, p 705; Aditya Behl, 'Poet of the Bazaars: Nazir Akbarabadi, 1735-1830, in Hansen and Lelyveld ed. *A Wilderness of Possibilities*, p 192; Sabir, *Gulistan e Sukhan*, pp 461-62; Karim ud din,*Tabqat Shoara e Hind*, pp 393-4
683 Tariq Rahman, 'Boy-Love in the Urdu Ghazal', *Annual of Urdu Studies*, vol 7, 1990, p 1; C.M. Naim, 'Homosexual (Pederastic) Love in Pre-Modern Urdu Poetry' in *Urdu Texts and Contexts: The Selected Essays of C.M. Naim*, Delhi 2004, pp 19-29
684 Tariq Rahman suggests that after 1830 particularly the expression of homosexuality was considerably muted, Rahman, in 'Boy-Love in the Urdu Ghazal', p 6
685 Frances W. Pritchett, *A Desertful of Roses* ghazal 173, verse 7; website of Frances Pritchett, http://www.columbia.edu/itc/mealac/pritchett/00ghalib/index.html
686 *Ghalib ke Khutut*, vol II, pp 519, 521, 533-35, 544
687 Mohammad Feroz, *Talmiz e Ghalib, Mir Mehdi 'Majruh': Hayat aur Tasanif*, Published with support of Urdu Academy Delhi, New Delhi 1999, pp 71-72; *Ghalib ke Khutut*, vol II pp 516, 527
688 Hali p 102
689 *Ghalib ke Khutut* vol 2 p 733
690 Sabir, *Gulistan e Sukhan*, pp 292, 444, 425, 484
691 C.M. Naim, 'Transvestic Words?: The Rekhti in Urdu', p 42; and 'Poet-Audience Interaction at Urdu Mushairas', p 110, in *Urdu Texts and Contexts*
692 Naim, 'Transvestic Words?', p 42; Sabir, *Gulistan e Sukhan*, pp 444-48; Karim ud din,*Tabqat Shoara e Hind*, pp 432-33
693 Naim, 'Transvestic Words?' pp 47-53
694 Naqvi, *Shoara e Urdu ke Tazkire*, p 707
695 Karim ud din,*Tabqat Shoara e Hind*, pp 444, 470
696 *Muhibb e Hind*, 1.1.1850
697 Sadiq ur Rahman Kidwai, *Hindustan mein fikri-o-tahzeebi islah ka aagaz aur Master Ram Chander*, Anjuman Taraqqi Urdu (Hind), New Delhi, 2007, pp 161-62

698 Karim ud din,*Tabqat Shoara e Hind*, p 444, Siddiqi, *Momin, Shaksiyat aur Fan*, p 116
699 Ali Safdar Jafri, *Nawab Mustafa Khan Shefta*, Azra Publications, Sutur Publications, Lahore, 1999, pp 53-54; Mustafa Khan Shefta, *Gulshan e Bekhar*, Uttar Pradesh Uttar Academy, Lucknow 1982, p 116
700 Pritchett, http://www.columbia.edu/itc/mealac/pritchett/00ghalib/index.html
701 Pritchett, *Nets of Awareness*, p 12, Syed Ahmad wrote a bit of poetry in Persian (see Sabir, *Gulistan e Sukhan*, pp 125-28)
702 Karim ud din,*Tabqat Shoara e Hind*, pp 470-71
703 *Journal of the Archaeological Society of Dehli*, Dehli Gazette Press, September 1850, Appendix
704 Ibid., pp 64-71
705 Fisher, *Counterflows to Colonialism*, pp 422-24
706 FP 15.3.1843, no.107; 27.1.1844, nos.210-11; 27.12.1845, no.2; Foreign Department, Secret Proceeding, National Archives of India, New Delhi, (henceforth FS) 28.12.1842, nos.482, 540, 675
707 FP 2.3.1844, nos.34-35; Mohan Lal, *Travels in the Panjab, Afghanistan and Turkistan, to Balk, Bokhara and Heart: and a visit to Great Britain and Germany*, W.H Allen, London, 1846, pp 480-528; National Galleries of Scotland, 40 amazing portraits of people who lived in and visited Scotland during the 1840s, https://www.vintag.es/2018/05/people-in-scotland-1940s.html
708 Fisher, *Counterflows to Colonialism*, pp 351-66; Mohan Lal, *Travels*, pp 480; FP 25.10.1845, nos.79-80; 27.12.45, no.2; 20.6.1846, nos.227-28
709 *Journal of the Asiatic Society of Bengal*, vol 5, Baptist Mission Press, Calcutta, 1836, pp 796-98
710 Hamida Sultan Ahmad, *Khandan e Loharu ke Shoara*, Ghalib Institute, New Delhi, 1981, pp 136-38
711 *Journal of the Archaeological Society of Delhi*, January 1853
712 *Qiran us Sadaen* n.d. 1854; Khan, *Asarussanadid*, pp 149-51, 167-8
713 Lelyveld, *Aligarh's first generation*, p 58; Hali, *Hayat e Javed*, pp 64-5
714 Hali, *Hayat e Javed*, pp 66-7
715 Hali, *Hayat e Javed*, pp 72-75
716 Hali, *Yadgar e Ghalib*, pp 84-6
717 For the events of the 11th May, see *Delhi Urdu Akhbar* 18.5.1857; Charles Theophilus Metcalfe, *Two Native Narratives of the Mutiny in Delhi*, Archibald Constable & Co., Westminster, 1898, Trial of Bahadur Shah, FMisc vol 376; George Wagentreiber *Our Escape from Delhi*, n.d.; Florence Wagentreiber, *Reminiscences of the sepoy rebellion of 1857*, Civil and Military Gazette Press, Lahore, 1911
718 Atiq Siddiqi, *Atthara Sau Sattavan: Akhbar aur Dastavezen*, Maktaba Shahrah, Delhi, 1966, pp 37-38; evidence of Jat Mall in the Trial of Bahadur Shah, FMisc vol 376
719 Evidence of Jat Mall in the Trial of Bahadur Shah, FMisc vol 376
720 Siddiqi, *Atthara Sau Sattavan*, pp 39
721 Evidence of Jat Mall in the Trial of Bahadur Shah, FMisc vol 376
722 Wagentreiber, *Our Escape from Delhi*; Wagentreiber, *Reminiscences of the sepoy rebellion*
723 Pramod K. Nayar, *The Penguin 1857 Reader*, Penguin Books, New Delhi 2007, pp 106-109, 112-115
724 *Dehli Urdu Akhbar*, 17th May 1857; Haq, *Marhum Dehli Kalij*, pp 72-73; Zahir Dehlavi, *Dastan e Ghadar*, p 98
725 Narrative of Muinuddin Hasan Khan, in Metcalfe, *Two Native Narratives*, p 47
726 The diary of Chunni Lal, in the Trial of Bahadur Shah, FMisc vol 376

727 The evidence of Gulab in the Trial of Bahadur Shah, FMisc vol 376
728 Metcalfe, *Two Native Narratives*, p 92, 100-101
729 The evidence of Mrs Aldwell and the diary of Chunni Lal, in the Trial of Bahadur Shah, FMisc vol 376
730 *Memoirs of Hakim Ahsanullah Khan*, edited by S. Moinul Haq, Pakistan Historical Society, Karachi, 1958, p 12
731 The diary of Chunni Lal, in the Trial of Bahadur Shah, FMisc vol 376
732 Metcalfe, *Two Native Narratives*, p 94
733 For the events of the day see the Trial of Bahadur Shah, FMisc vol 376, passim
734 The diary of Chunni Lal, in the Trial of Bahadur Shah, FMisc vol 376
735 The evidence of John Everett in the Trial of Bahadur Shah, FMisc vol 376
736 *Dehli Urdu Akhbar*, 31.5.1857
737 *Mutiny Records: Correspondence*, Sang e Meel Publications, Lahore, 2005, part 1, pp 151-52
738 The governor of Arabia and Iraq, Ibn Yusuf as-Saqafi, considered a tyrant by the Persians
739 *Dehli Urdu Akhbar* 24.5.1857
740 The diary of Chunni Lal, in the Trial of Bahadur Shah, FMisc vol 376; Siddiqi, *Atthara Sau Sattavan*, p 39
741 Metcalfe, *Two Native Narratives*, pp 43-46, 95
742 The evidence and diary of Chunni Lal, in the Trial of Bahadur Shah, FMisc vol 376
743 The diary of Chunni Lal, in the Trial of Bahadur Shah, FMisc vol 376
744 Said Mobarik Shah, 'The City of Delhi during the Siege'Mss Eur B 138, p 7
745 Metcalfe, *Two Native Narratives*, p 87
746 Ibid., pp 86, 95
747 The evidence of Jat Mall and the diary of Chunni Lal, in the Trial of Bahadur Shah, FMisc vol 376
748 Metcalfe, *Two Native Narratives*, p 96
749 Jivan Lal, *Sarguzisht e Dehli 1857 ke andolan ki kahani, Jivan Lal ki zabani*, edited and transcribed by Darkhashan Tajwar, Rampur Raza Library, Rampur, 2005, pp 113-14
750 For an English translation of the text of the document, see Mahmood Farooqui, *Besieged: Voices from Delhi, 1857*, Penguin, New Delhi, 2010, pp 56-58
751 *Dehli Urdu Akhbar*, 24.5.1857
752 Farooqui, *Besieged*, pp 58-60; Metcalfe, *Two Native Narratives*, p 90
753 The diary of Chunni Lal, in the Trial of Bahadur Shah, FMisc vol 376
754 Ibid
755 *Memoirs of Ahsanullah Khan*, p 16
756 Farooqui, *Besieged*, pp 72-72, 196, 228
757 Qureshi and Kazmi, *1857 ke Ghaddaron ke Khutut*, p 141
758 Metcalfe, *Two Native Narratives*, p 60; *Mutiny Records*, part 1, pp 429-32
759 Charles Ball, *History of the Indian Mutiny,* The London Printing and Publishing Company Limited, London, n.d., vol 1, pp 185-89
760 Metcalfe, *Two Native Narratives*, pp 61, 108-109; Ball, *History of the Indian Mutiny,* vol 1, pp 192-95
761 Ball, *History of the Indian Mutiny,* vol 1, pp 191-92, 195-200
762 Metcalfe, *Two Native Narratives*, p 122, 124, passim; *Mutiny Records*, part 1, passim
763 *Dehli Urdu Akhbar* 31.5.1857; Metcalfe, *Two Native Narratives*, pp 92, 110, 115, 121, 126-27, 133-35; Jivan Lal, *Sarguzisht e Dehli*, pp 83, 104-5, 116-17, 139, 149-50, 181-82, 243, 251, 263, 266, 274; S.M.Azizuddin Husain, *Dastavezat e Ghadar 1857*, Kanishka Publishers, New Delhi, 2007, pp 152-54, 157; Petitions

of Sheodial and Shadiram, merchants, and Dundiya Khan, farmer in the old fort, in the Trial of Bahadur Shah, FMisc vol 376; *Dehli Urdu Akhbar* 14.6.1857

764 Orders of Bahadur Shah to Mirza Mughal, in the Trial of Bahadur Shah, FMisc vol 376

765 Petition of the chaudhary of the managers of ice pits, and Syed Mohammad, an ascetic, in the Trial of Bahadur Shah, FMisc vol 376; Jivan Lal, *Sarguzisht e Dehli*, p 96; Husain, *Dastavezat e Ghadar*, p 154

766 Metcalfe, *Two Native Narratives*, p 117-32

767 Metcalfe, *Two Native Narratives*, pp 133-36; *Memoirs of Ahsanullah Khan*, pp 16-18

768 Metcalfe, *Two Native Narratives*, pp 134-35, 142

769 *Memoirs of Ahsanullah Khan*, pp 18-20; Metcalfe, *Two Native Narratives*, pp 134-36, 38-39; *Mutiny Records*, part 1, p 303

770 *Mutiny Records*, part 1, pp 230-33, 286-87

771 'Papers arranged under the head of Loan' Trial of Bahadur Shah, FMisc vol 376; Qureshi and Kazmi, *1857 ke Ghaddaron ke Khutut*, pp 95, 118, 160; Metcalfe, *Two Native Narratives*, pp, 96, 111, 113, 173-74; Jivan Lal, *Sarguzisht e Dehli*, pp 191-92

772 Qureshi and Kazmi, *1857 ke Ghaddaron ke Khutut*, pp 89, 93, 113, 148, 153

773 Metcalfe, *Two Native Narratives*, pp 92,110, 115, 121, 133-35; Jivan Lal, *Sarguzisht e Dehli*, pp 83, 104-5, 116-17, 139, 149-50, 181-82, 243, 251, 263, 266, 274; Husain, *Dastavezat e Ghadar*, pp 152-54, 157; Peition of Sheodial and Shadiram, in the Trial of Bahadur Shah, FMisc vol 376; *Dehli Urdu Akhbar* 14.6.1857

774 Diary of Chunni Lal, in the Trial of Bahadur Shah, FMisc vol 376; Qureshi and Kazmi, *1857 ke Ghaddaron ke Khutut*, p 88

775 Diary of Chunni Lal, in the Trial of Bahadur Shah, FMisc vol 376

776 Metcalfe, *Two Native Narratives*, pp 103-104, 107

777 *A short account of the life of Rai Jeewan Lal Bahadur and extracts from his diary*, by his son, Imperial Medical Hall Press, Delhi, 1888; Metcalfe, *Two Native Narratives*, pp 104, 107, 2, 77-78

778 Diary of Chunni Lal in the Trial of Bahadur Shah, FMisc vol 376; Metcalfe, *Two Native Narratives*, p 98

779 *Dehli Urdu Akhbar* 24.5.1857; Metcalfe, *Two Native Narratives*, p 100

780 Metcalfe, *Two Native Narratives*, p 121

781 Jivan Lal, *Sarguzisht e Dehli*, pp 125, 127, 185-86; Muir, *Records of the Intelligence Department* vol II p 38; Qureshi and Kazmi, *1857 ke Ghaddaron ke Khutut*, p 102, 112; Husain, *Dastavezat e Ghadar*, pp 56, 59, 67, 134; Sir Henry W.Norman and Mrs. Keith Young, *Delhi 1857*, Low Price Publications, Delhi, 2001, p 171; Metcalfe, *Two Native Narratives*, pp 143-44; Farooqui, *Besieged*, p 157

782 Metcalfe, *Two Native Narratives*, p 105

783 The evidence of Makhan, the mace bearer of Captain Douglas, in the Trial of Bahadur Shah, FMisc vol 376

784 *Memoirs of Ahsanullah Khan*, p 2

785 Petition of Kasim ud din, in the Trial of Bahadur Shah, FMisc vol 376, passim

786 *Mutiny Records*, part 1, pp 144-47

787 Ibid, pp 161-62

788 Order of Bahadur Shah date 11 August 1857, in the Trial of Bahadur Shah, FMisc vol 376

789 *Dehli Urdu Akhbar*, 17th May 1857

790 *Dehli Urdu Akhbar*, 5th July, 12th July 1857; Siddiqi, *Atthara Sau Sattavan*, gives a similar analysis of the evolution of the newspaper's stance in May 1857; see

pp 16-17. William Dalrymple's assessment that the newspaper's stance was stridently anti-British from the start of the revolt is untenable. The crucial paragraph he quotes in support of his theory is actually taken from the issue of the 31st of May. See Dalrymple, *The Last Mughal*, p 161, esp f.n. 41

791 *Dehli Urdu Akhbar* 31.5.1857, 14.6.1857, and 21.6.1857

792 Jivan Lal, *Sarguzisht e Dehli*, pp 168-69; Imdad Sabri, *1857 ke Mujahid Shoara*, Maktaba Shahrah, Delhi, 1959, p 150

793 Petition of Ram Baksh and Taley Yar Khan, in the Trial of Bahadur Shah, FMisc vol 376

794 Farooqui, *Besieged,* pp 257-58, 261

795 Metcalfe, *Two Native Narratives*, pp 125-26

796 *Memoirs of Ahsanullah Khan*, p 20; *Sadiq ul Akhbar*, 27.7.1857, in Siddiqi, *Atthara Sau Sattavan*, pp 198-99; Rashid al Khairi, *Dilli ki Akhri Bahar*, Urdu Academy Delhi, 1999, pp 68-69

797 *Dehli Urdu Akhbar*, 14.6.1857

798 Ibid

799 Summing up by the Deputy Judge Advocate Genreal, in the Trial of Bahadur Shah, FMisc vol 376

800 *Dehli Urdu Akhbar*, 31.5.1857, 5.7.1857 p 141, 21.6.1857

801 *Dehli Urdu Akhbar*, 14.6.1857

802 Farooqui, *Besieged,* p 229; Husain, *Dastavezat e Ghadar*, p 63

803 Zahir Dehlavi, *Dastan e Ghadar*, pp 108-9, 138

804 Metcalfe, *Two Native Narratives*, pp 68, 102, 118; W Muir, *Records of the Intelligence Department of the Government of the North Western Provinces of India during the Mutiny of 1857*, Edinburgh, 1902, vol I, p 495; Jivan Lal, *Sarguzisht e Dehli*, pp 162-63; Sabri, *1857 ke Mujahid Shoara*, pp 56, 124; Norman and Young, *Delhi 1857*, p 243

805 Said Mobarik Shah, 'The City of Delhi during the Siege', (translated by R.M. Edwards), 1859, British Library, Mss Eur B 138, p 3; Metcalfe, *Two Native Narratives*, pp 54, 90; Diary of Chunni Lal, in the Trial of Bahadur Shah, FMisc vol 376

806 Jivan Lal, *Sarguzisht e Dehli*, p 285-86; Sabri, *1857 ke Mujahid Shoara*, p 137; Order of Bahadur Shah to Mirza Mughal, and diary of Chunni Lal, in the Trial of Bahadur Shah, FMisc vol 376; *Dehli Urdu Akhbar*, 24.5.1857

807 Zahir Dehlavi, *Dastan e Ghadar*, pp 108-9, 138; Qureshi and Kazmi, *1857 ke Ghaddaron ke Khutut*, p 88, 100, 147, 183; FS 18.12.1857, no.407

808 *Dehli Urdu Akhbar*, 31.5.1857; Metcalfe, *Two Native Narratives*, p 61

809 Irfan Habib, 'The Coming of 1857', *Social Scientist,* vol 26, nos.1-4, Jan-April 1998, p 3

810 The diary of Chunni Lal, in the Trial of Bahadur Shah, FMisc vol 376; *Dehli Urdu Akhbar,* 24.5.1857

811 *Dehli Urdu Akhbar*, 24.5.1857

812 *Mutiny Records*, part 1, p 152

813 'Narrative of occurrences in Dehlee written by a Native residing within the walls of the city commencing from the 11th of May 1857', Showers Family Papers, Cambridge Centre for South Asian Studies

814 Farooqui, *Besieged*, p 236

815 *Dehli Urdu Akhbar*, 14.6.1857

816 Order of Bahadur Shah, to Jumma ud din (sic), in the Trial of Bahadur Shah, FMisc vol 376

817 Jivan Lal, *Sarguzisht e Dehli*, p 179

818 Petition of Ghulam Muiz ud din Khan, in the Trial of Bahadur Shah, FMisc vol 376; Qureshi and Kazmi, *1857 ke Ghaddaron ke Khutut*, pp 95, 101, 108;

Mobarik Shah, 'The City of Delhi during the Siege', Mss Eur B 138, p 126; FS 18.12.1857 no.407; Zahir Dehlavi, *Dastan e Ghadar*, p 138

819 Metcalfe, *Two Native Narratives*, p 127; Jivan Lal, *Sarguzisht e Dehli*, pp 128, 143, 208; *Memoirs of Ahsanullah Khan*, pp 20, 25; Mobarik Shah, 'The City of Delhi during the Siege', Mss Eur B 138, pp 155, 124-25

820 FS 25.9.1857 no.641; 18.12.1857 no.443

821 Qureshi and Kazmi, *1857 ke Ghaddaron ke Khutut*, p 101

822 Petiton of Nabi Baksh and others, and diary of Chunni Lal, in the Trial of Bahadur Shah, FMisc vol 376; Metcalfe, *Two Native Narratives*, pp 160, 172, 181-82; Jivan Lal, *Sarguzisht e Dehli*, pp 202, 205-6; Farooqui, *Besieged*, p 292

823 Farooqui, *Besieged*, pp 306-25

824 Major W.S.R. Hodson, *Twelve years of the soldier's life in India,* Ticknor and Fields, Boston, 1860, p 302; Farooqui, *Besieged*, p 326

825 *Mutiny Records*, part 1, pp 289, 297, 303; Peitions of Mirza Mughal, and of Khwaja Khairat Ali, clerk, in the Trial of Bahadur Shah, FMisc vol 376; Metcalfe, *Two Native Narratives*, pp 181, 195, 199-200

826 *Mutiny Records*, part 1, p 303; Metcalfe, *Two Native Narratives*, pp 152, 167, 179, 197

827 Metcalfe, *Two Native Narratives*, pp 188, 200, 211; *Memoirs of Ahsanullah Khan*, p 26; Qureshi and Kazmi, *1857 ke Ghaddaron ke Khutut*, pp 158-9; Jivan Lal, *Sarguzisht e Dehli*, pp 125, 239-41; Various documents attached under the head of 'loan' in the Trial of Bahadur Shah, FMisc vol 376

828 *Mutiny Records*, part 1, p 281

829 Metcalfe, *Two Native Narratives*, pp 191-92,199; Farooqui, *Besieged*, pp 293-94

830 Metcalfe, *Two Native Narratives*, p 202

831 Metcalfe, *Two Native Narratives*, p 215; Farooqui, *Besieged*, pp 60

832 Qureshi and Kazmi, *1857 ke Ghaddaron ke Khutut*, p 172, 213; Jivan Lal, *Sarguzisht e Dehli*, pp 276-78, 295-96; FS 30.10.1857 no.23

833 *Mutiny Records*, part 1, p 317; Farooqui, *Besieged*, p 74; Qureshi and Kazmi, *1857 ke Ghaddaron ke Khutut*, p 121-2, 128; FS 18.12.1857, no.411; Asadullah Khan Ghalib, *Dastambu*, edited and translated by Khwaja Ahmad Faruqi, Tarqqi e Urdu Bureau, New Delhi, 1994, p 32; Order of Bahadur Shah dated 9 August 1857, to the officers of the Volunteer Regiment, in the Trial of Bahadur Shah, FMisc vol 376; *Memoirs of Ahsanullah Khan*, p 21; Metcalfe, *Two Native Narratives*, pp 185-90

834 Hodson, *Twelve years*, p 303

835 *Mutiny Records,* part 1, p 365

836 *Mutiny Records*, part 2, pp 316-17

837 *Memoirs of Ahsanullah Khan*, p 24; Petition of Mukund Lal, in the Trial of Bahadur Shah, FMisc vol 376; *Mutiny Records*, part 1, pp 384

838 George W. Forrest, *Selections from the letters, despatches and other state papers preserved in the Military department of the government of India, 1857-58*, Military Department Press, Calcutta, 1893,vol *1,* pp 346-51, 357-64; *Mutiny Records*, part 1 p 408; Metcalfe, *Two Native Narratives*, p 203

839 Metcalfe, *Two Native Narratives*, pp 204-5; *Mutiny Records*, part 2, p 8

840 Jivan Lal, *Sarguzisht e Dehli*, p 187, 199, 253, 267

841 Husain, *Dastavezat e Ghadar*, pp 93-94

842 Letter of James Hare to his father, 23 August 1857, Hare Papers, Centre for South Asian Studies, Cambridge

843 Qureshi and Kazmi, *1857 ke Ghaddaron ke Khutut*, p 97, 118, 121, 128-29, 146; Jivan Lal, *Sarguzisht e Dehli*, pp 92-93, 148, 203-4

844 Qureshi and Kazmi, *1857 ke Ghaddaron ke Khutut*, pp 117, 131-33, 137-38,147-8, 153 156-161, 182, 187; Metcalfe, *Two Native Narratives*, p 65-66; FS

30.10.1857 no.50; Jivan Lal, *Sarguzisht e Dehli*, p 232; *Mutiny Records*, part 2, pp 13-14

845 Jivan Lal, *Sarguzisht e Dehli*, p 310; Qureshi and Kazmi, *1857 ke Ghaddaron ke Khutut*, pp 167, 178, 182, 188; FS 30.10.1857 no.50

846 FS 30.10.1857 nos.57-8, 81, 84; 18.12.1857, no.443; Mobarik Shah, 'The City of Delhi during the Siege', Mss Eur B 138, p 176

847 Hare to his father, 24th September 1857, Hare Papers; Surgeon General J. Fairweather, 'Through the Mutiny with the 4th Punjab Infantry, Punjab Irregular Force', Fairweather Papers, Centre for South Asian Studies, Cambridge

848 FS 30.10.1857 nos.86, 18.12.1857, nos.437, 443

849 Rashid ul Khairi, *Dilli ki Akhri Bahar*, pp 93-94; Sabri, *1857 ke Mujahid Shoara*, pp 268-71; FP 4.2.1859, no.56

850 FS 30.10.1857 nos.81, 778, 29.1.1858 no.524

851 *Ghalib ke Khutut* vol 1 p 267; Ghalib, *Dastambu*, pp 40-43

852 Khan, *Sirat e Faridiya*, pp 54-57

853 *Mutiny Records*, part 2, pp 225-26

854 FS 18.12.1857, no.443, 29.1.1858, no.21; Shah, *The City of Delhi during the Siege*, p 174; Nayar, *The Penguin 1857 Reader*, pp 143, 171-76

855 See Dalrymple, *The Last Mughal*, pp 462-63

856 FS 30.10.1857 nos.81, 686; 27.11.1857, no.12, 83, 27.11.1857, no.332; Raffi Gregorian, 'LOOT! The British Army and Prize Money in India, 1754-1864', senior honours thesis, University of Pennsylvania, 1986, pp 39, 41, 49

857 Muir, *Records of the Intelligence Department*, vol II p 288

858 Wagentreiber, *Reminiscences of the sepoy rebellion* pp 40-45

859 *Mutiny Records*, part 2, pp 290-91; FS 29.1.1858, no.28, 26.3.1858 nos.2, 4,18; FP 11.6.1858 no.38

860 FS 26.3.1858 nos.14, 18

861 Gregorian, 'LOOT!' pp 43-46

862 FS 29.1.1858, nos.520, 523-524

863 FS 18.12.1857, no.444

864 *Mutiny Records*, part 2, pp 323-27

865 Hodson, *Twelve years*, pp 340-41; FS 30.10.1857 no.686; 18.12.1857 no.439

866 *Mutiny Records*, part 2, pp 357-60, 363-64, 371

867 Charges, in the Trial of Bahadur Shah, FMisc vol 376

868 *Life of Rai Jeewan Lal Bahadur*, p 18

869 Evidence of Hakim Ahsanullah Khan and Mukund Lal, in the Trial of Bahadur Shah, FMisc vol 376; *Mutiny Records*, part 2, pp 391, 149-52, passim

870 FS 26.6.1857 nos.39-40, 28.8.1857 nos.71-72; Norman and Young, *Delhi 1857*, p 104

871 FS 25.9.1857 no.643, 666

872 The written defence of Bahadur Shah, in the Trial of Bahadur Shah, FMisc vol 376

873 Summing up by the Judge Advocate General, in the Trial of Bahadur Shah, FMisc vol 376

874 Ibid. emphasis added

875 Nayar, *The Penguin 1857 Reader*, pp 233-34

876 FS 31.7.1857 no.38

877 FP 10.12.1858, no.60; 7.1.1859, nos.55-56

878 Dalrymple, *The Last Mughal*, pp 45-52, 474, 480-81

879 FS 18.12.1857, nos.443, 445; FP 25.6.1858, no.429; 26.8.1859, no.44, 2.9.1859, nos.46, 48; Foreign Department Finance-A proceedings, September 1862, no.9. Also see Dlarymple, *The Last Mughal*, pp 424-26

880 Pritchett, *Nets of Awareness*, pp 22-25; Ram, *Qadim Dillii Kalij*, p.56

881 FS 29.1.1858, no.22; 25.6.1858, no.16. A fairly comprehensive list appears in Sabri, *1857 ke Mujahid Shoara*, p 203 onwards; R.M. Coopland, *A Lady's Escape from Gwalior*, Smith, Elder and Co., London, 1859, pp 268-69
882 *Mutiny Records*, part 2, p 266
883 Coopland, *A Lady's Escape from Gwalior*, pp 253-56, 263, 267; Norman and Young, *Delhi 1857*, p 297
884 FS 25.6.1858, no.16
885 Home Department Judicial Proceedings, National Archives of India, 10.6.1859, no.1
886 FP 1.4.1859, nos.113-15
887 Intezamullah Shahabi, *East India Company aur Baghi Ulema*, Deeni Book Depot, New Delhi n.d., pp 58,111; Syed Mohammad Miyan, *Ulema e Hind ka Shandar Mazi*, vol IV, pp 243, 258
888 Abdul Latif (trans. Khaliq Ahmad Nizami), *Atthara sau sattavan ka tareekhi roznamcha*, Union Press, Delhi, 1971, p 158; Russell and Islam, *Ghalib*, p 233
889 FP 13.8.1858, nos.440, 443, 446; *Mutiny Records*, part 2, p 320
890 A Hindu (S.C.Mookerjee), *The Mutinies and the People; or Statements of Native Fidelity exhibited during the Outbreak of 1857-58*, I.C. Bose & Co., Calcutta, 1859, pp 94-98
891 Nayar, *The Penguin 1857 Reader*, p 64
892 Sabri, *1857 ke Mujahid Shoara*, p 297
893 Muir, *Records of the Intelligence Department*, vol I, p 472; Norman and Young, *Delhi 1857*, pp 220, 222; Rashid ul Khairi, *Dilli ki Akhri Bahar*, pp 70-74
894 *Testimonials, Sanads and Letters of Munshi Nathmal and of his Descendants*, I.M.H. Press, Delhi, 1893
895 FP 26.8.1858, nos.38-39, 43-44
896 FP 12.3.1858, nos.161-62, 165, 177
897 Edwin Jacob, *A Memoir of Professor Yesudas Ramchandra of Dehli*, Christ Church Mission Press, Kanpur, 1902, vol 1, pp 103-04
898 Muir, *Records of the Intelligence Department*, vol II p 301
899 FS 29.1.1858, no.524
900 FS 18.12.1857, no.445; *Ghalib ke Khutut* vol 1 p 267; Ghalib, *Dastambu*, p 66
901 FP 30.12.1859, nos.82-86
902 FS 30.10.1857 no.186; 18.12.1857, no.43
903 FS 27.11.1857, no.83, 30.10.1857 no.686
904 FS 30.10.1857 no.686
905 Fairweather, 'Through the Mutiny with the 4th Punjab Infantry'
906 *Ghalib ke Khutut* vol 3 pp 993-4
907 FP 11.6.1858 no.322; *Munshi Nathmal*, p 6
908 Gupta, *Delhi Between Two Empires, 1803-1931*, pp 27-30
909 Deputy Commissioner's Office Records, Delhi State Archives, 11/1860
910 Ibid
911 *Ghalib ke Khutut* vol 1 p 384, vol 3 p 1203
912 Ibid., vol 3 p 992, vol 2 p 524
913 Gupta, *Delhi Between Two Empires*, pp 27-28
914 *Ghalib ke Khutut* vol 2 p 685
915 The evidence of Jut Mull, in the Trial of Bahadur Shah, FMisc vol 376
916 *Ghalib ke Khutut* vol 2 pp 504, 524, 596-7, 682, 695, 770
917 Letter to Mir Mahdi Majruh, dated 16th December 1862, Ibid., vol 2 p 539
918 *Ghalib ke Khutut* vol 2 p 508, vol 1 p 339
919 Ghalib, *Dastambu*, pp 85-88
920 *Ghalib ke Khutut* vol 2 p 624
921 Russell and Islam, *Ghalib*, pp 132-33, 152, 159, 172, 177

922 Introduction by Francis Robinson, pp viii-x, in Khan, *The Causes of the Indian Revolt*
923 Arifi, *Shahar Ashob*, p 22
924 Azurda, in Arifi, *Shahar Ashob*, p 180
925 Ghalib, *Dastambu*, pp 28-29
926 Mohammad Mohsin Khan 'Mohsin', in Arifi, *Shahar Ashob*, pp 183-4
927 Saghir Dehlavi, in Arifi, *Shahar Ashob*, p 198
928 Mirza Khan 'Dagh', in Arifi, *Shahar Ashob*, p 161
929 Qurban Ali Beg 'Salik', in Arifi, *Shahar Ashob*, p 165
930 Arifi, *Shahar Ashob*, pp 155, 180, 198
931 Mirza Khan 'Dagh', in Arifi, *Shahar Ashob*, p 161
932 Norman and Young, *Delhi 1857*, p 197
933 Ghalib, *Dastambu*, pp 25-27
934 Mohammad Taqi Khan 'Sozan', in Arifi, *Shahar Ashob*, p 167
935 Mohammad Zahur 'Zahur', in Arifi, *Shahar Ashob*, p 190
936 Zahur, in Arifi, *Shahar Ashob*, p 190
937 Syed Zahir ud din 'Zahir' Dehlavi, in Arifi, *Shahar Ashob*, p 171
938 Ghalib, *Dastambu*, p 38
939 Ghalib in Arifi, *Shahar Ashob*, p 195
940 *Ghalib ke Khutut* vol 1 p 281
941 Arifi, *Shahar Ashob*, p 220
942 Ghalib, *Dastambu*, p 70
943 Azurda, in Arifi, *Shahar Ashob*, p 182
944 Qadir Baksh 'Sabir', in Arifi, *Shahar Ashob*, p 225
945 Arifi, *Shahar Ashob*, p 222
946 Hafiz Ghulam Dastagir 'Mubin', in Arifi, *Shahar Ashob*, pp 156-57
947 Mirza Khan 'Dagh', in Arifi, *Shahar Ashob*, p 160
948 Translated by and quoted in Pritchett, *Nets of Awareness*, p 1
949 Quoted in Pritchett, *Nets of Awareness*, p 32
950 Kidwai, *Master Ram Chander*, pp 99-100
951 Maulvi Karim ud din, *Khatt e Taqdir* edited by Dr Mahmud Ilahi, Danish Mahal, Lucknow 1965, pp 37-39
952 Lelyveld, *Aligarh's First Generation*, pp 76-79, passim
953 Metcalf, *Islamic Revival*, pp 74-79, passim
954 Alexander Cunningham, *Archaeological Survey of India: Four reports made during the years 1862-63-64-65*, Govt. Central Press, Simla, 1871, vol 1, pp, i-iv, 132 onwards
955 *Ghalib ke Khutut* vol 2 p 525
956 C.M Naim, in a brief but perceptive article, 'Ghalib's Delhi: A Shamelessly Revisionist Look at Two Popular Metaphors', questions these assumptions; in *Urdu Texts and Contexts*, p 250. It is a thesis that definitely deserves to be taken further

Select Bibliography

UNPUBLISHED RECORDS

National Archives of India

Foreign Department, Political Proceeding (FP)
Foreign Department, Secret Proceeding (FS)
Foreign Department, Secret and Separate Proceeding (FS&S)
Foreign Department Miscellaneous Records (FMisc)
Foreign Department Finance-A Proceedings (FFinA)
Home Department, Public Proceedings (HPub)
Home Department Judicial Proceedings
North Western Provinces Papers, Abstracts of Proceedings of Charles Metcalfe (NWPAbs)

Delhi State Archives

Deputy Commissioner's Office Records
Residency Records

The British Library

India Office Records, Board's Collections volumes
Letters of William Linnaeus Gardner, Mss Eur C 304
Said Mobarik Shah, *The City of Delhi during the Siege*, (translated by R.M. Edwards), Mss Eur B 138
John Anthony Hodgson papers, Mss Eur D1200
Papers of Mountstuart Elphinstone, Mss Eur F88/383
William Dundas papers, Mss Eur F259/4
Raffi Gregorian, 'LOOT! The British Army and Prize Money in India, 1754-1864', senior honours thesis, University of Pennsylvania, 1986

Centre for South Asian Studies, Cambridge

Gardner Papers
Showers Family Papers
Hare Papers
Fairweather Papers

PUBLISHED GOVERNMENT RECORDS

Forrest, G.W., *Selections from the letters, despatches and other state papers preserved in the Military department of the government of India, 1857-58, vol 1*
General report on public instruction in the North Western Provinces of the Bengal Presidency for 1843-44, Agra Ukhbar Press, Agra
General report on public instruction in the North Western Provinces of the Bengal Presidency for 1844-45, Secundra Orphan Press, Agra
General report on public instruction in the North Western Provinces of the Bengal Presidency for 1846-47, Secundra Orphan Press, Agra

Muir, W. *Records of the Intelligence Department of the Government of the North Western Provinces of India during the Mutiny of 1857*, T&T Clark, Edinburgh, 1902

Mutiny Records: Correspondence, Punjab Government Press, Lahore, 1911, vol 1

Papers in the state and progress of education in the North-Western Provinces for 1854-55, Calcutta Gazette, Calcutta, 1856

Records of the Delhi Residency and Agency, Sang-e-Meel Publications, Lahore, 2006

Report of the General Committee of Public Instruction of the Presidency of Fort William in Bengal for the year 1836, Baptist Mission Press, Calcutta, 1837

Richey, J.A., *Selections from Educational Records, Part II, 1840-1859*, Bureau of Education, India, Calcutta, 1922

Selections from the records of the Government of the Punjab and its dependencies. New deries, no VII: Trial of Muhammad Bahadur Shah, titular King of Delhi, and that of Mogul Beg, and Hajee, all of Delhi, for rebellion against the British Government, and murder of Europeans during 1857, Punjab Printing Company Ltd. 1870

Selections from the records of the North-Western Provinces vol iv, Government Press, Allahabad, 1868

Selections from the records of the Government of the North-Western Provinces, Govt. Press N.W.P., Allahabad, 1867

Sharp, H., *Selections from Educational Records, Part I, 1781-1839*, Bureau of Education, India, Calcutta, 1920

Thornton, R., *Memoir on the statistics of indigenous education within the North Western Provinces of the Bengal Presidency,* Baptist Mission Press, Calcutta, 1850

NEWSPAPERS

Dehli Urdu Akhbar

Muhibb e Hind

Qiran us Sadaen

BOOKS AND ARTICLES

English

1857: Essays from Economic and Political Weekly, Orient Longman, Hyderabad, 2008

A Hindu (S.C.Mookerjee), *The Mutinies and the people; or statements of native fidelity exhibited during the outbreak of 1857-58*, I.C. Bose & Co., Calcutta, 1859

Andrews, Charles Freer, *Zaka Ullah of Delhi*, (edited by Mushirul Hasan and Margrit Pernau) Oxford University Press, New Delhi, 2003

Azad, Muhammad Husain, *Ab-e hayat: shaping the canon of Urdu poetry*, edited and translated by Frances W. Pritchett in collaboration with Shamsur Rahman Faruqi, Oxford University Press, New Delhi, 2001

Bacon, Thomas, *First Impressions and studies from nature in Hindostan*, W.H.Allen, London, 1837

Ball, Charles, *The History of the Indian Mutiny*, The London Printing and Publishing Company Limited, London, n.d.

Bates, Crispin, ed. *Mutiny at the Margins: New perspectives on the Indian uprising of 1857, Volume 1: Anticipations and experiences in the Locality*, Sage Publications, New Delhi, 2013

—— ed. *Mutiny at the Margins: New perspectives on the Indian uprising of 1857, Volume 5: Muslim, Dalit and subaltern narratives*, Sage Publications, New Delhi, 2013

Bayly, C.A., *Empire and Information: Intelligence gathering and social communication in India, 1780–1870*, Cambridge University Press, New Delhi, 1999

——, *Origins of Nationality in South Asia: Patriotism and ethical government in the making of modern India*, Oxford University Press, New Delhi, 1998

——., *Rulers, Townsmen and Bazars*, Oxford University Press, New Delhi, 1992

Bhattacharya, Sabyasachi, *Rethinking 1857*, Orient Longman, New Delhi, 2008

British India: the duty and interest of Great Britain, to consider the condition and claims of her possessions in the East, Clark and Baldwin, London, 1839

Chaghatai, Ikram, ed. *1857 in the Muslim historiography*, Sang e Meel Publications, Lahore, 2007

Chenoy, Shama Mitra, *Shahjahanabad: A City of Delhi, 1638-1857*, Munshiram Manoharlal, New Delhi, 1998

Coopland, R.M., *A lady's escape from Gwalior*, Smith, Elder and Co., London, 1859

Cunningham, Alexander, *Archaeological Survey of India: Four reports made during the years 1862-63-64-65*, vol 1, Govt. Central Press, Simla, 1871

Dalrymple, William, *White Mughals: Love and betrayal in eighteenth century India*, Penguin Books, New Delhi, 2002

——, *The Last Mughal: The fall of a dynasty, Delhi, 1857*, Penguin/Viking, New Delhi 2006

——, *The Anarchy: The East India Company, Corporate Violence, and the Pillage of an Empire*, Bloomsbury Publishing, New Delhi, 2019

Dean, A, *A tour through the upper provinces of Hindostan; comprising a period between the years 1804 and 1814*, C & J Rivington, London, 1823

Dyce Sombre, David Ochterlony, *Mr. Dyce Sombre's refutation of the charge of lunacy brought against him in the Court of Chancery*; Published by Mr. Dyce Sombre, Paris, 1849

Ehlers, Eckart and Thomas Krafft eds. *Shahjahanabad/Old Delhi*, Manohar, New Delhi, 2003

Farooqui, Amar, *Zafar and the Raj: Anglo-Mughal Delhi c 1800-1850*, Primus Books, Delhi, 2013

Farooqui, Mahmood, *Besieged: Voices from Delhi, 1857*, Penguin, New Delhi, 2010

Faruqi, Shamsur Rahman, 'A long history of Urdu literary culture, Part 1: Naming and placing a literary culture', in Sheldon Pollock ed. *Literary cultures in history: Reconstructions from South Asia*, Oxford University Press, New Delhi, 2004

——, 'Unpriviledged Power: The strange case of Persian (and Urdu) in nineteenth-century India', *Annual of Urdu Studies*, vol 13, 1998

Fisher, Michael, *Counterflows to colonialism: Indian travellers and settlers in Britain 1600-1857*, Permanent Black, Delhi, 2004

Franklin, Lieut. W., 'An account of the present state of Delhi', in *Asiatick Researches*, Vol 4, Vernor and Hood, London, 1799

——, *Military memoirs of George Thomas*, John Stockdale, London, 1805

Fraser, James Baillie, *Military memoir of Lt Col. James Skinner*, Smith, Elder & Co., London, 1851

Fusfeld, Warren, 'Communal conflict in Delhi: 1803-1930', *The Indian Economic and Social History Review*, Vol 19, No.2, 1982

Gaborieau, Marc, 'A nineteenth–century Indian 'Wahhabi' tract ggainst the cult of Muslim saints : *Al-Balagh al-Mubin*', in Christian W. Troll ed. *Muslim shrines in India*, Oxford University Press, New Delhi, 2003

Gooptu, Sharmistha, and Boria Majumdar, *Revisiting 1857: Myth, memory, history*, Roli Books, New Delhi, 2007

Gordon, Stewart, ed. *Robes of honour: Khil'at in pre-colonial and colonial India*, Oxford University Press, New Delhi, 2003

Greathead, H.H., *Letters written during the siege of Delhi*, Longman, Brown, Green, Longmans & Roberts, London, 1858

Gupta, Hari Ram, *Life and work of Mohan Lal Kashmiri 1812-1877*, Minerva Book Shop, Lahore, 1943

Gupta, Narayani, *Delhi between two empires, 1803-1931: Society, government and urban growth*, Oxford University Press, New Delhi, 1998

Habib, Irfan, 'The coming of 1857', *Social Scientist,* vol 26, nos 1-4

Hansen, Kathryn, and David Lelyveld eds, *A wilderness of possibilities, Urdu studies in transnational perspective*, Oxford University Press, New Delhi, 2005

Harris, Jonathan Gil, *The first Firangis*, Aleph Book Company, New Delhi, 2015

Hodson, Major W.S.R., *Twelve years of the soldier's life in India,* Ticknor and Fields, Boston, 1860

Holman, Dennis, *Sikander Sahib: The life of Colonel James Skinner, 1778-1841*, Heinemann, London, 1961

Husain, S.M. Azizuddin, *1857 revisited*, Kanishka Publishers, New Delhi, 2007

Husain, Iqbal 'The rebel administration of Delhi', *Social Scientist,* vol 26, nos 1-4

——, *The world of the rebels of 1857: proclamations, tracts and documents 1857-1859*, Primus Books, Delhi, 2019

Ireland, William Wotherspoon, *History of the siege of Delhi by an officer who served there*, Adam and Charles Black, Edinburgh, 1861

Jacob, Edwin, *A Memoir of Professor Yesudas Ramchandra of Dehli*, Christ Church Mission Press, Cawnpore, 1902

Jivan Lal, *A short account of the life of Rai Jeewan Lal Bahadur and extracts from his diary, by his son*, Imperial Medical Hall Press, Delhi, 1888

Journal of the Archaeological Society of Dehli, Delhi Gazette Press, September 1850, January 1853

Kaye, John William, *The life and correspondence of Charles, Lord Metcalfe*, Richard Bentley, London, 1854

Kaye, M.M. ed., *The golden calm*, Webb & Bower, Exeter, 1980

Lafont, Jean-Marie and Rehana, *The French and Delhi, Agra, Aligarh and Sardhana*, India Research Press, New Delhi, 2010

Lelyveld, David, *Aligarh's first generation*, Oxford University Press, New Delhi, 2003

——, 'Zuban-e Urdu-e Mu'alla and the idol of linguistic origins', *Annual of Urdu Studies*, Vol 9, 1994

Metcalf, Barbara Daly, *Islamic revival in British India; Deoband 1860-1900*, Oxford, University Press, New Delhi, 2002

Metcalfe, Charles Theophilus, *Two native narratives of the mutiny in Delhi*, Archibald Constable & Co., Westminster, 1898

Minault, Gail, 'Delhi College and Urdu' in *The Annual of Urdu Studies*, vol 14, 1999

——, *Gender, language and learning: Essays in Indo-Muslim cultural history*, Permanent Black, Ranikhet, 2009

—— and Christian W. Troll, 'Introduction' in Ian Henderson Douglas, *Abul Kalam Azad: An intellectual and religious biography*, Oxford University Press, Bombay 1988

Mir, Farina, 'Imperial policy, provincial practices: Colonial language policy in nineteenth-century India', *Indian Economic and Social History Review*, Vol 43, Issue 4, 2006

Mohan Lal, Munshi, *Journal of a tour through the Panjab, Afghanistan, Turkistan, Khorasan, and part of Persia in company with Lieut. Burnes and Dr. Gerard*, Baptist Mission Press, Calcutta, 1834

——, *Travels in the Panjab, Afghanistan and Turkistan, to Balk, Bokhara and Heart: and a visit to Great Britain and Germany*, W.H Allen, London, 1846

Mundy, Godfrey Charles, *Pen and pencil sketches: Being the journal of a tour in India*, John Murray, London, 1832

Muzaffar Alam, *The languages of political Islam in India, c 1200-1800*, Permanent Black, Delhi, 2004

Naim, C.M., Syed Ahmad and his two books called 'Asar-al-Sanadid', *Modern Asian Studies*, Vol 45, Issue 3, 2011

——, *Urdu Texts and Contexts: The Selected Essays of C.M. Naim*, Permanent Black, Delhi 2004

Nanda, Ratish and Narayani Gupta, *Delhi, The Built Heritage: A Listing*, vol I, INTACH Delhi Chapter, New Delhi, 1999

Nathmal, Munshi, *Testimonials, sanads and letters of Munshi Nathmal and of his descendants*, I.M.H. Press, Delhi, 1893

Nayar, Pramod K., *The Penguin 1857 Reader*, Penguin Books, New Delhi, 2007

Norman, Sir Henry W., and Mrs. Keith Young, *Delhi 1857*, Low Price Publications, Delhi, 2001

Nugent, Lady Maria, *A journal from the year 1811 till the year 1815, including a voyage to and residence in India, with a tour to the north-western parts of the British possessions in that country, under the Bengal Government*, London, T and W Boone (printer), 1839

Panigrahi, D.N., *Charles Metcalfe in India; Ideas and administration 1806-1835*, Munshiram Manoharlal, New Delhi, 1968

Pati, Biswamoy, *The 1857 rebellion*, Oxford University Press, New Delhi, 2007

Parks, Fanny, *Wanderings of a pilgrim in search of the picturesque*, Pelham Richardson, London, 1850

Pearse, Colonel Hugh, *Memoir of the life and military services of Viscount Lake*, William Blackwood and Sons, Edinburgh, 1908

Pernau, Margrit, *Ashraf into middle classes*, Oxford University Press, New Delhi, 2013

——'Multiple identities and communities; re-contextualizing religion', in Jamal Malik and Helmut Reifeld eds *Religious pluralism in South Asia and Europe*, Oxford University Press, New Delhi, 2005

——, ed. *The Delhi College: Traditional elites, the colonial state and education before 1857*, Oxford University Press, New Delhi, 2006

——, 'The Dehli Urdu Akhbar, Between Persian Akhbarat and English newspapers', *Annual of Urdu Studies*, vol 18, 2003

—— and Yunus Jaffery eds, *Information and the public sphere: Persian newsletters from Mughal Delhi*, Oxford University Press, New Delhi, 2009

Petievich, Carla, *When men speak as women: Vocal masquerade in Indo-Muslim poetry*, Oxford University Press, New Delhi, 2007

Powell, Avril A, *Muslims and missionaries in pre-mutiny India*, Routledge, London, 1993

Pritchett, Frances W., 'A long history of Urdu literary culture, Part 2: Histories, performances, and masters' in Sheldon Pollock ed. *Literary cultures in history: Reconstructions from South Asia*, Oxford University Press, New Delhi, 2004

Pritchett, Frances W., *A desertful of roses*; website of Frances Pritchett, http://www.columbia.edu/itc/mealac/pritchett/00ghalib/index.html

——, *Nets of awareness*, University of California Press, Berkeley, 1994

Rahman, Tariq, 'Boy-love in the Urdu ghazal', *Annual of Urdu Studies*, vol 7, 1990

Raina, Dhruv, and S. Irfan Habib, *Domesticating modern science: A social history of science and culture in Colonial India*, Tulika Books, New Delhi, 2004

Ramchundra, *A treatise on problems of maxima and minima solved by algebra*, W.H.Allen & Co., London, 1859

Rao, Vidya, 'The Dilli Gharana' in Mala Dayal ed. *Celebrating Delhi*, Ravi Dayal, New Delhi, 2010

Ray, Rajat Kanta, *The felt community: Commonality and mentality before the emergence of Indian nationalism*, Oxford University Press, New Delhi, 2003

Roberts, Emma, *Scenes and characteristics of Hindostan*, W.H. Allen, London, 1835

Robinson, Francis, *Islam and Muslim history in South Asia*, Oxford University Press, New Delhi, 2006

Ross, Major, of Bladensburg, *The Marquess of Hastings, K.G.*, Clarendon Press, Oxford, 1900

Roy, Kaushik, ed. *The uprising of 1857*, Manohar, New Delhi, 2010

Russell, Ralph, ed. *Ghalib: Life, Letters and Ghazals*, Oxford University Press, New Delhi, 2003

Sajan Lal, 'Professor Ramchandar as an Urdu journalist', *Islamic Culture*, Vol XXIII, Nos. 1-4, 1949

Sangin Beg, *Sair-ul-Manazil*, translated by Nausheen Jaffery, Tulika Books, New Delhi, 2017

Singh, Vir, *People's role in 1857 uprising–Delhi and neighbouring region*, Originals (an imprint of Low Price Publications), Delhi, 2010

Sleeman, W.H. *Rambles and recollections of an Indian official*, Hatchard and Son, London, 1844

Saroop, Narindar, *Gardner of Gardner's Horse*, Palit and Palit, New Delhi, 1983

Spear, Percival, *Twilight of the Mughals*, Oxford University Press, New Delhi, 2002

Stokes, Eric, *The English Utilitarians and India*, Oxford University Press, New Delhi, 1992

The annual biography and obituary for the year 1827, Longman, Rees, Orme, Brown and Green, London, 1827

Thompson, Edward, *The life of Charles, Lord Metcalfe*, Faber and Faber Limited, London, 1937

Thompson, George, *Debate at the India House, December 18th 1844, on the claims of the royal family of Delhi upon the justice of the British government and the East India Company*, William Congreve, London, 1845

Trevelyan, C.E., *On the education of the people of India*, Longman, Orme, Brown, Green, & Longmans, London, 1838

——, *Papers transmitted from India by C.E.Trevelyan, Esq.*, Printed by J.L.Cox, London, 1830

Wagentreiber, Florence, *Reminiscences of the sepoy rebellion of 1857*, Civil and Military Gazette Press, Lahore, 1911

Wagentreiber, George, *Our escape from Delhi*, n.d.

Wagner, Kim, *The great fear of 1857: rumours, conspiracies and the making of the Indian uprising*, Dev Publishers, New Delhi, 2014

Western, Frederick James, *The Early History of the Cambridge Mission to Dehli*, (for limited circulation), SPCK, London, 1950

Wilson, Horace Hayman, *Travels in the Himalayan provinces of Hindustan and the Panjab; in Ladakh and Kashmir; in Peshawar, Kabul, Kunduz, and Bokhara, by Mr. William Moorcroft and Mr. George Trebeck from 1819 to 1825*, John Murray, London, 1841

Urdu

Abdul Haq, *Marhum Dehli Kalij*, Anjuman Taraqqi Urdu (Hind), New Delhi, 1989

Abdul Latif, *Atthara sau sattavan ka tareekhi roznamcha*, Union Press, Delhi, 1971

Ahmad, Hamida Sultan, *Khandan e Loharu ke shoara*, Ghalib Institute, New Delhi, 1981

Ahmad, Mukhtaruddin, 'Mufti Sadr ud din Azurda ki kuchh nayab o kamyab tahrirein'

in Nazir Ahmad ed. *Tahqiqat: Intekhab maqalat Ghalib Nama*, Ghalib Institute, New Delhi, 1997
Arifi, Amir, *Shahar ashob, ek tajzia*, Saqi Book Depot, Delhi, 1994
Batin, Qutubuddin, *Gulistan e Bekhizan*, Uttar Pradesh Urdu Academy, Lucknow, 1982
Beg, Farhatullah, *Daktar Nazir Ahmad ki kahani, kuchh meri aur kuchh un ki zabani*, Anjuman Taraqqi Urdu (Hind), Delhi 1992
Beg, Mirza Sangin, *Sair ul manazil*, (edited and translated by Sharif Husain Qasimi), Ghalib Institute, New Delhi, 1982
Dehlavi, Syed Ahmad, *Rusum e Dehli*, Urdu Academy, Delhi, 1986
Dehlavi, Syed Zamir Hasan, *Dehlavi Urdu*, Urdu Academy, New Delhi, 2000
Dehlavi, Wazir Hasan, *Dilli ka akhiri deedar*, Urdu Academy Delhi, 1999
Faizuddin, Munshi, *Bazm e akhir*, Urdu Academy, Delhi, 1992
Feroz, Mohammad *Talmiz e Ghalib, Mir Mehdi 'Majruh': Hayat aur tasanif*, Published with support of Urdu Academy Delhi, New Delhi, 1999
Ghalib, Asadullah Khan, *Auraq e Ma'ani: Ghalib ke Farsi khutut, Urdu tarjuma*, translated by Tanvir Ahmad Alavi, Urdu Academy, Delhi, 2001
——, *Dastambu*, edited and translated by Khwaja Ahmad Faruqi, Taraqqi e Urdu Bureau, New Delhi, 1994
——, *Ghalib ke khutut*, Edited by Khaliq Anjum, Ghalib Institute, New Delhi, 2000
Hali, Altaf Husain, *Hayat e javed*, Qaumi Council Barae Farogh e Urdu Zaban, New Delhi 1999
Hali, Altaf Husain, *Yadgar e Ghalib*, Ghalib Institute, New Delhi, 1996
Khan, Ahsanullah, *Memoirs of Hakim Ahsanullah Khan*, edited by S. Moinul Haq, Pakistan Historical Society, Karachi, 1958
Husain, S.M. Azizuddin, *Dastavezat e Ghadar 1857*, Kanishka Publishers, New Delhi, 2007
'Insha', Mir Inshaallah Khan, *Dariya e Latafat*, Anjuman Taraqqi Urdu (Hind) New Delhi, 1988
Irtiza Karim, edited, *Dehli Urdu Akhbar, 1841*, Qaumi Council Barae Farogh e Urdu Zaban, Delhi, 2010
Islahi, Abdurahman Parwaz, *Mufti Sadr ud din Azurdah*, Maktaba Jamia, New Delhi, 1977
Jafri, Ali Safdar, *Nawab Mustafa Khan Shefta*, Azra Publications, Sutur Publications, Lahore, 1999
Karimuddin, Maulvi, *Guldasta e nazninan*, Azimushshan Book Depot, Patna, 1972
——, *Khatt e Taqdir*, Danish Mahal, Lucknow, 1965
——, *Tabqat Shoara e Hind*, Uttar Pradesh Urdu Academy, Lucknow, 1983
Kaukab, Tafazzul Husain Khan, *Fughan e Dehli*, Navrang Kitab Ghar, Noida, 2007
Khairi, Rashid al, *Dilli ki akhri bahar*, Urdu Academy, Delhi, 1999
Khan, Syed Ahmad, *Asarussanadid*, Urdu Academy, Delhi, 2000
——, *Sirat e Faridiya*, Mataba Mufeed e Aam, Agra, 1896
Kidwai, Sadiq-ur-Rahman, *Hindustan mein fikri-o-tahzeebi islah ka aagaz aur Master Ram Chander*, Anjuman Taraqqi Urdu (Hind), New Delhi, 2007
Masoom Moradabadi, *Urdu sahafat aur jang e azadi 1857*, Khabardaar Publications, New Delhi, 2008
Miyan, Syed Mohammad *Ulema e Hind ka shandar mazi*, Maktaba Burhan, Delhi, 1963
Momin, Momin Khan, *Insha e Momin*, edited by Siddiqi, Zahir Ahmad, Ghalib Academy, New Delhi, 1977
Naqvi, Haneef, *Shoara e Urdu ke tazkire, Nikat ush Shoara se Gulshan e Be Khar tak*, Uttar Pradesh Urdu Academy, Lucknow, 1998

Nasakh, Abdul Ghafur, *Sukhan shoara*, Uttar Pradesh Urdu Academy, Lucknow 1982
Nasim, A.D., *Barahvin sadi hijri mein Dilli ka shayarana mahaul*, Urdu Academy Pakistan, Lahore, 1999
Nasir Nazir, *Lal Qile ki ek jhalak*, Urdu Academy, Delhi, 2001
Nizami, Khwaja Hasan, *1857*, Khwaja Hasan Sani Nizami, New Delhi, 2008
Qureshi, Salim and Syed Ashur Kazmi ed. and trans. *1857 ke ghaddaron ke khutut*, Anjuman Taraqqi Urdu (Hind), New Delhi, 2001
Ram, Malik, *Qadim Dehli Kalij*, Maktaba Jamia Limited, Delhi, 1976
Sabir, Qadir Baksh, *Gulistan e sukhan*, Uttar Pradesh Urdu Academy, Lucknow, 1982
Sabri, Imdad *1857 ke mujahid shoara*, Maktaba Shahrah, Delhi, 1959
Shahabi, Intezamullah, *East India Company aur Baghi Ulema*, Deeni Book Depot, New Delhi n.d
Sharif Husain Qasimi ed and trans. Mirza Sangin Beg, *Sair ul manazil*, New Delhi, 1982
Siddiqi, Atiq, *Atthara sau sattavan: Akhbar aur dastavezen*, Maktaba Shahrah, Delhi, 1966
Siddiqui, Zahir Ahmad, *Momin, Shaqsiyat aur fan*, Ghalib Academy, New Delhi, 1995
Taimuri, Arsh, *Qila e moalla ki jhalkiyan*, Urdu Academy, Delhi, 1992
Yusuf, Mohammad, *Dilli mein Urdu sahafat ke ibtedayee naqoosh: Dehli Urdu Akhbar*, Educational Publishing House, Delhi, 2008
Zahir Dehlavi, Syed Zahiruddin, *1857 ke chashmdeed halaat: almaruf Dastan e Ghadar,* Adib Publications, New Delhi, 2008
Zaidi, Ali Jawwad, *Tarikh e mushaira*, Shan e Hind Publications, Delhi, 1992
Zakaullah, Mohammad, *Intekhab e Zakaullah*, (Asghar Abbas ed.) Uttar Pradesh Urdu Academy, Lucknow, 1983
Zill ur Rahman, Hakim Syed, *Dilli aur tibb e yunani*, Urdu Academy, Delhi, 1995

Hindi

Delhi Jain Directory, Jain Sabha, New Delhi, 1961
Jain, Jyoti Prasad, *Pramukh eitihasik Jain purush aur mahilayen,* Bhartiya Gyanpeeth, n.d.
Maheshwar Dayal, *Dilli jo ek shahar hai*, Hindi Academy, Delhi, 2005
Jivan Lal, *Sarguzisht e Dehli: 1857 ke andolan ki kahani, Jivan Lal ki zabani*, edited and transcribed by Tajwar, Darkhashan, Rampur Raza Library, Rampur, 2005

Index